Coalition Literature

Post•45 Loren Glass and Kate Marshall, Editors
Post•45 Group, Editorial Committee

Coalition Literature
Aesthetics on the Move in
Midcentury US Multiethnic Writing

Francisco E. Robles

Stanford University Press
Stanford, California

Stanford University Press
Stanford, California

© 2025 by Francisco E. Robles. All rights reserved.

No part of this book may be reproduced or transmitted in any form or by any means, electronic or mechanical, including photocopying and recording, or in any information storage or retrieval system, without the prior written permission of Stanford University Press.

Library of Congress Cataloging-in-Publication Data
Names: Robles, Francisco E., author.
Title: Coalition literature : aesthetics on the move in midcentury US multiethnic writing / Francisco E. Robles.
Description: Stanford : Stanford University Press, 2025. | Includes bibliographical references and index.
Identifiers: LCCN 2024041996 (print) | LCCN 2024041997 (ebook) |
 ISBN 9781503641877 (cloth) | ISBN 9781503641969 (paperback) |
 ISBN 9781503641976 (ebook)
Subjects: LCSH: American literature—Minority authors—History and criticism. | Immigrants in literature. | Aesthetics in literature. | American literature—20th century—History and criticism. | Liberalism—United States—History—20th century.
Classification: LCC PS153.M56 R63 2025 (print) | LCC PS153.M56 (ebook) | DDC 810.9/920693—dc23/eng/20240917
LC record available at https://lccn.loc.gov/2024041996
LC ebook record available at https://lccn.loc.gov/2024041997

Cover design: Lindy Kasler
Cover art: Ramiro Rodriguez, *A La Pisca*, 2001, linoleum relief print

Contents

	Acknowledgments	vii
	Introduction	1
	Speaking With and the Work of Coalitional Aesthetics	
1	Migrating Engagements	31
	Muriel Rukeyser, Zora Neale Hurston, and New Visions for Migrant Voices	
2	Movement Politics and the Politics of Movement	77
	Migrant Coalitions and Farm Labor in the 1940s	
3	Signs of Protest	119
	The Poetics of the Memphis Sanitation Strike and Gwendolyn Brooks's "Warpland" Poems	
4	Coalitional Aesthetics against Allegory	161
	Carlos Bulosan's and Tomás Rivera's Migrant Pizcaresques	
5	*This Bridge Called My Back* and the Shape of Dialectics to Come	202
	Notes	233
	Index	269

Acknowledgments

This book has been a long time coming, and I'm deeply grateful to a huge amount of people. I worked hard, alongside Erica Wetter and, in draft versions of chapters (including ones that don't appear in these pages), with Matt Gleeson, to curb my tendency toward volubility. In these acknowledgments, though, I'm afraid I won't be able to help myself.

First, thank you to Stanford University Press, and to Erica Wetter in particular, as well as to Loren Glass and, although you had to step aside for this project, Kate Marshall, for believing in this project since I showed you the proposal all those years ago. I'm so pleased that *Coalition Literature* is in the Post•45 series. Thank you to Caroline McKusick for ushering this manuscript over the finishing line. I'm grateful to Philip Leventhal for the feedback on the introduction, and for insisting that I focus myself by clarifying the stakes of this argument. I am also incredibly grateful to the reviewers of the book, who provided encouragement while also noting changes that would make the argument more cogent and urgent. Thank you for your editorial eye and for always excellent conversation, Matt Gleeson. Thank you to Sarah Osment for your labor indexing the book.

The first-ever version of this project was guided by Daphne Brooks, Alex

Vazquez, and Valerie Smith. I owe so much to you all. Thank you to Kinohi Nishikawa for pointing out an exciting seed of the new project in the old one; thanks to Bill Gleason, Starry Schor, Lee Clark Mitchell, Wendy Belcher, Joshua Kotin, Nigel Smith, Nick Nesbitt, and Simon Gikandi for being great advocates and mentors at various times while I was at Princeton.

I formed so many lasting attachments while in graduate school. Many of us have remained close, and though some of us stay in touch less often, I still think of you when doing my work. Jill Jarvis: our friendship grows deeper every year, which is hard to believe, but so sustaining. Brittney Edmonds: amiga, I'm so grateful for our intense friendship and our wide-ranging conversations. Rae Gaubinger, you have helped me grow into the person I am, and your friendship means the world to me. Ross Lerner, you are both the sweetest friend and the fiercest advocate, and so much of my life as a scholar is molded after the way you guide, build up, and support others. Katie Kadue: though not someone I knew in graduate school, you're part of it all now. The theory of the trash pocket will forever stand us in good stead. Mollie Eisenberg: every conversation picks up where we last left off, warming my spirit every time. Anjuli Gunaratne: half a world apart, and you're my forever-treasured friend. Kameron Austin Collins, Kelly Swartz, Priyanka Jacob, Emily Vasiliauskas, and Eric Miles Glover: I can't believe how lucky I was to have you all as friends and cohort-mates; I wouldn't be where I am without your steadiness, our conversations, and your brilliance. Tikia Hamilton, Gavin Arnall, Matthew Spellberg: you have each been a powerful friend to me in ways you might not know, but which matter deeply to me.

I would like to thank everyone who has been at Notre Dame's Department of English since I've been there: Laura Knoppers and Jesse Lander; Chris Abram, Laura Betz, Dionne Bremyer, Jacque Brogan, Noreen Deane-Moran, Margaret Doody, John Duffy, Chris Fox, Steve Fredman, Johannes Göransson, Barbara Green, Sandra Gustafson, Susan Harris, Romana Huk, Cyraina Johnson-Rouillier, Essaka Joshua, Gregory Kucich, Tim Machan, Joyelle McSweeney, Orlando Menes, Susannah Monta, Ernest Morrell, John Sitter, Steve Tomasula, David Thomas, and Laura Walls. Thank you to Eliot Visconsi, who is a model listener and mentor to graduate students and junior scholars. Thanks to Jason Ruiz and Ian Newman, for being my mentors. Chris Vanden Bossche, I'm proud to sit in the office that you sat in. Sara Maurer, Valerie

Sayers, and Steve Fallon: thank you all for actively showing what it means to stand up for others.

I would like to thank Lynn McCormack, Kelly Huth, Lisa Holderman, Paul Cunningham, Blake Holman, Alissa Doroh, Andrew Deliyannides, and Linnie Caye. Lynn, you have been showing me the (interminable) ropes since I arrived at Notre Dame, and you've forgotten more than I could ever know about how to make sure things run smoothly.

Ian Newman, Kate Marshall, Barry McCrea, Mark Sanders, Ranjodh Singh Dhaliwal, Michelle Karnes, Matt Kilbane, Mehak Khan, Liam Kruger, Xavier Navarro Aquino, and Yasmin Solomonescu: You all have made every day a delight in the English Department. I love talking and being with you all so much. Sara Marcus and Roy Scranton, you've been so welcoming since first greeting me at the South Bend Airport in early 2017; we've known each other for so long, and our friendship has grown and changed so much in the years since Princeton.

At the Institute for Latino Studies (ILS) at Notre Dame, I have benefited from the incredible generosity and mentorship of Luis Fraga. Thank you to Paloma Garcia Lopez, Maribel Rodriguez, Idalia (Laly) Rodriguez, Karen Richman, Tim Matovina, and José Limón as well. I have exceptional colleagues at ILS, many of whom I have had the pleasure of seeing on and off campus: Anne García-Romero, Maria Tomasula, Tatiana Ruiz, David Cortez, David Lantigua, Elena Mangione-Lora, Juanita Pinzón Caicedo, Yamil Colón, Alex Chávez, Ricardo Ramírez. Jenny Padilla and Woodrow, our horror movie nights make Indiana less scary. Jaime, Jenny, Andrés, and Maité Pensado: thank you for being familia; you've seen me at my silliest, and you've also seen me at my lowest, and you have fed me legendary food through all of it.

American Studies and Gender Studies at Notre Dame have also been hugely important for me; thank you for inviting me on board in the first place, Mary Kearney. I'm grateful to Africana Studies (thank you Dianne Pinderhughes and Richard Pierce), as well as to the Higgins Labor Program and the Center for Social Concerns, in particular Dan Graff and Judith Benchaar. I am also grateful to Jaimie Bleck, Susan Blum, Lionel Jensen, Katrina Barron, Vanesa Miseres, Juan Vitulli, Dianne Pinderhughes, La Donna Forsgren, Emiliano Aguilar, Katlyn Carter, Nikhil Menon, Jon Coleman, Annie Coleman, Darren Dochuk, Katie Jarvis, Rebecca Tinio McKenna, James Lundberg, Pam Wojcik, Ann Mische, John Deak, Paul Ocobock, Richard Williams, Susan Ostermann, Amy Mulligan, Mary O'Callaghan, Diarmuid Ó Giolláin, Brian Ó Conchubhair, Patrick Griffin, Sharon Yoon, Thomas Tweed, Nicole Woods, Mike Amezcua, John Betz, Kraig Beyerlein, Abby Córdova, Weibing Ye, Gail Bederman, Ashley Bohrer, Emily Remus, Dan Graff, Cecilia Lucero, Kevin Barry, Chris Hedlin, Joanna Want, Neil Chase, Diana Hess, the late Tony Flora, Kasey Swanke, James Creech, and Scott Barton for their friendship and camaraderie. Provost John McGreevy has been a steady advocate since he was my dean when I arrived, and thank you to associate provost Maura Ryan, who provided crucial support for faculty of color and international faculty in my first year at Notre Dame, which started things off on the right foot. I am deeply grateful to dean Sarah Mustillo, not only for supporting the English Department but also for having an extensive vision of the humanities, as well as to Margaret Meserve and Ernest Morell.

Thank you to the Nanovic Institute of European Studies for funding its 2022/2023 Signature Conference Grant for "Reimagining Europe from Its Peripheries," which I co-organized with Korey Garibaldi and Perin Gürel. Particular thanks go to Clemens Sedmak, Grant Osborn, Mel Webb, and Rebekah Prince. Thank you to the Institute for Scholarship in the Liberal Arts (ISLA) at Notre Dame, particularly former director Alison Rice, who supported the Desert Futures: Sahara/Sonora conference in November 2021. This was one of the most significant events of my scholarly career, and an extraordinarily meaningful several days in South Bend. I'm especially grateful to Kristen Garvin-Podell, who was an extraordinary administrator and a delightful person throughout the process.

Francisco Aragón, the work you do for the world of Latinx poetry can never be fully calculated, but the depth of your impact in the wider world and in my particular life has been enormous. Jason Ruiz, Juan Albarracín, Ian Newman, Kate Marshall, Barry McCrea: you all have been family to me, and have made South Bend feel close; I am enormously fond of you all and owe much of my happiness in South Bend to you. Marisel Moreno and Tom Anderson: being in community with you means the world to me. Pam Butler, Karen Graubert, and Ricky Herbst: I adore hatching plans and laughing with you all—above everything, laughing and caring. Jennifer Huynh, thank you for always knowing what to say, and for being so generous. Korey Garibaldi,

Sara Marcus, Roy Scranton, and Chanté Mouton Kinyon: I want every day to be like the days I spend with you, especially when the sun is shining and the wine is flowing. Azareen van der Vliet Oloomi and Leo Francalanci: I know love the most when I am with you. I am also enormously grateful for the friendship of Sarah Shortall, Josh Specht, Alison Rice, Joseph Rosenberg, Father Paul Kollman, Madison Mainwaring, Pedro Mellado, Tarryn Chun, Anne García-Romero, Tobias Boes, Tracy Bergstrom, Julia Kowalski, Alexander Hsu, Sarah McKibben, Pete Cajka, Zachary Sell, and Tamara Kay. Frances Jacobus-Parker, Marius Hauknes, Jude, and Bodie, I can't express enough how much joy it brings me to be with you all. I feel beyond sustained; I feel understood and free.

Thank you to the graduate students at Notre Dame, current and former, whom I've had the pleasure of advising: Dominique Vargas, Chamara Moore, Sara Judy, Ruth Solarte-Hensgen, Mayra Cano, Hades Chavanne, Kristen Carlson, Oliver Ortega, Heidi Arndt, Zay Dale, Noemí Fernández Labarga, Hyunsoo Kim, Karla Maravilla, and Paulina Hernández-Trejo. All of my undergrads, current and former, thank you. I've taught students at Princeton University, Garden State Correctional Facility, Albert C. Wagner Correctional Facility, Cheshire Correctional Institution, York Correctional Institution, Connecticut College, and the University of Notre Dame. I'd especially like to thank Alexa Rojas-Monsivais, Alan Avalos, Anna Staud, Sabrina Takagishi, Joshua Kuiper, Phoebe Corde, Clyde Meikle, James Jeter, Tracie Bernardi Guzman, and Khalil Lockett (RIP). You all in particular have shifted how I think about literature and how I see it—you've shaped my scholarship in ways you might never even know, but your insights stay with me whenever I write and teach, especially when I see my lesson plans bearing the marks of your teaching.

Michelle Huang, Harris Feinsod, and Charif Shanahan, I am beyond grateful for our friendship and conversation. Paulina Jones-Torregrosa, Mariana Gutierrez Lowe, and Viola Bao, thank you for being so kind to me. Thank you to Sara Dimick, Tina Post, Emily Hyde, Sarah Wasserman, Adrienne Brown, Andy Ferguson, Jarvis McInnis, Julius Fleming, James E. Ford III, GerShun Avilez, Bill Mullen, and Christopher Pexa. I'm grateful to have shared conversations, spaces, and drinks with Maia Gil'Adi, Tommy Connors, Dixa Ramírez-D'Oleo, Ren Ellis Neyra, Renee Hudson, John Ribó, Sarah Quesada,

Josie Saldaña, Patricia Stuelke, David Vázquez, Bill Orchard, Marcela DiBlasi, Salvador Herrera, Christofer Rodelo, Daniel Borzutzky, Jennifer Harford Vargas, Elda María Román, Marion Christina Rohrleitner, Marta Caminero, Kirsten Silva Gruesz, Fede Aldama, Arturo Aldama, and Mary Pat Brady. I'm grateful to Marcos Gonsalez, Tommy Connors, and José A. de la Garza Valenzuela for enjoying conferences as much as I do! Erick Rodriguez: the City of Night lives on. Rachel Galvin: I'm so grateful for the generosity you show as a scholar and the kindness you embody as a friend. John Alba Cutler, thank you for taking me seriously, and also for not—you always know which way to be, and it gladdens me deeply. Michael Dowdy, thank you for the expansiveness of your scholarship, for being a gentle listener, and for being both a great and a kind person.

Bharat Ranganathan, your gifts as a scholar are exceeded only by your gift as a friend. Barbara Abadia Rexach, Claudia Mosquera Rosero-Labbé (mi alma géminis!), Yomaira Figueroa, Tacuma Peters, Paul Joseph (Pablo José) López Oro, Omaris Z. Zamora, Yoallí Rodríguez Aguilera, Amarilys Estrella, Nicole Fleetwood, Jorge Giovanetti, Michelle McKinley, and Zuleica Romay Guerra: fue un honor conocerles en Tepoztlán.

Gloria Fisk, Dan Sinykin, Michael Docherty, Tyler Tennant, and Noah Gounoue: *Contemporaries*! Arthur Wang, Mary Esteve, Annie McClanahan: I've loved being part of the larger Post45 editorial collective with you all, with *Contemporaries* and *Peer Reviewed* building a larger body of lasting scholarship. Thank you to Sarah Chihaya, Tim Aubry, Florence Dore, J. D. Connor, Rachel Greenwald Smith, Jane Hu, Brian Jacobson, and Sean McCann. Thank you, also, to Carlos Nugent, Jordan Brower, Gerónimo Sarmiento Cruz, Xander Manshell, Hayley O'Malley, Cara Lewis, Daniel Valella, Justin Mitchell, Laura McGrath, and Kyle Frisina.

Thank you to Cristina Pérez Jiménez and Bret Maney for welcoming me into your home, especially near the tail end of the project's writing. Thank you to David Witzling and the Manhattan College English Department for the invitation to give the Third Annual June Dwyer Lecture. The legacies your department has built exceed the bounds of short-sighted administrations, and I am honored that I was able to learn from you in my short time on your campus. This was also the occasion that prompted me to finish the final section of my book, and I am enormously grateful for that kindness.

Paul Nadal and Johaina Crisostomo: You're the best writing pals anyone could ask for. I look forward to many, many more years of friendship, camaraderie, and co-writing. Briallen Hopper: thank you for being a friend; travel down the road and back again; your heart is true, you're a pal and a confidante. Julie Rivkin, Lina Wilder, Blanche Boyd: thank you for mentoring me so gently and with such perspicacity in the year I was at Connecticut College. Liz Reich, Rijuta Mehta, Michelle Neely, and Natalie Avalos: I am grateful for your friendship since 2016, and for the fact that we have found new ways to grow. Natalie Koch, your work inspires me, and I learn from your example as a scholar, an advocate, and someone whose ethics guide their work. Joey Hurchings, I'm glad we met in 2006; over the years we keep returning to the basics of our friendship, and that's been such an anchor for me.

To my desert studies folks, and the collectives that keep growing and growing: Jill Jarvis, Brahim El-Guabli, Natalie Koch, Martín Camps, Daniela Johannes, Eda Pepi, Argyro Nicolaou, Teresa Villa-Ignacio, Tom Lynch, Robin Reineke, Melina Vizcaíno Aleman, Tom Lynch, Suban Nur Cooley, Simón Ventura Trujillo, Jamie Fico, Michele Sollai, Brittany Meché, Ingrid Nelson, Bobby Lee, and Anne Marie McManus. Celina Osuna, whose art and scholarship I admire so much. To Ofelia Zepeda: your work continues to sustain me, and to draw me in new and more conscious ways toward loving the world; thank you for honoring us in South Bend.

In South Bend, I have gotten to know so many people: Bettina Spencer, Ernesto Verdeja, Molly Gower, Dan Newton, Zach Schrank, Rachel Schrank, Alan Lindsay, Neil Lobo, Brian Kane, Jayleen Santiago Díaz, Idrissa Sidibé, and Adam Schelle, and so many others. Bridget and Andrew Hoyt, art and neighborliness combine to make you wonderful. Benjamin Balthaser, Jake Mattox, Paul Mishler, and Gerrie Casey, you welcomed me so early on when I came to South Bend, from talking Ben Shahn to the Marx reading group. The AAUP work you all do (and which I admire beyond inspiration) makes IUSB the center of our city, and may it remain that way. Thank you to April Lidinsky and Ken Smith. Kacie Klamm, Patrick Klamm, Wrigley, and Moira: being your neighbors has been a joy; merci. Fred Slaski and Lucky: you were Merci's first friends, right when we brought her into our lives after the pain of losing Zorro. Sandy Carmichael: thank you for saving my life. Romana Huk, Peter Holland, Joyelle McSweeney, Johannes Göransson, Kevin O'Chap and

Stan Molenda, Ted and Marie Benchik, Mark and Hillary Doerries, Chad and Alex Savage: hello, neighbors!

To my departed grandparents—Primitivo Robles, Virginia Robles, Ignacio Gomez, and Maria Luisa Gomez—I dedicate this work. I also dedicate this work to Mildred Pettis, who taught me to wander with love and insight.

Mi tocayo, tío Frankie Mireles, tío Ray Duran, and my cousins Mark Mireles and Solomon Hernandez have passed on; I was glad to know all of you. My work is also dedicated to my Gomez and Robles sides: my tías Cruz Mireles, Gloria Duran, Josie Soto, Carmen Gomez, Olivia Hernandez, tío Eligio Gomez, and tía Maudi Gomez, as well as Tony Hernandez, Nancy Gomez, and Kevin Neil; my tía Norma Milum, tío Luis Robles, and tía Josie Robles. My cousins, first and once- and twice-removed: Melissa, Jessica, Macalynn, Michelle, Victoria, Luca, Veronica, Dalia, Delilah, Julius Drake, Cisco, Sergio, Andres/Andy, Stefanie, Dea, Rachel, Johnny, Michael, Jaime, Jordan, Aramis, Demetrius, Joseph, Daniella, Vince, Samuel, Emilia, Alex, Michael, Luci, Liliana, Gabriel, and Adrianna; thank you to Kate, Norm and Nissa, Jerlean and Josh; also, thank you to Louis, Luis, Juan and Stacy, Jose and Rosana, and Elena.

Yolanda and J.R.: thank you for being my parents. We've grown so much over the years, and it feels like every year is a new moment in our relationship, one that I'm so excited about. You've been so supportive and encouraging, and my love of music (and my ability to play it!), my love of reading, and my zest for life all come from you. Thank you.

Zorro and Merci: you have been the best friends I could ask for. Zorro, your death is still so deeply felt. Although it's hard, I try to love like you loved: with every fiber of my being, and with an abiding, deep purr. Merci, I didn't know what the world around me looked like until you showed me. When I'm with you, I can see clearly. Everything looks richer, smells earthier, sounds more detailed, and feels nearer when you show me where it all is. My heart bursts with the love from you both.

Brandon, we've been together for half our lives now. We've grown, we've changed, we've become more ourselves and less ourselves, and through it all: I can depend on you every step of the way. I knew I liked poetry before I met you, but loving you has shown me the poetry of everyday life; I owe so much of my scholarship to the life we've envisioned in union.

Thank you all.

Acknowledgments

Parts of this book have been published in very different but still pertinent iterations. Part of chapter 3 appears as "Transformation and Generation: Preliminary Notes on Reading the Poetics of the Memphis Sanitation Strike," in *Post45: Peer Reviewed*, issue 5 (Fall/Winter 2020). Part of chapter 4 appears as "Communal Imagination and the Problem of Allegory in Tomás Rivera's . . . *y no se lo tragó la tierra*," in *Twentieth-Century Literature* 68, no. 1 (Spring 2022). I have presented portions of the book at the American Comparative Literature Association, the Post45 Annual Symposium, the Association for the Study of the Arts of the Present, Shapeshifters: Recycling and Literature Conference at Yale University, the American Studies Association, the Modern Language Association, and the Manhattan College Department of English's Third Annual June Dwyer Lecture.

I gratefully acknowledge the generosity of archivists and archives for the use of the following: "1913 Massacre" and "Farmer-Labor Train" by Woody Guthrie. © Woody Guthrie Publications, Inc. Used by permission. "The 23rd Slum," "Sanitation Workers' Prayer," "Why should we sit and wait?," "A Black Poem," and "There Was a Man" used by permission of the University of Memphis Special Collections.

Introduction
Speaking With and the Work of Coalitional Aesthetics

IN MARTÍN ESPADA'S POEM "Floaters," from the 2021 collection of the same title, the poet offers an enraged lament built through specificity and combination. Written about a father and daughter who drowned in the Rio Grande, Espada's poem refuses to accept the lyrical position of elegy while at the same time insisting on poetry's reparative possibilities, especially in the realm of aesthetics as an embodied experience of art. The poem's language attempts paradoxically to structure an awful loss, to build lines that can sustain something larger than themselves. The poem achieves this not by striving for sublime unity, but instead through specific details that generate a diffused, differential sensibility. The second stanza begins with the evergreen, ever-anaphoric "and," enumerating people whose names threaten to remain unknown:

> And the dead have names, a feast day parade of names, names that
> dress all in red, names that twirl skirts, names that blow whistles,
> names that shake rattles, names that sing the praise of saints:
> Say *Óscar Alberto Martínez Ramírez.* Say *Angie Valeria Martínez
>   Ávalos.*
> See how they rise off the tongue, the calling of bird to bird somewhere
> in the trees above our heads, trilling in the dark heart of the leaves.[1]

The dead, including Óscar Alberto Martínez Ramírez and Angie Valeria Martínez Ávalos, join "a feast day parade." Their names dance vibrantly, and "twirl skirts," "blow whistles," and "rise off the tongue," becoming "the calling of bird to bird somewhere / in the trees above our heads." The names of

Martínez Ramírez and Martínez Ávalos become—and are not just *like*—"the calling of bird to bird." The names, and not just the act of naming, become communications through and across difference, "trilling in the dark heart of the leaves."

This stanza from "Floaters" participates in a method of literary innovation whose very impetus emerges from the desire to maintain difference as a necessary component of expression. The goal is not unity or totality, and it is not identification. Espada asserts that we cannot assimilate the dead even as we must never forget them. This poetry emerges from what Espada's contemporary John Murillo calls "the tradition of the witness," which includes some expected names (that is to say, putatively canonical in the context of US poetry), but which Murillo understands as international and continuous, rather than as bounded by literary historical expectations. He includes voices such as "Walt Whitman, Pablo Neruda, Audre Lorde, Czeslaw Milosz, Gwendolyn Brooks, Etheridge Knight, Nazim Hikmet, Sonia Sanchez, and Grandmaster Melle Mel," as well as "Aracelis Girmay, Suheir Hammad, and the Mighty Mos Def."[2] This expanded tradition interests me not only because it reframes questions of literary influence as well as the chronological, racial, national, gender, and genre makeup of literary history, but also because it reaches back and transforms aesthetic inheritances in order to generate resonant forms. This is not an abjuring of literary form, and it is not a complicity with historical assumptions about who and what matters; it is, instead, an active sense of literary transformation and generation that frames art as an act of *speaking with* its audience, of authors writing through and with difference rather than striving for unity and similarity.

I begin with this discussion of two contemporary Latinx poets and their poetic sensibilities in order to show that the philosophical and aesthetic preservation—indeed, privileging—of difference is the foundation of literary representation, mediation, and formal literary expression, and that this is part of a long-standing argument in which many multiethnic US writers have participated. Espada and Murillo, as well as writers such as Karen Tei Yamashita, Gayl Jones, Valerie Martínez, and Aracelis Girmay, offer notable continuations of and innovations in this tradition. In *Coalition Literature: Aesthetics on the Move in Midcentury US Multiethnic Writing*, I lay out an even more specific argument about literary history, explaining how questions of difference and a shared aesthetics of *speaking with* in multiethnic US literature took shape as a result of philosophical engagements with the Popular Front, and how these ideas shifted into multiculturalism.

Speaking With, Not For

From 1935 to 1981, Popular Front–influenced multiethnic literature flourished, and its aesthetic sensibilities developed along shared political impulses toward coalition, relation, connection, and communality. This midcentury stretch of decades provides crucial insight into how multiethnic coalitional aesthetics transformed gradually into the language of multiculturalism, a scalar shift of aesthetic and political horizons from transnationally inflected labor politics articulated through the grammar of coalition to goals of institutional inclusion prioritized by multiculturalism's politics of representation. The idea of coalition that this book holds, and according to which I shape my discussion of coalitional aesthetics, is this: coalition is a method and relation that operates to bring distinct people together precisely through their difference, and as such it is a process whose directions and outcomes must always be renewed and reimagined.

As I define it here, coalition rejects stability and stasis as critical endpoints, since it must accommodate shifting relations between authors and literary objects as well as generative emergences of connection and thought. Karma R. Chávez notes that "coalition is a present and existing vision and practice that reflects an orientation to others and a shared commitment to change. Coalition is the 'horizon' that can reorganize our possibilities and the conditions of them. Coalition is a liminal space, necessarily precarious, and located within the intermeshed interstices of people's lives and politics."[3] For Chávez, coalition is a process on the edge that works through a "shared commitment to change," particularly because coalitions must imagine beyond the given world, even as they work through that very world. What I see occurring in coalition-informed literary works—by luminaries such as Muriel Rukeyser, Zora Neale Hurston, Woody Guthrie, Sanora Babb, poets of the Memphis Sanitation Strike, Gwendolyn Brooks, Carlos Bulosan, Tomás Rivera, and the contributors to the anthology *This Bridge Called My Back*—anticipates Chávez's observations about coalition as a "horizon," precisely because they develop and participate in new aesthetic forms influenced by a visibly multiethnic world.

More properly, my work is guided by attention to literary forms developed through a coalitional ethos. Building on Matthew Beeber's coinage of coalitional aesthetics, which he uses to theorize how modernist, leftist literary anthologies of the 1930s and 1940s developed "a set of formal techniques that emphasizes rather than smooths over incongruities between constituent parts," I offer resonant pairings of midcentury multiethnic literary experiments that bear witness to a perduring commitment to difference as a foundation upon which to build literary expression.[4] Working with and alongside difference becomes *the* constitutive and shared ethos through which every text in this study connects. The goal for coalitionally oriented multiethnic US writers, as with the Popular Front literary anthologies Beeber discusses, is not smoothness, but instead the building of something new from many constitutive voices. For these writers, the hope is not to come to the same conclusion or to reduce everything to a singular and strongly shared point of view, but to build a more robust structure through the embrace of difference. In examining how this took shape from the 1930s to the 1980s, I offer an in-depth exploration of how literary style, form, and political intention produce intriguing new connections.

In finding these novel circuits of meaning, I think through the ethics of comparative work by refusing the language of analogy; instead, I turn to moments of surprising connection to develop this literary historical analysis of midcentury US coalitional aesthetics. In making this metacritical comparative turn, I join María Eugenia Cotera's emphasis on literary critics taking up a "coalitional ethos." Cotera asks, "How do we elaborate a mode of comparative analysis across race, nation, and historical context that does not assimilate the experiences of 'others' to our own? How might we respect the particularities of different historical experiences even as we mine the similarities of these experiences for key points of connection that reveal the systemic working of patriarchal, heteronormative, colonialist, racist, and classist networks of power?"[5] Cotera's questions antiprescriptively outline conditions for producing a new grammar of comparative inquiry, one that can account for coalitional aesthetics without producing positivist wagers or purity tests. Coalition emerges as a thing or process created through labor, one that can be studied and outlined but never tabulated or fully accounted for.

By developing the idea of coalition as a conversation that courses through the multicultural US literature discussed in this book, I'm proposing aesthetics as a distinctive means of theorizing, understanding, and elaborating coalition, especially as it turns on labor politics, migration, gender, and race in twentieth-century US writing and art. In this, I add bricks to the bridges between the social sciences and the humanities, especially as coalition moves from a distinctly political category into a sensibility that informs aesthetics. Karma Chávez, Ki Namaste, Erin M. Adam, Elena Gambino, and Deborah Gould theorize coalition through the interactions of queerness, ethnicity, and migration, especially coalition that is built as a response to specific political actions or problems.[6] Gould, for example, argues that the coalitional housing activism performed by Queer to the Left and Jesus People USA, in "Chicago under the auspices of a grassroots activist group, Community of Uptown Residents for Affordability and Justice (COURAJ)," affords a particular mode of willful intellectual possibility, "not because it had tremendous effects, but because it still might." She thus leans into the Blochian idea that "the not-yet exists in the present as potentiality, meaning that rather than seeking transcendence, we can look to the world *as it is* for sources of change."[7] I thoroughly examine this antitranscendental model of transformation in my final chapter on *This Bridge Called My Back*, and Gould's argument furnishes a sense of coalition's perduring draw as a mode of organization across political registers and scales.

This sensibility shares the philosopher Frédéric Neyrat's "atopian" philosophy and politics. For Neyrat, coalition offers a powerful reorientation of being through the idea of the "*trans-ject*," a term that ought "to be developed alongside forms of animal subjectivation, not to impose human subjectivity onto them, but in order to show that a subject is not set in opposition to animality: *A subject is that which situates itself at the edge of an existential trans-ject. A trans-ject is not a trajectory, something flexible, to be modified at will, but persistence, marked by a history that characterizes each existence in its own way.*"[8] Neyrat's philosophy of excessive difference demands coalition, connection, and relation, especially against forms of perception and consideration that understand comparison as a form of hierarchy. The payoff, for Neyrat, is "an *adventurous coalition*," or a "form of community created by those who are subject to the trans-jects of existence."[9] An "adventurous coalition," argues Neyrat, generates an "ensemble of beings inclined one on the other, an ensemble bearing uncertainty without undermining the possibility of a being-in-common." This is opposed to *"confused coalitions*, which deny thresholds, smother singularities, produce hybrid confusions in which each object would be lost in another object, where the absence of One has become the nightmare of a malleable diversity."[10] Although Neyrat and Gould offer distinct contexts for their coalitional thinking—Neyrat's is joyfully abstract, Gould's is insistently concrete—the refusal to accede to "malleable diversity" means embracing difference, positionality, and connection through the organizational and, importantly, *aesthetic* encounters that affirm political agency as a matter of relation rather than as something merely inherent. Coalition, in this sense, requires an actively extensive political framework, one that shapes the relations between its members according to a transformative project. In this way, coalition contains an expansive framework for understanding difference.

I conjoin writers through related practices of what I call *speaking with*, this book's key term. *Speaking with* denotes a shifting set of styles, tones, and positions that cohere—sometimes loosely, sometimes tightly—through specific formal literary engagements that theorize meaning as an interrelated process between author, text, and audience.[11] As a distinctly coalitional practice, *speaking with* requires that engagement be shaped by the ethical acknowledgment of difference as a constitutive element of any relation, rather than something to be smoothed over through assimilation or inclusion. The cultural and aesthetic modes of *speaking with* examined in this book illuminate a new way of approaching and organizing US midcentury multiethnic literature around coalitional aesthetics. A striking number of aesthetic practices emerge from *speaking with*, and they flexibly shift according to context and coalitional need, such as constructing a narrative from folk stories gathered in Florida lumber camps (Zora Neale Hurston's *Mules and Men*) or developing a literary anthology that pulls together essays, letters, poems, and interviews that emerge from variegated cultural contexts (*This Bridge Called My Back*, edited by Gloria Anzaldúa and Cherríe Moraga). Practices of *speaking with* evade representational capture, especially in the sense that their very production and use works against the static logic of representation as an end in and of itself.

From the Popular Front to the 1980s

At its core, the Popular Front was the Communist International's advice, to its various constituent national parties the world over, to pursue the building of broad coalitions to oppose the rise of fascist and explicitly anticommunist political movements. In Spain, for example, the Popular Front became a key element of the brief but influential Spanish Republic; indeed, many Popular Front tendencies around the world—including in the US, Mexico, the USSR, France, Germany, Cuba, and other nations in the Americas and Europe in particular—sent financial, material, and military support to the Spanish Republic during the Spanish Civil War, as the republic struggled against and ultimately fell to Francisco Franco's fascist forces. A short-lived political strategy enacted by the Third Communist International that began in 1934, the Popular Front had a remarkably long life as a political and aesthetic influence in the United States, and it especially resonates in midcentury multiethnic literatures. The texts I take up in this book use various grammars of *speaking with* that extend our understanding of the radical coalitional consciousness of the Popular Front beyond its typical periodization in the United States. Although the Communist International's official Popular Front strategy ended in 1939, many critics—including Michael Denning, Bill Mullen, Alan Wald, Mary Helen Washington, Robert Reid-Pharr, and Erin Royston Battat—have demonstrated a Popular Front culture that lasted into *at least* the mid-1940s, with the end point usually identified as the conclusion of World War II or the defeat of Henry Wallace's 1948 Progressive Party campaign for president of the United States. For critics such as Kate A. Baldwin, Kimberly Springer, Cheryl Higashida, and Bettina Aptheker, the resonances—whether subdued or explicit—lasted even longer: they have found important structural, aesthetic, and philosophical residues of Popular Front thought in the 1960s, 1970s, 1980s, and 1990s.[12]

In theorizing *speaking with* as a coalitional practice, I join these theorists of the long Popular Front by identifying a literary historical narrative of radical democracy's intersection with aesthetics, one that spans from the Popular Front to multiculturalism, from the mid-1930s to the early 1980s. *Coalition Literature* takes a carefully attuned look at the continued resonances, in different guises and formations, of enormous cultural forces that produced the legacies of the Popular Front, and posits that these can best be seen in multiethnic US literature. In addition to the above critics, I agree with and extend the arguments of Mary Helen Washington, Cristina Pérez Jiménez, Benjamin Balthaser, Margo Natalie Crawford, and James Smethurst, who have shown that Popular Front modes of organizing and aesthetic production have been especially pertinent within African American literature and Latinx literature, as well as for writers concerned with joining their work to a broader multiethnic ethos, such as Muriel Rukeyser, Sanora Babb, and Carlos Bulosan.[13] In a different iteration of this book, Hisaye Yamamoto, the band Los Lobos, and the folk singer Odetta would have found their ways into distinct chapters: there are many, *many* other writers, musicians, and artists who contributed to the coalitional ethos of midcentury multiethnic modernism, but whose case studies could not be fit into *Coalition Literature*.

To the multiethnic midcentury writers I discuss in this book, the Popular Front and its cultural resonances are far more interesting than many more visibly enduring institutions that make room for progressive thought, such as the twentieth-century US Democratic Party and the big tent that (often, but not always) made space for leftists. Although the Popular Front became intimately linked with Franklin Delano Roosevelt's New Deal and its legacies, especially for racial minorities who took up the promise of Johnson's Great Society policies, there emerged a decisive split away from the Popular Front due to the presence of communists within the large coalition. Michael Denning, Michael Kazin, Michael K. Honey, and others have pinpointed the attention paid by the Congress of Industrial Organizations (CIO) to interracial organizing, in particular, as a driver of the Popular Front's widely flung and widely appreciated democratic ethos. Kazin, for example, argues that for "most CIO leaders, interracial organizing was both a practical necessity and an ideological calling. Millions of Black people toiled in the steel mills, auto plants, packinghouses, tobacco factories, and other industries that made up the core of the American economy."[14] As Kazin details, the CIO's organizing tendency led to enormous gains among migrant workers of every race, and especially among African Americans. Indeed, as Michael Szalay has shown, the Democratic Party gathered progressive and leftist novelists in particular "within a larger 'coalition culture,'" which he describes as containing "a range of expressive forms—jazz, rhythm and blues, and rock and roll prominent among them—that militated on behalf of new unions between Black and white voters and, more broadly, the ends associated with the Civil Rights Movement and the larger project of integration."[15] For Szalay, the Democratic Party's vision of racial integration and alliance fell apart as an aesthetic project due to a poisonous compromise in which novel after novel of "middle-class self-liberation" emerged to "reassure their readers that white professionals and managers have it in their power to become owners and capitalists, in ways that Black workers do not."[16] Szalay's observation notes a particular racially oriented discomfort among white liberals; more broadly, this unease became antagonism toward people of color in the big tent coalition. This led to a decisive shift in the Republican Party's political base, as well as to the separation of Southern white Democrats—the Dixiecrats, as they came to be called—from the larger Democratic Party's umbrella. Andy Hines notes that in the postwar era, the "fractious coalition Franklin Delano Roosevelt had established between Southern Dixiecrats, labor advocates, and corporate liberals in the Democratic finally cracked," and that the "breaking point was an effort to unionize industrial workers both Black and white in the South."[17] For primarily left-oriented midcentury multiethnic writers, the Popular Front's resonances inspired work that could offer striking alternatives to the Democratic Party's status quo. Midcentury multiethnic writers and artists, from the East Coast to the West Coast, from Ben Shahn to John Fante, and, in this book, from Muriel Rukeyser to Cherríe Moraga and from Carlos Bulosan to Estela Portillo, found continued inspiration in the Popular Front's legacies of coalitional aesthetics.

I have also set out to explain my curiosity about how these novels, poems, and songs resist the analogical impulses that have undergirded liberal narratives of progress, turning instead to the difficult work of building a coalitional aesthetics by developing new infrastructures that could provide a foundation for their visions of belonging. By showing how multiethnic literature of this midcentury cultural period was characterized by attempts to develop aesthetic strategies that relationally represented their subjects on a scale that attended to the ethnic and racial diversity of American letters, I offer an account of how Popular Front–derived coalitional approaches to race, ethnicity, labor, migration, and gender shaped the sensibilities of writers such as Muriel Rukeyser, Zora Neale Hurston, Woody Guthrie, Sanora Babb, the poets of the Memphis Sanitation Strike, Gwendolyn Brooks, Carlos Bulosan, Tomás Rivera, and the contributors to *This Bridge Called My Back*. I fully agree with Michael Denning's argument that the Popular Front was a structure of feeling that outlived its historically established time frame, and that it must be seen "as a political and cultural charter for a generation," a cultural mode that resonated into and beyond the 1960s and the 1970s.[18] For Denning, "that the moment of the Popular Front—the age of the CIO—is usually visible only as an interregnum, a dead end, the 'thirties,' is a result . . . of its seeming to fall outside those larger stories of modernism and postmodernism, Fordism and post-Fordism. However, the Popular Front, the age of the CIO, stands, not as another epoch, but as the promise of a different road beyond modernism, a road not taken, a vanishing mediation."[19]

The writers who saw "the promise of a different road beyond modernism" as a distinctive, alternative midcentury American modernism were decidedly shaped by the Popular Front and its legacy, finding ways to consciously incorporate its organizing methods into their artistic practices. The coalitional aesthetics that emerge along this "different road" work through the structural, syntactical experiments of *speaking with* as attempts to expand lyric voice, to reimagine proletarian engagements with literary and institutional history, and to make polyphonic or multivocal prose distinctly political in its coalitional character.

Coalitional and Multicultural Aesthetics on the Move

In a section from Rukeyser's 1938 suite of poems *The Book of the Dead*, entitled "Absalom," we can see an example of mid-1930s coalitionally shaped *speaking with* at work. Tapping a family's voices, Rukeyser works through a series of lyric relations to build a layered testimony to the devastating effects of silicosis, which was killing hundreds if not thousands of primarily Black tunnel workers in Gauley Bridge, West Virginia:

> Shirley was my youngest son; the boy.
> He went into the tunnel.
>
> > *My heart my mother my heart my mother*
> > *My heart my coming into being*
>
> My husband is not able to work.
> He has it, according to the doctor.

> We have been having a very hard time making a living since
> this trouble came to us.
> I saw the dust in the bottom of the tub.[20]

Of the nine verbs and verb phrases in the above selection, five involve iterations of "to be," and Rukeyser depends on drawn-out grammatical constructions ("is not able to work" and "have been having") in key moments to emphasize the infringing nature of the industrial disaster on the migrants' bodies and lives. The lineation, spacing, indentation, and typography produce different tonal and formal qualities, suggesting the blending of different voices into one combinatory and coalitional lyric voice generated through the dialogic labor of the poetry itself. The complicated redistribution of the speaking voice, oscillating between a mother's memory and her son's fragmented and repetitive couplet, suggests that this multiply lyrical poetry depends on bearing witness as a polyphonic structure crafted by *speaking with*, perhaps the only way to express the interconnectedness of the disaster's consequences.

Four decades later, in *This Bridge Called My Back*, Cherríe Moraga's poem "The Welder" shows another distinctive use of *speaking with* as a means of generating and constructing coalitional verse; especially notable is its shift toward a multiculturalist lyric position. Whereas Rukeyser's melding of lyric voices suggests a lyrical and vocal interplay—but also perhaps submerges or naturalizes the poet's role in the process of crafting this polyphony—Moraga's stanzas more thoroughly examine the distinctions between poets and their comrades in coalition, situating coalition as a distinct set of relations rather than containing it in a mellifluous lyric voice. Moraga declaims,

> I am a welder.
> Not an alchemist.
> I am interested in the blend
> of common elements to make
> a common thing.

> No magic here.
> Only the heat of my desire to fuse
> what I already know
> exists. Is possible.

> We plead to each other,
> *we all come from the same rock*
> *we all come from the same rock*
> ignoring the fact that we bend
> at different temperatures
> that each of us is malleable
> up to a point.[21]

What is common and blended gets resolutely imagined as part of what already "exists" and "is possible," a steadfast materialism that grounds the welding metaphor. The lyric voice in Moraga's poem develops through a dramatized dialogue, an examination of positionality and political speech as necessary and difficult components of a coalition attentive to the imperatives of inclusion that shape multiculturalism. The transition in the form, appearance, and direction of *speaking with* from "Absalom" to "The Welder" shows how *with* is perhaps always already transforming into—and in dialogue with—*to*, and illuminates the distinctive position each preposition represents as a matter of writerly address. The grammar of multiethnic coalitional aesthetics, of *speaking with*, overlaps with multiculturalism's grammar of *speaking to*, and perhaps always has, to a certain degree. This prepositional distinction indexes the perceived relationship between a collectivity's members, shaping the horizons of aesthetic and political belonging.

Even so, the line from Rukeyser's poem to Moraga's—from the 1930s to the 1980s—shows a continuity or spectrum in *speaking with*. This genealogy of coalitional literary thought, organized by experiments in *speaking with*, troubles 1945 as a line of demarcation, as well as accounts of midcentury African American and Chicanx literature that understand their examinations of race, migration, and gender through the lens of a nascent multiculturalism interested primarily in inclusion through representativeness. My account of coalitional cultural production attends to communities whose pre- and postwar lives were shaped by continued state oppression, labor violations, immiseration, and racism. Practices of *speaking with* show that aesthetics is on the move, traveling Denning's "different road" through aesthetic strategies that actively work against forms of statal, capitalist, gendered, and racist violence, especially in the space of literature. This "different road" was not and has not been lost: we just haven't used the right lenses to see it, and have not turned to the writers who kept the engines of coalition turning, sparking into life. Coalitional thought has found an enduring home in multiethnic literatures of the United States, although it has been transfigured into a residual presence in multiculturalism, as well as an organizing structure that haunts contemporary discourses of intersectionality.

This "different road" parallels how Shu-mei Shih redescribes the concept of the "literary arc," which is a critical modality of envisioning "a network of texts as a study" that "is not a closed circuit but an extendable and contractable trajectory that connects texts along an arc, elucidating certain problematics." This idea of the literary arc provides a spatiotemporal metaphor that visualizes and connects "multiple nodes" through which "a text can enter into relation with other texts anywhere along [the arc], illuminating specific issues within a time period or across time periods."[22] *Speaking with*, as a means of naming a set of interrelated coalitional aesthetic practices, offers a clear constellation of these "multiple nodes" of relation and connection within US midcentury multiethnic literature. In each instance of *speaking with*, an aesthetic practice emerges that connects specifically to another example, generating within my book a critical method that traces, case by case through midcentury American literature, a long-obscured lineage of creativity influenced by coalitional aesthetics that operates through relationality.

Extending Coalitional Aesthetics

The coalitional aesthetics I examine, from the 1930s until 1981, have much more in common with the Popular Front coalitional imaginary than with later forms of organizing (and institutionalizing) difference within texts and across groups: multiculturalism and intersectionality. Benjamin Balthaser describes the aesthetic sensibilities of the Popular Front and its emphasis on solidarity most aptly, arguing that the "modernism of the Popular Front was a language of the global Left, its radical style a way to signify bonds of solidarity while also recognizing that the very global order that connects them is the one that they oppose."[23] The works I gather in *Coalition Literature* precede multiculturalism's influential (and since problematized) discourses of the 1980s and 1990s; furthermore, these works offer a radically different intercultural vision of organizing from that of intersectionality, especially in how the latter has become firmly ensconced within the framework of the individual subject. I do not quibble with intersectionality as a critical legal heuristic, especially as a descriptive and prescriptive category. Still, studying midcentury multiethnic coalitional aesthetics does reveal how often intersectionality has been co-opted to signal the formations and limits of empathy, especially within broken structures of discursive recognition. The problem is that neoliberal forms of recognition operate through identity and similarity, rather than by recognizing difference as the absolute foundation of any possible connectivity.

Bill Mullen and Mary Helen Washington, among others, have brought important attention to the postwar influence of Chicago's Popular Front cultural institutions, and James Smethurst has provided important evidence of the Popular Front's widely felt infrastructural influence on the Black Arts Movement in the US South, building on work by Margo Natalie Crawford and Robin D. G. Kelley.[24] This confluence of scholars takes up Alan Wald's important provocation to critics in his essay "The 1930s Left in U.S. Literature Reconsidered," in which he urges scholars to "contextualize the Thirties experiences within the following decades of the 1940s, 1950s, and 1960s, when many of these same cultural workers continue to produce under new conditions, and, also, interact with younger writers."[25] Smethurst, for example, traces how the internationalist orientation of 1960s activism emphasizes the viability of Popular Front cultural institutions, especially given the role of Old Left intellectuals and activists as professors and administrators at historically Black colleges and universities (HBCUs), particularly in the South, many of whom formed "important bridges between the Popular Front and Black Arts, providing some institutional continuity between different generations of Black radicals."[26] The persistence of coalitional tendencies centered on Black workers, often hidden in regional plain sight, means that viable resistant and oppositional art foundationally ushered leftist art and politics through the anticommunist 1950s and into the efflorescence of left-oriented activism in the 1960s. For Rachel Ida Buff, in her study of left-of-center and socialist-adjacent immigration organizations of the twentieth century, the Popular Front forms a necessary fundament. Using "the history of the American Committee for the Protection of the Foreign Born (ACPFB), a multiracial organization with a broad national network among foreign-born communities" as a crucial example, Buff insists that the ACPFB's existence—from 1932 to 1982—shows how deeply its organizing tendencies were "emanating from the liberal-left coalitions of the Popular Front era."²⁷ For Buff, the continuities of the ideological conditions of coalitional resistance, traceable through historical distance, are demonstrated by the fact that "the anticolonialism prevalent in the 'New Left' was preceded by a fierce anti-imperialism on the part of the 'Old Left.'"²⁸ While anticolonialism and anti-imperialism index different moments of resistance to the development of global capital as well as residual (imperial) and dominant (national) formations of sovereignty, tracing their historical continuity, for Buff, shows the persistence of coalitional thought, especially as it is refracted through historical and social conditions.

I extend the above arguments, and offer answers to the following questions: In the US, how did we get from Popular Front coalitions to multiculturalism? How do literary form and literary content in particular help us trace movements, their continuations, their overlaps, and their influences? How does coalition shape literary texts as aesthetic objects, and what might multiethnic midcentury modernism's deeply political character have to do with coalitional thought? How did specific Anglo-American writers use coalitional aesthetics to discuss the intersections of labor, race, and gender against the common sense of the racist imaginaries they inherited and consciously opposed themselves to, and how might we understand their work as being shaped by and participating in an emergent canon of multiethnic literature? How does the Civil Rights Movement factor into this timeline, not as a bridge or a break and thus as ancillary to literary and political history, but as an important refinement and continuation of antiracist coalitional aesthetics? How can the coalitional aesthetics of *speaking with* offer a way to think about the watershed year of 1968 in important new ways? How might a turn to the coalitional aesthetic strategies midcentury multiethnic writers often used to shape novels, poems, and songs from the 1930s to the 1980s provide an insight that has so long been missing?

Coalitional thinking helps reconceptualize the broad category of ethnic literature against the grain of its academic reception, particularly regarding how this literature gets disseminated through consumption and pedagogy. I am not alone in this, of course: many scholars argue against the reifying impulses of pedagogy as a mode of ethnographic affirmation, especially in the age of an expanding canon. Works of ethnic literature too often become ethnographic testimonials assessed apart from aesthetic criteria rather than through them—the aesthetic is improperly separated from the political, to the detriment of both. I distinguish sharply between representation as a fact of linguistic life (in that all language is representative) and representation as an act determined within aesthetic practice (in that linguistic choices work together with formal parameters to produce desired affective, sensual, and intellectual effects). The mere presence of an underrepresented person in a text is never simply enough, and a casual perusal of American literary history shows this to be the case. More important is the labor done within the work of art as a conduit of readerly, writerly, and textual perspectives in a vibrating web of related aesthetic practices. To put it simply, dismissing something by calling it political or social-justice-oriented is a careless sleight of hand that betrays the intellectual smallness of those who make this sort of claim.

I therefore dedicate much of my energy to critiquing the general disciplinary record pertaining to the reception of ethnic American literature, and I insist on emphasizing novel modes of relation generated by coalitional thoughts and feelings. This is a reading practice that does not seek to totalizingly comprehend and master literary texts. Each author featured in *Coalition Literature* creates a set of related coalitional aesthetic practices that generate material, textual spaces for the voices and self-determined narratives of their subjects. This is done against the representation of social or cultural identity as an end in and of itself, which might initially seem contradictory: How can a text generate the voice of an un- or underrepresented person or people, yet also avoid the framework of what Amy Hungerford has called "the identity plot"—the narrative impulse to resolve tensions between the individual and their ethnic community?[29] To misread ethnic literature and ethnic studies as being devoted simply to expanding representation as such is to continuously center an unimaginative canon whose framework goes continually unchallenged (even when there are changes to the texts that constitute it).

Emergent Critical Practices and Positions

While I often focus on the figure of the migrant and the problems that migrancy reveals for political and artistic representation, I also offer a broader, interrelated series of case studies through which to understand the diverse, coalitional aesthetics of *speaking with* that shape literature, culture, and politics from the 1930s into the very early 1980s. I unfold a series of readings that concretely elaborate the legacies of midcentury, generally leftist thought, experimentation, and artistic creation, especially within literature. As I argue throughout the book, the granularity of this difference requires flexible and careful attention to how writers stage new ways of *speaking with*. To develop connections—rather than straightforward comparisons—it is necessary to generate artistic constellations and creative dialogues that trace previously unseen critical, material, and social relations between authors, as well as between theorists. Though the connections that enliven each chapter might at first seem willful, paying close attention to how authors used *speaking with* helps build a latticed argumentative structure that attends to how coalition unfurls as a polymorphous and deeply contextual experimental grammar.

I organize *speaking with* according to two connected but still independent modes: the grammars of relation and of generation. Conceptually, I mean relation as it is theorized by Édouard Glissant. Even with a specific conceptual foundation, though, relation does not operate as a generalizable theory but instead as a method for observing and remarking upon sets of contingent and surprising connections. These relations, unlike more academically traditional comparative heuristics, offer new versions of encounter and definition: these connections allow scholarship to revel in contingency and the joy of realization, rather than establishing stable sets for comparative consideration. In this way, relation can itself become a coalitional mode of scholarly inquiry, and this comes forth most clearly in my pairings of Zora Neale Hurston with Muriel Rukeyser, and Sanora Babb with Woody Guthrie. Generation, like relation, describes a contingent tendency of emergence as literary creation, especially within midcentury multiethnic US literature. In particular, generation names the process of meaning-making that comes from novel aesthetic practices in relation to literary tradition. In this sense, generation links works such as the poems of the Memphis Sanitation Strike, Carlos Bulosan's and Tomás Rivera's remixing of the literary genres of allegory and the bildungsroman, and the deep philosophical interventions offered by *This Bridge Called My Back*.

For Glissant, relation "does not act upon prime elements that are separable or reducible. If this were true, it would itself be reduced to some mechanics capable of being taken apart or reproduced. It does not precede itself in its action and presupposes no a priori. It is the boundless effort of the world: to become realized in its totality, that is, to evade rest."³⁰ Glissant suggests that nothing in relation can be understood in isolation; there are no terms in relation that can be "reduced to some mechanics capable of being taken apart or reproduced." Relation is also not solely an ontological category, and it defies stasis: in relation there are no "prime elements," nothing is "separable or reducible," nothing can "precede itself in its action," and nothing can be stilled or stopped, since "totality" in relation means "to evade rest." Everything in relation is revealed *in* and *as* relation, in perpetual motion and visible only in partial forms that can only be understood as connected to each other—fractals, in other words.³¹ This sense of contingency and interdependence does not make connection or analysis impossible, though; instead, intellectual labor becomes responsive in generative new ways: "Relation is learning more and more to go beyond judgments into the unexpected dark of art's upsurgings. Its beauty springs from the stable and the unstable, from the deviance of many particular poetics and the clairvoyance of a relational poetics."³² There is perhaps no stronger intellectual inspiration for my conceptualization of *speaking with* than Glissant's antipodal philosophy. Glissant finds beauty in multitude, contradiction, and aesthetic diffusion, all of which coincide in the generation of nearly infinite modes of relation. This is precisely—or, better yet, imprecisely—how authors use a constantly shifting, constantly renewing variety of practices that generate *speaking with* and its expansive, coalitional aesthetics.

I acknowledge, indeed, that the novel connections between, and pairings of, writers and cultural figures who imagine relationality along aesthetic and cultural continuums can only come into being through a certain degree of critical willfulness. The connections and resonances between Zora Neale Hurston and Muriel Rukeyser, two fiercely critical artists searching for justice who are the focus of my first chapter, are extremely strong. Embracing a flexible, coalitional praxis means opening oneself up to the many meanings and possibilities contained within each text. It means resisting unidirectional or preordained readings of texts and following instead the various, often subtle shapes taken by *speaking with*, including confusions and complications. I complicate readings of Zora Neale Hurston, whose work has too often been utilized as an ethnographically unified representation of Black Southerners. The same impulse undergirds my turn to the poems written during and immediately after the 1968 Memphis Sanitation Strike: in attending to the spirit of poets and activists who imagined the present and future through a critical relationship to the past and its canons of thought, I argue for a sensitive formalism couched in nuanced and collaborative meaning-making. The refusal of the singular is also my strategy when I assess and correct the dominant literary criticism of Rivera's . . . *y no se lo tragó la tierra* and Carlos Bulosan's *America Is in the Heart*, and when I perform undercommons readings of songs by Guthrie.[33] Complication and uncomplication are related critical outcomes in this book, largely because both processes, in their specific application, develop each text in relation to another and strive to make each text *more* readable, though not simpler. In this, I align myself with Monika Gehlawat's critical study of dialogue in midcentury US literature, in which she traces a continuity of authors who "showcase dynamic plurality through literary representations of speaking subjects engaged in dialogue, direct address, debate, and self-testimony."[34] The point, for Gehlawat, is a plurality that cannot be settled or captured; the same holds true for the authors in my book, and it is this sparking aliveness that prompts me to pursue the resonances I have found.

The authors I discuss consciously work to avoid any personification of a fictitious person or entity as a representative of a whole, as well as any reduction of a person's or a people's multiplicity. In this, I find important precursors in Walt Whitman's hugely influential embrace of contradictions and multitudes; Yiddish modernism centered around Abraham Cahan's *Forverts* and continuing through brothers Isaac Bashevis Singer and Israel Joshua Singer (who were contemporaries, in part or in whole, of many of the authors in my study); and, especially, the history of multilingual modernism that Joshua L. Miller aptly describes as "kinetic expressive forms [that] lent credence to alternative angles of literary perspective, enabled insight into diverse U.S. communities, and generated critiques of racialized national Anglo-Saxonism."[35] *Speaking with* brings to light and helps analyze the vastness of interpretive possibilities, demanding that textual encounters between readers, writers, and literary subjects remain open and transformative. *Speaking with* urges the unsettling of assumed fantasies of sovereignty, power, and representational promise, instead looking for conjunctions in the otherwise, in what is beside the point, in what is almost missed. This is the case when Zora Neale Hurston and Muriel Rukeyser criticize the idealization of the "folk" that prevailed in their time, which suggested the folk were an untouched and simple category of regional humanity. Thus, even as Hurston and Rukeyser explore folk ideas and popular knowledge, they do so in order to raise up the voices of people directly impacted by ecological and capitalist destruction—to bring them into a coalitional fold. This is also the case when I correct for allegorical (mis)readings of Tomás Rivera's . . . *y no se lo tragó la tierra* and Carlos Bulosan's *America Is in the Heart*, or when considering Sanora Babb's *Whose Names Are Unknown* and its signal attention to Dust Bowl migrants and their lives. These texts refuse totalizing allegorical readings even as they offer distinctly collective visions of coalitional belonging. Even as I acknowledge irrepressible yet doomed political hope—which, as Sara Marcus reminds us, means we might see "disappointment not merely as a reaction to failure but as a form of survival"—in so many texts, I find beauty and justice in the shared struggle to reshape the very possibilities through and under which art and politics revolutionize each other.[36]

As a spatial and literary heuristic, placement is crucial to establishing an interpretive praxis crafted through literary and cultural studies within the book. Thus, to pay attention to the various modalities of *speaking with*, especially as they are registered across cultural, literary, and musical discourses, is to commit to a praxis that allows for critical flexibility—that is, an aesthetics on the move. The various modes of *speaking with* present in this book reveal itinerancies of being and belonging that produce relation through coalition's often fitful, often exciting generation. Incomplete, flexible, and open-ended coalition emerges in the radical yet subtle experimentation behind Rukeyser's *The Book of the Dead* and Zora Neale Hurston's *Mules and Men*, the peregrinations and melodrama of Bulosan's *America Is in the Heart*, the aesthetics of a community-in-formation that run through Tomás Rivera's . . . *y no se lo tragó la tierra*, and the dialogic construction of prose, poetry, and art in *This Bridge Called My Back*. These texts experiment with new models of reading and literary representation, all of which offer complicated hermeneutical revisions of how the world and its many entities and places get encountered. Hermeneutics is not a synonym for interpretation, but a revitalized, urgent ethical project for living in a world encountered through dialogic negotiation.

A major feature of *Coalition Literature* is its attention to how certain textual and artistic practices open up interplays between texts as speaking objects, textual subjects as speaking subjects, audiences as listeners, and authors as active and responsive participants in a dialogue. This depends on deliberate acts that make texts present, sometimes through multimodal writing, sometimes by deauthorizing or collectivizing lyrical subjectivity or narrative authority, sometimes by embedding a song so specifically within the local that it opens a brilliantly lit causeway between the particular and the universal. These strategies—what Jessica Berman identifies as "narrative strategies that allow many of the radical writers of the 1920s and 1930s to incorporate working-class voices, rhythms, and experiences into narrative fiction and also resist a dominant, unified perspective that might silence those voices"—endure beyond their moment of modernist experimentation.[37] Although works like *Whose Names Are Unknown* and *Mules and Men* are more chronologically relevant to Berman's point, *America Is in the Heart*, songs by Guthrie, the poems of the Memphis Sanitation Strike, and *. . . y no se lo tragó la tierra* also generate related but quite unique strategies that allow them to not only "resist" but also *refuse* altogether the possibility of "a dominant, unified perspective." These texts labor to create a coalitional difference in their approach to creating nonsingular narrative, articulating togetherness while avoiding homogeneity. Relatedly, Alexandra Vazquez, using criticism as a dialogic model of relational meaning-making rather than as an instrument of pure interpretation or explication, provides a generative and flexible methodological example for the undertaking of critical cultural studies and textual interpretation. For Vazquez, "listening in detail," as a critical ethos, requires "a set of necessary protocols: one must be able to adjust to a different sense of time, be eager to go to unexpected places, remain open to being altered, ready to frame a project in the diminutive, and prepared to assume there is always some other way."[38] Adhering to protocols rather than methodological truisms (reminiscent of Hortense Spillers's critique of methodology and discipline as such[39]), Vazquez sees listening in detail as an *ethos*, or a form of critical engagement that produces new critical inflections.

This critical practice of "listening in detail" moves me toward a critical position that James Baldwin, in his essay "Everybody's Protest Novel," names when defining truth: "truth, as used here, is meant to imply a devotion to the human being, his freedom and fulfillment; freedom which cannot be legislated, fulfillment which cannot be charted."[40] Within coalitional aesthetics, "devotion to the human being, [their] freedom and fulfillment" is taken as the primary and foundational logic of expression: there cannot be utterance or art without devotion to freedom and fulfillment within a relational framework. Furthermore, it is not the artist who instantiates freedom and fulfillment through art; instead, freedom and fulfillment precede and precondition any act of artistic creation. However, as Gayatri Spivak warns, the conflation of aesthetic and political representation is one of critical theory's most persistent problems. By understanding how *speaking with* radicalizes existing notions of political representation through a praxis of revolutionary (re)presentation, we can sketch a route alternative to the one critiqued by Spivak when she questions the efficacy of discussing the representation of the other—whether defined as the subaltern, the proletariat, or the colonized—without determining a consistent or specific meaning of representation as a term or notion. Although Spivak's focus is on a dialogue between Michel Foucault and Gilles Deleuze published in *Power/Knowledge*, she signals that her intervention is meant to be more broadly instructive, since the problem is widespread in politically oriented criticism and philosophy. Says Spivak,

> Two senses of representation are being run together: representation as "speaking for," as in politics, and representation as "re-presentation," as in art or philosophy. Since theory is also only "action," the theoretician does not represent (speak for) the oppressed group. Indeed, the subject is not seen as a representative consciousness (one re-presenting reality adequately). These two senses of representation—within state formation and the law, on one hand, and in subject-predication, on the other—are related but irreducibly discontinuous. To cover over the discontinuity with an analogy that is presented as a proof reflects again a paradoxical subject-privileging.[41]

Spivak comments on the critical habit of representing others' voices through the un-reflected-upon position of the author or the critic, a habit that reinscribes the already oppressive framework of power that separates the critic as a speaking subject and the reification of the *who* about which the critic speaks into a *what*.[42] By speaking "benevolently" about the oppressed—by representing their concerns—the critic presents him- or herself as one who knows, as a privileged voice. But, as Spivak points out, we must remember that the critic or author is not only representing the other in the realm of politics but also engaging in aesthetic "re-presentation."

The "other" is too often spoken for by benevolent critics, and Spivak points out that what emerges is always a matter of representation: a literary figure or figuration, an emptying out of content, has occurred. This constructed lack becomes a space in which the critic can unfold the argument they wish to prove. This produces, as Rey Chow observes, an interminable loop in which the native informant is inscribed and iterated ad nauseam:

> Thus one of the most important enterprises nowadays is that of investigating the "subjectivity" of the other-as-oppressed-victim. "Subjectivity" becomes a way to change the defiled image, the stripped image, the image-reduced-to-nakedness, by showing the truth behind/beneath/around it. The problem with the reinvention of subjectivity as such is that it tries to combat the politics of the image, a politics that is conducted on surfaces, by a politics of depths, hidden truths, and inner voices. The most important aspect of the image—its power precisely as image and nothing else—is thus bypassed and left untouched.[43]

Through their critiques of critical theory's imprecise grasp of representation as a political as well as aesthetic form, Spivak and Chow urge us to imagine anew the relationship between art and interpretation. Following Spivak and Chow, my wager is that the coalitional aesthetics of *speaking with* emerge from the entangled labors of writing and interpretation that refuse the singularity of the author as well as the reader. There is, and always will be, more than one of each—especially as coalitional texts produce multiple sources of meaning and authority, forging new collective possibilities through relation and generation.

The political or aesthetic message in a work of art emerges from the encounter across difference, whether this is a difference between the writer and the text's subject(s), or between the reader and the text. In this way, *speaking with* describes a coalitional critical position, as well as the structuring impulse of coalitional aesthetics. A text's moments of *speaking with* register the necessity of difference and mediation, highlighting the necessity of understanding one's position or placement within the world and its complicated networks of power. I consider *speaking with* as requiring an analysis of difference and mediation akin to Simone Weil's radically unsettling idea of "force" within a work of art. For Weil, the knowledge of "force" and its structuring of individual relationships to political or world-historical moments of crisis comes with a critically important burden: "Only [s]he who has measured the dominion of force, and knows how not to respect it, is capable of love and justice."[44] The structuring grammar of *speaking with* emerges always through the specificity of the intervention that each text performs within its respective generic constraints, attending to the capacities "of love and justice" that come from, in Weil's terms, knowing "how not to respect" any "dominion of force." In the realm of literary criticism, I find a sensibility related to Weil's in Paula M. L. Moya's claim that "as a medium of communication that involves the active use of imagination—on the part of the reader as well as the author—literature is one of the key sites in which the social order can be imaginatively examined and reshaped."[45] In developing a literary history of this active sense of transformation in US multiethnic literature, my own formal analyses and contextualizing arguments build a lattice of comparative readings that supports the efflorescence of this genealogy of texts in relation to one another. Each text I discuss *deforms* form: from *Mules and Men*'s experimental ethnography to the aslant documentary of *The Book of the Dead*, from Woody Guthrie's geographically dependent themes and variations on dignity and democracy to Sanora Babb's multimodal representations of the desire for dignity in *Whose Names Are Unknown*, from the enormously capacious collective lyric field of the Memphis Sanitation Strike's poetics to Gwendolyn Brooks's multiform lyric voice in her three "Sermon on the Warpland" poems, from the genre-bent narratives of labor power and migration in Carlos Bulosan's *America Is in the Heart* to the anti-allegorical development narrative of Tomás Rivera's . . . *y no se lo tragó la tierra*, each text conducts a reflective enactment of and engagement with its respective artistic forms by *speaking with*, rather than for, its subjects.

Two caveats emerge, however. First, these radical experiments in coalitional aesthetics do not in and of themselves perform coalitional activism, except insofar as they elaborate a philosophical and artistic foundation for digesting how coalition might be represented and considered. Nevertheless, even though they do not take the actual place of coalitional activism, *speaking with* offers intriguing continuations of—if not important alternatives to—dominant American aesthetic methods of articulating multiplicity, from Whitman's multitudes to Sandberg's place-based folk democratic lyrics, from Edgar Lee Masters's epitaphic lyrical communities to the montage-based free indirect discourse in Dos Passos's early novels, from Anderson's *Winesburg, Ohio* and its community of grotesques to Faulkner's segmented, familial stream of consciousness in *The Sound and the Fury*. The texts take up and expand Whitman's important sense of "multitudes," and given the Brooklyn bard's centrality to the Popular Front's aesthetic sensibilities, it is well worth noting the many paths taken toward plural expression and *speaking with*. Second, I do not dwell on failure as a method, model, or critical concern, even if this analytical position remains important to literary criticism that takes up leftist writing and art. While asserting failure's centrality certainly resonates in an academic world where hope, joy, and courage are seen as various stages of false consciousness, the coolness of this critical stance imposes critical cynicism over popular sentiment. Failure certainly seems easier in the face of fascism's shocking reappearances across the twentieth and twenty-first centuries; yet I cannot help but see, through the idea of *speaking with*, the powerful hope Sanora Babb asserts at the end of *Whose Names Are Unknown*:

> South to north the valleys curved in a long green flowering bowl, filled with food enough for a nation, while hunger gnawed these workers' bodies and drained their minds. An old belief fell away like a withered leaf. Their dreams thudded down like the over-ripe pears they had walked on, too long waiting on the stem. One thing was left, as clear and perfect as a drop of rain—the desperate need to stand together as one man. They would rise and fall and, in their falling, rise again.[46]

The Sisyphean resonances of this passage—particularly in the desire to rise and rise again—deepen with the knowledge that Babb's hoped-for farmworker's utopia has never emerged. What is required, first and foremost, is an unsettling of the very idea of hope: it is not merely a fantastical replacement for what does not work, and it is not a synthesis of the contradictions that prevent us from truly understanding the world we inhabit. Hope is not transcendence as either an external or internal force. I see *hope* instead as a word for what we do not yet know and what cannot be known *yet is felt*, with the demand for dignity as its heart and soul. As Stefano Harney and Fred Moten put it, "We're already here, moving. We've been around. We're more than politics, more than settled, more than democratic. We surround democracy's false image in order to unsettle it. Every time it tries to enclose us in a decision, we're undecided. Every time it tries to represent our will, we're unwilling. Every time it tries to take root, we're gone (because we're already here, moving)."[47] Hope is not a demand for what has been promised in a systemic imaginary; rather, it is what undoes systematically homogenized and flattened arcs of possibility. As with the striking workers in Babb's novel, hope, at its best, generates uncapturable narratives of dignity and empowerment.

Every writer discussed in this book offers textual spaces for encountering multiple discourses, voices, and stories, all of which critically imagine the varied terms of community formation and postulate other possibilities that can shape belonging. The texts I explore are most concerned with the people(s) and communities with whom they engage. I am further concerned with the dialogic nature of the coalitional aesthetics developed in these works, especially in their imagining of spaces that enable being and belonging outside of extant political structures. By voicing manifold subjectivities, the authors and songwriters in *Coalition Literature* craft textual encounters that enact coalitional aesthetics through their own varieties of *speaking with*.

The House *Coalition Literature* Lives In

I have structured *Coalition Literature* as a five-chapter book whose literary chronology begins in 1935 with the publication of Zora Neale Hurston's *Mules and Men* and ends in 1981 with the publication of *This Bridge Called My Back*. In the first chapter, I perform a contrapuntal reading of Zora Neale Hurston's *Mules and Men* and Muriel Rukeyser's *The Book of the Dead*, offering important new connections between these hugely influential writers, one a Black writer and ethnographer largely associated with the Harlem Renaissance and the other a Jewish writer and reporter firmly associated with leftist experimental poetry. Whether the oppression is political (as in the case of laborers who have no recourse to political power or belonging), economic (as in the exploitation of injured laborers for the benefit of others), or discursive (as in the stereotype of the Black folk, in which certain classes of people are relegated to the status of historical oddity or absurd remainder), Rukeyser and Hurston work against strictures that bind people to representational dead ends. By including and experimenting with the voices of their subjects in their work, Hurston and Rukeyser insist on the plural, multivocal, and dynamic lives of their characters, exploring the particularities of the people they have encountered, studied, and come to know, and with whom they have allied. What Rukeyser and Hurston reveal is a deeply multivocal humanity that lives, dies, struggles, weeps, laughs, and thrives in the everyday. Through the representation and centering of marginal peoples, Hurston and Rukeyser engage in the lexical and political praxis of *speaking with*, offering new hermeneutic methodologies with which to ethically encounter others and stage new versions and visions of democratic community.

My second chapter is a critical consideration of the work of Sanora Babb together with that of Woody Guthrie. During the time she spent in migrant "Okie" camp communities in the 1930s as part of her FSA work, Babb collected notebooks full of information on the lives and experiences of these migrants throughout their travels, travails, and encampments. Her boss, Tom Collins, read these notebooks and decided to forward them to John Steinbeck, who he knew was conducting research on white migrants in California. In *Whose Names Are Unknown*, Babb develops a descriptive praxis that utilizes but also quite radically departs from realism, and which is oriented toward consciousness raising and political transformation. This is a praxis that one finds in the music of Woody Guthrie, in that Guthrie invokes grand historical narratives while still singing about and representing his audiences. Guthrie often chose which verses to perform (of the many that his songs contain) almost on the spot, depending on the historical, political, or regional context. These songs, whether originals or standards, took on many shapes and sounds as they moved from setting to setting and from person to person, as they were learned and listened to across the country.

Chapter 3 continues the previous chapter's preoccupation with imagining new possibilities of ethical and political feeling through art, moving into an extended discussion of the Memphis Sanitation Strike and Gwendolyn Brooks's poetry from 1968. To do this, I look at direct action as both a mode of coalitional aesthetics and an inspiration for activist poetry within and in response to one of the most consequential labor strikes in American history. Memphis, Tennessee, shaped by post–Civil War migration to the city and industrialization, came directly to the fore of the American consciousness in February through April 1968, when the Memphis Sanitation Strike took place. Although I gesture to the interactive iconography of the Memphis Sanitation Strike, including protest signs, flyers, leaflets, poems, and student reactions to the March 28 police riot against a demonstration in support of the sanitation workers, I focus primarily on the poetry that emerged during the strike.

This "striking" poetry forms an especially capacious lyric field through which questions of speaking position and subjective responsibility come to the fore of political poetry. My analysis demonstrates the deeply coalitional and dialogic nature of the strike's poetry. The lyric field of the sanitation strike contains a multitude of lyric positions: poetry written by students in Memphis middle schools, high schools, and colleges, newspaper remembrances (including poetry), hymns and songs, slogans, placards, and picket signs. Studying this vernacular poetry in combination with Gwendolyn Brooks's three "Sermon on the Warpland" poems, which span *In the Mecca* and *Riot*, I tell a new story of Brooks's emergent lyrical mode after her experience at the Second Black Writers' Conference at Fisk—a story often told, but not in direct relation to the Memphis Sanitation Strike's expansive lyric field. The "Sermon on the Warpland" poems look to sources of communal and coalitional power that, when considered together with the poetry of the Memphis Sanitation Strike, expand poetic possibilities through a coalitional aesthetic that both takes up and supplements the idea of a collective lyric.

My fourth chapter takes a slight turn in terms of the book's chronological orientation. I turn back to a friend and contemporary of Sanora Babb's, Carlos Bulosan, arguing that his magnum opus *America Is in the Heart* can, when put into conversation with Tomás Rivera's *. . . y no se lo tragó la tierra*, shed important insight into migrant literature that has undertaken the difficult process of unsettling received literary forms such as the picaresque and the bildungsroman. I begin the chapter with Bulosan's *America Is in the Heart*, arguing that the memoir-adjacent novel uses *speaking with* to produce a remarkable new form: the migrant pizcaresque, with a z. In offering this term, *the pizcaresque*, I combine the words *pizca*—the Spanish word for "harvest" or "picking"—and *picaresque*, the literary form of peregrination, encounter, and discovery. With its pizcaresque shaped through a colonial migrant's encounter with the United States, *America Is in the Heart* is a text filled with heartache and degradation, but it also offers a singular and transnational expression of *speaking with* as generative of a necessarily coalitional aesthetic. I conclude with an extended reading of how Rivera constructs diasporic consciousness and diasporic memory, especially as these concepts interact with geographies of power, ethnicity, and capital, forming a significant echo of Bulosan's novel from twenty-five years earlier. In my reading of both texts, I find important points of view that insist on rethinking representations of the lives of migrants as Bulosan and Rivera knew them (both were migrant laborers and farmworkers). Rivera's novel is polyvocally composed of *estampas* (a regionally specific Spanish language literary form) and short stories, spanning various lives, locations, ages, and genders. In representing a wide picture of migrant life, Rivera opens up a complex critique of capital along several lines: gender relations, worker exploitation, religious fear and faith, and racial tension, to name a few. These two migrant pizcaresques show how coalitional aesthetics can allow authors to generate new ways of representing flows of people, affects, and memories through communally derived and community-inflected rhetoric.

In my final chapter, which functions as an extended conclusion through the addition of a coda, I argue that we in academia have too often used the monumental anthology *This Bridge Called My Back* as a stand-in for diversity, difference, and inclusion. We need to take quite seriously the anthology's incisive and radical contributions to theory and political action: its labor must not be attributed solely to the presence of diverse voices—though this is undeniably important, especially given the enforced exclusion of women of color in so much of academic discourse. Rather, these many voices enact coalition, rather than merely representing diversity. Ultimately, *Bridge* must be considered a monumental intervention in literary theory and philosophy that outlines specific practices for imagining new systems and canons of thought, one that emerges distinctly from the coalitional ethos of the Popular Front even as it lays the foundations for multiculturalism as an institutional logic and ethos. To a large degree, this takes place on the level of the anthology's shape. By shape, I mean *Bridge*'s argumentative and narrative arc; its organizational tactics, in the sense of how conversations and dialogues are situated and practiced within and throughout the text; and, finally, its radical and radicalizing arguments against verticalized, teleological theorizations of revolution and progress, instead insisting on a reevaluation of transformation as a horizontalized praxis of revolution. In these ways, *Bridge*'s formal and thematic construction establishes a praxis for deliberately and deliberatively creating a critical space in which transformative thought and action, and therefore transformative justice and politics, can take place.

Even if this chapter on *Bridge* ends the book, I do not consider the anthology to be the logical end point or ultimate exemplar of my argument, especially because it informs so much of subsequent activism and aesthetic practices in the 1980s, 1990s, 2000s, and 2010s (and, hopefully, the 2020s and beyond). Situating the anthology at the end of my discussion indicates the residual existence of a culturally resonant mode of coalition building based on the Popular Front. This is not the capstone or terminus of coalition building writ large, however. Concluding this way reveals my intention to revel in the difficult, circuitous, anachronistic possibilities contained within history and its interpretation, to see putative endings as beginnings, especially if viewed from every relevant perspective. *Bridge* by no means contains or indicates the end of radical coalition's history, or, indeed, a dialectical end point through which an emergent synthesis can be assumed, even as I take it up at the conclusion of my *particular* account of an era's literature. In this sense, *Bridge* is an example of coalitional literature at a significant waning point of the Popular Front's cultural and aesthetic influence, yet it uses that influence to build a vision of what multiculturalism would become, and how it would continue, even if disappointingly, the legacies of midcentury coalitional aesthetics.

With the book's coda, I look to emergent modes of coalition building in the US that coalesce under and against multiculturalism's tendencies toward representational inclusion. As the Soviet Union collapsed and the idea of international communism seemed to fade from possibility, emergent modes of union began to reimagine how to think broadly, particularly by refusing to let go of coalitional aesthetics. *Bridge* offers a particularly strong case for what this coalitional thinking might look like: thinking together through difference by remaking the parameters of the concept of unity. As *Bridge* shows, even as the matrix of multiculturalism determines so much of the coalitional imagination, radical organizing still takes place. Groups and alliances such as ACT UP, by criticizing mere representation and insisting on rethinking justice, make a case *against* multiculturalism as an organizing logic. Looking forward into the twenty-first century, I find that the radical legacies of multiethnic midcentury writers devoted to coalitional aesthetics have taken on new life, informing urgent new modes of imagining the present and the future. Though still emergent, these modes, like those that precede them, imagine open-ended, coalitional structures for inhabiting a difficult world in union with one another.

Migrating Engagements
Muriel Rukeyser, Zora Neale Hurston, and New Visions for Migrant Voices

ZORA NEALE HURSTON'S *Mules and Men* (1935) and Muriel Rukeyser's *The Book of the Dead* (a suite of poems that forms part of her 1938 collection *U.S. 1*) are powerfully informed by the authors' encounters with migrant workers.[1] Rukeyser's *The Book of the Dead* lyrically incorporates the voices of Black migrant workers and their families in West Virginia who became the victims of one of the US's most deleterious industrial disasters. Hurston's *Mules and Men* includes residents of her hometown of Eatonville, Florida, migrant workers in Everglades lumber camps, and people who moved in and out of New Orleans. Both authors found ways of *speaking with* the people they encountered on their respective research trips, and both reimagined—and often eschewed the norms of—literary representation, narrative form, and genre structure.

Hurston and Rukeyser felt the *need* to imagine new aesthetic possibilities for remarkably similar reasons: to ensure that Black migrants could openly express their desires and epistemic frameworks to a receptive audience, and to use aesthetics to understand Black history, Black diaspora, and migration as historically and geographically concrete processes as well as larger, transhistorical modes of indexing communal feeling and self-identification. *Mules and Men* and *The Book of the Dead* model the feeling of *speaking with* others, not in order to offer a sheer (or mere) representation of community, but to give a sense of with-ness that approaches something like a communal phenomenology. Several key questions guide my investigation of *speaking with* in *Mules and Men* and *The Book of the Dead*. What makes a story or a poem communal or coalitional? What does a story or poem look like when it is told by many, and how does that process of telling—as an act of *speaking with*—shape internal and external perceptions of community, especially when imagined through coalitional aesthetics? Any possible answers hinge on rethinking authority as a structuring concept.

Hurston and Rukeyser, though contemporaries, might not seem like the most obvious writers to bring together as originary figures in a story about aesthetic experiments dedicated to building a coalitional imagination. Tantalizingly, though, according to Rowena Epstein-Kennedy, "Hurston asked Rukeyser to accompany her on an ethnographic trip to the south in the mid-1930s."[2] Although the joint trip did not occur, it's quite exciting to imagine their potential encounter. Hurston, who is central to the literary historical account of the Harlem Renaissance, turned her attention to theorizing and describing Black aesthetics, thus forming part of a long bridge spanning the work of Paul Laurence Dunbar, James Weldon Johnson, Alain Locke, Langston Hughes, Margaret Walker, Gayl Jones, Toni Morrison, and Toni Cade Bambara, among many others. Rukeyser, for her part, condenses two strands of literary tradition, both of which formed dominant modes of poetic expression in the 1930s: documentary poetics or the poetics of witness, and high modernist poetic innovation. Both authors were considered idiosyncratic within the larger milieus in which they wrote, and were often charged with being out of step with the prevailing aesthetic tendencies.

I link the two through a variety of shared impulses, which initially shaped my theorization of *speaking with*. In particular, I consider what might bridge two writers of such shared aesthetic preferences who were quite far apart, politically speaking: Hurston's later move toward libertarian polemic is particularly troubling for the connections between them. However, the Popular Front's enduring influence, and the possibilities it opened for radical connections and affinities, offers an important structuring model for connecting Hurston and Rukeyser. Mary Helen Washington and James Smethurst argue that the Popular Front must indeed be understood as extensively influential, particularly in leftist Black artistic spaces and coteries. Washington argues that literary critics and historians must "extend the period of the Black Popular Front to 1959" because, as she shows, many artists and authors "continued to work collectively on the Left in Popular Front-style organizations."[3] For Smethurst, the internationalist orientation of 1960s activism—particularly in its antiwar, anticolonial, and antiracist formations—shows the persistence of the Popular Front. In particular, Smethurst notes that HBCUs, especially in the South, form "important bridges between the Popular Front and Black Arts, providing some institutional continuity between different generations of Black radicals," especially in arts and literature departments.[4] In examining Jewish migrant modernism's influence on US letters, Jonathan Freedman offers a bidirectional extension of the impulse toward continuity, noting that "Jewish writers, artists, and intellectuals helped transform the ways in which Americans imagined Otherness itself—the concept in the abstract, to be sure, but—of equal or even greater importance—the specific contours that other Others took in the unfolding ethnoracial drama" of US cultural production of the twentieth century.[5] For Alan Wald, a significant aspect of leftist midcentury political and cultural organizations was "cultural pluralism," which "was opposed to assimilation and the concept of the 'melting pot'" while also being "equally opposed to cultural and ethnic parochialism, positing as an alternative the future achievement of cosmopolitan values . . . as well as a willingness to borrow from all cultures to achieve the richest blend."[6] I turn to these expansive extensions of the Popular Front's aesthetic and structural influence, particularly in the purview of African American and Jewish American literary culture, to affirm just how perduring it was as a font of inspiration. Given the coalitional aesthetics of *speaking with* that Hurston and, slightly later, Rukeyser develop in their work, the Popular Front is significant in theorizing their aesthetic work together.

Washington's, Smethurst's, Freedman's, and Wald's arguments echo Denning's description of the "Cultural Front": "under the sign of the 'people,' this Popular Front public culture sought to forge ethnic and racial alliances, mediating between Anglo American culture, the culture of ethnic workers, and African American culture, in part by reclaiming the figure of 'America' itself."[7] Just as the Popular Front indicates a coalitional tendency of authors and artists, the Harlem Renaissance, as a literary critical and historical term, names what Alain Locke called "a fusing of sentiment and experience" within "the laboratory of a great race-welding," coalescing in Harlem in the first third of the twentieth century.[8] (Notably, Locke himself referred to the movement he was theorizing as "the New Negro Renaissance.") Locke theorized the Harlem Renaissance in its moment, and subsequent generations of scholars have examined the implications of this "fusing" and "race-welding": what emerged were modernist sensibilities of literary innovation, migration, and diaspora, as well as political sensibilities responsive to urbanization, industrialization, and the growing discourse of rights. Taking up the connections between these two tendencies, even though they differ in scale and intention—the Popular Front was a national political platform, while the Harlem Renaissance was characterized by the formation and interaction of many local coteries—reveals a shared dedication to fusion and representativeness in the process of relationally oriented institution building.[9]

Locke's language of "fusing" and "welding" describes Popular Front writing as well: the Harlem Renaissance and the Popular Front sought to engender the combination and complementarity of a multitude of places, spaces, communities, and political aims. These two movements are linked by the particular influence of what Steven S. Lee describes as "the dream of advancing simultaneously ethnic particularism, political radicalism, and artistic experimentation, debunking the notion that particularism yields provincialism."[10] Mary Helen Washington, Bill Mullen, Bill Maxwell, Lawrence P. Jackson, Robert F. Reid-Pharr, Steven S. Lee, Erin Royston Battat, and Abigail Manzella have all shown that the aims attached to Popular Front writers and to writers grouped under the umbrella of the Harlem Renaissance overlap significantly, particularly their political aims, and particularly insofar as these aims shared a commitment to expansive labor politics symbolically represented by the more racially diverse CIO—the Congress of Industrial Organizations, which splintered from the AFL (American Federation of Labor) and competed with it from 1938 until 1955, when the two rejoined. The Popular Front had broadly antifascist commitments, which often meant theorizing capitalism, racism, and sexism in the US as facets of worldwide fascism; this critique was often tempered by the political persuasion of the critic, of course, and the US was still much more often seen as a land of promise than a compromised political project. The reclamation of, as Denning puts it, "the figure of 'America' itself" was well under way, and Hurston and Rukeyser show two distinct modes of setting about to achieve this aim.

Reading Hurston and Rukeyser side by side reveals just how deeply the formal and conceptual connections run, beyond neat political links and archival evidence of belonging or membership. More than just similarities or resonances between the two authors' works, these formal and conceptual connections are relational, working in tandem to offer important new insights. Considering Hurston's *Mules and Men* together with Rukeyser's *The Book of the Dead* does not mean making connections on the order of the metaphysics of representation, as it were, but instead illuminating the related practices of representation that the two authors undertake to renew and reconsider how readers might conceptualize Black migrants in concrete settings—Florida, Louisiana, and West Virginia—as well as a broader claim to dignity and justice as transhistorical concepts.

Writing about Hurston and Rukeyser together illuminates a conceptual arc for coalitional aesthetics in the 1930s, an arc based on understanding how each author uses aesthetic practices, particularly narrative and lyric voicings, that emerge from migrants themselves. These voicings seek to evade representational capture. In addition, these overlapping aesthetic concerns underscore the continued need to differentiate among US modernisms while also offering new ways of conceptualizing the multiple relations between and confluences of these various regional, aesthetic, political, and social milieus and coteries, specifically by taking a motivated look at the modes of writing Hurston and Rukeyser generated.

When considered together, the distinct way in which each elaborates her approach—Rukeyser through the collectivized poetics of (bearing) witness and Hurston through experimental ethnographic narrative—speaks to the manifold possibilities in the praxis of *speaking with*. Still, both share important aspects of working with and through relation. Both Hurston and Rukeyser open textual space for the men and women they encounter, making it possible for these people's voices to resonate. They juxtapose the authorial voice with these other speakers' voices by means of different formal methods and visual cues, creatively reimagining and resituating documentary information and data. Hurston and Rukeyser insist on the irreducible complexity of the lives they represent on the page—lives that are always represented in relation to, and in dialogue with, other lives. Monika Gehlawat notes that certain literature "intentionally *represents*" what she, following Jürgen Habermas, calls practices of "communicative action," and that in doing so, this literature thematizes "such practices, their consequences, and reasons for failure," thus embracing "an ethical commitment to the practice of dialogue."[11] Hurston and

Rukeyser utilize this devotion to dialogue, described by Gehlawat, to explore the particularities of the people they have encountered, studied, and come to know, and with whom they have developed a rich imagination in common. What results is two texts that imaginatively embed voices into the labor that constitutes them, such that ethnographic voice and plot (in the case of *Mules and Men*), and poetic form and lyric voice (in *The Book of the Dead*), must be experimented with and reimagined as coalitional in order to function.

In addition, both *The Book of the Dead* and *Mules and Men* contain a documentary impulse and ethos, but it is not accurate in either case to characterize the work as straightforwardly documentary.[12] While Hurston and Rukeyser both went on fact-finding research journeys, and both collected stories which they then included in their work, their texts do not represent stories, experiences, or observations as standing alone or exemplary. Instead, each instance or moment relies on context and situatedness revealed through its interplay with a larger narrative or lyrical structure. Both writers enliven facts and data—but this is not merely a representational choice meant to entice readers; rather, it is a way of generating an ethical imperative, an act of treating aesthetics as an embodied and relational politics. For both Hurston and Rukeyser, there is no prototypical folk or citizen, no "real American," that predetermines identitarian possibilities and affiliations and excludes anyone who does not fit the mythical image. Instead, both authors generate a kaleidoscopic sense of possibility and construct a different basis of belonging to a community. Indeed, each author deforms form: *Mules and Men*'s experimental ethnography takes apart ethnographic conventions regarding the categorization of people as the "folk," and the aslant documentary style of *The Book of the Dead* forms an instance of lyric poetry made up of multiple levels of individual and collective discourse. Each text conducts a sideways and self-reflective performance of its respective form, *speaking with*, rather than for, its subjects and its audiences.

Both *Mules and Men* and *The Book of the Dead* reveal a deeply multivocal humanity that lives, dies, struggles, weeps, laughs, and thrives in the everyday—and always, always in relation, which is revealed as a dignity whose expression emerges in surprising ways, from brawls to burials. Through the presentation and centering of putatively marginal persons and their lives, Hurston and Rukeyser engage in a lexical and political praxis of ethically encountering others by following them as they stage new versions and visions of community. By insisting that the voices they present in their works must be listened to, Rukeyser and Hurston refuse to present people as mere objects for audiences to feel sympathy for, or symbols whose narratives and postures signal folksiness. Going further, they suggest that the very framework of representation—both aesthetic and political—needs to be revolutionized in order to place author, reader, and textual subject *beside* one another, in dialogue with one another, rather than treating them according to informational flows that depend on their authority as writers.

Zora Neale Hurston's Aslant Ethnography

The purpose of Zora Neale Hurston's ethnographic trips to Florida and Louisiana for *Mules and Men* (as well as her trip to Haiti a year after the book's publication) was to gather material for a robust study of Southern Black life and culture. *Mules and Men* is no typical ethnography, though. As one of Franz Boas's mentees, Hurston was at the forefront of developing the discipline of ethnography, but her book departs from his methods—particularly standard notions of distance, objectivity, and familiarity—in significant ways. As María Eugenia Cotera argues, Hurston's extraordinarily complicated relationships to Franz Boas and her financial patrons occurred because of her work's dedication to complication, pleasure, and imaginative scholarship.[13] Even Hurston's particular method of participation violates codes of conduct within the participant-observer construct that establish the applicability and repeatability of ethnographic data. The first leg of her research trip—a stop in Eatonville, Florida—was also a return to her hometown, which her forebears helped build into one of the first incorporated all-Black towns in the United States. In Florida, where Hurston already knew many of the stories she recorded, she told people she would be recording their stories and embedding them within representations of their lives, and she actively participated in the social life of her friends, family, and neighbors. In New Orleans, an important city for intra-Southern migrants, Hurston went even further by complicating herself as a source of expertise: she embarked on a lengthy tutelage as a student of Vodun, unlearning her previous beliefs and social mores, her university education, and her social life in Harlem (as well as the social life she reveled in while in Eatonville, in the first half of the book).

The entire narrative construction of *Mules and Men* blends fiction with nonfiction in striking ways. The text lives in a space beside genres such as memoir, novel, ethnography, and historiography, offering a distinctly relational method of representing its subjects through the practice of *speaking with*. Hurston embedded stories she heard on her trips within a broader narrative she largely constructed, animating them within a vivid framework. In the Florida section, this embedding takes place in order to index Hurston's interaction within larger conversational communities and contexts. While in Louisiana, she participates in a small, esoteric community devoted to Vodun. If Mark Twain's *Adventures of Huckleberry Finn* famously has problems stably reaching its conclusion, *Mules and Men* takes the difficulty of conclusion to a stranger, more speculative level. Hurston's book ends with the departure of the author altogether: she has been semiotically transformed into, and semiotically displaced by, an image of a black cat sitting on its haunches and licking its paws. Importantly, this image picks up a preceding moment in the text: a black cat that she buried alive during a ritual that was part of her training in Vodun (or, as she calls it throughout, Hoodoo). This reanimation of the black cat at the end of *Mules and Men*—the continuation of Hurston the author within the reawakened image of the formerly sacrificed cat, and the combination of unmistakably metaphorical and even surreal elements with the ethnographic language she depends on to contextualize her Louisiana journey—crafts an altogether magical combination of fiction and nonfiction.

Hurston's ethnographies, novels, and memoirs were critical interventions in their time. Each one of these works was certainly meant to enlighten audiences and preserve certain folkways and folk forms, as part of Hurston's larger project of describing the Black South and cataloguing some of its unique aesthetic practices and experiences. Contrary to what several of her contemporary critics accused her of (the most famous criticism came from Richard Wright), Hurston's representations of African Americans in *Mules and Men* and other texts detail the richly textured, imaginative lives of the people she grew up among, knew, loved, and ultimately wrote about. While some critics perceived Hurston's texts as unabashed and uncritical folk portraits operating through ethnographically justified axioms about rural Black life, Rosemary V. Hathaway argues that "the very issues about which Hurston's critics took her to task, and the very things that make [*Their Eyes Were Watching God*] vulnerable to touristic reading—its representation of folklife, its use of dialect, and its apparent lack of political grounding—are the same issues that can be reread and reinterpreted to create a more complex understanding of the novel, and of Hurston's view of tradition."[14] While it might feel justified to teach Hurston's texts as historical or ethnographic portraits that widen students' understanding of diverse American experiences, Hathaway suggests we reread Hurston's work and reinterpret it as knowingly working against modes of "touristic reading" in which comprehension becomes a means of suitably categorizing knowledge. In other words, touristic reading understands culture as an unchanging piece of a larger mosaic, a system of relations that may be networked but which remains uncomplicated and stable.

While insisting on cultural distinctiveness, Hurston refrained from simplistic, atavistic, or straightforwardly nostalgic arguments about Southern Black people: in other words, she problematized the production of the "folk" as a stable, reified category of cultural purity. Hurston's work defies comprehension as a means of achieving epistemic certainty, instead pointing to the contingencies of relation: communities constantly shift and remake themselves. With its playful and polyphonic sense of cultural life, Hurston's *Mules and Men* glitters with possibilities that emerge from *speaking with* as a highly contextualized, participatory, and flexible process.

The book's many energetic narrative centers, which I refer to as speakers, compete with each other as storytellers. This produces a text of many authors, leading the ethnography into novelistic terrain. However, the dynamic does not function as a competition for narrative space on a metafictional level, à la Alex Woloch's *The One vs. the Many*, or Marta Figlerowicz's study of character and narrative attention in *Flat Protagonists*. Being both ephemeral and integral, the speakers in *Mules and Men* enable the text to develop its fullness and narrative arc through the relation and accretion of *speaking with*, rather than hinging on independent character development or the competition for narrative space. By framing ethnographic anecdotes through her own narrative process of self-making in Florida and self-unmaking in Louisiana, Hurston utilizes and redistributes the author function to build a fiction-adjacent, networked story of communality that truly cannot establish stable ethnographic truth outside of itself. This becomes coalition building: *speaking with* elaborates a narrative in which belonging and truth-telling become multiply possible. In other words, Hurston's method of *speaking with* can be distinguished from other communal narrative impulses and even other ethnographic and anthropological texts, particularly in how she makes *Mules and Men* truly collaborative, rather than observing so-called native informants and converting their lives into exchange-value for scholarship.

The ethnographic data she collects—tales or stories, colloquially called "lies" by those who share them, which I will discuss at length below—are not kept within the framework of anthropological methodology but are instead used to imagine an enlivening, participatory, and collaborative context for each story. By producing an ethnographic monograph that fictionalizes her experiences and properly but creatively contextualizes the stories she is told, Hurston undoes the singularity of the monograph and its fiction of authority, ceding space to other storytellers. In this, she prefigures a tendency Gehlawat observes in Grace Paley; namely, that Paley prefers "communal to autonomous narrative authority," and that she uses "literary craft" as a formal strategy of demonstrating "political empowerment" for characters within their embedded narratives.[15]

Turning to an example of this redistributed ethnographic method in Hurston's book, we can see how she generates an improvisational, dialogic process through which one can actively participate in the building of community. She first elaborates this practice in a section of the text in which she hangs out with laborers in Loughman, Florida, at the Everglades Cypress Lumber Company's work camp. The encounter begins with none of the ease or smoothness of her encounters in Eatonville, her hometown. The men and women at the camp are from all over Florida and the South, and they have come together to dredge swamps, chop trees, and mill lumber. None of the workers or their family members will approach Hurston, given her beautiful new car and expensive Macy's dress. She weaves a tale of herself as a bootlegger's girlfriend and gradually makes inroads with some of the men around a campfire. Soon, a man named Pitts approaches her, letting her know the fine way he would treat a woman of her class and bearing. Hurston recounts,

> I laughed and the crowd laughed and Pitts laughed. Very successful woofing. Pitts treated me and we got on. Soon a boy came to me from Cliffert Ulmer asking me to dance. I found out that was the social custom. The fellow that

wants to broach a young woman doesn't come himself to ask. He sends his friend. Somebody came to me for Joe Willard and soon I was swamped with bids to dance. They were afraid of me before. My laughing acceptance of Pitts' woofing had put everybody at his ease.

James Presley and Slim spied noble at the orchestra. I had the chance to learn more about "John Henry" maybe. So I strolled over to James Presley and asked him if he knew how to play it.

"Ah'll play it if you sing it," he countered. So he played and I started to sing the verses I knew.[16]

Hurston conveys the vivacious, engaging quality of the camp celebrations, which were often coincident with payday. Throughout the book, Hurston often describes her own immense, intense feelings of joy as she both participates in and bears witness to the telling of stories, dancing, fighting, singing, gambling, and eating. Indeed, this passage neatly conveys how Hurston uses *speaking with* to represent the community she has encountered. The use of "and" in the first sentence resists the grammatical separation of clauses through commas; this is a small observation, but the breathlessness of conjunctive grammar indicates the process of connection and causation Hurston wants readers to observe. Although her laughter directly responds to Pitts's "woofing"—his hitting on her—she nevertheless produces a layer of mediated connection between herself and Pitts through "the crowd." As part of her conversation with Pitts, a communal connection forms. Hurston continues to develop the necessarily relational and improvisational communal sensibility throughout the passage.

Daphne Brooks argues that Hurston finds ways to both spatialize and historicize Black cultural life. While Hurston's attention to sound and orality has been well catalogued, her self-archived performances and her own involved musicality during ethnographic trips (particularly to Jamaica and to Haiti, which formed the basis of her 1938 book *Tell My Horse: Voodoo and Life in Haiti and Jamaica*), as Brooks points out, have not often been considered by scholars as methods of participation or, indeed, as the development of novel ethnographic methods. Brooks argues that in Hurston's singing, "with that weird, quirky, piercing voice, Zora folds the folk musically into the realm between head and heart and sonically mediates that space through her own form of what cultural critic Sonnet Retman refers to as 'signifying ethnography.'"[17]

Brooks's brilliant observation about Hurston's "own form" is in reference to her personhood, her bodily sense of moving through the world and placing herself in the context of ethnographic fieldwork such that knowledge's appearance is always as a result of participation and communality, rather than of distance and observation. Indeed, when in the above passage Hurston asks the musician James Presley about the classic folk song "John Henry," she finds that in order to "learn more about" the song, she must actively participate in the communal joy of the gathering. Presley assents to Hurston's larger project by challenging her to become part of the community and its knowledge. Rather than an extractive intellectual economy or a commercial relationship based on the exchange-value of the community's knowledge, this interaction shows that Hurston's work falls more along the lines of gift-giving and equivalent participation.

In her interaction with James Presley, Hurston actively situates the pursuit of historically important knowledge as being bound up in the space of living culture. Indeed, the only way to access what she deems ethnographically important is to re-create the "data" in an active, living context. Importantly, though many of the incidents related in *Mules and Men* certainly happened, many likely did not, and the book's plot most certainly did not proceed precisely the way it is related, especially in terms of each chapter's internal chronology. Fictional strategies structure the book, as they give a *truer* portrait of the stories and exchanges Hurston relates. This gets at the heart of the distinction between "truth" and "authenticity": in order to cut through this Gordian knot, Hurston's *Mules and Men* shows that "authenticity" can emerge only if it is in the pursuit of a larger "truth," a pursuit that requires fictionally resituating interactions so that the ethnographic data can be vividly and contextually represented. To enable this larger pursuit of truth, Hurston relies primarily on one form of ethnographic data: what she truthfully, authentically, and playfully calls "lies."

For Hurston, "lies" are regionally and ethnically specific, which is why she has traveled to Florida to investigate and collect them. In *Mules and Men*, lies are deep sources of historical knowledge, and they function as tales and tools of survival. They relate humorous anecdotes, serve to pass the time, provide mnemonic structures for cultural exchange and continuation, and, through all of this, strengthen familial, communal connections and genealogies (in terms of both family trees and epistemic histories). They can be affirmative tales of enslaved people tricking enslavers, of a hero named John, of the Devil, or of God; they can be admonitory stories that enforce social codes and mores; they can be explanatory and Genesis-type stories about various biological or cosmic facts. Lies contain larger truths—about memory, about faith, about race relations, about the experiences of enslavement and forced diaspora, about humor, about knowledge, about present conditions, about good and evil, about futurity. As deliberate fictions, lies operate like a Central and South Florida iteration of what Roland Barthes would later in the century call "myths," in that they form a textual and semantic layering around objects, ideas, and communal experiences. In these ways, lies open up and are (re)presented to *Mules and Men*'s readers as experiences to be hermeneutically approached and encountered.

Recall that in the context surrounding the music-making passage above, Hurston lucidly illustrates her very self-conscious, self-aware method of creating trust and confidence: she creates a fiction in order to facilitate the appropriate context for storytelling and exchange. She does not disavow her nice clothes or her nice car, but instead finds a way to explain them that is reasonable and interesting to the people around her—indeed, her lie here functions somewhat like the "lies" she's dedicated to collecting, in that it serves an explanatory purpose that confirms a communal epistemology. While this is indeed dishonest (and just one of the many methods Hurston employed that Franz Boas objected to), it signals her desire to place herself within and according to the community's sensibilities. This means that Hurston erases her status as an academic (while still functioning as an academic) in order to establish an egalitarian relationship between herself and the people at the lumber camp. She does not completely erase her purpose for coming to the camp, though:

> After [the first celebration] I got confidential and told them all what I wanted. At first they couldn't conceive of anybody wanting to put down "lies." But when I got the idea over we held a lying contest and posted the notices at the Post Office and the commissary. I gave four prizes and some tall lying was done. The men and women enjoyed themselves and the contest broke up in a square dance with Joe Willard calling figures.
>
> The contest was a huge success in every way. I not only collected a great

deal of material but it started individuals coming to me privately to tell me stories they had no chance to tell during the contest.[18]

In establishing both her bona fides and the contest, Hurston creates a space in which the community members feel their stories can be respected. Indeed, it is the *actual* truth that the lumber camp denizens have trouble accepting: they "couldn't conceive of anybody" seeing the "lies" as culturally or academically valuable. Leaving aside the question of their academic publication and the role Hurston's work has long played in legitimizing ethnography and anthropology, the situation she creates enables the storytellers to feel they are *speaking with* Hurston, and that their stories are interesting in and of themselves. This shift from individual purpose—"when I got the idea over"—to communal ownership and participation—"we held a lying contest and posted the notices"—is replicated through the grammatical shift from "I" to "we." Thus, while perhaps the community members initially saw lies as irreverent and culturally esoteric, Hurston's contest prompts people to come forth—"coming to me privately to tell me stories they had no chance to tell during the contest"—and distribute their knowledge to a larger, clearly more visible cultural project.

In setting up the contest, Hurston establishes an internally coherent and internally objective measure through which to rate and remunerate the "lies." This certainly explains the success of the contest and people's subsequent willingness—indeed, by her recollection, their eagerness—to share their lies with Hurston. By ingratiating herself to the laborers and their families, Hurston gains access to the spaces and statements of everyday life that contextualize the "lies" and bring to life the many people with whom she interacts. In the chapters that follow, Hurston gets to accompany the laborers out to the swamps and hears many more "lies" on various treks and adventures. This enlivening means of *speaking with* shows the work Hurston does in creating a shared space of experience, which Retman argues is an effective rhetorical strategy of subtly foregrounding the positionality of the author, and, by identificatory and participatory extension, the reader: "As she drives, talks, and sings with her informants, she shares contemporary time with them. By proxy, so do we."[19]

In the process of writing *Mules and Men*, Hurston incorporated a "great deal of material" she collected from the contest—very little of which she shares at the time of the contest's occurrence in the narrative—as well as some of the other "lies" privately related to her. Sidestepping the possibility of a perfect memory, it is quite likely that Hurston restaged and enlivened the stories by incorporating them within believable, living contexts. As a result of any given chapter's plot structure, the "lies" are often thematically and epistemologically related. That is, by using the "lies" to build an entirely new narrative arc appropriate to their content as well as their telling, Hurston helps rethink the possibilities of story and community as overarching concepts. She builds narrative around the "lies," suggesting that they are both the focus and engine of storytelling's form: the fictionalized or temporally resituated plot serves to provide an interactive context for the epistemologically and categorically grouped stories. In fact, these "lies" *generate* the very possibility of the book's framework, and *Mules and Men* hangs entirely on the structural progression in which Hurston situates the stories she collects. In Chapters 5, 6, and 7 of *Mules and Men*, when the workers at the Everglades Cypress Lumber Company progressively discover they do not have to work for the day and make their way to a nearby river to fish, the tales and lies are often cued by the sights and sounds of nature, especially as they relate to the conversation's shifting contours. Leaving the camp, Hurston and the workers experience a shift in the scope and type of stories being shared. James E. Ford III observes that the surveillance and control of laborers in camps is a broader preoccupation of Hurston's (a concern that Muriel Rukeyser, Sanora Babb, Carlos Bulosan, Tomás Rivera, and others actively share). Reading through Hurston's reflections on Nietzsche and Spinoza, Ford argues that, like her other prose work more broadly, her novel *Moses, Man of the Mountain* "exposes a most pernicious feature of the camp, which tries to throw a wrench in the development of a collective critical consciousness among laborers. . . . Hurston reveals how a disunited multitude reacts passively to labor exploitation by a surveillance regime shrouding itself in mystery."[20] This "pernicious feature of the camp" featured in *Moses, Man of the Mountain*, however, is pointedly avoided in *Mules and Men*: rather than "a disunited multitude" that "reacts passively to labor exploitation," Hurston represents the laborers removing themselves from the camp. To Ford's point, they are not leaving the camp to discuss forming a union or meet with labor organizers. Yet they pass the time in their own way: in particular, fishing very likely reduces the need to rely on company stores and in-town suppliers whose wares are marked up for the seasonal workers. The "lies" the workers tell contain this contradiction of freedom and surveillance, of joy and oppression, of spiritual concerns and material complaints, and the narrative framework generates constant ongoing cues for the stories they tell.

It is telling that Hurston chooses chapters 5, 6, and 7 to tell this story of workers "at rest." Mirroring the biblical creation story—on the fifth day, Yahweh created the creatures of the water and the sky; on the sixth, Yahweh made the creatures of earth, including the first human; on the seventh day, a day of divine rest was decreed—this short sequence of "lies" spans discussions of heaven and hell, theories of labor and theodicy, and long-standing cultural norms, woven together through competitive, ecological, and narrative cues. For example, the lack of mockingbird calls on that Friday awakens the interest of the small group of men and women on their way to the river, and a man named Eugene Oliver says the silence of the birds is unnatural. Big Sweet, one of Hurston's friends and her chief protector in the camp, contradicts him, stating that it *is* natural. Big Sweet proceeds to enlighten her fellow travelers with a story about mockingbirds helping a hell-bound human friend of theirs: every Friday, they're in hell ferrying grains of sand to quench the fires of perdition in order to rescue their immoral friend, thus explaining their absence.[21] Much like the workers, whose fishing trip both is and is not related to the camp, these mockingbirds take their day off to do a different form of labor—one of love and sustenance.

In situating this "lie," Hurston has Big Sweet establish three strands of epistemological and narrative framework that the other people in the group take up, play with, and extend in immediate response to her tale. First, the "lies" establish mythical human-animal interactions, framing their causes and consequences. Second, and perhaps tautologically, observed animal and human behaviors, especially as they fictionally interact, are explained within stories as responses to human morality or immorality. Third, days of the week—particularly weekends—are confirmed in their importance in relation to work, time off, and worship. The lies told may incorporate one, two, or all three of these elements within their narrative framework.

Big Sweet's story leads to humorous, competitive storytelling about catfish when Joe Wiley responds with his own addition to the larger discussion about animals assisting humans. Joe Wiley prefaces his catfish "lie" by saying,

"If them mockin' birds ever speck to do dat man any good they better git some box-cars to haul dat sand. Dat one li'l grain they totin' on their bill ain't helpin' none. But anyhow it goes to show you dat animals got sense as well as peoples."[22] Wiley establishes a competitive stance here with his criticism of the mockingbirds (or, more accurately, criticism of the story told about mockingbirds) but acknowledges the broader premise of animals having sense. He introduces his own story as one about animal cleverness, and then segues into the tale itself: "Now take cat-fish for instance. Ah knows a man dat useter go fishin' every Sunday."[23] His story carefully and cunningly weaves together the same three strands established by Big Sweet's story—human and animal encounters, along with immoral behavior exhibited by ignoring the importance of a certain day of the week (Sunday as a day of worship)—but upholds its own narrative and thematic logic, transitioning from mockingbirds to catfish, from robbing and stealing (but treating birds with kindness) to the immoral flouting of church worship, from Friday to Sunday. Although the "lies" diverge, they emerge from shared discursive and cultural preoccupations.

The series of "lies" told on the trip to the river are representative of the stories in *Mules and Men* more generally. In each chapter, "lies" can be clustered into a number of shared—and often competing—sets of preoccupations, pedagogical intentions, and discursive explorations of cultural epistemologies. The breadth of preoccupations spans the entire book, from the Florida section all the way into Louisiana, when *Mules and Men* takes a decidedly mystical turn.

Hurston thus assembles a "dissembled" narrative, providing an enlivening, narratively oriented contextualization of folk culture. She is informant and tourist, borrower and lender, author and reader, teller and listener, gift receiver and gift giver. This is a particular mode of *speaking with*, and the text's formal functioning emerges from Hurston's demonstration of the stories in a communal and participatory setting, rather than as points of ethnographic data. By producing a living context, she establishes a dialogic form in which "lies" emerge in relation to each other: they come after each other; they spring up after suggestions, experiences, or mnemonic and environmental triggers. Indeed, David Todd Lawrence argues that "without the fictional contextualization, the isolated tales would provide only a partial understanding of how they function in a dynamic discursive moment. So the material Hurston adds does not just link up two folktales, it instead provides a colorful and plausible scene in which the folktales are situated."[24] As Lawrence points out, by situating the "lies" in a living context, Hurston gives readers an idea of how they construct folk epistemologies, and how these ways of knowing occur within the world. Indeed, as Lawrence claims, "in order to effectively employ the stories in this ethnographic model, they must be thought of as complete performance activities rather than just isolated textual recordings of single events."[25] Thus, rather than functioning as an anthology of folk stories, *Mules and Men* (re)presents knowledge through linked performances placed within an "extended context" to better establish not just what is told but how stories happen, as well as why they continue to explain the world and build relations within and across a community. More than simply remaking ethnography (and more than just violating ethnography's putatively objective boundaries), Hurston's writerly strategy makes *Mules and Men* not quite ethnography, not quite novel, not quite memoir, not quite performance, and entirely a practice of *speaking with*.

The "lies" show a vibrant, tenacious complexity that postures as a stable set of indexical representations emerging from a large set of community informants. Many of Hurston's readers initially saw her work as a set of fixed, typical portraits (Franz Boas's introduction to the text is representative of this viewpoint), and saw the "lies" as documentary evidence of a fading folk culture. Yet, as we will see with Rukeyser's disruption of documentary's formal expectations, Hurston's own methods destabilize the very ideas of folk purity that a cursory reading might accuse her of. As Michele Wallace has observed, Hurston's men and women fight, curse, and behave badly, even while they provide a pathway to putatively fading folk wisdom.[26] These men and women are *alive*—not representations or representatives, regardless of how much others at the time would have liked them to be either bucolic folk figures or model minorities. The very specificity with which Hurston imbues these subjects is what gives them their living textual splendor, and also what releases them from the boundaries of readerly expectation. *Mules and Men* revels in this articulated messiness of humanity—for Hurston, dignity arises from this very state of imperfection, from the deep contextualization she offers.

Sonnet Retman points out that *Mules and Men* is best read with an ear attuned to the atypical, boundary-pushing means through which Hurston redefines and signifies upon the conventions of ethnography, folk studies, and anthropology. Focusing on the problems and critiques engendered by the 1930s and 1940s cultural milieu that gave birth to documentary as we now know it, a world in which authenticity was a prized category, Retman shows how Hurston uses "signifying ethnography" to satirize and complicate the very notions of folk authenticity she was widely understood to be verifying. In her signifying ethnography, Retman argues, "Hurston shows her readers how these conventions produce images of the folk—and she makes them aware of their own complicity in the process."[27] For Retman, understanding Hurston's method can help "shed light on our contemporary negotiations with mass-mediated identity and consumer culture, and our grappling with the 'real' and the 'authentic' in narratives of self, community, and nation."[28] Awareness of complicity transforms understanding into a practice of perceptive reading, rather than of mastery or comprehension. Retman posits, indeed, that Hurston wants readers to see "how these conventions produce images of the folk," thus prompting a reflection on how textual encounters produce knowledge. Interpretation requires imagination—the making of images, literally—and we create these images according to previous experiences, cultural expectations, genre conventions, and the discursive possibilities offered by syntax and semantics and their interplay within the readerly community. Thus, by unsettling preconceived images of compliancy (through a careful elaboration of survival strategies and their explanations, as well as celebrations of time off), violence (which becomes central and necessary to the fictionalized narrative framework, rather than pathological or merely entertaining), and religiosity (by showing a wildly expansive theological structure that accommodates the agency and contradictory natures of humans, Yahweh, and Satan), *Mules and Men* opens up new possibilities.

The purely textual—that is, interpretable and interactive—representation of cultural life in *Mules and Men* eluded one of its most famous early champions, however. Franz Boas, in his preface to the text, suggested that it was "the charm of a loveable personality and of a revealing style which makes Miss Hurston's work an unusual contribution to our knowledge of the *true inner life of the negro*."[29] However, the interiority Boas thinks he sees, if it is understood as synonymous with essentialism, is clearly withheld in favor of a relational picture that tells a broader truth about communal knowledge. Hurston does not deny either interiority or agency, but insists instead on the need to see representation as a discursive amalgam. Rather than giving readers a folk portrait of "true inner life," Hurston confronts the expectation of and desire for authenticity with a vision of community as an interpretable, interactive whole, creating a text that consistently moves away from comprehension as a totalizing force. Hurston reroutes the question of authenticity through a textual alchemy of *speaking with* that produces an idea of truth even while it unsettles authenticity.

In contradiction, then, to the assumption that *Mules and Men* is an easy-to-digest ethnographic text that reveals representative authenticity—that the people in the text are precise portraits of Florida's Black folk—we can instead see it as a revealing and revelatory presentation of representation's impossibility. The liveliness of context in *Mules and Men* gives us a radical image of participatory art. Beyond ethnographic preservation of a fading or lost state of society, Hurston's work constitutes a vital political praxis that takes up the "folk" and their knowledge in order to make an argument about how communities function beyond essentialism, beyond how they might be seen by a world intent on studying or encapsulating them.

The recurrent, renewing relation between the reader and the text, mediated by Hurston's central role in collecting, framing, and disseminating the folk tales she has heard, generates a decentralized authority that unsettles any pretense of the text's unity of meaning. John Laudun argues Hurston's work often presumes that "human subjectivity . . . is dialogically constituted to the extent that sometimes readers are at a loss to know who exactly is speaking. And that would seem to be the point."[30] Hurston's staging of the encounter between the reader's interpretive subjectivity and that of the textual subject unmoors the reader from straightforward apprehension of a sequential or consecutive order according to which the folk tales ought to be catalogued. In *Mules and Men*, therefore, the route of interpretation is characterized by forms of slippage and can never be unidirectional.

Shifting the critical discourse around Hurston's ethnographic technique, Autumn Womack argues that the broader context of Hurston's practices—especially her use of film technology and ethnography—means we must move our "focus away from a politics of representation that takes for granted the representability of Black social life, and toward a concern with what visual technology can and cannot convey."³¹ Hurston does not merely produce documentation according to ethnographic standards of observation. Indeed, per Womack, in the few extant ethnographic films that Hurston made during the 1930s, there emerges "a filmic grammar that oscillates between the recognizable and the uncontrollable, producing visually discordant and disruptive effects at the very moment when coherence is at stake." In this way, Womack continues, "the films unhinge the putative relationship between spectator, film, and subject and clear a space for the emergence of social formations, political narratives, and ways of seeing that move outside the terms of positive, good, and real, unhinging the authoritarian perspective of both the camera and the spectator."³² Turning on the idea of "unhinging," Womack's argument emphasizes the uneasy relationship between ethnography's representation of people as data and Hurston's representational "overabundance." Meaning operates through a surplus that cannot be easily reinvested in the reproduction of expected knowledge.

With this in mind, we might turn to the terminal logic of chapters in *Mules and Men*, especially in the first section, set in Florida. In the course of wrapping up each chapter, Hurston produces a variety of conclusory contradictions: Sequences are neatly brought to an end, while still containing un-remarked-upon and uninterpreted folk tales. Endings include hasty departures and hazy nights and mornings: "Then somehow I got home and to bed and Armetta had Georgia syrup and waffles for breakfast"; "Bonnie Lee tried to ask his well-known question but the coon dick was too strong. He mumbled down into his shirt bosom and went to sleep"; "A hasty good-bye to Eatonville's oaks and oleanders and the wheels of the Chevvie split Orlando wide open—headed south-west for corn (likker) and song"; "The sparse contribution taken, the trio drifted back into the darkness of the railroad, walking towards Kissimmee"; "I fell out of the door over a man lying on the steps, who either fell himself trying to run or got knocked down. I don't know. I was in the car in a second and in high just too quick. Jim and Slim helped me throw my bags into the car and I saw the sun rising as I approached Crescent City."³³ And, in the final, inscrutable line of the book, after Hurston has done ethnographic work in Florida and learned Vodun in Louisiana, *Mules and Men* concludes with, "I'm sitting here like Sis Cat, washing my face and usin' my manners."³⁴

These sudden and often enigmatic chapter endings show Hurston engaged in an estranging realism, a representational overabundance of contextual details that rejects analogy even as it operates through contextualization and substitution. This refusal to reproduce essentialism becomes another means for Hurston to counteract what Retman has described as the dominant idea of "the folk." In her analysis of Federal Writers' Project (FWP) state guides and their reification of folksy uniqueness, Retman shows how Florida's rural people, for example, became "designated as authentic examples of Florida's 'native life'" for tourists or scholars who might use those guides. This tendency toward exemplarity paradoxically meant that "the laborer's poverty makes them all the more vulnerable to the guide's gaze: they become a central spectacle within the text." The Florida guide, therefore, often "quickly forecloses the possibility of a more thorough analysis of social and economic exploitation."[35] Hurston's *Mules and Men* is decidedly against the foreclosure of this possibility. Its focus may not be a direct or "thorough analysis of social and economic exploitation," but Hurston's book becomes an imaginative exploration of folklore as a method of making sense of a complex world. By refusing the ossification of folklore and its contexts, Hurston makes it possible to see the people she writes about beyond the boundaries of their locales, even while, importantly, it is impossible to theorize them outside of their concreteness.

The contradiction contained in this movement toward and away from representational inscrutability reveals *Mules and Men* as an aesthetic and political project of contradiction devoted to complex representations of dignity. This dignity emerges from the textual interactions of labor, playfulness, difficulty, and didacticism, especially as Hurston seeks to provide contexts for the "lies." *Speaking with* illuminates the exciting, generative thorniness of these many contradictions that work together to produce a remarkably vibrant text, rather than miring us in either unknowability or absolute comprehension.

Muriel Rukeyser's Migrant Witness through *Speaking With*-ness

In the late 1920s, Black migrant workers, largely from Georgia and Mississippi, arrived in Gauley Bridge, West Virginia, hired to dig the Hawks Nest Tunnel as part of Union Carbide's new dam project on the Kanawha River. As the project developed, Union Carbide's refusal to adhere to labor protocols—their workers were made to dry-drill through almost pure silica discovered during digging and construction, without masks or adequate training—resulted in thousands of cases of silicosis and hundreds of documented deaths. Three years after the publication of *Mules and Men*, Muriel Rukeyser's *U.S. 1* (1938) poetically revealed her own journey down the length of US Highway 1, which runs from Maine to Florida. In its trajectory, Rukeyser's trip was very similar to the one Hurston took in the first half of *Mules and Men*, and Rukeyser too took care to produce a communal, polyvocal text, one in which poetic voices cascade like the West Virginia cataracts she observed on her travels. *U.S. 1* has three parts: first comes *The Book of the Dead*, the second is *Night-Music*, and the collection ends with *Two Voyages*. Rukeyser's most celebrated and discussed sequence of poems, *The Book of the Dead* (which I italicize when referring to the suite as a whole) focuses primarily on the disaster in Gauley Bridge, both in its particularities and in a longer, nearly mythopoetic historical arc.

In 1935, *New Masses*, the leading leftist publication of the time and a frequent publisher of Rukeyser's freelance writing, had published "Man on the Road," a story by Albert Maltz that railed against Union Carbide, the utility company running the operations at the Hawks Nest Tunnel (and whose subsidiary, Union Carbide India Limited, would be responsible for the horrific Bhopal disaster in 1984). While the cases of silicosis began unfolding in 1930, as Tim Dayton has succinctly noted, "news of this disaster in remote West Virginia spread slowly."[36] This subsequently generated quite a bit of interest regarding what many publications referred to explicitly as an industrial disaster, a term Union Carbide emphatically resisted by claiming that reports of rising casualties among the tunnel workers were exaggerated.[37] The disaster at Hawks Nest did not lie in any dramatic tunnel collapse or cataclysmic explosion, but in the large number of silicosis deaths—a catastrophe obscured by the fact that silicosis was not yet recognized as an industrial hazard that employers were legally required to prevent or be liable for.[38]

As Martin Cherniak carefully proves in *The Hawk's Nest Incident: America's Worst Industrial Disaster*, the labor contractors—Rinehart and Dennis Company—did all they could to avoid hiring trained, experienced miners, who would never have dry-drilled through silica; instead they recruited through word-of-mouth advertising and rumor mostly in Georgia, among primarily Black communities.[39] Dayton notes,

The inability of the tunnel workers to resist the abuses inflicted by their employers may in part be explained by the nature of the workforce. To drive the tunnel through more than three miles of solid rock, a workforce was assembled that was largely though not exclusively migrant in character. . . . Fewer than 20 percent of the men who worked inside the tunnel—the only place where dust concentration made silicosis a danger—were locals, according to Union Carbide's records. Most of these migrant workers were Black. As a result, the majority (around 75 percent) of workers inside the tunnel were Black. By recruiting Black laborers into mostly (80 percent) white Fayette County, the employers sought to ensure some distance between the tunnel workforce and the population. This plan worked to a great extent.[40]

Telling the story of this industrial disaster and the concentrated harm visited upon the mostly Black workforce, Rukeyser sought to develop a distinctive synthesis of documentary poetics, reportage, and lyric poetry, and in doing so forged a manifold lyric voice devoted to *speaking with* the people harmed due to the tunnel work. Using a variety of typographic and tonal strategies to distinguish between voices, Rukeyser embeds polyphony within the very structure of her poetry of witness, offering a complicated lyrical stance that could speak truth in the face of injustice: *speaking with*. In her use of ephemera, interviews, data, journalism, and what might most conveniently be called "found poetry" to construct *The Book of the Dead*, she creates a method of building coalitional lyric that distinguishes itself from other forms of collective verse or lyrical multitude that preceded her work. Consider Edgar Lee Masters's satirical epitaph-like poetry from the grave in *Spoon River Anthology*, Walt Whitman's ecstatic sense of the multitude in *Leaves of Grass*, or Carl Sandburg's imagistic, proletarian poetry–influenced *Chicago Poems*.

The closest analogue to her work, though, might be Charles Reznikoff's *Testimony*, whose many volumes appeared between 1934 and 1978, finally reissued as a collected volume in 2015. The poetics of witness as elaborated by Reznikoff and Rukeyser takes a specifically Jewish form, in the sense that it emerges from a shared theological foundation. Although Rukeyser had a notably complicated relationship to Judaism, it is undeniable that her theological understanding of being Jewish in the twentieth century—to borrow one of her poems' titles—led her, as Sara Judy describes, "to both participate in and challenge the prophetic tradition as she participates in and challenges traditional notions of what it might meant to be a politically engaged poet in America."⁴¹ Matthew Baigell, in the context of leftist Jewish modernist visual culture, notes that the Popular Front was particularly able to accommodate Jewish artists who saw their religion as "concerned with union organizing in early-twentieth-century America, to prevent industrial accidents, to aid the impoverished, and not stand idly by if somebody's life is in danger"—a description as apt as any that has been intentionally made of Rukeyser's *The Book of the Dead*.⁴²

While Rukeyser's work was decidedly antifascist, it roused the ire of some fellow leftists. In the *Partisan Review*, John Wheelwright preferred an aesthetic driven by historical materialism's direct explanatory power.⁴³ Wheelwright's 1938 review of *U.S. 1* insisted that Rukeyser's "socialism belongs to the inexperienced school—pre-war."⁴⁴ Alan Wald reframes this claim, stating that "in a 1980 interview, Rukeyser insisted that she had desired to be part of the Communist movement, but its political zig-zags made any stable relationship impossible. In particular, she was inspired by a pre-Popular Front vision of militant antifascist and anticapitalist collaboration by a range of radical tendencies she witnessed at the outset of the Spanish Civil War."⁴⁵ Indeed, as Julius Lobo notes, Rukeyser "witnessed the carnage and loss of life in Gauley Bridge and Barcelona in quick succession," and, as he convincingly demonstrates, these nearly simultaneous experiences exercised an enormous influence on her.⁴⁶ Also of note, Baigell traces a complicated relationship between Jewish leftist artists and the Soviet Union in particular, observing that Ben Shahn, Harold Rosenberg, Robert Warshow, and many fellow artists and critics in their circles "were unwilling to conventionalize" their sensibilities and responses to Earl Browder and the Communist Party USA (CPUSA), especially "according to party exhortations." Furthermore, "many artists, whatever their commitment to left politics, were . . . not ready to submerge their sense of individuality within the mass or to give up the notion that their own life was not their real life."⁴⁷ While this broad rejection became more focused in light of Soviet famines as well as disagreements with Browder's leadership of CPUSA, Baigell's remarks remain nonetheless descriptive of Rukeyser's own complicated relationship to party politics more broadly, a sensibility she shared with other modernist writers (and one that Hurston famously shared as well, though far more vituperatively).

Wheelwright's ire extended beyond incoherent charges of naïveté, however. He insisted that Rukeyser's "limited philosophy limits poetry," leading him to summarize his statements with the pithy claim that "political and aesthetic failings have one root."[48] In his conclusion, Wheelwright broadens his admonition, stating testily, "Leave the timid their obscurity. Confront communication. It devolves upon us to rediscover clarity. Revolutionary writing in the snob style does not reach a proper audience."[49] Taking up critiques such as Wheelwright's in his reading of *The Book of the Dead*, Walter Kalaidjian asks, "Why exactly did Rukeyser's long poem provoke such universalizing expressions of resistance on both the left and the right?"[50] His answer rests on Rukeyser's resistance to orthodoxy: "Rukeyser elicited such aggressive responses, arguably, because she embraced a new, revolutionary mode of cultural identity—one that departed from the late nineteenth- and early twentieth-century figurehead of what Michel Foucault would dub some forty years later the 'universal' intellectual: the one who 'spoke and was acknowledged the right of speaking in the capacity of master of truth and justice.'"[51] Lisa Siraganian argues that Rukeyser's contemporary critics generally "failed to grasp" that *The Book of the Dead*'s "unusual literary form *was* her aim: to challenge the disturbing phenomenon of actions occurring without defined intentions," which is a particular feature of corporations such as Union Carbide.[52] I concur entirely with Siraganian and Kalaidjian here, and further suggest that this "revolutionary mode of cultural identity" comes through in her poetry's embrace of *speaking with* against "speaking *in the capacity* of master of truth and justice."

By developing *speaking with* against the singular voice of authority or truth, Rukeyser undertakes a poetic rendering of her trip to Gauley Bridge and articulates West Virginia's historical roots, from its First Peoples to the settlers—especially farmers and miners—who moved through the land. In "West Virginia," the second poem in *The Book of the Dead*, Rukeyser condenses the history of the state in a rapid cascade of lines:

They saw rivers flow west and hoped again.
Virginia speeding to another sea!
1671—Thomas Batts, Robert Fallam,
Thomas Wood, the Indian Perecute,

and an unnamed indentured English servant
followed the forest past blazed trees, pillars of God,
were the first whites emergent from the east.
They left a record to our heritage,
breaking of records.⁵³

Of especial import for Rukeyser, as for many others during the Popular Front, was the haunting presence of John Brown, whose courageous, divisive, and inspirational 1859 uprising put Harpers Ferry squarely into the enduring national consciousness; in her 1944 collection *Beast in View*, for example, Rukeyser has a poem entitled "The Soul and Body of John Brown," showing a longer preoccupation with Brown's cultural centrality for leftist poetry, as well as democratic poetry more broadly. Michael Denning identifies John Brown as indicative of the Popular Front's radical shifting of symbolic Americanness: "It is worth noting that this appropriation of American mythologies had a more radical edge than usually admitted. Whereas the official Americanisms of the Depression usually invoked the figure of Lincoln, the Popular Front was more likely to invoke John Brown."⁵⁴ Rukeyser monumentalizes John Brown in *The Book of the Dead*, typographically indicating the enormity of the man's legacy:

War born:
The battle at Point Pleasant, Cornstalk's tribes,
last stand, Fort Henry, a revolution won;
the granite SITE OF THE precursor EXECUTION
sabres, apostles OF JOHN BROWN LEADER OF THE
War's brilliant cloudy RAID AT HARPERS FERRY.⁵⁵

The capitalized font, which quotes a historical placard in Charles Town, West Virginia, prominently cuts through the poem and bespeaks the enormity of John Brown's legacy. The words make their own sense, residing perpetually in and yet overwhelming their specific poetic context.

Rukeyser's mythical envisioning of Gauley Bridge within a grand historical arc can also be seen in her sweepingly romantic description in "Story Outline for *Gauley Bridge*," a proposal she sent in 1939 or 1940 to Columbia Pictures for a feature film about the same disaster, which likely would have featured a professional cast—though perhaps not, as films like *Bicycle Thieves* (1948) and *The Salt of the Earth* (1954) relied extensively on nonprofessional actors. Lobo notes, as do Anne F. Herzog and Janet E. Kaufman, that this proposal was published in 1940 in the short-lived journal *Films* (in volume 1, issue 3). The proposal begins broadly while also observing the cyclical nature of migration: memories, bodies, and roots can never be disentangled.

> The story is a chapter of the great American migration. It is not concerned with the westward sweep of the frontier-breakers, or, in our own day, of the dust bowl refugees—but rather with one of the shifts that feed and follow such sweeps.... This is a story of one of these shifts; of how several thousand Americans arrived, for one reason or another, in a beautiful valley in West Virginia where there was a job to do, and where hope was held out to them.... [T]his land knew the struggle with itself and for itself, in pioneer and farmer and miner, and this struggle for power—water-power and man-power—was only a new phase of the story.[56]

Rukeyser gestures here to the broad stakes of the Hawks Nest disaster, but also claims that this "was only a new phase of the story" of the "struggle for power" in the United States. The particulars—"several thousand Americans arrived ... in a beautiful valley in West Virginia"—ground the disaster within its place and time, showing how Rukeyser's consideration of the Hawk's Nest disaster embeds the specific situation of the tunnel workers in a historical, almost mythical narrative.

Although nothing grand came of "Story Outline for *Gauley Bridge*" (except, as noted above, its publication in 1940 in the evanescent journal *Films*), the text shows the continuity of Rukeyser's thinking about what she learned and wrote about the tunnel workers. Even more notably, the response letter from Eve Ettinger at Columbia Pictures notes, "I read your outline for a picture on silicosis very carefully, and I am sure it has swell possibilities for a documentary film."[57] For Ettinger, a film executive, a feature film about laborers could not register as anything but a documentary. This confusion is the result of a thirst for and expectation of authenticity, a demand that obscures Rukeyser's emphatic pluralism. As a result, her contemporary critics generally could not see her *speaking with* as a genuinely radical and concrete political practice; indeed, Lobo argues that the film story outline was likely unable to find a home due to Rukeyser's "complex documentary practices," in which a "multiplicity of voices forms the voice of the American people."[58] As with Hurston's writing, the aesthetic experimentation Rukeyser worked through was often read as an attempt at mimetic authenticity, when in fact it was a radical attempt to reimagine the relationships between author, textual subject, and audience, a broader aesthetic tendency toward multiplicity of which *The Book of the Dead* is a signal piece.

Raphael C. Allison claims that "for Rukeyser, 'imagination' entails complex examination, multiple perspectives, and a pluralist belief that such multiplicity yields strengths."[59] It is in this dedication to specificity, complexity, and multiplicity that Rukeyser is closest to Hurston's ethos as an artist. As with Hurston, Rukeyser's idiosyncrasy lies in her approach to politics and poetics. She demands openness—both of herself and of her readers and listeners, a point that Christa Buschendorf links to Rukeyser's poetics of witness, in which the poet "expands the reader's functions within the triangle of author, work, and reader to include both subjective experience and objective testimony. In the creative process the reader is no longer condemned to passivity."[60] This "creative process" of *speaking with* resists the certainty of conclusion, replacing it with a poetics of witnessing that is active, relational, and impossible to enclose or neatly encapsulate. As Allison further points out, "Rukeyser believed that her task was to produce texts that dramatized this process of plural forms and experiences in order to challenge fascistic fantasies of total domination."[61] In Allison's estimation, Rukeyser's political orientation could best be characterized as a leftism driven above all by a resistance to singularity, domination, and determinism. Rukeyser does not affirm others by *saying so*; rather, she affirms others by effacing the idea of a metaphysical or authoritative voice even while she grants specificity to the citizen subjects of her poem—the direct result of *speaking with*. What Kalaidjian calls Rukeyser's "specific cultural critique" and the poem's "dialogic mix of the period's representative discourses and rhetorical styles" are the result of her dedication to *speaking with* as a transformational and coalitional aesthetic practice.

The poem "Mearl Blankenship" demonstrates *speaking with* through multiple lyrical voices and its use of typography, particularly in relation to how the poem repurposes the document it incorporates. Rukeyser conjoins her voice and the voice of a laborer who wrote a letter (of somewhat unclear destination) to New York City describing the situation in Gauley Bridge.[62] As Catherine Venable Moore has painstakingly traced and documented, the person who signed the letter as Mearl Blankenship was very likely a man named Oran Mearl Blankenship, who died from the effects of silicosis in 1950.[63]

Rukeyser's means of distinguishing between voices is superficially evident: Blankenship's letter is indented, while the lyric speaker's words appear in short, nonindented stanzas. The first five stanzas of the seven-stanza poem read:

> He stood against the stove
> facing the fire—
> Little warmth, no words,
> loud machines.
>
> Voted relief,
> wished money mailed,
> quietly under the crashing:
>
> "I wake up choking, and my wife
> rolls me over on my left side;
> then I'm asleep in the dream I always see:
> the tunnel choked
> the dark wall coughing dust.
>
> I have written a letter.
> Send it to the city,
> maybe to a paper
> if it's all right."
>
>> Dear Sir, my name is Mearl Blankenship.
>> I have worked for the rhinehart & Dennis Co
>> Many days & many nights
>> & it was so dusty you couldn't hardly see the lights.
>> I helped nip steel for the drills
>> & helped lay the track in the tunnel
>> & done lots of drilling near the mouth of the tunnell
>> when the shots went off the boss said

> If you are going to work Venture back
> & the boss was Mr. Andrews
> & now he is dead and gone
> But I am still here
> a lingering along.⁶⁴

The lyric speaker and Mearl Blankenship are placed in conversation with each other through this formatting, and what strikes me is the depth of sympathy and imagination that occurs through this structure. Rukeyser begins by giving a succinct description of Blankenship—his exhaustion, the machinic loudness surrounding him, and his political beliefs and actions. She then imagines Blankenship's words through direct discourse, enclosing them in quotation marks. She also imagines Blankenship's letter anew, breaking it into verse and subtly altering it. As Dayton observes, regarding the six final lines of the letter, "Rukeyser makes the lines into coherent phrasal units . . . and establishes a rough regularity: two four-stress lines followed by two three-stress lines, each with a pyrrhic foot [two unstressed syllables], and two syllabically shorter three-stress lines."⁶⁵ Dayton also notes that Rukeyser largely maintains the language of the original letter—for example, the alternative spelling of "tunnell"—but, oddly enough, capitalizes some words that aren't originally capitalized (such as "Many days"), adds periods (the original letter has no periods at all), omits certain words, and alters some phrases (she changes "mixed the steel for the drills" into "nip steel for the drills").⁶⁶ These changes heighten alliteration, assonance, and consonance, increasing the poetic effect. This is quite literally an act of *speaking with*, in that the poet and the letter writer have their texts expanded by each other. The sorrowful letter is given the drama of poetic progression through reformed lineation: some lines from the letter are expanded (the lines in the original letter are on the shorter side, given space constraints and Blankenship's handwriting), and then the lines are gradually narrowed at the end of the poem to visually reproduce the gasps of a silicotic migrant laborer. This is poetics as dramaturgy, a staging of *speaking with* achieved by formally melding the poet's voice with Mearl Blankenship's, thus creating a different poetic speaker altogether. Yet the poem insists on specification and formal distinction, as it becomes literally reformed and reshaped by its uneasy but insistent epistolary reconstitution. The prosody itself becomes migratory, capable of *speaking with* the worker whose language creates the possibility of the poem itself.

Rukeyser gives over much of the poem to Blankenship's voice, with the poet's own lyrical position largely reduced to (admittedly loaded) description. One could argue that in loading her descriptions with emotionally powerful images—such as the way Blankenship "leaned against the stove / facing the fire" and hopes for redress "quietly under the crashing"—she engages in what Kalaidjian has called "proletcult" verse, an aesthetic tendency, criticized by William Stott and Retman among others, that imagines the masses as messianic (and often unconscious) harbingers of the revolution to come. Michael Thurston, for example, argues that "many poets on the left experimented with dialect and vernacular verse forms to demonstrate solidarity with blacks and other marginalized groups," and that Rukeyser did this "with varying success and with the corollary drawback of apparent condescension."[67] Proletcult texts offer narratives of political transformation, often rely on stereotype or portraiture to emphasize sociological arguments, and often assert proletarian innocence or naïveté, which is related to idealized notions of "the folk." As Stott argues, this tendency often means that "social documentary is instrumental, and its people tend, like the innocent victims in most propaganda, to be simplified and ennobled—sentimentalized, in a word."[68] Following Stott, one could argue that this may indeed be one of the limits Rukeyser runs into: "documentary treats the actual unimagined experience of individuals belonging to a group generally of low economic and social standing in the society (lower than the audience for whom the report is made) and treats this experience in such way as to try to render it vivid, 'human,' and—most often—poignant to the audience."[69]

In the sixth stanza of "Mearl Blankenship," Rukeyser imbues description with deathly strangeness, focusing the imagery on catastrophic bodily and ecological injury:

> He stood against the rock
> facing the river
> grey river grey face
> the rock mottled behind him
> like X-ray plate enlarged

diffuse and stony
his face against the stone.[70]

Stone and grayness dominate here. Images of landscape and figural description index the circumstances of Blankenship's exploitation. The simile "the rock mottled behind him / like X-ray plate enlarged" moves beyond mere affective fallacy and parallelism by raising an ethical question: How can you look at a man suffering from silicosis, his head against a spotted rock, and not see that his world—and, of course, our world—is splitting apart? The descriptive merging of landscape and worker shows the binding nature of oppression. Exploitation of the earth and exploitation of the human are one and the same. Mearl Blankenship's face has turned gray from his sickness, from anxiety, from staying underground to dig out silica. Rukeyser reprises the theme of uniformity of color by referencing "white dust" over and over in the course of *The Book of the Dead*. In "George Robinson: Blues," the speaker is the organizer of the workers in the laborers' camp, and he says, "Looked like somebody sprinkled flour all over the parks and groves, / it stayed and the rain couldn't wash it away and it twinkled / that white dust really looked pretty down around our ankles."[71] In "Alloy," whose title not only denotes the compounding of metals but also one of the sources of exploitation (Alloy being the name of the town where the unearthed silica was shipped for Union Carbide's use), these lines appear: "Crystalline hill: a blinded field of white / murdering snow, seamed by convergent tracks; / the travelling cranes reach for the silica."[72] The white covers everything like a dispersed sprinkling of flour in the form of "a blinded field of white," just as gray becomes ubiquitous and assimilative in "Mearl Blankenship," coloring the stone as well as Blankenship's face. This chromatic uniformity connects everything as parts of a networked degradation brought about by the overwhelming exploitation of the land and the people. Rukeyser seems to be saying that if everything is connected—no matter the measure or the moral condition of that connection—then it is near impossible to separate oneself.

In the particular way in which she incorporates political speech and action across the suite of poems, Rukeyser weaves an aesthetic structure whose sense of authority is diffused and expansive, rather than neatly folded into the lyric speaking position's meaning-making processes. In "Praise of the

Committee," for example, Rukeyser extends the formal and visual presence of *speaking with* utilized in "Mearl Blankenship." As Dayton observes, the chief committee that appears in this poem is not the congressional committee that was later convened to investigate the incident—although the congressional committee's discussions and procedures do appear in one stanza made up of direct discourse, as well as in the poems "Statement: Philippa Allen," "The Disease," "The Doctors," "The Dam," "The Disease: After-effects," and "The Bill."[73] Rather, the principal committee in "Praise of the Committee" is a people's defense committee organized by the laborers, their families, and their allies. As with "Mearl Blankenship," Rukeyser splits the poem and its stanzas using indentation, but in this instance she also adds italicization, as she does in "Absalom." "Praise of the Committee" begins with a declaration:

> *These are the lines on which a committee is formed*
>   Almost as soon as work was begun in the tunnel
>   men began to die among dry drills. No masks.
>   Most of them were not from this valley.[74]

The formation of the committee is given spatial and temporal priority, occurring before we are told *why* the committee is formed. The "lines" on which the committee is formed become connotatively doubled through the poem's quasi-journalistic poetic lines, which elaborate grievances and political-economic facts: "freights brought many every day"; "The ambulance was going day and night, / White's undertaking business thriving and / his mother's cornfield put to a new use"; "No reply. Great corporation disowning men who made."[75] Above these lines of explanation, which pervade the poem and describe a catastrophic injustice driven by corporate greed and the exploitation of workers and their families, the committee itself is given (poetic) form. Subsequent italicized declarations enumerate the purposes of the committee, before the work is illustrated in the many lines that follow each: "*The committee is a true reflection of the will of the people*"; "*The Committee meets regularly, wherever it can*"; "*This is a defense committee. Unfinished business.*"[76] When the fifth italicized declaration appears, at first it seems to follow the same pattern, but in fact it signals a shift in the type of committee being described: "*This is the procedure of such a committee:* / To consider the bill before the Senate. / To discuss relief.*"[77] The phrase "*of such a committee*" may seem to signal continuity, but while the first four declarations name the people's committee, the fifth is describing the procedure of a Senate subcommittee. What follows is a tangle of two different committees whose work is connected yet occurs on different scales:

> Active members may be cut off relief,
>   16-mile walk to Fayetteville for cheque—
>   WEST VIRGINIA RELIEF ADMINISTRATION, #22991,
>   TO JOE HENIGAN, GAULEY BRIDGE, ONE AND 50/100,
>   WINONA NATIONAL BANK. PAID FROM STATE FUNDS.
> Unless the Defense Committee acts;
> the *People's Press*, supporting this fight,
> signed editorials, sent in funds.
> Clothing for tunnel-workers.[78]

The defense committee actively works to defend the laborers, while the Senate committee considers the bill before it: both necessary, one to redress the moment, the other to consider the future of such moments. Melding the two committees, Rukeyser bolsters *speaking with* as a necessary, coalitional aesthetic whose different voices and registers are blended formally on the page. Following Siraganian, this purposeful blending of committees might well share in modernist US literature's "early workshop of thought experiments on how seemingly authorless entities make meaning."[79]

At stake is the very real matter of reparation within a larger structure of representation. Certainly the political and the aesthetic are not one and the same, and justice articulated in terms of one form of representation is not equivalent to justice achieved in the other. Yet Rukeyser offers *speaking with* as a mode that works across the slippery conjunctions of politics and aesthetics, demanding reparation as a matter of linked imaginative desires. Mrs. Jones, one of the mothers Rukeyser includes in *The Book of the Dead*, reports that she went around the state looking for medical and political support for her sons. She tells her story:

> The youngest boy did not get to go down there with me,
> he lay and said, "Mother, when I die,
> I want you to have them open me up and

> see if that dust killed me.
> Try to get compensation,
> you will not have any way of making your living
> when we are gone,
> and the rest are going too."[80]

Who is left to speak for the dead? As Rukeyser claims near the end of "Praise of the Committee,"

> These men breathe hard
> but the committee has a voice of steel.
> One climbs the hill on canes.
> They have broken the hills and cracked the riches wide.
> In this man's face
> family leans out from two worlds of graves—
> here is a room of eyes,
> a single force looks out, reading our life.[81]

The steel-voiced committee—which one, however?—speaks with the men who "breathe hard." The stanza reaches completion with the curious phrase "our life," referring to an unmoored first-person plurality whose contours are not clear: is it "these men," "the committee," the readerly community enabled by the poem, or humankind? An answer, by way of further deviation, may lie in the method that underlies the poem "Absalom," which, as mentioned above, brings forth the voice of "Mrs. Jones." As Thurston notes, "Rukeyser edits to strengthen the discursive authority of a sympathetic speaker. This is nowhere more apparent than in the crucial poem 'Absalom,' where Rukeyser melds the testimony, spread over forty pages of congressional hearings, of three different speakers—social worker Philippa Allen; the poem's speaker, Mrs. Jones; and her husband, Charles Jones—into the single speaking voice of Mrs. Jones."[82] Thurston's description of the lyric voice as an artifact of poetic melding in "Absalom" also identifies precisely this unmoored yet strangely powerful "our" that appears in "Praise of the Committee."

By giving the laborers their proper place in history, Rukeyser invites us, as Stephanie Hartman points out, to "reach beyond grim facts to imagine a conceivably better future."[83] In *The Book of the Dead*, this futurity is possible only through redress and reparation, and this in turn is achieved through Rukeyser's focused use of "who" and "whose." These pronouns insist upon a naming or filling in. In "Praise of the Committee," we read the following cascade of questions:

> Who stands over the river?
> Whose feet go running in these rigid hills?
> Who comes, warning the night,
> shouting and young to waken our eyes?
>
> Who runs through electric wires?
> Who speaks down every road?
> Their hands touched mastery; now they
> demand an answer.[84]

Who? Rukeyser insistently demands. *Who* stands, *whose* feet go running, *who* comes, *who* runs, *who* speaks? No one, everyone, and the specific people named in *The Book of the Dead*, such as Philippa Allen, Mrs. Jones, George Robinson, and Mearl Blankenship. As laborers, "their hands touched mastery"—the awesome and terrible power of Earth, as well as the power of human skill in shaping the earth. As migrants, they arrived in a state whose "rigid hills" once echoed the voices of different, non-European peoples of the Susquehannock, Monongahela, Tutelo, Moneton, Monacan, Shawnee, and Cherokee nations, as well as subsequent refugees and migrants of other Indigenous nations, in addition to maroon communities of Africans and African-descended peoples. In these ancient hills and mountains, workers breathed silica into their lungs, silica that was used to temper the steel to create dams, factories, and other structures in the region. Their bodies, with lungs shredded by the silica dust, are buried in a cornfield before their families can dress them in finer clothes or address them one final time. "Dust to dust," indeed.

Yet Rukeyser shakes us, asking us to move out of complacency. What do we feel when we poetically witness the scenes of industrial terror in *The Book of the Dead*? Rukeyser offers up the voices of the laborers and their families in order to make us not only witness, but *listen*. And not only listen, but *respond*. *The Book of the Dead* indeed warns us against the mere act of merely seeing, of merely witnessing, and calls upon us instead to actively bear witness:

> Words on a monument.
> Capitoline thunder. It cannot be enough.
> The origin of storms is not in clouds,
> our lightning strikes when the earth rises,
> spillways free authentic power:
> dead John Brown's body walking from a tunnel
> to break the armored and concluded mind.[85]

Rukeyser reminds us that bearing witness means "to break the armored and concluded mind." No longer "a-mouldering in the grave," as the Civil War–era song puts it, John Brown's body walks forth from the same West Virginia soil in which he and his fellow fighters died, and in which the Gauley Bridge laborers are buried, revenants whose presences make evident the long history of struggle the poem reminds us of.[86]

In the opening stanza of her poem "The Soul and Body of John Brown," published in her collection *Beast in View* six years after *The Book of the Dead*, Rukeyser announces, in language reminiscent of the ancient Hebrew prophets, what it means to bear witness to the dead:

> His life is in the body of the living.
> When they hanged him the first time, his image leaped
> into the blackened air. His grave was the floating faces
> of the crowd, and he refused them in release,
> rose open-eyed to autumn a fanatic
> beacon of fierceness leaping to meet them there,
> match the white prophets of the storm,
> the streaming meteors of the war.[87]

"F" and "m" are the dominant sounds, a consonant mixture of thickly ethereal air pushing through lips and an earthy humming into closed lips—all of it fulminating in a condemnation of a nation whose prosperity has rested upon dispossession, genocide, and chattel slavery. "He refused them in release," an "open-eyed" revenant who spoke of the indignation and violence faced by the nation's enslaved and who demands continual recognition: John Brown's "grave was the floating faces / of the crowd." As in *The Book of the Dead* and its speakers, John Brown is not—and cannot be—dead. He makes the crowd bear the shame of his execution, but, as Brown would say, any shame at his death pales in comparison to the great shame of the nation—the bondage and destruction of millions, the transformation of the nation's hills and prairies into monuments of genocide.

The Book of the Dead similarly challenges us to bear shame, implying that the laborers who died from silicosis have been actively executed through negligence and face being doubly executed through their fading from national memory. *Never forget*, dares Rukeyser. At *The Book of the Dead*'s conclusion, in the eponymous poem, Rukeyser implores readers to see with and then also begin *speaking with*:

> What one word must never be said?
> Dead, and these men fight off our dying,
> cough in the theatres of the war.
>
> What two things shall never be seen?
> They : what we did. Enemy : what we mean.
> This is a nation's scene and halfway house.
>
> What three things can never be done?
> Forget. Keep silent. Stand alone.
> The hills of glass, the fatal brilliant plain.[88]

Rukeyser warns us against proclaiming the laborers done and dead—in this case, it's an invocation against forgetting. Thurston reads this poetic logic of memorialization, also central to the poem "Absalom," as a direct invocation of the "Egyptian myth system" of the suite of poems as a whole, especially given its title. Thurston points out that "Mrs. Jones takes on the role of Thoth, the Egyptian scribe god. Naming the dead, she exercises the right to give them new life. She also attains, by calling this role, a vantage point that commands the entire valley, shifting the names of the men to the names of the towns they come from, broadening her scope to show how 'the whole valley is witness.'"[89] Rukeyser wants us to memorialize the workers into an active montage of reparative recollection, rather than monumentalizing them into perfect identity with their graves. That is, memorialization is to speak their memory and commit their lives to memory, rather than to rest content with etching their names into static slabs of stone or, for that matter, merely printing their names onto pages.

Furthermore, "these men fight off our dying, / cough in the theatres of the war." Gauley Bridge is established as a theater of war; not only that, but, as Tim Dayton and Anne Herzog remind us, Rukeyser connects the migrant laborers in West Virginia with the Republican soldiers of the Spanish Civil War, whom she constantly honored in her life and poetry.[90] Both wars were lost: the migrant laborers got about $22 each after all was said and done, while the Spanish Republic fell to Franco and lost Spain to decades of fascism.

"What two things shall never be seen?" Rukeyser asks, suggesting the buried lives of the workers and the hidden costs of their labor; she also knows that the enemy will not reveal what they "mean." In contrasting the "enemy" to "they," Rukeyser also overturns the logic of opposition in which "we" are against "them." Indeed, "they" names the laborers, who know that what will never be seen is "what we did." "They" and "we" form part of the same collectivity. What cannot be seen, however, creates "a nation's scene and halfway house": a purgatory of sorts, where what cannot be *seen* becomes the *scene*, entrapping us by revealing the evidence of horror while still obscuring the horror itself. To refuse this, Rukeyser names the three things that "can never be done": "Forget. Keep silent. Stand alone."

The poem—and the suite of poems as a whole—concludes by linking *speaking with* to love within a never-ending flow of dialectical motion:

> Voices speak to us directly. As we move.
> As we enrich, growing larger in motion,
>   this word, this power.
>
> Down coasts of taken countries, mastery,
> discovery at one hand, and at the other
>   frontiers and forests,
>
> fanatic cruel legend at our back and
> speeding ahead the red and open west,
>   and this our region,
>
> desire, field, beginning. Name and road,
> communication to these many men,
> an epilogue, seeds of unending love.[91]

Rukeyser's voice is not the primary invocative voice of this poem: neither the voice that calls to the muses nor the voice whose lyric power creates the poetry's movement. The voices come from beyond her, and here at the end, she lets us know that she is as much a witness as we are: in this, she and Hurston are aligned. She has been listening and reading just as we have. "This word, this power" remains oblique: what is the singular word to which she refers? This word reaches out to us, and, as we keep expanding the frontiers of human existence and capacity with "fanatic cruel legend at our back," we are told that we must still recall "name and road"—to always dwell in the particular and specific, to never forget.

Sarah Ehlers argues that "one of the aspirations of [*The Book of the Dead*] itself is a totalizing vision that is indelibly marked by the events in West Virginia. In so doing, Rukeyser emphasizes that the plane of expressions is a complex material assemblage, another form of the alloy, that has historical meaning but that also exceeds existing representational boundaries. In a landscape where 'a gradual scar formation' will eventually 'block the air passageways,' a new mechanism for voicing must be discerned."[92] Extant conceptions of the lyric, of subjectivity, of representation, and of "voicing" cannot adequately apprise readers of what Rukeyser wants them to see. She therefore rejects typical routes of writerly empathy-building in *The Book of the Dead*. Ehlers likens Rukeyser's representational strategy to an alloy throughout her engagement with the poet's work, and while this emphasis on creativity and newness does Rukeyser's work a great justice, my own emphasis on *speaking with* suggests a critical metaphor more directly invested in bodily engagement. Perhaps, then, collaboration retains the distinctiveness of the conversational participants rather than having the radically renovative powers of alloying's admixture. For Hartman, Rukeyser "counters the focus on the isolated individual . . . by using montage to put individual 'portraits' such as those of Blankenship and [Arthur] Peyton into a larger context, indeed, into relationship: she presents the workers both as named individuals and as members of their class."[93] Hartman's description of *The Book of the Dead* as montage is more apt than any turn to modernist collage aesthetics, and complements Ehlers's evocative paralleling of the poem to the alloy that appears throughout it. Movement and relation, rather than combination or synthesis, constitute the primary method of Rukeyser's coalitional aesthetics.

As Ehlers shows, ultimately, "*The Book of the Dead* does not make documents poetic, nor does it poeticize documentary; rather, the very materials of 'poem' and 'document' dissolve into particles as finely grained as silica dust."[94] Ehlers's point is that distinguishing between "poem" and "document" produces an unknowable difference, while also eliding important distinctions between the two in *The Book of the Dead*. Something new is needed. While Ehlers's preferred term for the needed poetic energy is "alloy," I emphasize instead the coalitional nature of the text, as a result of multivocality as well as the formal(ist) relations among and across the various poems in the larger whole. Ehlers convincingly claims, I acknowledge, that "the sequence challenges readers to imagine the poem as a conglomeration of materials that refuses familiar parameters of poetic and, consequently, political subjectivity."[95] And, as Buschendorf suggests regarding the poet's larger philosophy, "in Rukeyser's poetic concept the confessional mode transcends subjectivity as it bears witness to the veracity of the poet's experience that allows for generalization; the poet's confession necessarily turns into a public act."[96] Buschendorf's point that Rukeyser's lyric speech becomes "a public act" resonates with Ehlers's claim that *The Book of the Dead* "refuses familiar parameters" of poetics and politics. Indeed, as Ehlers notes, the suite of poems "imagines conglomerations of materials—bodies, histories, languages, texts, textiles—that constitute human subjects and lay the ground for alternative modalities of representation and expression."[97] The unanchoring of authority from a central lyric voice—whether that of the prophet, or the witness, or the judge, or even the *poet*—is central to the building of a coalitional aesthetics whose contours shift and whose aims remain committed to *speaking with*.

Seeds of Unending Love

To a large degree, *The Book of the Dead* musses the line between fact and imagination in a way that echoes *Mules and Men*. However, in altering the words of her interlocutors, Rukeyser is potentially attempting to obscure her role as a lyric poet and observer, which offers a contrast to Hurston's method of situating herself within and in observation of the community she writes about. Even if she largely disappears from the text (outside of the opening drive to West Virginia and the declamatory, prophetic final section of the sequence), Rukeyser establishes a dialectic between the individual and society, testifying against a national and industrial history that is all too willing to marginalize and forget the Black migrant laborers in Gauley Bridge. *The Book of the Dead* contextualizes these laborers partly to forward a larger revolutionary history of class struggle, and partly to understand how the US is a project of political power built through enduring coloniality. Rukeyser gives weight to individual stories, providing concrete particulars that anchor universal struggle in the world as it is lived, using a poetic process of continual movement and montage rather than any achievable synthesis. Much as I discuss in subsequent chapters, this is a vision of what Gwendolyn Brooks names "love like morningrise" and "love like black, our black— / luminously indiscreet; / complete; continuous."[98] It also looks forward to Audre Lorde's argument that theorizing community through difference helps generate "a fund of necessary polarities between which our creativity can spark like a dialectic."[99] Movement and continuity—and, importantly, not totalizing conclusion—become the point of politics and aesthetics, and *The Book of the Dead* and *Mules and Men* offer us examples of what a "complete; continuous" work of art can look like.

Recent work by Yomaira C. Figueroa-Vásquez and John E. Drabinski expands upon relation as theorized by Édouard Glissant and puts into motion Glissant's argument that "in the poetics of Relation, one who is errant (who is no longer traveler, discoverer, or conquerer) strives to know the totality of the world yet already knows he will never accomplish this—and knows that is precisely where the threatened beauty of the world resides."[100] Another discourse of relation that parallels this decolonial framework emerges from what Kandice Chuh et al. call a sense of "being with," developed in queer theory and performance studies through the work of José E. Muñoz. (A similar refusal of totality can be found in Eve Sedgwick's phenomenological turn in *Touching Feeling*.)[101] For Figueroa-Vásquez, relation enables a combination of precision and capaciousness necessary for "reckoning with the *longue durée* of our histories as well as a commitment to seeing relations and disjunctures across the Black Atlantic and across the world."[102] A flexible yet coherent concept, Figueroa-Vásquez's description of relation reorients interpretive protocols, destabilizing the criteria long upheld by literary studies as indicative of influence and importance. Relation privileges movement over stability, embeddedness over radical individuation, and connection over distinction. Indeed, says Glissant, "Relation is learning more and more to go beyond judgments into the unexpected dark of art's upsurgings. Its beauty springs from the stable and the unstable, from the deviance of many particular poetics and the clairvoyance of a relational poetics. The more things it standardizes into a state of lethargy, the more rebellious consciousness it arouses."[103] Considering Figueroa-Vásquez and Glissant together, relation is both ever-reinventing and historically embedded; it is always in motion and unsatisfied with the ossification of social forms. *Mules and Men* and *The Book of the Dead* take up this contingency by relying on concreteness while refusing to cede the terms of justice and labor dignity to capriciousness or arbitrariness—in other words, contingency is understood as the basis for all relations in the world, but not seen as a justification for violence or injustice. The world is what it is, but it does not have to continue to be so, especially if it is unjust.

Mules and Men and *The Book of the Dead* carefully articulate a vision of coalitional possibility that can only be expressed through relation. Representation is not alienated or abrogated, as in a system wherein a "representative" speaks *for* a specific polity. Hurston and Rukeyser situate neither themselves nor the people they write about as "representative" in any robust sense. By moving away from representation (and representativeness) as a ruling logic for ethnic literature, Rukeyser and Hurston make the case for alternative, communal, and coalitional grammars of belonging: belonging is expressive, of course, but does not rely on signification through the logic of representation—which is so often the calling card of ethnic literature.

This radically democratic impulse is particularly important given the context in which Rukeyser and Hurston wrote: 1930s segregated communities in which African Americans were consistently denied access to political representation and afforded only various degrees of alienated aesthetic representation. Even if *Mules and Men* is not political in any expected way—and even more, definitively *not* leftist in the way *The Book of the Dead* definitively *is*—the praxis through which the text is created helps us craft a vision of how American institutions and aesthetics might be radicalized. In *The Book of the Dead*, the work's poetics bend toward the creation of a space for justice's political achievement, and Rukeyser achieves this through a subtle experimentation that undoes the poet's lyrical authority and aestheticizes political demands for dignity by deferring to her subjects' actual voices, rather than speaking on their behalf through assumption and co-optation.

Rukeyser and Hurston commit to relational writing as an expression of aesthetic imagination and sensibility. Each author seeks to revolutionize the formal structures of representation, imagining and creating flexibility where there might formerly have been loops of stereotyped feedback and acceptance or representational cul-de-sacs in which what is expected occurs over and over again, according to a predetermined set of signifiers that restrict and control human dignity. Although in literary studies forms are most broadly considered restrictive and enclosing (and thus formalism as a descriptive term is incorrectly understood as requiring a distinctively constrained and conservative form of criticism, though Caroline Levine has rather capaciously reopened the potentiality of studying forms[104]), Hurston and Rukeyser understand the encounter as an intriguing form in itself—one that is entirely open-ended and generative, one that can give rise to novel forms of expression and representation.

Thus, rather than dismissing or undoing forms as such, Hurston and Rukeyser understand how certain forms—especially the encounter—have affordances that have been hitherto unnoticed, dismissed, rejected, and unimagined (both in the sense of *not* imagined and in the sense of the undoing of imagination). Textual encounters should require insistent capaciousness and eternal motion. Recall the closing lines of Rukeyser's poem "The Book of the Dead": "Name and road, / communication to these many men, / as epilogue, seeds of unending love." Communication must take place among the living and dead "as epilogue, seeds of unending love"—that is, as potentiality and emergence, not as fully grown flowers. Rukeyser finishes this poem with *love* envisioned as ever-shifting dialectical motion: the revolutionary call to movement—and to be part of a movement—that we must heed.

In *Methodology of the Oppressed*, Chela Sandoval calls love an interpretive practice that we bring to others and ourselves in order to move beyond the discourses that bind us. She argues that love is "a 'breaking' through whatever controls in order to find 'understanding and community': it is described as 'hope' and 'faith' in the potential goodness of some promised land."[105] *The Book of the Dead* gestures to the promised land in the perpetual motion of the poem's finale, the "desire, field, beginning" of movement and migration. Importantly, this motion predicated on "beginning" and "seeds of unending love" does not hope for conclusion or totalizing comprehension. Such a teleologically oriented desire would risk falling into the snarls of what the late Lauren Berlant calls "cruel optimism," a relationship to desire in which "the *affective structure* of an optimistic attachment involves a sustaining inclination to return to the scene of fantasy that enables you to expect that *this* time, nearness to *this* thing will help you or a world to become different in just the right way."[106] The "thing" in *The Book of the Dead* is not an object or a readily articulated ideology, but rather the moving dialectic of relations within and beyond communality. Perhaps, as Hurston's final image in *Mules and Men*—of a black cat sitting on its haunches and licking itself—reminds us, the ease and unease with which we fit or fold images within their frames must remain ever unsettling. Hurston gives us no answer for the image's meaning, and there likely *is* no answer. But the encounter with the image was, is, and will be the point, no matter how many times we read it.

Movement Politics and the Politics of Movement
Migrant Coalitions and Farm Labor in the 1940s

CENTRAL TO UNDERSTANDING the cultural representations of Dust Bowl migration is the enduring attempt to resignify the needs and desires of people moving throughout the country, particularly those moving from the Midwest, the South, and the Plains states to the West Coast. In 1941, Henry Hill Collins Jr. argued that the "migrant of today would, seventy-five years ago, have been a pioneer. Securely imbedded in our traditions and folkways are the tales of these pioneers and settlers that followed them."[1] For Collins, the political problem of migration is one of misrecognition and, perhaps, untimeliness: the westward-moving migrants carry the spirit of "pioneers and settlers," even if they are not granted the national and ideological respect Collins feels they are owed. Within this recoding, Collins's assumption of the affinity between internal Dust Bowl migrants and pioneers relies on whiteness. As an American leftist of his time with a relatively uncritical eye toward progress, and especially as a New Deal supporter in Franklin Delano Roosevelt's administration, Collins insists upon the continuous line of nation building produced by white settlement.

The "cluster of metaphors" surrounding white pioneer life, in Henry Nash Smith's terminology, generated enormous symbolic energy in support of a settler colonial project that was subsidized and enforced by the federal government and nascent state governments. In *Virgin Land*, Smith describes this settler ideology:

> With each surge of westward movement a new community came into being. These communities devoted themselves not to marching onward but to cul-

tivating the earth. They plowed the virgin land and put in crops, and the great Interior Valley was transformed into a garden: for the imagination, the Garden of the World.... [T]he master symbol of the garden embraced a cluster of metaphors expressing fecundity, growth, increase, and blissful labor in the earth, all centering about the heroic figure of the idealized frontier farmer armed with that supreme agrarian weapon, the plow.[2]

By the time of the Great Depression and the Dust Bowl, this vision of white settler continuity was firmly ensconced in the national imaginary. Unfortunately, this ideological superstructure based on the image of the fecund garden led demonstrably toward ecological destruction in a concrete sense, as the practical reality of white settlement became cash crop dependence, plant monoculture, and agricultural tenancy. The result was the desperate futility of small farmers in what would become the Dust Bowl, especially as they struggled to reconcile their failing farms with the national symbol of "the heroic figure of the idealized frontier farmer."

As Abigail G. H. Manzella puts it, "The myths of possession of the yeoman and of the white settler society equate power and success with landownership and self-possession. This ideal is framed through an imagined individual who moves where there is economic opportunity to cultivate and possess the land and himself."[3] Sarah D. Wald asserts that the erosion of the yeoman farmer myth's stability "reveal[s] the ideological crisis that ensues when white US citizens lose their farmland. When white farmers become exploited farmworkers, it threatens the nation's foundational myths."[4] As Wald shows, in general, "Dust Bowl migration narratives conveyed anxieties not only about the nation's prosperity but also about the crisis that the Dust Bowl migration and the exploitation of white migrants in California's fields posed for national agrarian fantasies."[5] Manzella and Wald both note the broad diminishment of private agricultural land ownership in the 1930s, specifically as it overlapped with whiteness, settlement, independence, and the shifting basis of agrarianism. The fact of the Dust Bowl erupted into public consciousness thanks to harrowing representations of poor white farmers driven to despair and driven off their homesteaded land. The certainties of whiteness, especially as this racial construct was used (incorrectly and generally) to identify farmers from the South, the Midwest, and the Dust Bowl, became attenuated, generating political responses and anxieties that often attempted to shore up assumptions of whiteness. In this chapter, I am interested in how the singer and writer Woody Guthrie and the author Sanora Babb use varying methods of *speaking with* to imagine whiteness as something that needs to be understood in coalition, rather than as a foundation of normative assumptions about belonging, ownership, and entitlement(s).

The alternative imaginaries of utopian idealism that Guthrie and Babb offer are expressed through a multiracial syndicalism undergirded by aesthetic visions of coalitional, cross-racial political belonging that emerge from farmworkers. These coalitional visions generate alternatives to anxieties about cultural loss, political disenfranchisement, and the future. Manzella, for example, urges scholars to understand "large-scale displacements in the twentieth century while acknowledging the voices of women, the laboring class, and various racial groups that narrate and people these incidents," especially in light of "the complex logic behind mass movements with causes that are natural, governmental, and societal." This means specifically naming "those outside [natural, governmental, and societal] forces" while illustrating "acts of resistance from within the communities affected, which include the developing empowerment of women as a result of different strategies of movements and conceptions of community."[6] For Wald, an alternative runs beside dominant cultural myths about independent settler farmers, such that "a parallel between Jeffersonian agrarianism and industrial unionism" becomes possible as "a communism that is truly American."[7]

Babb and Guthrie link their radically democratic ideals to agricultural labor, thus directly responding to and reimagining the national(istic) image of the yeoman farmer as the heart and soul of the nation. Wald puts it best: attending to precisely how the farmer is imagined and reimagined helps us see "the importance of American agrarianism for producing, contesting, and affirming the categories of abject alien worker and white citizen farmer."[8] Against the predominant and fundamental image of the independent farmer whose liberty is the nation's lifeblood, Guthrie and Babb transform racial assumptions about *who* labors in America's fields; this is an idea I will develop even further in chapter 4, through Carlos Bulosan's and Tomás Rivera's work.

In each of the textual encounters in this chapter, I work to build a story of the connected vision of *speaking with* shared by Babb and Guthrie. Babb's

Whose Names Are Unknown and Guthrie's body of musical work are directed toward the attaining of a communal voice. Each could be effectively described by Gustavus Stadler's assertion that "no term in Guthrie's lexicon has as much range, potency, or alchemical potential as union."[9] For Guthrie (and Babb, for that matter), connection—union—relies intimately and sensitively on the possibilities offered by relation. Guthrie wrote and performed popular folk songs with a distinct Popular Front flavor. Babb's Dust Bowl novel, based on her experiences working at migratory camps in California (and her own experience as a denizen of the Dust Bowl region), insists that any solution to the agricultural crisis must be coalitional and multiracial.

What I will mostly be exploring in this chapter is the space where grief, disaster, anger, joy, failure, and promise converge into localized moments of labor-oriented, radically democratic politics with a distinctively coalitional, union-inflected bent. I am particularly interested in how Babb and Guthrie engage in Popular Front–influenced "new coalitions, mass organizations, and rhetoric."[10] Babb and Guthrie each demonstrate how "the Popular Front social movement grew out of the crisis of Fordist modernism, and it built a remarkable coalition for economic justice and civil rights and liberties."[11] This "remarkable coalition created and nurtured a new culture, a distinctive sensibility, aesthetic, and ideology, embodied in stories that were told again and again.... [I]t left its mark on the institutions of American culture—from broadcasting and Hollywood to the novel and the universities—and it influenced those who grew up among the subaltern classes of US society."[12]

In this chapter, I also examine Guthrie's and Babb's responses to the racial politics of Popular Front coalition building, shedding important light on antiracist white leftists as a countervailing force to prevailing sentiments among white liberals of their era.[13] The Popular Front in the US, characterized by its strategic attention to interlocking theoretical and practical resistance to international antifascism, often struggled with questions of race as it sought to build its big tent. Michael Kazin enumerates the many partners in Popular Front organizing: "all sorts of small businesses and unions, churches and synagogues, liberal and moderate newspapers, professional organizations, even elected leaders like FDR.... [I]n the United States, the [Communist Party] embraced the Popular Front as a politics and culture with a zeal unmatched by comrades in other nations. The new strategy allowed rank-and-file radicals to make America's ideals and culture their own."[14] Of course, in the name of beating fascism, explicit concessions were made, particularly regarding racial justice—lest it be forgotten, FDR's New Deal policies were enormously beneficial for white, "yeoman"-class farmers and industrial laborers, often at the expense of African American, Native American, Asian American, and Latinx workers. Ideas of the "everyman" in popular culture of the time, especially in the strongly burgeoning film industry—whether the elderly, kindly protagonists in *Make Way for Tomorrow* (1937, dir. Leo McCarey) or the wealthy man pretending to be a hobo in order to learn the truth about the common man, fallen (briefly) on hard times, in *Sullivan's Travels* (1941, dir. Preston Sturges)—inevitably centered whiteness, either ignoring race altogether (*Make Way for Tomorrow*) or making race a simultaneously ancillary and narratively momentous concern (*Sullivan's Travels*). A later Popular Front–inflected film, *Salt of the Earth* (1954, dir. Herbert J. Biberman), offers a quite different perspective on race as a necessary concern within coalitional politics, and if this book had taken a slightly different path, Biberman's film about New Mexican mine workers and their communal labor movement would have its own chapter.

Aesthetically, the Popular Front ushered in a new populist, demotic framework for creative writing, dramaturgy, journalism, music, and the visual arts. This framework developed a number of political concerns characterized mainly by, as Lieberman notes, "a focus on American democracy which stressed the virtues of the common man and the dignity of oppressed groups such as the Negro, the functional character of folk music as a response to the particular experiences of American history, and the relationship of American folk [art] to its prototypes in the cultures of other nations."[15] Such art often took the shape of so-called "proletcult" creativity, in which largely middle- and upper-class artists utilized "folksy" sounds, styles, and words to create politically conscious versions of realism.[16] "A romantic view of the American past and present permeated Popular Front culture," therefore, and, as Lieberman argues, this had the result of "focusing on the people and their democratic traditions and heroes, the natural resources of the country, and the potential richness of life in America for every individual. The American land and people were glorified by the radio plays of Norman Corwin, the films of Pare Lorentz, the writings of John Steinbeck, and the ballads of Woody Guthrie."[17] This socialist realism, however, often exploited its subjects, rendering them objects of political knowledge—and, as Lieberman suggests, Guthrie has been accused of this. In this chapter, however, I argue that Guthrie's work is invested in *speaking with* "the American land and people," and that the glorification Lieberman notes is much closer to acknowledgment or recognition than to mythification. And, much as Hurston and Rukeyser did, Guthrie and Babb strongly resist such objectification; both created coalitional work deliberately committed to preserving the dignity of their subjects.

Guthrie and Babb were quite aware of the intersecting lines of class, race, and poverty that shaped the social and economic impact of the Great Depression. They also believed that, ideologically and economically—as Rukeyser and Hurston argued in the previous decade—the United States was invested in maintaining a "folk class" of poor white workers whose fortunes were tied to, but too often set against, Mexican American, African American, Filipino, and Native American laborers.[18] Both Guthrie and Babb articulate a belonging that does not suggest that the migrant laborers they are *speaking with* are ideological or mythical descendants of white settler pioneers. In a sense, these artists argue that the problem of whiteness is a problem of democracy and its limits, as well as a problem of racism and a problem of labor. Guthrie and Babb see hope within Popular Front coalitional politics, yet still offer critiques of the white racial roots of the Popular Front as a cultural influence. Whether embracing the possibilities of coalitional aesthetics by showing their difficulty and precarity, or demonstrating how Popular Front coalitional politics run up against and reckon with the problems of nationalistic incorporation (especially considering the nationally bound character of Popular Fronts across the world), Babb and Guthrie urge readers and listeners to fully embrace an ethos of attention as crucial to the objective of *speaking with*. Whether we succeed or fail, we come to understand, we must do it together.

Woody Guthrie's Performances of Migrant Representation

To approach Woody Guthrie, I want to start by dipping briefly into Babb's *Whose Names Are Unknown*, specifically a moment that dramatizes the role of music in migrant camp life. This shows the sympathy between Babb's and Guthrie's views and also signals their deeply overlapping commitments to togetherness.

Just after his family arrives at the government camp in California, Milt

Dunne—Babb's yeoman-farmer-turned-migrant—walks through it as a flaneur of sorts, exploring the atmosphere and noting various scenes. Then he is surprised by the sound of music:

> Suddenly he heard the small picks and rings of an orchestra tuning up, then a burst of gay music. Unbelieving, he looked toward the tent the sound came from, and through the wide flaps pinned back he saw a boy of about eleven standing by a huge bass fiddle, seeming to pound the strings with his small right hand, bringing forth grave and wonderful tones. Below him sat another boy, about nine, strumming a mandolin. A young girl with her back to the door was playing a violin. Deep in the dusk of the tent a man played a banjo. Over and through it all the heavy, somber strings throbbed like a great heart.[19]

Happening upon a family's music making, Milt is drawn to the "somber strings" beating a pulse "like a great heart," a simile that imagines circulation and dispersal linked through a central engine of connection. As Milt continues to watch the band, he is brought into a meditative reverie by the wafting music:

> They played on, not resting, and Milt watched the small boy's pliant hand rising and falling on the responsive strings. He felt the dizziness again, swinging across his eyes and through his ears in time with the music.... He thought of Lonnie, sleeping all day to forget her hunger. He thought of Julia and Mrs. Starwood forgetting theirs. He thought of the carrots tomorrow, the weeds in the carrots. He thought of Friday and surplus commodities. His mind was clear and light like air. Music wafted through it like a feather. He felt very tall. His broken shoes whispered in the soft dirt far below. *Lonnie sleeping Friday weeds carrots three feet wide a woman screaming quarter of a mile tomorrow surplus commodities walking music water running forgetting forty cents a day sleeping forgetting forty cents floating like air clear water running sparkling through the brain surplus brain commodities sleeping a feather of music tickling this is my tent sitting down like a cloud floating music faces fluffy sound in my ears flying away.*[20]

The music brings Milt into a fugue, wherein he initially thinks of his and his family's troubles in direct-discourse narration; then the text breaks into stream-of-consciousness narration as he recapitulates these worries together with earlier scenes from the novel in fragmented, italicized words and phrases with nonstandard spacing between them. The susurrus of the music is revealed in repeated words, such as "sleeping," and an emphasis on "s" and "f" sounds: "a feather of music tickling," "fluffy sound in my ears flying away." The music alternately grounds and lifts Milt, making him think, *this is my tent*, even while, in a wonderfully contradictory image, he meditatively imagines himself "sitting down like a cloud floating." Immediately prior to the stream-of-consciousness section of the passage, we read that Milt's "broken shoes whispered in the soft dirt," whispering, perhaps, along with the family band's music. As above, so below, and the grounded sound of Milt's shoes—which are "far below"—becomes transposed into musicality, along with everything else he experiences. What we see here is a moment of reflection and heightened consciousness, narrated in harmonically oriented language.

More than an ephemeral enjoyment of music, this passage illustrates the importance of music in migrant life. Music gives voice to migrant life, while also enabling scenes of communal listening and engagement—the family is equipped to practice and play, and this forms a sonic space for any of the other migrants in the camp who hear and engage with the music. Music is a gift shared by and between migrants, an integral part of the communal fabric. Such an image of music as gift giving and sharing, to me, forms the undercurrent of Woody Guthrie's music writing and music making, and the political project he envisioned through his art. Guthrie's musical imaginary, motivated by his desire to politicize struggle through balladry and psalmody, is often expressed through the language of gift, harmony, and dignity.

In *Bound for Glory*, Guthrie's 1943 "fictionalized autobiography," he lays out a long scene of listening to two sisters at a work camp in Redding, California, playing music for their baby brother.[21] Guthrie writes, "One of the sisters turned a string or two, then chorded a little. People walked from all over the camp and gathered, and the kid, mama, and dad, and all the visitors, kept as still as daylight while the girls sang."[22] Guthrie links the different participants and actions with multiple uses of the conjunction "and." The description is filled with walking and gathering, reminiscent of both a pilgrimage and a concert. This scene coalesces the many into one crowd, but they are, nonetheless, individuated. As Guthrie continues, he notes that he "just reared back and soaked in every note and every word of their singing." He immediately goes on:

> It was so clear and honest sounding, no Hollywood put-on, no fake wiggling. It was better to me than the loud squalling and bawling you've got to do to make yourself heard in the old mobbed saloons. And, instead of getting you all riled up mentally, morally and sexually—no, it done something a lot better, something that's harder to do, something you need ten times more. It cleared your head up, that's what it done, caused you to fall back and let your draggy bones rest and your muscles go limber like a cat's.[23]

This passage bears and privileges an affect remarkably similar to that found in Babb's description of Milt Dunne responding to the family band's music. When Guthrie writes, "It cleared your head up . . . and let your draggy bones rest and your muscles go limber like a cat's," it might as well be Milt trying to explain his feeling of the music *"floating like air clear water running sparkling through the brain."* Both images of clarity describe music as acting on the individual mind, while also grounding that individual mind within a networked sense of sound and belonging.

Guthrie extends the scene of listening beyond the crowd surrounding the girls, though. He writes:

> Two little girls were making two thousand working people feel like I felt, rest like I rested. And when I say two thousand, take a look down off across these three little hills. You'll see a hat or two bobbing up above the brush. Somebody is going, somebody is coming, somebody is kneeling down drinking from the spring of water trickling out of the west hill. Five men are shaving before the same crooked hunk of old looking-glass, using tin cans for their water. A woman right up close to you wrings out a tough work shirt, saves the water for four more. You skim your eye out around the south hill, and not less than a hundred women are doing the same thing, washing, wringing, hanging out shirts, taking them down dry to iron. Not a one of them is talking above a whisper, and the one that is whispering almost feels guilty because she knows that ninety-nine out of every hundred are tired, weary, have felt sad, joked and laughed to keep from crying. But these two little girls are telling about all of that trouble, and everybody knows it's helping. These songs say something about our hard traveling, something about our hard luck, our hard get-by, but the songs say we'll come through all of these in pretty good shape, and we'll be all right, we'll work, make ourself useful.[24]

These songs, expressive of the difficulty of working-class migrant life, speak with the "two thousand" people in the space, whether they are sitting and listening, shaving, working, washing, or whispering. Guthrie's thick description of the crowd suggests that listening and connecting take on as many aspects as there are members of a crowd. Like the story of Jesus feeding a multitude with two fish and five loaves of bread, the two girls give sustenance to the many. Indeed, Guthrie suggests a communion-like atmosphere, a ritualistic partaking of a sacred substance—song—that brings the multitude together through shared pain and shared experiences. Yet he also uses apostrophe to indicate how listening becomes observation, how observation becomes participation, and how participation becomes political: "take a look down off across these three little hills," where you'll see "a hat or two bobbing," somebody "going," "coming," "kneeling," or "drinking," and a woman who "wrings out a tough work shirt" and makes sure that she "saves the water for four more." Indeed, all over, "women are doing the same thing, washing, writing, hanging out shirts," and all of them are speaking at a "whisper" (just as Milt Dunne's shoes lower their sound to a whisper in Babb's passage). Nearly all are "tired, weary, have felt sad," and have done anything "to keep from crying." Yet, as he notes, "the girls are telling about all of that trouble, and everybody knows it's helping."

Guthrie decides to join in with the two girls' music. He gives, at the end of this section, a strong ethical motive for his memorization of the countless songs he played on his travels:

> I let them run along for a little while, twisted my guitar up in tune with theirs, holding my ear down against the sounding box, and when I heard it was in tune with them I started picking out the tune, sort of note for note, letting their guitar play the bass chords and second parts. They both smiled when they heard me because two guitars being played this way is what's called the real article, and millions of little kids are raised on this kind of music. If you think of something new to say, if a cyclone comes, or a flood wrecks the country, or a bus load of school children freeze to death along the road, if a big ship goes down, and an airplane falls in your neighborhood, an outlaw shoots it out with the deputies, or the working people go out to win a war, yes, you'll find a train load of things you can set down and make up a song about. You'll hear people singing your words around over the country, and you'll sing their songs everywhere you travel or everywhere you live; and these are the only kind of songs my head or my memory or my guitar has got any room for.[25]

Here, Guthrie links the process of music making and composition with the issue of reception and listening. What interests him, he explicitly says, is the synthesis of "your words" and "their songs," such that an entire musical corpus is built from the everyday and political concerns of working people. Guthrie's emphasis on pronouns, wherein "your words" signifies the speaking self—he's referring to himself in the second person, albeit in the capacious way in which spoken language often combines the first and second person through "you" and "your" as empathetic pronouns—and "their songs" signifies the voices that have informed and shaped the conscious self's repertoire, signals the fundamentally, unalterably relational notion of composition that underlies his work. Interestingly, his guitar, which during World War II Guthrie labeled with a sticker proclaiming, "This machine kills fascists,"[26] is here given agency in musical selection, when Guthrie states that "my head or my memory or my guitar" only have room for songs dedicated by and to the people whose voices, words, and lives inform them. Bryan Garman, linking Woody Guthrie to Bruce Springsteen through the "hurt song," describes the social, performative nature of these songs: "Written in working-class language, hurt songs express the collective pain, suffering, and injustice working people have historically suffered, and articulate their collective hopes and dreams for a less oppressive future."[27] Hurt songs explicitly articulate class concerns as a means of simultaneously thinking about injustice and hope. Garman argues that "Guthrie was convinced that only folk music, a form which captured the voice of the people, could represent 'the real stuff' of class struggle and 'use the Truth . . . like a spring of cold water' to bring about social reform."[28]

Like Milt Dunne's "clear water" and Guthrie's "cleared head," the idea of expressive, affective, socially oriented music leading to political effectiveness reveals the foundation of an artistic praxis that sees art not as secondary, ornamental, or "merely" entertaining; instead, in this view, art is primary, substantial, and *of course* entertaining. Entertainment and enjoyment become political, become expressive of dignity, especially in the face of degradation. Guthrie reimagines folk music and balladry as more than a connection to the past through a sustained tradition; rather, he thinks of his music as an oral history of the present. Guthrie's music often offers a new set of particulars through which people can articulate themselves, especially since his broad vision of this music's circulation among people embraced new (or, indeed, perduring and ancient, if no longer valorized) types of performance venues as well as mass media.[29] Richard Reuss argues that "spatial isolation and relatively simple technological and communications systems have formed the basic criteria for determining folk society in the United States," a definition he finds far "too limited."[30] Reuss, like scholars who take up Hurston's *Mules and Men*, pinpoints the problematic scholarly criteria for defining "the folk," which seemingly hinges upon a desire to maintain an impoverished, isolated class of people whose cultural, folkloric contributions are valued above their own needs. This is not to say that isolated communities who wish to remain so do not have that right—rather, it is to say that the desire to preserve a culture "like it used to be" or as "authentic" while partaking of that culture from a distance, and especially while maintaining class difference, produces a highly problematic relationship of production and consumption.

Guthrie was uniquely situated in his ability to spread his musical and political message. Finding himself in Los Angeles at a time when radical radio allowed for music and political commentary to seamlessly mix, Guthrie was able to develop a popular personality that he claimed led thousands of admiring letters to be sent to him care of his radio station, KFVD.[31] Edwin Cohen notes the enormous effects of technological change during the Depression years: the growth of the radio and phonograph recording industries created large new listening audiences, and electricity became far more widely available in rural areas. This, Cohen argues, fundamentally changed folk music: "The American folksong because of these influences did one of two things in the 1930's and 1940's: it became virtually extinct in all but some of the more rural, backward areas of the country; or, it changed its form to accommodate some of the aspects of song previously reserved for the popular song; that is, it became a popular song with a folk feeling and folk sense."[32]

Serge Denisoff takes a different view, arguing that politically charged folk songs by known and recorded artists "reflected a fusion of social movement technique, ideology, and traditional folk material. . . . [T]he songs were no longer folk songs but, rather, examples of folk consciousness. Folk songs had become 'songs with *conscious messages*, composed with calculated awareness.'"[33] Denisoff's issue is that Guthrie's songs, especially the political ones that dominate his oeuvre, are no longer "informant" texts that provide unconscious, unmediated windows into folk life and folkways. Denisoff's ire toward

Guthrie in particular focuses on a city-country divide, such as when he levels the criticism that Guthrie's songs were enjoyed "predominantly by urban radicals and Communists in New York and elsewhere."[34] Gene Bluestein, on the other hand, rejects this critique as overdetermined:

> Because Guthrie was born of middle-class parents in a small Oklahoma town, academic folklorists have viewed him as inauthentic; his traditional-sounding, folk-based work cannot be folk song because it has clear authorship and lacks the requisite lower-class antecedents. From this point of view, Guthrie is obviously a "revivalist," a pernicious term that implies lack of association with the folk process.[35]

Bluestein finds this binary between "folk song" and "folk revivalist" untenable, along with the assumption that because Guthrie made up his own songs, they could not possibly have been popular with the people among whom he performed. For Bluestein, the most specious claim made by Denisoff and others is that "clear authorship" equates to a "lack of association with the folk process." Such arguments treat the folk as having no capacity for authorship, as having no politics and no desires outside of the quotidian and domestic—a claim belied by the long tradition of border ballads from Scotland to Spain to Mexico to California, and even more so by the songs sung by the enslaved the world over, especially in the Americas.

To counter the assumptions behind folk authenticity, Bluestein coins the term *poplore*, which describes the incorporation of folk culture and material into popular culture.[36] Observing that mass media has indelibly changed the ideal of the untainted or undiscovered musician (merely consider Guthrie, who had a popular L.A.-based radio show at the outset of his career), Bluestein argues, "All the notable figures of twentieth-century folk fame (including white rural singers and black blues people) are actually poplorists.... Grounded in a kind of double helix of black and white source material, these tunes, rhythms, texts, and vernacular styles (especially the blues) have been the basis for all musical developments since. They have been copied, extended, and often, like bluegrass, totally re-invented by such talented and creative poplorists as Guthrie."[37] The reincorporation of and significant borrowing from previous styles is explicitly named by Guthrie as the primary propulsion and reason behind his music. Guthrie performed in interracial musical groups such as the Almanac Singers, played with Huddie "Lead Belly" Ledbetter and Josh White (both of whom are also sometimes accused by scholars and listeners of "selling out" and becoming political once they began performing and recording with Guthrie, Seeger, Cisco Houston, the Lomaxes, and others), and, more than can be said for many of his successors in the folk revival, publicly acknowledged and gave performance space to singers and artists whose work influenced his.[38] In Bluestein's assessment, "Poplorists such as Guthrie have been the most important figures in bringing together the musical and ideological implications of folk and popular culture in our time."[39] This was certainly also true of Bessie Smith, for example, or Lead Belly, and later on Sister Rosetta Tharpe, Johnny Cash, and groups like Los Tigres del Norte. Ultimately, Guthrie's important bridging of Anglo folk-music culture and popular culture, especially through his savvy use of media technologies, reveals not exploitation and crass commercialism, but an esteem based on a "sense of popular culture as the culture actually made by people for themselves, which is different" from ideas of popular culture as a manifestation of mass cultural entertainment.[40] Artists like Guthrie tapped into the voices and desires of their listeners—not only those who listened to them on the radio or bought records, but those who came to see them in concert halls, saloons, billiard halls, dance halls, union halls, open-air concerts, camp tents, and impromptu performances—prompting sing-alongs, lyric memorization, imitation, and affective engagement.

Guthrie used these voices and desires to advance a particular mode of politics. In his lyrics, he so capably moves from mountains, dams, grand historical narratives, and factories to people, local places, and specific times that he gives the audience a dynamic mix of imaginative possibility and calls to action. Guthrie saw performance as a political *and* musical process, and he sought to cultivate a quite radical relationship between himself and his audience that modeled a utopian, direct form of democracy. This audience relationship, in combination with his musical style—his idiosyncratic guitar playing and his many collaborations, duets, and group performances—directly informed his performance ethos.

Guthrie's songwriting was geared toward creating affective, collectively driven political solidarity, in its means as well as its message. Joe Klein, in his biographical study of Guthrie, argues with respect to Guthrie's theory of writing lyrics, "He took a classic high-culture position arguing against agitprop exhortation. You didn't have to slam people over the idea; it was more artful and effective to *show* than to *tell*. He argued that writing a ballad was the ultimate test of a songwriter."[41] Klein focuses on Guthrie's lyrical chops, especially his ability to tell a story. This balladic impulse led Guthrie to "cover" John Steinbeck's 1939 novel *The Grapes of Wrath* in his 1940 album *Dust Bowl Ballads*, and to spread news about anti-labor incidents in the cultural (though not exactly musical) style of the Mexican and Mexican American corrido, such as the infamous Italian Hall disaster he sang about in "1913 Massacre." Paired with this straightforward balladic lyricism, Guthrie's fairly schematic use of chords in his songs generates a musical style that draws audiences in through memorable narratives and recognizable melodies, while also making it more likely that audiences learn, copy, and spread the songs.

Most Guthrie songs vary between two and four chords. Essentially, he often goes between G major, D major or D7, and C major, one of the most common chord combinations in many a guitar repertoire (this "I–V–IV" harmonic structure is foundational to blues and rock, for example). Combined with his narratively driven lyrics, these simple chords make it quite possible for a song to catch on, to be learned and spread. Also, if the chords are easy to remember, then rhythms can be improvised and melodies can be altered to suit each player's own preferences in delivery. Craig Werner, tying Guthrie's style to the call-and-response tradition, notes that "once the call has been issued, the audience is free to respond in any way it sees fit. . . . Other voices, each drawing on its own vertical process, can agree, argue, redirect the dialogue, raise new questions. . . . The position of leadership can pass from individual to individual, community to community."[42] Werner's point is well taken, especially given how many song melodies Guthrie borrowed from the Carter Family, from traditional hymns, from folk songs such as "The Wabash Cannonball," and more. Guthrie's "simple" songs were easy to learn, but the complexity of their situatedness, of their contextualization within shifting scenes of performance, bespeaks a deep commitment to making sure songs are always *speaking with*—rather than *for*—audiences, and that they can, in turn, be used in further scenes of *speaking with*.

Denisoff recognizes the transmissibility of Guthrie's straightforward chord schemas but argues that it served other purposes.[43] Specifically citing

1939 to 1942, a period aligned with the heyday of Guthrie's popularity, Denisoff argues, "During this time 'folk music' became what one listened to at informal gatherings and social affairs given by radicals. Folk entrepreneurs were featured performers at benefits for migratory workers, refugees of the Spanish conflict, and fund-raising drives for militant unions.... Woodrow Wilson Guthrie, known simply as 'Woody,' idealized the renaissance."[44] Denisoff further argues that a major weapon in the folk entrepreneur's arsenal, coinciding with the entry of the US into World War II, is what he calls the "song of persuasion":

> A song of persuasion may be thought of as a propaganda song which employs the instrumental and stylistic techniques generally associated with folk songs.... The structure of the music frequently is tied to a three-chord progression such as G-C-G-C-G-D7 or E-A-E-A-E-B7, with lyrics being stressed. This latter feature makes it ideal for propaganda purposes, since the music does not detract from the message. Equally, the lyrics in many cases are easily adapted to contemporary situations.[45]

Leaving aside Denisoff's marked distaste for political folk music, his description largely fits Guthrie's style of songwriting and performing. Though Denisoff interprets Guthrie's motives uncharitably, the simple harmonic structure of the three-chord progression allows for great iterability and improvisation of melody, facilitating memorization of both tune and lyrics.

Generally speaking, Guthrie didn't mind that people played his music, and didn't care when they played it or if they credited him (unless it was a corporation seeking profit). In providing his audiences with "free gifts" through his performances, Guthrie often short-circuited usual notions of ownership: he invited his listeners to sing along, to learn the songs, and to perform on their own.[46] Guthrie's songs were passed around, communally heard, and disseminated in both public and private across America, achieving a variety of shapes and sounds as they moved from mouth to mouth, from setting to setting, and from person to person. Guthrie's own flexible and improvisatory performance style also enacted localized moments of radical democratic thought and feeling, largely because he let people around him at any given performance influence how that performance went. Reuss notes, "For Guthrie, as with other traditional artists, the composition or performance of a song was a creative act born out of the dynamics of a given moment in time.... To Woody, each draft or performance of a song was a new creative experience rather than the revision of an old one."[47] Guthrie's legendary memory allowed him to memorize hundreds of songs and dozens of verses for each song, and he performed songs differently according to the crowd, his feelings, and the political situation at hand and abroad. A famous raconteur, Guthrie was also able to make up verses on the spot. In several of his recorded songs this can be heard in his hesitations (both lyrical and melodic—this is exemplarily evident in his recording of a children's song, "Why, Oh Why"[48]), his laughter, his muddled words, and his heavy rhyming. In his joy and genuine pleasure, Guthrie cultivates endearment.

The United States that Guthrie's musical utopias imagine, one where everyone's stories are sung and woven together into new sorts of ensemblic performances, is a nonexistent America, a possible America that he exuberantly declares inevitable. This music, borrowing from Josh Kun, "gives us the feelings we need to get where we want to go."[49] In his musical performances, Guthrie embodies and subjectivizes the "great historical bum," his archetypal characterization of a peripatetic prophet. Always marginalized and radically conscious, the great historical bum appears in his songs as a working person who connects to the great many other migratory workers throughout history. He wonders what it means to be a worker who travels throughout space and time, declaring solidarity with fellow working people from the Garden of Eden to the titanic industrial war economy of the early 1940s. What Guthrie asks us to hear in his music is the promise of economic and historical change. Greil Marcus argues that this prophetic mode of criticism (akin to Cornel West's critical reinvigoration of prophetic discourse[50]) often arises from a single person's drive to voice justice: "Out of a throng of selves, what is one body of prophecy? Before it is anything else it is a single American, claiming his or her birthright, as a single body standing in, if only for a moment, for all other Americans. People are out there; someone has to hear. And then what?"[51] Rather than taking up Marcus's idea of "a single body standing in" for many others, I would like to locate Guthrie's intervention in relation to Marcus's subsequent question—"And then what?" By way of response, Guthrie sees the "throng of selves" he sings to and about as "one body of prophecy" (which Marcus quotes from Allen Ginsberg)—as a listening public whose songs and lives he sings.

A more specific answer Guthrie might be said to proleptically provide to Marcus's "And then what?" takes shape in his song "Farmer-Labor Train." In this driving, upbeat song, modeled directly on the folk standard "The Wabash Cannonball" (a tune and theme he would reuse for "The Wallace-Taylor Train," in support of Henry Wallace's 1948 presidential campaign), Guthrie's unrestrained, joyful voice combines with Cisco Houston's rollicking, foot-stomp-inducing, cut-time guitar playing, Guthrie's joyful harmonica, and the two men harmonizing their voices at various nonlyric points of the song to channel the train's wailing whistle. The music's indignation and righteous optimism envisions a new concept of participatory, popular democracy:

> There's folks of every color and they're ridin' side by side
> Through the swamps of Louisiana and across the Great Divide,
> From the wheat fields and the orchards and the lowing cattle range,
> And they're rolling onto victory on this Farmer-Labor train.
>
> This train pulled into Washington a bright and happy day,
> When she steamed into the station you could hear the people say:
> "There's that Farmer-Labor Special, she's full of union men
> Headin' onto White House on the Farmer-Labor train."[52]

Guthrie's vision of farmworkers joining union workers and chugging into the nation's capital speaks to the radical politics he supported and expressively sang about throughout his career. This train, defiantly leftist and defiantly desegregated, rides into the US's political center with an agenda of fighting for the rights of working-class men and women. The train pulls "*onto* victory," "*into* Washington," and "*onto* White House": the workers insert themselves into and onto spaces of hegemony, and even victory is treated as a place in and of itself. Furthermore, seeing as Washington, DC, was a segregated city, this integrated train insists upon being recognized by both Washingtonian onlookers and Washingtonians who make political decisions. Syntactically, Guthrie pulls together the various workers and various actions through the repetition of the conjunction "and"—a radical unifier of difference, tying together while still maintaining the particularity of clauses and actions. With its syntax and diction, "Farmer-Labor Train" weaves together a narrative of alliance and political empowerment in the utopian space of song and future action. By the end of the song, after enumerating various types of workers and their locations, Guthrie imagines the admiration of a people that respects the rights of all workers, positively construing and calling forth an American public that did not quite (and still does not always) seem to persist or exist: an(other) America that fights against class hierarchies, racism, and other forms of chauvinism.

This desire to sing the songs and tell the tales of the undercommons activates much of Guthrie's habits of *speaking with*, and a paradigmatic example of this tendency is "1913 Massacre."[53] In his introduction to this song, Guthrie slowly and melancholically plucks individual notes from a chord for two bars. He then begins singing a recitative melody, a staple of ritualistic religious song in which a cantor sings around a sustained note structure. In this song released in 1945—the year of his marriage to Marjorie Mazia Greenblatt—the influence of a Jewish cantor can indeed be strongly felt.[54] Using his thumb to pluck out a walking line in "common time," he gives the song a swaying, slow beat.[55] The song's opening is an invitation to the audience: "Take a trip with me in 1913, / To Calumet, Michigan, in the copper country. / I will take you to a place called Italian Hall, / Where the miners are having their big Christmas ball." The use of prepositions here is unusual, as in "Farmer-Labor Train." Rather than inviting listeners to take a trip with him *to* 1913, he says "*in* 1913." This folds the listener into Guthrie's powerful and anachronistic imagination as another example of the "great historical bum" who moves through history as an empathetic fellow laborer and traveler. In this place and time, Guthrie is guide and fellow observer. After setting the scene and laying out the working conditions and pay structure for the miners ("less than a dollar a day"), he tells us, "There's talking and laughing and songs in the air, / And the spirit of Christmas is there everywhere, / Before you know it, you're friends with us all, / And you're dancing around and around in the hall." No longer asking questions of the miners or merely watching from the wings, we are now part of the ball itself, ensconced in the milieu as part of Guthrie's mode of *speaking with* both the audience and the subjects of the song. The internal rhymes (talking, laughing; there, everywhere) and end rhymes (air, everywhere; all, hall) emphasize the community being actively built in that specific hall.

As we are in the midst of enjoying ourselves, dancing with the miners and their families in 1913, the "copper boss' thug men" falsely "scream, 'There's a fire,'" and cause a stampede that kills dozens of celebrants. Children, especially, get smothered in the crush.[56] Recitatively delivering the sorrowful lyrics, Guthrie wails, "Such a terrible sight I never did see, / We carried our children back up to their tree, / The scabs outside still laughed at their spree, / And the children that died there were seventy-three." While Guthrie "never did see" this incident, he demands that we place ourselves directly in the midst of this violence and imagine the terrifying specter of crushed children, a consequence of anti-labor brutality and vigilantism. He imagines that we all—the miners, himself, and his listeners—carry the victims "back up to their tree" (the Christmas tree), gathering together in a scene of sorrowful martyrdom. The piano that earlier played joyful Christmas tunes is now playing songs of mourning: "The piano played a slow funeral tune, / And the town was lit up by a cold Christmas moon, / The parents they cried and the miners they moaned, / 'See what your greed for money has done.'" The final word coincides with the final note of the song, which ends on this accusation of greed. In the recording, "your greed" is multidirectional: the words "moaned" by the miners might also be addressed to the listeners. Though within the space of the song we have been dancing and witnessing, we might also be guilty of greed—it is up to us, then, to move or be moved, to affect or be affected. Our involvement in the song, as listeners, runs from the beginning to the end, from invitation to potential accusation, from joy to sorrow. The question of what side we're on dominates the song's conclusion.

Indeed, for Guthrie, not seeing injustice is no excuse to avoid engaging with it. As Stadler, Kaufmann, and Klein have shown, a formative moment in Guthrie's biographical sensibilities was the 1911 lynching of Laura Nelson and her son, Lawrence, who lived near Okemah, where Guthrie was born a year later. Klein describes the lynching and its lead-up very matter-of-factly: "a mob burst into the jail one night—a mob composed of many of Okemah's finest citizens, including Charley Guthrie [Woody Guthrie's father]—and dragged Laura Nelson, her son, and her baby to the bridge over the Canadian River about six miles west of town, where she and Lawrence were lynched and the baby left crying helplessly by the side of the road." Klein further notes that the town's newspaper "also published a grisly photo of the lynched bodies, which later was reprinted as a postcard and became a popular novelty item in local stores."[57] The circulation of the Nelson family's lynched bodies in the form of the souvenir postcard operates by means of commerce and exchange, a ritualized reminder and remainder of the catastrophic violence behind the photograph. This postcard, in emphasizing the coming together of a community through catastrophic anti-Black violence, was part of a broader lynching cultural economy in which, as Harvey Young points out, "the lynching keepsake . . . is incomplete and finds a sense of wholeness through an embrace of an accompanying narrative."[58] The community's whiteness is ritually constituted and ideologically sanctified through the murder of the Nelsons, and the justificatory narrative of the lynching provides the photograph with a parallel "sense of wholeness" that allows it to metonymically stand in for Okemah as "a popular novelty item in local stores," as Klein puts it above. Stadler suggests that Guthrie's political and aesthetic idea of union theorizes against violent forms of wholeness. In elaborating this point, Stadler argues that the Nelson family's lynching, and anti-Black violence more broadly, preoccupied Guthrie's last years, a point he emphasizes through careful attention to the notebooks Guthrie kept while hospitalized by the rapid progression of his Huntington's disease over the last several years of his life.[59]

Ultimately, Guthrie's radically imaginative musical praxis invokes movement politics through the politics of movement—the politics of being *moved*, as well as acknowledging the artistic, creative, and political potential of the migrating, rambling people he sings about. For Werner, Guthrie is "at his best when he sounds most like himself, most like the singer who welcomed the actual sounds of those voices into his own consciousness. . . . Democracy sings in each of us individually, Woody intimates, as long as we understand who we are—what we sound like—is shaped by and at best responds to everyone we hear."[60] Notably, Guthrie always imagines others as fellow musicians and fellow travelers, whether they are requesting published versions of his songs, or picking up on his songs' easily memorizable lyrics and chord structures, or playing their own beautiful music that he wants to join in with, as when he plays alongside the two little girls in the California field.

The enduring power of his music shows that Guthrie's sense of union was not only consistently active, but activatable in perpetuity. For Cantwell, "to be precisely what Guthrie was demanded the precise pattern of his tragic exile, which equipped him to mediate imaginatively, in his person and his works, between the world of the poor and the dispossessed and those who had never touched that world except as readers, tourists, journalists, artists, or photographers."[61] Guthrie's songs bridge experiences and actions, spanning difficult distances through his hard traveling and freely circulating musicking. Ultimately, Guthrie's music creates spaces for encounter, for knowledge, and, most importantly, for the acknowledgment of coalitional difference that makes us and others subjects who *speak with*, together.

Sanora Babb and the Interracial Roots of Radicalism

At the same time that Hurston and Rukeyser engaged in ethnographic and documentary research to visibilize Black migrant workers in the American South and Appalachia, Sanora Babb was working in the western states, documenting the migrant work camps that sprang up among people fleeing the wrath of the Dust Bowl. In doing this work, Babb hewed her path through the aesthetic and political wilds of the 1930s, 1940s, and beyond.[62] While Babb may not have attained the stature of Hurston and Rukeyser, her lengthy career as a writer and the quality of her work, particularly her development of a coalitional aesthetic of *speaking with* that actively works against the whiteness of Popular Front political imagery (evident in literary texts by her white contemporaries), has inspired growing interest.[63]

It might be said that Babb's aesthetics are quite similar to the documentary ethos Rukeyser and Hurston applied in developing their practices of *speaking with*. Babb utilized documentary and journalistic modes in her fiction, as well as in her work as a Farm Security Administration (FSA) educator and employee. At the heart of her novel *Whose Names Are Unknown* (published by University of Oklahoma Press in 2004, and completed in manuscript form by Babb in 1939), we encounter the struggles of working men, women, and children as they strive to make themselves legible to a system that sees them as nothing but expendable, interchangeable labor. In particular, Babb's descriptive praxis—her attention to small details that enable us to see familial and communal dynamics—labors to raise consciousness and produce political transformation, especially when coupled with her use of free indirect discourse as a connective narrative device. This is a praxis that one also finds in Guthrie's music: invoking grand historical narratives and dialectical materialism while still representing reported stories by people without privileged access to established musical or literary production through which to disseminate their narratives.

In *Whose Names Are Unknown*, expressions of desire for social and political change are represented through intimate engagements with the lives of people affected by oppressive social, economic, and political systems. Babb relies on information she gathered in her FSA fieldwork, weaving documented experiences and documentary representations with lyrical prose, moving between expansive, abstract description and the concrete struggles of a specific family, the Dunnes, and of their friends and fellow workers. (In terms of concreteness, *Whose Names Are Unknown* is similar to but more specific than Steinbeck's *The Grapes of Wrath*—the influence, as will be discussed below, ran from Babb to Steinbeck.) Babb's novel mixes these concrete and abstract reflections within the text, utilizing free indirect discourse, "found object" inclusion (the use of text from handbills and eviction notices, as well as likely fictionalized epistles), and diaristic writing to make a case for proletarian power while also demanding the recognition of individual migrants.[64] Babb does not seek to (re-)create a folkloric migrant culture, though, and the Dunne family—Julia, her husband Milt, and their daughters Myra and Lonnie—is not like Steinbeck's archetypal and symbolically load-bearing Joad family.

The Dunne family *does* depart the Dust Bowl, heading west with friends and working fields in California after valiantly attempting, for roughly half the book, to save the farm they rent from the bank in town. They leave behind their beloved Konkie, Milt's father, whose final gesture is perhaps one of the most heartbreaking in US literature in its sublime specificity: "Tears ran down his brown weathered face as he loosed [Myra's] arms and lifted her into the backseat where Lonnie was already squeezed among the quilts. He closed the door and pecked on the glass with his long bony fingers trying to make them smile."[65] The family and their friends make it to California, struggle in the orchards and the fields, join a failed labor action, and resolve to stay in the union and fight.

I am particularly invested in exploring and writing about Babb, having first learned of her from Ken Burns's 2012 documentary *The Dust Bowl*. Her field notes and research notebooks were lent without her permission to John Steinbeck (by Babb's boss, Tom Collins, who is the dedicatee of Steinbeck's novel) to aid the writing of *The Grapes of Wrath*.[66] In a terrible blow that revealed the sexist, consumer-driven culture in which Babb was writing, her own novel, which was already under contract and whose manuscript was essentially complete, was shelved a year after Steinbeck's novel was published.

Whose Names Are Unknown was seen as piling on to a literary "trend" that had, with the presence of a single tome, already been cornered—publishers said there was no more room for another Dust Bowl novel.⁶⁷ In terms of my own scholarly growth, when I searched for more work on Babb after learning of her from Burns's documentary, I initially came across Abigail Manzella's dissertation, which has been transformed into the excellent *Migrating Fictions*, as well as Douglas Wixson's enormously influential and committed work expanding Babb's legacy.⁶⁸ Later in graduate school, I encountered Sarah Wald's *The Nature of California* and Erin Royston Battat's *Ain't Got No Home*, both of which, alongside Manzella's work, are significant achievements in elaborating the literary history of a consciously literary, interracial left. I lay out this history in order to acknowledge my significant debt to this work, which has painstakingly and lovingly sought to remedy Babb's outrageous exclusion from US literary history.

Babb, like Steinbeck, was interested in exploring the lives of men and women from the agriculturally devastated American heartland. Unlike Steinbeck, she hailed from the Dust Bowl herself. Whereas for Steinbeck it could be (and, in fact, *is*) argued that he sees the Joad family as political symbols that could be exchanged with any number of other families, the intimacy Babb establishes with the fictional Dunnes and other families, such as the Brownells and the Brennermans, speaks to the vibrant community she envisioned as part of her fictional praxis. *Whose Names Are Unknown* is a direct attempt to make the existences and particularities of the farmers and laborers *known*, rather than interchangeable. Evident from the very first—the novel's title— Babb's commitment to telling a specific story of people whose names were unknown works alongside, but far more specifically than, the stories that so often functioned as Popular Front encapsulations of the mythical yeoman farmer fallen on hard times. Specificity, for Babb, best expresses the degradations and deprivations of the Dust Bowl disaster.

Wixson, in his invaluable studies of Sanora Babb's life and work, notes that refugees from the High Plains often embraced Babb with open arms, specifically because she was one of them.⁶⁹ Growing up in Oklahoma, Kansas, and southeastern Colorado, Babb moved with her family through the part of the nation that would become known as the Dust Bowl, which acquired its name largely due to the destruction of its topsoil, the uprooting of its native grasses, and the subsequent dust storms that swept across hundreds of miles of inhabited land. Knowing firsthand the privations of the small farmers on the High Plains, Babb became a trusted and reliable worker for the FSA in 1938 and 1939, especially as it worked to establish government camps for Dust Bowl refugees and migrants seeking work in California's massive agribusiness industry. Exploited white farmworkers, whose faces were most famously photographed by Arthur Rothstein and Dorothea Lange, generated enormously empathetic public responses. This process in turn led to the creation of specifically targeted social and economic "safety nets": government-run camps that could each house hundreds of migrant workers (although, as was quite evident, these "safety nets" provided at best temporary shelter and food, since migrants still had to move to find work). Tom Collins worked alongside Babb and other FSA workers to convince the people moving through California to rely on FSA camps to find reliable food, shelter, services, and facilities (such as toilets, showers, and water pumps). These camps offered important alternatives to the growers' camps with their company stores and scrip, or their wages-in-credit, and were far safer (in particular from the infamous vigilante men) than most of the squatter camps that the majority of the migrants lived in.[70] Wixson notes that the government camps were incredible resources for the migrants, while also observing the specifically racialized impetus behind the establishment of the FSA and its projects. He says, "Founded in 1934 as the Resettlement Agency, the FSA was established to aid dispossessed Anglo farmers, not the migrant workers, mainly Mexican and Filipino, who had done the harvesting in the years before the diaspora of Dust Bowl migrants flooded California's Central Valley in the 'dirty thirties.'"[71]

In *Whose Names Are Unknown*, Babb gives a direct account, using a shifting narratorial voice and various interlaid sources of italicized free indirect discourse, of why these camps provided such a boon to the migrants and proved such a thorn in the side of the California growers and their allies. Often relying on a distanced narrative voice when conveying facts and observations, Babb describes strategies by which migrant workers were disenfranchised in order to actively disempower them:

> Of course, there were other means of preserving the migratories as such. One of the most effective was a particular system of bookkeeping, ordained to keep

migratory workers from registering and voting. All members of an organization of big farmers kept a record of their workers' car license numbers and the date they entered into the state. When a worker had been in a county for six months, by law, he could register. If convenient for the crop at hand, the worker was let out just before that time. As he moved on asking for work from other farmers, their records showed he should be on his way to another county.[72]

The hyperbureaucratic means through which workers were kept track of—even as they were disallowed from registering as voters—bespeaks the types of organization that were allowed: "big farmers" were allowed to form collectives that actively prevented their workers from organizing into unions or collectives, while migrants were not allowed to exercise their right to a public voice through the ballot. Migrant populations are often used to sharpen the logic of expulsion in binarizing arguments about citizens versus noncitizens, bearers of rights versus disposable people. For Paul Virilio, this tendency to consider migrants as separate from citizens creates a "stable or enclosure" in which the former are often contained: "the temporary lodging of the migrating masses implies their relative distance from the dwellings of men, in other words from the city."[73] Temporariness is opposed to permanence; camps for migrant outsiders are opposed to defended settlements for citizens. Elaborating the idea that California was a new "city on a hill," the growers and politicians in California actively refused to allow migrants to settle, to be inhabitants within the state.[74] This, at its heart, provides for Babb the most important argument for direct democracy. Or, as noted in the novel with documentary accuracy by means of a leaflet slipped under a door, "D.F. means Democracy Functioning."[75]

Given the trust that Babb earned from the many migrants she encountered, she was able to compile detailed notes, reports, and observations about their lives. Her notebooks, as mentioned above, were given to Steinbeck. There is some confusion about how her notebooks came into Steinbeck's possession, and whether or not she approved of their going to the other writer. In his PBS special, Ken Burns suggests that Collins lent Babb's notes to Steinbeck without her knowledge. Wixson is suspicious of this explanation and gives a different account, arguing that there is a strong possibility that Babb's political ideals were knowingly manipulated:

Collins and Babb met frequently to exchange their views on what they had experienced and on ways of improving the conditions in the camps. Collins asked her to share her field notes with Steinbeck, as he had done with his own. The success of the theater version of *Of Mice and Men* (1937) had vaulted Steinbeck into literary prominence. The spirit of little magazine contributors had deeply influenced Babb: to view writing as a common enterprise, to share ideas and to criticize one another's work were her apprenticeship in writing. She had gone to "school" on the steps of the Los Angeles Public Library, where she had spent afternoons with John Fante, Carlos Bulosan, and other young writers discussing their work, trading tips, and enjoying one another's success in placing a story. Now she felt the urgency of making known the plight of the "Okies." It was in this spirit that she lent her field notes to Collins, who passed them to Steinbeck.[76]

This version attributes volition and idealistic selflessness to Babb, whose friendship with leftist writers Bulosan and Fante shaped her sense of political commitment and its relationship to aesthetic development. Wixson convincingly suggests that Steinbeck *still* flouted her expectations of the exchange. For Babb, the most important consequence of her writings was "making known the plight" of the High Plains migrants, and, as Wixson puts it, "it was in this spirit" that she shared her notes with Steinbeck, as it would would help as many people as possible. Steinbeck's blockbuster *The Grapes of Wrath*, along with Guthrie's *Dust Bowl Ballads* and John Ford's film adaptation (both from 1940), certainly made a powerful and widely known case for the Dust Bowl refugees. The personal cost to Babb was, of course, enormous. Significant, too, was the cost of privileging the archetypal generalizations of Steinbeck's novel over the specificity that defines Babb's aesthetics.

As Wixson, Manzella, Battat, and Sarah Wald have noted, Steinbeck's highly successful and powerful novel differs significantly from Babb's *Whose Names Are Unknown*, even if they share source material. All four locate this difference in Babb's personal experience, as well as her attention to the migrants' lived experiences. The minstrel-adjacent use of dialect Steinbeck attributes to the Joads (and the painful way these accents made their way onto the silver screen in Ford's uneven but sometimes magnificent filmic adaptation) is largely absent in Babb's novel, even as naturalistic speech patterns and dialogue prevail. Indeed, there are only two places where dialect is used at length. One is in a letter a character receives from a sister (discussed at length below); another is due to a questionable decision by Babb when a Black character speaks in the text. Wixson argues that Babb's "literary radicalism is a form of critical realism in which the characters and events problematize social and political realities, based upon her own reportorial observation and personal experience. The refugees, she perceived, were not hapless, uninformed 'Okies' who came late to political consciousness."[77]

The idea of "hapless, uninformed 'Okies'" is central to *The Grapes of Wrath*. What Babb instead saw was an already politically conscious, intelligent, and aware group of people who were wary of outsiders, even if those outsiders were radicalized labor organizers or CPUSA party members. Denisoff calls approaches such as Steinbeck's the "'simple Americans' technique. This technique was designed to appeal to the masses, transcending class and political divisions."[78] What this means, beyond an economy of style and a simplicity of presentation, is that symbolic, largely mythological representations of real, "simple Americans" produce a conceit of common sense and folk wisdom. This precise intersection of mythological style and symbolic expectation is where Rukeyser and especially Hurston radically intervened in the process of literary representation. Babb also asserts a different, more empathetic vision of "the folk," such that there emerges a particularism or specificity, an antimythic means of asserting the universal dignity of concrete persons. Using a style different from Steinbeck's formal dialectical materialism in *The Grapes of Wrath*, which occurs on the level of the oscillation between Joad family chapters and the universalizing sections that critics generally refer to as "intercalary chapters," Babb does not separate out the concrete and the abstract in order to suggest a transcendental synthesis. Rather, she intently and consistently develops an aesthetic dialectical materialism devoted to upholding the dignity of the individual in connection to and combination with larger communal concerns. Yet she does not subsume the voices of her characters to these larger concerns; even as these characters speak to experiences, movements, and ideas that are "larger than life"—such as revolution, political organization, agrarian justice, and racial justice—they do not become metonyms or avatars for these political ideas. They remain humans in the mantles of their dignity, rather than reduced, idealistic spokespeople or folksy representations.

Perhaps nowhere is this more evident than in the fact that Babb goes to great lengths to name most of the characters in *Whose Names Are Unknown*. Her novel defies the anonymity-inducing eviction notices beginning with the words "To John Doe and Mary Doe, whose true names are unknown," which she includes to great effect in the novel. She also resists the impulse to subordinate real lives to the demands of symbolic political certainties.[79] Babb's tactic of naming characters is especially profound when compared to *The Grapes of Wrath*, in which perhaps the most powerful and dynamic character, the Joad family's matriarch, is only and forever known as "Ma Joad." Regardless of all her strength and dignity, Ma Joad is consistently reduced to—and solely identified with—her role within the nuclear family. Julia Dunne, the Dunne family's matriarch, is not only a wife, a mother, and a worker (like Ma Joad), or a decision maker and a mythicized, rooted political conscience (which is also Ma Joad's role). Julia is also a purposeful creator of writing and possesses an acknowledged first name (unlike Ma Joad). Indeed, Julia's diary entries shape a significant (albeit short) part of the novel; here in particular her role departs quite radically from that of Ma Joad, whose dialect is often reduced, like Mrs. Rachel Poyser's in George Eliot's *Adam Bede* (1859), to expressions of mawkish "aw shucks" folk wisdom. Julia is given the chance to represent her own world, and the reader's encounter with this act of creation is one of many examples of how the space of the novel offers a manifold, multiply realized series of scenes of radically democratic relationships and ideas. This move, on Babb's part, constitutes an important praxis for *speaking with* the migrants she is writing about.

Rather than writing through an archetypal lens, Babb focuses on the particular workings of identity construction and negotiation taking place in the Anglo-American migration from the Plains to California. Babb's book focuses on a white family, and one way she goes beyond the myths of whiteness is by taking up the issue of nonwhite labor organizing, as practiced by Filipino, African American, and Mexican American union members within the text.[80] Sarah Wald argues that "in contrast [to *The Grapes of Wrath*], Babb's *Whose Names Are Unknown* . . . refuses to affirm Dust Bowl migrants' white privilege. Babb's novel focuses on white landless workers' similarity to other oppressed groups, including Mexicans, Filipinos, and Blacks. *Whose Names* suggests that all workers deserve dignity, freedom, and security."[81] Babb subtly lays out an indication of the intersecting nodes of need that drive farmworkers to work in horrible conditions, implying that racial difference, as Wald has shown, lies almost entirely in the privilege to work or not work in such conditions. Self-consciously ironizing her descriptions of "fast-working and nimble-fingered Filipinos, the resident hardworking Japanese and Mexicans," Babb writes:

> The terrible summer desert heat drove the white men out of the valley, but these men could endure it, partly because they were conditioned to stand it, partly because they must if they were to earn a living. The need that forced the Filipinos into the scorching fields was the same that sent them to the loneliness and alien cold of Alaska, into the stinking, sweating fish canneries to work days and nights without sleep when the fish were running.[82]

Perhaps influenced by Carlos Bulosan, one of her literary interlocutors and friends, Babb gives a broad description of the Filipino diaspora and its importance to industrial food production in the United States.[83] Tying the exploitation of Filipinos in particular to the broader means of agricultural production and consumption, Babb remarks upon the "need" that forces Filipino workers into extreme and "alien" labor contexts. Importantly, she includes a subtle critique of white privilege (although certainly not discussed as such) along the lines of racial expectations and norms related to labor, suggesting that Filipino workers forge into hostile environments in order to make a living, while white farmworkers journey to less climatically severe—that is to say, greener—pastures.

Themes that trouble the racial myths of whiteness are present in other scenes of the novel as well. The first occurs when some white farmworkers, including Milt, are at a town store in California. They are confronted by vigilante men: armed, Pinkerton-like brutalizers of workers whose sole role is to intimidate union efforts and terrorize marginal laborers into submission.[84] These vigilante men have been hired by an unnamed grower who does not want the workers buying goods in the grocery store or discussing the possibility of organizing against him and other growers in the county. When the workers resentfully refuse to show deference, the vigilante men, angry, shout, "Get out of the way, okies, or we'll give you some."[85] This anger builds in the scene, exploding forth when the farmworkers refuse to acknowledge the commands: "The men did not move. 'Git outta the way, you white niggers!' "[86] The racial epithet with the modifier "white" in this passage viscerally reveals two things: first, how white migrant farmworkers were flatly discussed as racially inferior, largely because of their class position and their marginal status as nomadic laborers without permanent homes; second, the deeply anti-Black logic behind the class-based racialization of the workers, such that downward mobility forms a kind of race betrayal.

This scene is directly referenced later in the text, as Milt begins working in cotton. When he begins talking to "a tall Negro [who] worked alongside Milt keeping the same pace," he consciously works through his received expectations and racial assumptions: "Milt waited automatically to hear the 'suh' and when it did not come, he was relieved. He had been wondering how he would say it, tell him not to. *We're both picking cotton for the same hand-to-mouth wages. I'm no better'n he is; he's no worse.* The memory of being called a white nigger in Imperial Valley lay in his mind unforgotten, sore, like an exposed nerve. Milt looked at him. Garrison looked back, his eyes straight, and there was no difference."[87] This scene, and the chapter as a whole, does quite a bit with a Hegelian framework of mutual recognition, in which each person constitutes the other as a subject, rather than an object, resisting the "master-slave" or "lord-bondsman" subject-object relationship. This process of mutual recognition is carefully articulated through, first, Milt's desire to remove class and race distinctions, indicated by his unvoiced desire to "tell [Garrison] not to" call him "suh" (rendered, in his imagination, in dialect), and then their direct eye contact, in which "Garrison looked back, his eyes straight, and there was no difference." This gaze *does* contain difference, though, in that Milt looked at Garrison, and "Garrison looked back": it is a difference that requires each person to exist in their specificity.

While important in expressing the Popular Front view of racial equality, on an initial read this passage seems to elide the differences in likely lived experience between Milt and Garrison. It is interesting, indeed, that Dunne remembers, "like [it was] an exposed nerve," "being called a white nigger in Imperial Valley." The passage, in the finality of "there was no difference," seems to complete the circuit of the elision, offering a statement of similarity that seems to avoid the presence of racial whiteness in favor of solidarity. The attempt to locate solidarity in and through proximity becomes clunky when Milt's experience of being called a racialized epithet is linked to Garrison's experience as a Black farm laborer; the attempt to empathize, though genuine, simplifies the diversity of working-class experiences. Yet, as Milt thinks about Garrison, he realizes, "*I'm no better'n he is; he's no worse.*" Milt seems to locate the similarity primarily in their mutual labor, side by side, "*for the same hand-to-mouth wages.*" It is not simply proximity in the cotton field that drives this connection. Unlike Steinbeck's murdered Indians on hills or even Guthrie's rather generalized references to African American experiences, Babb shows Garrison to be an experienced farmworker who speaks for himself, whose respect Milt craves, and who, it turns out, is an important local leader in the labor union that the Dunne family joins.

At the end of the conversation, Milt reveals his naïveté to Garrison, specifically with regard to the racial segregation enforced upon the workers in their living quarters: "'You're not in camp?' Milt asked. 'No-o,' Garrison said smiling in a way that Milt did not understand. 'We got a camp of our own three miles away.' Milt understood the implication then, but he dared not voice his sympathy in the face of this man's dignity."[88] Presumably, the camp mentioned by Garrison was established for people of color who worked at several nearby farms, for reasons of segregation as well as to provide safety from angry whites, both migrants and locals.[89] As in the previous passages, communication takes place between the lines of the spoken: silence, understanding, and empathy make up the language that does the work between two people.[90] When Milt comes to understand that segregation is at work, he does not extend verbal sympathy, most likely because it will sound like pity or hollow verbiage, undercutting "this man's dignity."

Later, after Milt agrees with several hundred of his fellow workers to sit down and refuse to work, though without consulting with the labor leadership first (thus not ensuring that the workers can receive union funding for food and material support), he realizes that he has involved himself in an action that disappoints Garrison. Though Garrison, as one of the labor leaders, sits down alongside his fellow workers, he knows the action has been conducted too soon: "Milt looked at Garrison and saw his face was serious, worried. He glanced sideways at Milt and shook his head slowly. . . . When Garrison was ahead of him, it seemed to Milt he could guess by the tired stoop of the man's burdened shoulders that he was disappointed in him. Milt felt sorry. Somehow he wanted this man's respect, and suddenly he was not ashamed to acknowledge it to himself."⁹¹ Rounding out the passage, again, is a direct reference to mutual recognition and respect. Communication, once more, emerges through physical movement and language. Furthermore, Milt realizes that he is "not ashamed to acknowledge" that he wants Garrison's respect—that he wants to be held *up* to and achieve Garrison's standards and expectations, rather than demanding that Garrison respect him by dint of racial difference.

While these passages indicate Babb's idea of racial solidarity, the text somewhat sabotages its desire for representational equality through one of the most popular writing strategies of the 1920s and '30s: the use of dialect to render Black voices. *Whose Names Are Unknown* generally refuses to render white speech in dialect, which glaringly highlights Babb's choice to represent Garrison's speech, as well as his wife's, this way. This decision folds Black speech into the novel's examples of "found speech," since the only other times when dialect is explicitly used are in written letters included in the text, such as a letter Mrs. Long—a friend of the Dunne family—receives from her sister. The novel's other characters of color, Garrison's wife and a Filipino labor organizer named Pedro, both speak "in accents." In Pedro's case, his speech is rendered normatively in standard English, but we are told, "His English was precise and clipped by his accent."⁹² An accent is noted but not reproduced—a simple gesture of representational equality. Alfred Maund's 1957 novel *The Big Boxcar*, for example, refuses to use reductive dialect.⁹³ In Babb's novel, why are only Mrs. Long's sister's letter and Garrison's and his wife's speech rendered this way? That Babb was self-consciously pushing against the stereotype of the uninformed "Okie" remains a potent answer—so then it is more interesting that through narratorial intervention she makes sure we know Pedro's English is "clipped by his accent," and that she directly and without comment renders Garrison's speech dialectally. The implications seem rather clear, even if Babb may not have considered them: for all of her attempts to represent Garrison as a fellow person, she formally and syntactically aligns him with the objects—such as the long letter—within the text, using Black speech as a Barthesian reality effect along the lines of regionalist literature (and not, as Hurston does with dialect in her own work, as part of a distinctly modernist project). Less than a complete and damning failure, however, this artistic decision shows that *Whose Names Are Unknown*, though a progressive and racially democratic text organized by *speaking with* as an aesthetic mode, is still hindered by some of the limits of the white imaginary. Even as I point out this subtle but illustrative complication, I maintain that Babb *does* succeed in providing a progressive, egalitarian view of what she believes race relations could be.[94]

Given that the other instance of highly visible dialect is Mrs. Long's sister's letter, sent from California in the first part of the novel, it is interesting to trace how found materials participate in the novel's production of realism. Two pages long, this letter is formatted differentially, both in terms of indentation and font size. It is included in full, from salutation to valediction, and is characterized by misspellings, nonstandard punctuation, run-on sentences, and a wide variety of important material information, such as prices, wages, and concrete factual observations.[95] The nonformal, nonstandard English of the letter is meant to indicate Mrs. Long's sister's educational and class status, and as a "found object," the letter provides realistic detail (and, no doubt, is an outlet for Babb's FSA research). The letter's fidelity to realism, expressed through imperfect punctuation and dialect, produces a gap between the forms of mediation that constitute *speaking with* in Babb's work. This helps Babb acknowledge that perfect representation is impossible and highlights difference as a necessary effect within realism. The textual moment certainly resonates with Rukeyser's incorporated letters and Hurston's reproduced tales. This very difference between narrative voice and epistle, indeed, produces a formalistically appreciable coalitional effect in the novel.

The most conspicuous "found object" in the novel is Julia Dunne's journal of the month of dust—possibly, though not certainly, the monthlong series of dust storms of April 1935 at the height of the Dust Bowl disaster. This period became known for the "Black Sunday" dust storm of April 14, during which enough dust was produced to completely cover the High Plains and even travel as far as the East Coast.[96] The farmer Lawrence Svobida, in his Kansas memoir *Farming the Dust Bowl*, describes this 1935 storm through a catalogue of survival strategies, physical ailments, and psychological tolls, claiming that he felt, like many of his neighbors, "that here even the dead cannot rest in peace with the dust blowing over their graves—until Judgment Day—in a land where living men and women go insane from the strain."[97] Julia's diary makes up almost all of chapter 17 of Babb's novel, notably setting this chapter off from the rest of the novel even while embedding the putatively found material into the very fabric of the narrative. The diary leads the reader into intimacy, subjectivity, and the granting of greater depth and completeness to Julia's character. The diary's moments of privacy, shared with the reader, symbolically link to moments of carnal intimacy in the novel, such as when Julia and Milt have sex at a work-camp bungalow, or when two minor characters, Max Brownell and Anna Brennerman, make love in a field. Privacy, when shared, becomes transformative for the novel by providing enormous insight that works alongside its otherwise observational narration.

Introducing chapter 17—and the diary entries within it—is the novel's standard narratorial voice, which reports that Julia, while cleaning around the house, sees the diary and rereads it. After—and only *after*—she rereads it within the time-space of the narrative's imagination, do we get to turn to the diary: "She read her description of the first storm and felt frightened, and pleased with herself. She closed the tablet and placed it on a shelf and went about her work." Immediately after this sentence the diary begins, offering an entirely different narrative voice that signals a difference between Julia the character and Julia the writer: "*April 4. A fierce dirty day.*"[98] The rest of chapter 17, from pages 90 to 95, contains Julia's entire account of the rest of the month. Julia's creative work contains her thoughts and her feelings, but we do not share the process of thought (which elsewhere is often encountered in direct description and italicized free indirect discourse). Rather than being directly involved in her consciousness *as* she writes or *as* she thinks—an access we are given in other places in the novel, particularly (though not exclusively) through Milt's italicized, stream-of-consciousness irruptions into the narratorial flow—we examine her writing after it has been completed. This distancing is not disempowering; rather, it gives us access while not giving us complete transparency. For Babb, it is important that Julia is creative, that she makes language and text.

This long example of creative observation within the text is contrasted to artists whose engagement with the Dust Bowl refugees Babb critiques in the novel. As an FSA worker whose commitment to the agricultural laborers was evident in her involvement in the day-to-day operations of the FSA's government camps, Babb was skeptical of artists who came and went. These photographers, journalists, and writers collected images and then left—and beyond providing shocking and sensational narratives for the media, Babb was not sure whether these visits materially benefited migrants. Near the end of the novel, Babb, filtered through Julia's point of view, provides a criticism of these artistic practices. As Julia considers stealing a loaf of bread from an unattended grocery store basket bearing the storekeeper's daily delivery of bread, she remembers when a young man was sentenced to eleven years for the theft of groceries:

> That was the day the famous writer and the photographer from the big picture magazine were along, so they went to the judge at his house and told him how hungry the old woman was. The judge thanked them and said he thanked them again because it was the first time he had thought of these okies as human beings. The writer and the photographer and the government man felt happy that everything was understood, and the people in camp felt better. When the boy came up for trial right away, the judge sentenced him to eleven years in San Quentin. Breaking into, stealing, transporting to another county. But most of all being an okie. But the judge remembered the visitors. He went with two more men to see the mother, and they took her a basket of groceries.
>
> Julia was frightened, remembering how the old woman howled at the men and chased them away, how she shook her fist and fell down in the mud. She could hear her howling, far away in her mind, and the tears started to her eyes in awe and fear.[99]

Babb satirizes the judge's satisfaction, following up the phrase "the writer and the photographer and the government man felt happy" with the judge's almost immediate, astonishing sentence for the theft of groceries: eleven years in San Quentin for "most of all being an okie." Ultimately, the "famous writer and the photographer"—Steinbeck and Rothstein? Agee and Walker?—have made no significant impression on Julia, but she clearly remembers "how the old woman howled at the men and chased them away." The specificity of "how she shook her fist and fell down in the mud" causes Julia to cry in "awe and fear." The shallowness of the other writers' involvement and the hypocrisy of the judge, while enraging, fade in the face of Julia's memory of the old woman's "howling, far away in her mind."

This awe and fear generated by the old woman's refusal of the judge's conditional and performative kindness, so devastating and motivating for Julia, becomes the affective register and seed of the revolutionary democratic politics that the migrants begin to enact by the novel's end. A few pages after

Julia remembers the old woman, the migrants gather and decide to fight back against the eviction and incarceration of their fellow workers, especially those who have done the dangerous work of organizing their labor. Gathered together, vibrant with outrage and hope, the migrants take an eviction notice given to one of their members and repurpose it as a letter of solidarity. The notice, a historical document that Babb has worked deliberately into the novel, states, "To John Doe and Mary Doe, whose true names are unknown."[100] The migrants, in their anger and brilliance, take "John and Mary Doe, whose true names are unknown" as a call to arms, and they identify with the undercommons possibility within the reclamation of this enforced anonymity. The eviction notice is turned over—literally overturned—and on the back is written a letter to "Sister Martha Webb," a young girl who has been helping the farmworkers organize. "The rest of the page was filled with 'Mary Doe' and 'John Doe,' written many times in as many different handwritings. They each signed in the same way and passed the letter on."[101] Crafting a political bloc out of enforced anonymity, the workers announce themselves as one—a one that is nevertheless numerous. They announce, through their uniform signatures, that their union will be strong, that they will take the impersonal, alienating names they are given by state power and use them.

Manzella reads this moment with skepticism, asserting that "by claiming the terminology of naming already available, though, their imagined element does not consider who is left behind."[102] By pointing out that the workers writing the letter address it to a woman who is one of the labor organizers, and that the other organizers—Lacy, Pedro, and Garrison—remain in jail for their roles in the strike, Manzella makes a strong point that the only possibilities for successful radical action belong to the white workers at the end of the novel. Wald, in contrast, sees the novel offering a radical alternative imagination: "Rather than reify the migrants' whiteness in the face of their dispossession, Babb disrupts the boundary between white farm owner and nonwhite farmworker. *Whose Names* suggests that the dignity and purpose that Jeffersonian democracy once offered white Oklahomans can be rebuilt through multiracial industrial unionism."[103] For Battat, "Babb creates a vision of Popular Front unity not only by insisting on the shared class interests of migrant workers but also by suggesting their shared status as ethnic outsiders. While her liberal peers defended the Okies' rights as white citizens, Babb highlighted the permeable boundaries of whiteness in order to make room for class-based unity."[104] While Manzella's skepticism is certainly warranted, especially given the general historical collapse of white solidarity with working-class African American, Filipino, and Mexican workers in California, the novel's coalitional aesthetics firmly place it as an idealistic document of "unionism" and "unity," as Wald and Battat put it. For Babb, whiteness is not a given, and it is not a political status to be defended or achieved. Rather, it becomes a matter of lived experience whose relative privileges must be resisted, especially in the name of building a stronger union through the coalitional aesthetics of *speaking with*. This is particularly true in one of the novel's most explicit discussions of dignity, an oratorical flourish at the end of chapter 41: "Let no one ever think himself apart in this. Let him sit down and talk to any man and feel his shame; the unsayable things come out as clear and simple as a bell at night in every word he speaks. He wants more than bread and sleep; he wants himself—a man to wear the dignity of his reason."[105]

Near the end of the novel, right after the workers have signed the letter with many lines of John Doe and Mary Doe, they remain gathered and speak together, not hushed, not rushed, yet maintaining an urgent desire to stay together and fight for their dignity. Babb narrates:

> One of the men—whose father died of pneumonia when he was moved from camp, and who with his two brothers took care of his mother and her old sister—leaned back on the bed and spread his arms out in a stretch that looked like a wide embrace.
>
> "Gee, it's a good feeling to be together. It's sure good to feel the love of one another." The word *love* lay in the warm air of the little tent for each of them to feel in the unashamed and simple truth of his knowing. No one spoke for a long time.[106]

After an entire backstory is given for the man within em dashes, the description of his "wide embrace" gives weight to the capacious sentiments he then expresses: "It's sure good to feel the love of one another." In this passage, love becomes actual, a combination of "spirituality and sense of purpose," and something that can be felt "in the warm air," like a substance or physical reality: "*love* lay in the warm air of the little tent for each of them to feel in the unashamed and simple truth of his knowing." Like Milt's realization that he is not ashamed of wanting Garrison's respect, here the workers are "unashamed" of knowing exactly what the man who declares "the love of one another" means. Love becomes a gift, more than a representation of feeling, in this passage. It is what constitutes the gathering, it is what connects the men and women in the tent; even more, it is something that is admired and that is felt by each person, even as it is the thing that makes them one.

This moment of love—warm, affective, unashamed, simple, and truthful—becomes the essential component of *Whose Names Are Unknown*'s radical democracy. A praxis built of love and geared toward truth through specificity becomes the defining moment of the novel. This scene does not have the same shocking symbolic value of Rosasharn (Rose of Sharon) breastfeeding a dying man with the milk that would have sustained her dead baby, at the conclusion of *The Grapes of Wrath*; nor does the novel contain the utopian potential of a radicalized Tom Joad leaving a womb of bushes and brambles that he's created, in the dead of night, to organize workers in some unnamed future, thus completing the utter dissolution of the Joad family even while symbolically self-birthing toward a hopeful future. Wald reads the end of *Whose Names Are Unknown* as a suggestion by Babb that "humanity is reborn," and argues that the "novel finds the possibility for human potential, the ability to simultaneously achieve freedom and security, in multiracial revolutionary unionism. Multiracial revolutionary unionism offers the spirituality and sense of purpose that Dust Bowl migrants once found in their relationship to the soil."[107] While largely agreeing with Wald, I find the "rebirth" motif unsatisfying. Rather, there's a covenantal continuity—perhaps like the rainbow after the deluge in Genesis—that is and is not another moment of creation. Rather than rebirth, the novel emphasizes a return to an original promise with a difference: there is no messianic rebirth needed, no symbolic futurity that needs to be activated. Rather, a full embrace of lived, communal union becomes the answer. By reproducing the scene of organization, of workers' dignity and will, Babb's novel provides *actual* labor, labor built out of love, giving a clear image of workers uniting, loving, fighting, and staying together.

A Final Word

"Together" is the word with which each section of this chapter has concluded so far. This word might represent the defining political and personal motive behind both Babb's and Guthrie's work; certainly, it describes the thematic bond that links their texts. More importantly, "together" furnishes a name for the writerly affect (in the Barthesian sense, indicating the openness of a text whose meaning is made through the reader's interpretation, rather than through a closed system of obviously intended meaning) through which readers, encountering and interpreting each artist's work, are able to work themselves into these constructed worlds of fiction and music. In other words, Babb and Guthrie create political feelings, and these feelings are the basis of an invitation to feel with, to locate oneself *beside*, the texts at hand.

Babb and Guthrie crack open the limitations of aesthetic representation by crafting an aesthetics of affect. Babb does this through a variety of aesthetic methods, from documentary poetics to imagined journals, from free indirect discourse and stream-of-consciousness narration to a reimagining of the Hegelian dialectic. Through this diversity of methods, Babb constructs a praxis that radicalizes democracy, bringing the reader into the work alongside the workers, who themselves have been brought into the text alongside the author. No paean to pity, this Dust Bowl text urges us to consider how love might be used to construct the revolutionary politics of our utopian desires. For Guthrie, a crafty destabilization of prepositions, along with music made and delivered specifically for communal engagement, offers up new ways of imagining oneself, both historically and in the present moment. Not only that, but the "free gift" of his music ensured its wide and joyful dissemination.

Although the concept of the nomad is frustratingly unspecific in critical theory, especially in the wake of Deleuze and Guattari's deracinated abstraction of the term, May Joseph's theorization of "nomadism" nevertheless offers a useful reevaluation of unsettled belonging:

> Nomadic citizenship fractures coherent categories of belonging, offering instead the incomplete, ambivalent, and uneasy spaces of everyday life through which migrant communities must forge affiliations with majority constituencies. Nomadic citizenship comprises a series of unstable relations through which ideas of citizenship, nationality, and sovereignty are invented along the road to statehood.[108]

Within similar "uneasy spaces of everyday life" that emerge in the fracture of "coherent categories of belonging," Babb and Guthrie find the lives and labors they felt compelled to represent. Though both were born to stably middle-class families, in both cases a father ruined the family's fortunes and the children were cast out into the world as travelers (Babb's father was an addict; in addition to likely being a lyncher, Guthrie's father was a land speculator who couldn't stop until he was dead broke). In each case, these travelers became deeply invested in the crumbling world they knew, of men and women whose lives were wrecked by the Dust Bowl. Thus, partially through personal experience and identification with the plight of the Dust Bowl migrants, and partially through a fierce commitment to people who had little access to unalienated or nonexploitative textual mediations and renditions of their lives, Babb and Guthrie fashioned unique modes of speaking *with*, rather than *for*, the people they wrote and sang about.

At the end of their edited collection of Guthrie archival materials, *Pastures of Plenty*, Dave Marsh and Harold Leventhal include one of Guthrie's final diary entries, written through the crushing pain of his Huntington's disease with its attendant chorea. This disease ensured he could never play the guitar again; it stopped this paradigmatic "rambling man" from ever easily moving on his own again. The pain through which he wrote these words, his by then always shaking hand working across the page, is unimaginable. Yet the scene of creation must be imagined, just as he tried to envision a just, dignifying world when writing his desires out in his painfully executed longhand. Entitled "The Word I Want to Say," this journal entry imagines an absolutely sacred, unifying word that keeps everyone together through love and dignity:

> The odd thing is about this word that it is no one certain word, but fits in the ring and tone sound of every word. It is the word inside of all of our other words, the word that gives our words a shape and a form, and a clearer sense. This is the free word that no jail can hold, no cell can keep, no chain drag down, no rope can lynch, no weapon can hurt or hinder. I say this word is that one word that makes all democracy clear, plain, and keeps democracy alive, and I keep this one word alive. I will die as quick and as easy as I can to keep this one word living, because it keeps my whole race of people living, working, loving, and growing on to know more and to feel more. This is the word I want to say.[109]

"The one word"—like Rukeyser's "one word" at the end of "The Book of the Dead"—is sacred, is dignifying, is entirely and radically creative. Imagined as an unspoken, unifying signifier, this is a word that "fits in the ring and tone sound of every word," a description of language usually befitting theological views of a prelapsarian or post-rapture world. The influence of Judaism is again apparent in Guthrie's thinking, given the unnamed and unsayable nature of the word he thinks of and will not say, even as he is determined to "keep this one word alive." It is covenantal, as is the mutual sustenance of Yahweh and man. Guthrie knows that this word actually and potently exists, that it "*is*"—not that it was or will be. It is a word that makes a world. It is a word that refuses sanctuary to none and offers love to all.

Signs of Protest
The Poetics of the Memphis Sanitation Strike and Gwendolyn Brooks's "Warpland" Poems

BY THE 1960S, the coalitional aesthetics that had expanded during the 1940s had gone through the trials of the fiercely anticommunist 1950s. The crushing defeat of Henry Wallace's progressive campaign for president in 1948 became a bellwether of the decade to come, particularly given the anticommunist resentment that dogged Wallace's supporters. Even more, losing a viable leftist alternative meant the contraction of a vital part of antifascist coalition building, especially in the turn toward the anticommunism of Cold War culture. Thus, much 1950s art with Popular Front tendencies was produced in exile (Elizabeth Catlett's work in Mexico, for example) or had radically limited distribution and engagement (such as the film *Salt of the Earth*). Yet the presence of leftist cultural production driven by coalitional aesthetics remained, and its regional contours are ripe for further scholarly discussion.

Bill Mullen and Mary Helen Washington, among others, have brought important attention to the postwar persistence of Chicago's Popular Front culture, and James Smethurst has shed new light on the Popular Front's widely felt infrastructural influence on the Black Arts Movement in the US South, particularly in New Orleans, Atlanta, Louisville, Nashville, and the Gulf Coast of Mississippi. Smethurst's work builds on Margo Natalie Crawford's *Black Post-Blackness: The Black Arts Movement and Twenty-First-Century Black Aesthetics* and Robin D. G. Kelley's seminal *Hammer and Hoe: Alabama Communists during the Great Depression*.[1] For Smethurst, the internationalist orientation of 1960s activism—particularly in its antiwar, anticolonial, and antiracist formations—shows the persistence of Old Left cultural institutions; Smethurst further credits HBCUs, especially in the South, as "important bridges between the Popular Front and Black Arts, providing some institutional continuity between different generations of Black radicals," especially in arts and literature departments.[2] Andy Hines further confirms this observation, noting the literary and paraliterary critiques of New Criticism spearheaded by Black leftist critics and writers, specifically in the postwar period, and how this geographically dispersed critical tendency shaped African American literary studies.[3] The persistence of coalitional tendencies centered on Black workers, often hidden in regional plain sight, suggests that viable institutional and para-academic settings for oppositional art helped usher leftist art and politics through the anticommunist 1950s and into the efflorescence of left-oriented activism in the 1960s.

Thus emerging from the nadir of the anticommunist 1950s, the 1960s were filled with art and politics shaped by an openly resurgent leftism. The long Civil Rights Movement came to the fore in the 1950s and 1960s, and was central to subsequent political and institutional developments—sometimes by way of critique—such as Black nationalism, ethnic studies, women's studies, anti–Vietnam War activism, antinuclear activism, the late-decade emergence of the gay rights movement, and the continuing struggle to assert the dignity of migrants and the poor. Yet the 1960s seem to culminate symbolically in the metonymic and overdetermined year of 1968. Countless studies of 1968 have been written from a number of national and transnational positions, most of which show the broadly connected struggles of people battling the convergent globalisms of US-led capitalism and Soviet-style communism. 1968 also encapsulates, in the worldwide protests against the US invasion of Vietnam, a longer history of armed anticolonial and decolonial struggles in earlier decades, particularly in Southeast Asia, Morocco, Algeria, and Kenya, along with other conflicts that concluded after 1968, such as the anticolonial wars of liberation undertaken by Mozambique and Angola. None of these conflicts, and none of the longer labor struggles and protests against capitalism, colonialism, sexism, and racism, can be confined solely to 1968, except perhaps in quite specific moments: for example, the violent police reaction to protests at the Democratic National Convention in Chicago or the murderous quelling of student-led protests in the Plaza de las Tres Culturas in Tlatelolco prior to the Olympic Games in Mexico City. April 4, 1968, of course emerges as a historical flash point, with the assassination of Martin Luther King Jr. galvanizing worldwide protests and mourning. Yet in the typical accounting of 1968, Memphis is treated as a backdrop to world history, the almost accidental site of world-historic catastrophe.

To tell a new story of 1968, I suggest centering Memphis in the story of global political struggle. I focus on the sanitation strike that brought King Jr. to Memphis, considering it *in addition to* the catastrophe of his assassination at the Lorraine Motel, and here I provide a contextual discussion of poems that emerged from the strike in order to expand the discussion of how Memphis matters in and to 1968. To center the Memphis Sanitation Strike of early 1968 means to set the city in relation to Paris, Chicago, Mexico City, Prague, and Warsaw, in addition to its acknowledged connections to the many US cities that moved into protest following King's assassination. Adding Memphis to the geography of 1968 as anything other than catastrophe means understanding the work of the strikers in another way, particularly as they interwove Black nationalism, demands for adherence to civil rights legislation, religious feelings rooted in hemispheric liberation theology, complex antiwar sentiments, and a desire to eradicate poverty. Even so, the assassination of Dr. King has shaped our understanding of Memphis such that the city has become indelibly connected with national tragedy, and this must be acknowledged too.

Seeing the sanitation strike as world historic beyond the frameworks of catastrophe and trauma means attending to the vision the strikers had of their role in a broader struggle over civil and labor rights. To do this, I trace a brief history of twentieth-century Memphis labor politics, civil rights activism, and religion. I then turn to four poems of the sanitation strike, each of which emerged from the context of civil rights labor struggles in the city. In assembling these works here, I concur with Julius B. Fleming Jr.'s advice that "in lieu of sidelining the [Civil Rights Movement's] classical phase, we should work toward building more multidimensional histories of this period through a willingness to expand the archival and conceptual schemas that have heretofore shaped traditional histories of the movement."[4] This desire to "expand the archival and conceptual schemas" of civil rights activism is of particular import in this chapter, given the broad historiographical assumption that the 1960s, in particular, were characterized by a widening gap between class-based and race-based political organizing, a stance that Robert Rodgers Korstad sums up when arguing that the "disintegration of the movements of the Popular Front era ensured that when the civil rights struggle of the 1960s emerged it would have a different social character and a different political agenda, which in the end proved inadequate to the immense social problems that lay before it."[5] Michael K. Honey nuances this claim about separation or disintegration by noting, instead, that due to the "legacy of slavery and the persistence of segregation, 'race' remained the defining question over which industrial unionism succeeded or perished throughout much of the South."[6] The difference between these perspectives is subtle, especially since neither is condemnatory, and hinges on the question of whether a given tactical focus could compensate for the distortive power of racism in the midst of political organizing. In Memphis in particular, the problems faced by civil rights activists were exacerbated by a New Deal–influenced Democratic Party machine, which saw the fortunes of all workers rise, though quite differentially, as Honey notes.[7] Yet, as I show, the poetry on the ground suggests a concerted, coalitional aesthetics that borrows directly from the Popular Front–influenced, long Civil Rights Movement lexicon to demand racial and economic justice as deeply connected activist pursuits.

My goal in discussing several short lyric poems from the Memphis Sanitation Strike's archive of actions is to provide another look at the long Civil Rights Movement according to the poets' highly specific yet world-historically-attuned texts. These poems take connected—though sometimes oppositional—stances toward religion, national as well as worldwide revolution, Black nationalism, and Memphian politics, offering a sense of how the sanitation strike must be understood within local as well as global frameworks. Indeed, the argument in this chapter sees the sanitation strike's aesthetic expressions as continuations of the city's history of migration and labor struggle led by Black Memphian workers, and also as connected to a broader framework of revolutionary thinking, exemplified at the end of this chapter by Gwendolyn Brooks's three "Sermon on the Warpland" poems. Linking these sets of poems—the sanitation strike poems and Gwendolyn Brooks's Black Arts–influenced innovative poetry from *In the Mecca* and *Riot*—is not as tall an order as it might initially seem: three of the sanitation strike poems fall squarely within vernacular poetry traditions of biblical engagement and emphatic rhyme, and Brooks's "Warpland" poems take up the sermon form; all of the poems discussed in this chapter turn on "we" or "us" as the most significant marker of lyric speech and subjectivity; and finally, as Smethurst and others have shown, the interpenetration of art forms, the muddling of highbrow-middlebrow-lowbrow distinctions, and the impulse toward social realism as expressive of political ideology all fall within the larger structural influence of Popular Front coalitional aesthetics. For the purposes of this chapter, I suggest that social realism and innovative lyrical forms within ostensibly divergent political poems can be linked through the conceptual framework of *speaking with*. In the case of the poems I discuss, understanding them through the lyric "we" of collective political expression in 1968 means also understanding how they each take up and transform extant poetic traditions—such as biblically oriented satire and midcentury experimental poetry—to generate important forms of political and aesthetic expression.

Centering Memphis, 1968

Although the story of African American migration is often framed as movement *away* from the South—from Mississippi to Chicago, Detroit, New York, or Los Angeles, say—it is important to acknowledge that migration took (and takes) place *within* the South. Mississippians moved to Memphis, as did rural Tennesseans, Arkansans, Alabamians, and Kentuckians. Similar migrations occurred to and from Richmond, Atlanta, Washington, DC, Nashville, Houston, Dallas, Birmingham, and New Orleans, as well as between other, smaller metropoles. This multidirectional framing is crucial for understanding just how strategies of *speaking with* during the Memphis Sanitation Strike were part of the long Popular Front.

Historians Laurie B. Green, Steve Estes, Joseph B. Atkins, and Michael K. Honey provide deep historical context for the Memphis Sanitation Strike, showing how the strike emerged from the long history of civil rights and labor struggle in Memphis. The Democratic machine in Memphis—dominated by E. H. "Boss" Crump and his extensive system of political patronage—ensured that Black Memphians could vote in the city several decades before the passage of the Civil Rights Act of 1964 and the Voting Rights Act of 1965. This did not ensure political power for African Americans in the city, but it meant a system of political participation—Crump considered it patronage—that acknowledged the importance of civic belonging. This took place out of necessity given Memphis's large Black population, as well as out of cynical preservationist instincts on the part of the Crump machine and later Democratic leaders in the city. Crump's leadership and his patronizing attitude toward Black voters is certainly of a piece with Mayor Henry Loeb (mayor of Memphis from 1960 to 1963 and 1968 to 1971) referring to Black Memphians as "my Negroes," as Honey and others have pointed out. Michael Szalay argues that Southern "local machines and landowners generated and sustained virulent racism in working-class whites, especially those living in the black belts once central to the region's plantation economy."[8] This possessive and patronizing position, couched in the history of the plantation, became a catalyst for Memphian activists as they focused their efforts toward civil rights with an emphasis on their emergent political autonomy, their desire for labor dignity, and their dignity as human beings.

Thus, after decades of supporting Democratic politicians, and after the passage of the Civil Rights Act and the Voting Rights Act, by 1968 Black Memphians were urgently and directly demanding egalitarian employment and promotion opportunities. The primary impetus for the sanitation strike was the collective decision to demand access to the job of driving sanitation trucks, rather than being restricted to jobs hauling and dumping individual trash cans into a truck's garbage compactor. The sanitation truck jobs were not the only ones segregated according to race in Memphis, but they enabled a particularly powerful strike, one that created an infrastructural and sensory crisis for the city as a whole. This protest about sanitation, jobs, and infrastructure struck at the heart of the biopolitics that produce the geographies of city and citizenship.

The city's churches—AME and Pentecostal in particular—furnished spaces for protest gatherings. Before, during, and after the sanitation workers' strike of 1968, Memphis was sustained through the activist energy of the AME Clayborn Temple and especially the powerful apparatus of the Church of God in Christ (COGIC). COGIC's headquarters was Mason Temple, which hosted Dr. King several times, including for his famous final speech, "I Have Been to the Mountaintop." Clayborn Temple and Mason Temple worked together to elaborate a message about labor dignity in Memphis that to the world became a call for democratic and interracial syndicalism: unions now, unions forever. Explaining the AME and Pentecostal influences on Memphis politics means understanding a complex web of relational action and thought elaborated through theology, liturgical practice, and church-oriented community building.

Pentecostalism, for example, becomes partially explanatory but never overdeterminative of the shape taken by political and artistic expression. Ashon Crawley argues that turning seriously to Blackpentecostalism—"Blackpentecostalism" being the term he develops to signal important spiritual, experiential, and political dimensions of Pentecostalism that are not contained by its denominational practices—and the shape of its worship community helps us understand "the extra-subjective mode of being together that is the condition of occasion for envisioning, and living into such envisioning, a critique of the known—the violent, oppressive, normative—world."[9] This is particularly important in the context of Memphis, where the Civil Rights Movement was heavily focused on the Protestant church tradition, and Blackpentecostalism in particular. This metaphysical understanding runs alongside the social fact of injustice and requires a real-world commitment to the active seeking of justice. It is within this (non)contradiction that we can see the materialist spin in the discussion of dignity, as there cannot be a separation of race, class, and infrastructure within analysis and action—a quotidian embrace of the biblical story of the Pentecost, in other words. Although the foundations of the sanitation strike's demands might be metaphysical—all people are equal in the eyes of Yahweh—the practice of freedom demands a material and materialist answer. An insistence on equality becomes the insistence that metaphysical recognition be realized as economic and labor opportunity, which becomes the declaration "I AM A MAN" held aloft on thousands of picket signs.

More than equality based on basic democratic ethos, however, the sanitation strike was influenced by the emergent ethos of Black nationalism. As Evie Shockley, GerShun Avilez, Margo Natalie Crawford, Fred Moten, and James Smethurst have shown, Black nationalism is categorically important to understanding literature of the late 1960s, particularly as elaborated through what we have come to call the Black Arts Movement. Smethurst points to the distinctive but related character of Black Arts literature in various regional iterations, arguing that there is no single unifying characteristic that constitutes a Black Arts text, other than a shared devotion to Black empowerment within an anti-Black cultural and economic system. The presence of the Black Arts Movement in the South, Smethurst observes, facilitated important "ideological and institutional spaces in which young, and not so young, Black artists and intellectuals [would] come together and organize, study, and think about what a new Black art (and a new Black politics) might be."[10] These spaces, additionally, "were largely found in what remained of the formal and informal networks (study groups, bookstores, forums, lectures, educational associations, magazines, and so on) of the Old Left, networks that were often subterranean but nonetheless present in the Cold War South, and those of what might be thought of as the old nationalism of Garveyites, Pan-Africanists, and so on."[11] Especially in the 1960s, broader leftist tendencies, such as Students for a Democratic Society (SDS) and other multiracial leftist organizations, saw the Black Arts Movement as a direct aesthetic corollary of Black power and, often, the Black Panther Party (BPP) more specifically. Benjamin Balthaser notes that for "SDS and other organizations of the New Left, Black Power was not seen as threatening, but rather a welcome advance over what before had been understood as partial and far too slow progress on civil rights." As Balthaser shows in his analysis of theoretical statements and positional articulations of New Left groups in relation to the question of Palestine, "rather than perceiving Black Power as harmful to the New Left, organizations such as the BPP were seen as advancing the racial and political analysis in the movement by embracing Third World revolutionary politics over the civil rights frame of the nation-state."[12] In this sense, the Black Arts Movement is precisely *a movement* and a mode more than a solidified or rule-bound set of texts. Turning to Memphis shows how the Black Arts Movement could furnish the broader set of connections and relations for the sanitation strike's methods of *speaking with*—of finding ways to speak coalitionally with fellow strikers, readers, and generations prior to and subsequent to the actions of 1968. Transforming extant texts and styles, and finding ways to generate new aesthetic perspectives on mass collective action, the poems I discuss in this chapter offer important perspectives on 1968, on literature informed by the Black Arts Movement, on the legacies of migration, and on the cultural persistence of Popular Front modes of building and maintaining coalitions.

Labor tactics in Memphis insisted on connecting racial justice to workers' rights, thereby participating in a well-defined argument made by Black thinkers for centuries: capitalism and anti-Blackness are deeply imbricated sociocultural structures, working in tandem through the objectification of life under the guise of value. In demanding the right to equal wages for Black sanitation workers, as well as the rights to drive garbage trucks, to ascend the city sanitation department's leadership ladder, and to overhaul the intensely segregated public works department, Black Memphians unified labor justice and racial justice in the face of segregation's sociopolitical continuation despite its supposed legal and juridical conclusion. In this way, the Memphis Sanitation Strike linked specific labor demands to a longer struggle for reparation and reenvisioned justice. Very important for Memphis, too, was the presence and support of Martin Luther King Jr., especially his full, vocal turn toward linking antiracism with pacifism, labor rights, and the eradication of poverty. And, in the wake of King's assassination in Memphis, the city came to symbolize both locally and nationally the catastrophic persistence of anti-Blackness.

The Memphis Sanitation Strike was made up of an enormous coalition of educational, labor, cultural, religious, and political organizations, all of which sought an antiracist, pro-labor world in common. This coalition was assembled from masses: of people, of related languages and ways of thinking, of mutual political goals and complementary (or at least nonexclusionary) activist philosophies, of shared desires. Important to this process was the development of a striking language during—and as—protest. Most famous, of course, were the "I AM A MAN" placards that marchers wore on the picket lines, and which often functioned as mass, serial poetry during protests (see figure 1).[13] Laurie B. Green argues for a nuanced understanding of the sanitation strike's most enduring visual, since strikers and protesters "combined formal issues of rights with cultural problems of self-definition" in order to successfully advance their claims.[14]

The famous placards hold a central iconographic place in the long Civil Rights Movement, and scholars have often tied them to the famous abolitionist rhetoric of the nineteenth century, particularly as represented by Josiah Wedgwood's impressive "Am I Not a Man and a Brother?" medallion, which featured a kneeling enslaved man supplicating an unrepresented but assumed audience. This medallion, worn by abolitionists, circulated widely—an iconographic commerce whose semiotic parallel to the exchange of living humans has not gone unremarked. Lynn Festa notes how the medallion partook in a larger colonial imaginary in which the bonds of sympathy often operated to

Figure 1. "The Massive March." Photograph by Rut Tufts of *The Sou'wester*, 1968. The Search for Meaning Archive, Special Collections Department, University Libraries, University of Memphis.

maintain a rigid hierarchy of worth and belonging, such that the reduction of a Black man to an exchangeable icon became unremarkable: "Colonial expansion means that readers must find ways of recognizing human likeness while maintaining other forms of difference. The sentimental community upholds a common identity, not by forging bonds directly between seemingly like individuals, but by creating a shared relationship to a common but excluded object about which the community has feelings."[15] Festa's point about the substitution of "a common but excluded object" for a fellow (racially marked) human would suggest that the Memphian picket signs move the needle by undoing the iconographic substitution while creating their own iconic language. The connection between Wedgwood's medallion and the "I AM A MAN" signs is compelling, especially if we read the signs as pointed appropriations of a longer abolitionist iconography that often lurched into sentimental condescension.

Yet, as Green has pointed out, the origins of the "I AM A MAN" signs lie in activist Cornelia Crenshaw's insistence on using this phrase as a slogan for the sanitation strike; most intriguingly, Crenshaw's emphatic arguments hinged on a poem given to her by a fellow labor activist named Robert Worsham. The poem was entitled, fittingly, "I Am a Man," and was written as a response to the indignities of busing segregation. The history of the signs, then, has direct links to local Memphian poetry, even if its resonance is global both in terms of the history of the phrase and the enduring legacy of the sanitation strike. This is a thread I will continue to tease out in this chapter.

The Poetics of the Memphis Sanitation Strike

The examples of striking poetry I focus on in this chapter are not like these signs and their moving concrete poetry, however. The poems I work with here live on through their archival presence—unlike the signs and their iconicity—even as they create meaning through conventional poetic forms and the historical poetry of the Bible. Through my readings of verse poetry produced within the collective struggle of the Memphis Sanitation Strike, I propose a repertoire of linguistic gestures, lyrical postures, and formal expressions of mass strike that constitute a specific poetics of the strike, one based on the coalitional aesthetics of *speaking with*.

I look at four poems in particular: the first a satire based on Psalm 23 that was often spoken at rallies; the second a transformed prayer written by an angry high-school student in the aftermath of a brutal police riot against a protest on March 28, 1968; the third a critique of passivity as a civil rights tactic, written by a man named Joe L. McKinnie; and the fourth a poem written by a student named Morgan McCraw for a student publication at Memphis State University (now the University of Memphis, though I will use the institution's 1968 name throughout the chapter).

The presence in particular of "The 23rd Slum" and "Sanitation Workers' Prayer" in several different folders in the Search for Meaning Archive at the University of Memphis, as well as in archivally recorded interviews and recollections, shows that the poems' circulation generated a relational sense of protest poetics during the strike. The poems connect to each other through their religious and semantic registers, as both are satirical poems that condemn Memphis mayor Henry Loeb and contextualize their critiques within well-known biblical texts. Working through religious and poetic discourses, the poems excel as critiques largely because they do not utilize a singular lyric speaker, but instead erect an angry collective voice that is both assumed and generated in each instance. "Why should we sit and wait?" and "A Black Poem" both also work through a lyrically constructed collective sensibility, though they do not index their semantics through specific transformations of biblical texts. These two poems instead generate their critiques by leaning on differing approaches to political poetry: "Why should we sit and wait?" works through straightforward rhyming couplets to tell a story of how the sanitation strike could succeed, and "A Black Poem" uses free verse to express Black power through unity of action, with the sanitation strike's political situation as its background. These four texts offer divergent yet related examples of Black Arts Movement aesthetics couched in specific Memphian contexts, providing insight into the sanitation strike's political messaging and activism and broadening the spectrum of Black Arts–influenced literary activity, especially as this activity moved outside of widely read literary publications and the recognition they provided.

In these four poems, Memphis strikers and their supporters produced a justice-oriented poetic corpus through the techniques of transformation and generation, especially in regard to biblical allusion and vernacular poetic traditions. *Transformation* here means each poem's formal and thematic engagement with well-known texts and poetic strategies, and *generation* signals a production of semantic possibility to create both material and imaginative space for previously unconsidered meanings and contexts, especially through the poetic juxtaposition of seemingly contradictory ideas. Each of these poems powerfully generates a sense of political relation that takes an expansive, nonindividuated lyrical form, particularly by relying on first-person plural pronouns to enunciate a unified but not ossified lyrical position based on collective desire and action.

While specifically grounding these poems in the strike, I suggest larger implications for literary studies. The appreciation of nuance as a critical mode of attention means understanding meaning-making as a formally determined communal exercise, one that is particularly driven toward the somewhat compromised but still necessary idea of liberation. The generative movement between satire and religious allusion within these poems opens up intriguing possibilities for lyrical position and form, especially given the poetry's topicality, evident political stances, and consciously literary historical self-contextualization.

Reading this intersection between politics and poetics in the context of the Memphis Sanitation Strike requires working through an unapologetic yet sensitive formalism. Sensitive formalism works as an emotionally attuned reading exercise couched in collaborative meaning-making. It emerges from interpretive humility, which means listening carefully and intently to what the work of art can teach: what it says, when it says it, where it says it, and why it might be trying to say it. Sensitive formalism takes seriously Alexandra Vazquez's description of "listening in detail," in which critical interpretation works by accepting that "one must be able to adjust to a different sense of time, be eager to go to unexpected places, remain open to being altered, ready to frame a project in the diminutive, and prepared to assume there is always some other way."[16] For this critical attitude to work, "openness," says Vazquez, is an "inarguable condition. One has to go beyond reliable critical locations, listen a little harder, feel comfortable with flexible theories."[17] The question, then, is whether literary criticism can be literary criticism without "reliable critical locations." Or, perhaps, whether literary texts contain some immanence or aura (in the Benjaminian sense) whose surplus generates a value that we must not reinvest to maintain our disciplinary formations, but instead must use toward liberation from restricted systems of predetermined meaning.

In looking at the potential for collective lyrical sentiment and expression, I build on Theodor Adorno's observations about lyric poetry's dialectical containment of the individual and/as the social. Refusing to cede the power of lyric poetry to the concepts of individualized expression and the lyric speaker, Adorno insists that even at its most solitary and alienated, "this very lyric speech becomes the voice of human beings between whom the barriers have fallen."[18] The poems I read here stake their lyrical power and their poetic claims in the search for political justice; the position of the lyric is found in its collective enunciation. The implications are clear for critical interpretation, and I propose an analogy to other forms of organizing and action. We need to open ourselves up to the nuances of what we're reading, because this means understanding the nuances of our comrades, particularly as we work toward liberation. Clarity, in this sense, is mutually built, not expected or imposed.

As popular poems read privately and publicly during the strike, these works circulated a sense of collective ire couched in satire. The first example—written by a high-school student—is entitled "The 23rd Slum" (see figures 2a and 2b).[19] It clearly transforms the Twenty-Third Psalm, one of the Bible's most famous passages.[20] Establishing the drama of the sanitation strike through the biblical chiaroscuro of the King James translation of Psalm 23, "The 23rd Slum" also takes up some of the key metrical and syntactic resonances of that famous psalm. As a poem about faith and courage, Psalm 23 has long been a cultural and literary touchstone; thus, revising the "Psalm" into a "Slum" posits the sanitation strike as a contemporary struggle with historical and cultural significance.

The transformations of Psalm 23 made in "The 23rd Slum" reveal difference as a generative force, and these alterations occur through contextually shifted allusions, as well as through an implicit argument about the original psalm's applicability to the situation in Memphis. As Mike Chasar notes, poetry in the American popular imagination has been "written, published, and consumed in relation to a range of different aesthetic systems and expectations," and, as is the case with literary critics, "uncredentialed or ordinary readers" are often "concerned with the subjects of poetic genre, form, tradition, and taste."[21] Chasar also argues that popular practices of appropriation, reappropriation, quotation, and improvisation show how "poetry became, over time, a repository or magnet for other values (such as love, patriotism, religion, friendship, and so on) that were incompletely capitalized as well."[22] The surplus within the "incompletely capitalized" poetry becomes a form that is not quite akin to exchange-value or use-value, but which certainly takes on elements of both.

The poem's transformations present an argument about race, religion, protest, and liberation, and these generative poetic moves invite a critical labor that does not extract value in order to reinvest it, but instead reimagines to what ends aesthetics might labor. As a political appropriation of a popular religious text, "The 23rd Slum" reorganizes poetic value through the recombination of sacred and secular verse, and this accumulation of literary transformations voices collective rage against Henry Loeb, the police, and the racist labor practices that begat the Memphis Sanitation Strike in the first place.

The poem transforms the biblical psalm's metaphorical language of faith

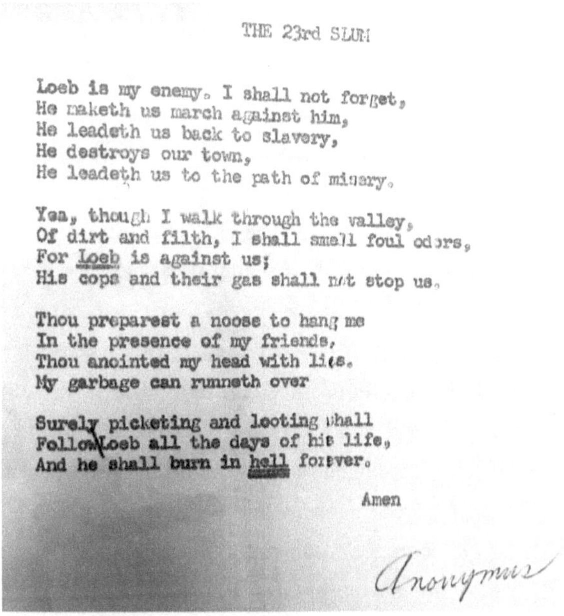

THE 23rd SLUM

Loeb is my enemy. I shall not forget,
He maketh us march against him,
He leadeth us back to slavery,
He destroys our town,
He leadeth us to the path of misery.

Yea, though I walk through the valley,
Of dirt and filth, I shall smell foul odors,
For Loeb is against us;
His cops and their gas shall not stop us.

Thou preparest a noose to hang me
In the presence of my friends,
Thou anointed my head with lies.
My garbage can runneth over

Surely picketing and looting shall
Follow Loeb all the days of his life,
And he shall burn in hell forever.

                           Amen

                           Anonymus

Figure 2a. "The 23rd Slum." Anonymous, 1968. The Search for Meaning Archive, Special Collections Department, University Libraries, University of Memphis.

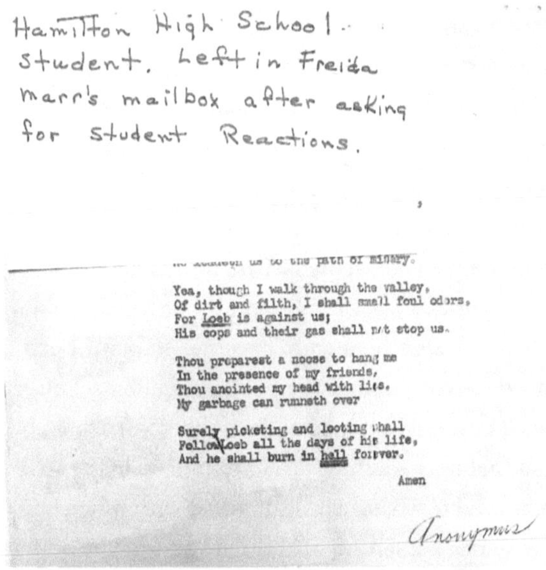

Hamilton High School.
Student. Left in Freida
Marr's mailbox after asking
for Student Reactions.

...leadeth us to the path of misery.

Yea, though I walk through the valley,
Of dirt and filth, I shall smell foul odors,
For Loeb is against us;
His cops and their gas shall not stop us.

Thou preparest a noose to hang me
In the presence of my friends,
Thou anointed my head with lies.
My garbage can runneth over

Surely picketing and looting shall
Follow Loeb all the days of his life,
And he shall burn in hell forever.

                       Amen

                       Anonymus

Figure 2b. Contextualizing the origins of "The 23rd Slum." Anonymous, 1968. The Search for Meaning Archive, Special Collections Department, University Libraries, University of Memphis.

into a site-specific semantic web, uncannily transmuting the original's abstract figurations into concrete action. "The valley of the shadow of death" is converted into "the valley, / Of dirt and filth," which resonates with the redolent consequences of the strike: uncollected garbage piled on Memphis streets. The psalm's famous opening, "The LORD is my shepherd; I shall not want," has been rendered, "LOEB is my enemy. I shall not forget." Turning LORD into LOEB, while of course a cheeky barb unfavorably comparing Loeb to Yahweh, also significantly redirects the poem's apostrophe. Psalm 23 is a supplication to God, a request for courage; "The 23rd Slum" is no supplication—it is a declaration and a demand. "I shall not want," a statement of dependence and faith, here becomes "I shall not forget." The clauses of the original psalm's translation are connected by a semicolon. "The 23rd Slum" transforms this single sentence's continuity by separating the two clauses with a period, producing two clipped sentences that emphasize the line's poetic fury: Loeb is the enemy. This will not be forgotten. Importantly, the functional pronoun is maintained in this first line—the speaking voice is mainly linked to the poem's "I" (compare this to the next poem's consistent "us" and "our"). However, the first stanza follows "I shall not forget" with "He maketh us march against him, / He leadeth us back to slavery, / He destroys our town, / He leadeth us to the path of misery." Turning to the collective "us" and "our" for the remainder of the first stanza, "The 23rd Slum" completes the semantic shift from LORD to LOEB, from individual supplication to collective demand. Unlike the deity of Psalm 23 (who "maketh me lie down in green pastures: he leadeth me beside the still waters. / He restoreth my soul: he leadeth me in the paths of righteousness for his name's sake"), Loeb does not produce solace or calm in the community. Instead, "lie down" becomes "march" and "still waters" threaten to become "slavery." Loeb does not "restore" but instead "destroys," and the poetic voice finds "misery" instead of "righteousness." Thus, in addition to unfavorably comparing Loeb to Yahweh, the poem shows that Loeb's authoritarian responses to the strike must be resisted: though he might try, the mantle of power with which he cloaks himself is nothing more than a perversion of Yahweh's restorative powers outlined in Psalm 23.

Crucially, the poem's critical direction works by keeping the action focused against Loeb. He is the poem's other—but not the desired other of a short love lyric or the sacred focus of psalmody. Strikingly similar to the Pharaoh of the Book of Exodus, Loeb narratively and poetically functions as a unifying external evil. The imprecatory action of the poem works against him, as does the combined semiotic force of the poetic language. In Psalm 23, the speaker walks "through the valley of the shadow of death" and "will fear no evil: for you art with me; thy rod and thy staff they comfort me." In "The 23rd Slum," however, the corresponding lines read, "though I walk through the valley, / Of dirt and filth, I shall smell foul odors, / For Loeb is against us; / His cops and their gas shall not stop us." Using assonance to convert Yahweh's "rod" and "staff" into "cops" and "gas" (the Memphis police used military-grade Mace to assault marchers supporting the striking sanitation workers), the anonymous poet—a high-school student, recall—names and condemns the tyrannical power held by Memphis's white power structure and wielded by Loeb and the city government. The sonic connection made between the rod and staff and the cops and gas suggests power run amok, power that must be curbed.

The next stanza, "Thou preparest a noose to hang me / In the presence of my friends, / Thou anointed my head with lies. / My garbage can runneth over," almost straightforwardly reverses the corresponding lines from Psalm 23. Yahweh's prepared table "in the presence of mine enemies" becomes a terrifying lyncher's noose, meant to hang the poem's speaker—presumably as a violent example—in front of their friends. Rather than finding sanctuary when ringed by enemies, the speaker fears being murdered even when surrounded by friends. Loeb's lies, in turn, viciously anoint the speaker's head, and the speaker's vessel overflows not with blessings, but with the noxious spillage of uncollected garbage. The poem's fourth and final stanza hardens its concrete address to Memphis's present. In Psalm 23, "goodness and mercy shall follow me all the days of my life"; in "The 23rd Slum," "picketing and looting shall / Follow Loeb all the days of his life." The poet asserts the strikers' fortitude, as well as the righteousness of the struggle, by transforming the "me" of the psalm into "Loeb." Additionally, "goodness" becomes "picketing," "mercy" becomes "looting"—playing (perhaps unintentionally) on the Latin *merx-*, which is the etymological root of both *mercy* and *commerce*—and "my life" becomes "his life." As the poem suggests, there can be no end to the struggle—not as long as segregated employment, anti-Black violence, and police militarism remain the structuring forces of everyday life in Memphis. Fittingly, eternity is where the poem ends—the contradictory (in)finitude of "forever" as a signal of conclusion, as well as an insistence upon endlessness. Unlike the psalm, in which the speaker "will dwell in the house of the LORD for ever," Loeb "shall burn in hell forever."

The double underscoring of "hell" wrathfully emphasizes the poem's vengeful bent—we should not avoid its enraged emotional field. This doubled gesture, small as it is, might be understood as a moment of inspired typographic nuance, or perhaps what Shockley theorizes capaciously as innovation.[23] Anthony Reed calls such moments "unthought components" that purposively escape disciplinary boundedness or lyrical enclosure in experimental poetry.[24] Fred Moten, seeking to describe the conditions of emergent emancipatory being within the matrix constructed of social life and social death, of citizenship and its (im)possibilities, suggests that criticism's attention to this type of gesture reveals "new things, new spaces, new times [that] demand lyrical innovation and intervention, formal maneuverings that often serve to bring to the theoretical and practical table whatever meaning can't. Phrasing, where form—grammar, sound—cuts and augments meaning in the production of content, is where implication most properly resides."[25] With its phrasing and typographical emphasis, the entire final line of "The 23rd Slum" "augments meaning in the production of content" as the anonymous young poet categorically condemns Loeb to eternal damnation in the Christian vision of the lake of fire. Especially given that this poem is a response to the police riot on March 28, 1968, that broke up the enormous march to Beale Street, for which King Jr. had flown into Memphis, the final line becomes a "formal maneuvering" that furiously asserts retribution for Loeb's violent, racist response to the sanitation strike. The virulent police response, which ended with dozens injured and one—a teenager named Larry Payne—murdered by a policeman, becomes the poem's central hinge. Lines 8 and 9 ("For Loeb is against us; / His cops and their gas shall not stop us"), at the center of the poem, take us from the poem's alpha—"Loeb is my enemy. I shall not forget"—to its omega—"And he shall burn in hell forever."

"The 23rd Slum" invokes civil and uncivil rage as a poetic muse. More than an ugly feeling, rage is putatively antisocial. Yet in the case of "The 23rd Slum," rage "defies those dominant modes of description that are paradoxically subordinate to an assumed natural history that understands deviance as derivative positioning," as Fred Moten describes deviance in the face of anti-Blackness.[26] In the case of the anonymous Hamilton High School student from Memphis, the poem becomes a virtuously angry condemnation of a vicious anti-Black society that continually enacts its murderous intentions both structurally (in the world) and specifically (in Memphis, 1968).[27] "The 23rd Slum" takes rage and converts it into a transformative poetic engine: the poem generates meaning by anchoring itself onto the poetic unity of Psalm 23, and also insists, by example, that this unity can be thoroughly undone and reconceptualized in order to address the material exigencies of the sanitation strike.

Another striking poem, "Sanitation Workers' Prayer" (figures 3a and 3b), transforms the Lord's Prayer as laid out in Matthew 6:9–13.[28] As a transformation of the Lord's Prayer, this poem perhaps seems straightforward. However, like "The 23rd Slum," the differences that emerge from transforming institutional prayer into protest poetry speak to the occurrence of a potent, generative act. The author, as with "The 23rd Slum," is unknown. Yet the same religious background undergirds the poem, and this same religious anchoring imagines the Christian God as a deeply material presence.[29]

The "Sanitation Workers' Prayer" unmoors the Our Father in two ways: First, it changes its addressee to "Our Henry." This mockery of Loeb rehearses the "King Henry" motif established by strikers during protests, as well as the shift of "LORD" to "LOEB" in "The 23rd Slum." Indeed, "who art in City Hall" becomes a reduction of station, even as it parallels "who art in heaven." City Hall is no "heaven," and this is emphasized through the near-homophony of "Hall" with hell. Second, the poem's use of "thy" works through a bidirectional deixis. It is Loeb, of course, whose name is modified by "Hard-headed"; more importantly, though, "thy" points to the strikers: "Thy kingdom C.O.M.E., / <u>OUR</u> will be done, / In Memphis, as it is in heaven." Heaven, it turns out, *does* exist in the poem's imaginary. It is a space of dialectically conceived justice, as the poem insists on underscoring an isomorphic relationship between the concreteness of Memphis and the abstractness of heaven. The stewards of this earthly "kingdom," the poem asserts, are the members of COME—Memphis's own Committee On the Move for Equality.[30] The poem leaves open the suggestion that COME and "<u>OUR</u>" indicate different, albeit allied, entities.[31] More

SANITATION WORKERS PRAYER
——————————————————————

Our Henry, who art in City Hall,

   Hard-headed be thy name.

Thy Kingdom: C.O.M.E.,
   OUR will be done,

In Memphis, as it is in heaven.

Give us this day our dues check-off,

And forgive us our boycott,

As we forgive those who spray Mace
     against us.

And lead us not into shame,

But deliver us from LOEB;

For ours is Justice, Jobs and Dignity;

Forever and ever.

FREEDOM!

Figure 3a. Version 1 of "Sanitation Workers' Prayer." Anonymous, 1968. The Search for Meaning Archive, Special Collections Department, University Libraries, University of Memphis.

SANITATION WORKERS' PRAYER
——————————————————————

Our Henry, who art in City Hall,

   Hard-headed be thy name.

Thy kingdom C.O.M.E.,

   <u>OUR</u> will be done,

In Memphis, as it is in heaven.

Give us this day our Dues Checkoff,

   And forgive us our boycott,

As we forgive those who spray MACE
     against us.

And lead us not into shame,

   But deliver us from LOEB!

For OURS is justice, jobs and
     dignity,

Forever and ever.

<u>F R E E D O M !</u>

Figure 3b. Version 2 of "Sanitation Workers' Prayer." Anonymous, 1968. The Search for Meaning Archive, Special Collections Department, University Libraries, University of Memphis.

importantly, the "our" maintained throughout raises the question of whether the poem has a lyric speaker, and sensitive formalism notes this distinction between different possibilities for building the first-person plural: it can be all-enveloping, it can be coalitional, or it can be diffuse.

As collective verse, presumably spoken aloud, does this poem signify a different set of interpretive assumptions and operations than a poem anchored to a single consciousness? "Sanitation Workers' Prayer" suggests that the purview of the lyrical—the presence of a speaker's desire, the addressee or object of apostrophe—might be a matter of multiple positions rather than of the essentially solitary individual. Ashon Crawley's *Blackpentecostal Breath*, in its expansive engagement with aesthetics and enactment, touches on Bishop Charles Harrison Mason—the founder of the COGIC denomination of Pentecostal churches—and his desire to create collective belonging in his worship community. Crawley's discussion describes almost exactly the sensibility of the Memphis Sanitation Strike poems as a whole, and of "Sanitation Workers' Prayer" in particular. Mason, who resisted lynching and mob violence in Tennessee, had a "conceptualization of personhood" that "was not grounded in the capacity to produce mob and lynching violence, but was an ethical stance of how to be together in an unjust world."[32] In Crawley's description, the namesake of Memphis's Mason Temple conceived of acting together as "an ethical stance" for being "together in an unjust world." This dedication to each other—the "our" of the "Sanitation Workers' Prayer"—is demandingly enacted in each moment.

I would suggest that to speak together is a lyrical action. "Sanitation Workers' Prayer" does not call an abstract "us" into being, but rather, in its speaking, generates community *through* the presence of the "us." In enumerating the strikers' and protesters' duties—"our Dues Checkoff" and "our boycott"—the poem points to the necessity of collective action. A dues checkoff maintains the financial viability of the union, particularly during a strike. A boycott cannot succeed without enough participation. Yet, the "boycott" of "Sanitation Workers' Prayer" parallels "our trespasses" against "Our Father," suggesting a violation of the established order. This violation—the boycott as a "trespass"—is willful and necessary, given capitalism's structuring of commerce as a sacred and protected social good. Additionally, unlike the Lord's Prayer, the "Sanitation Workers' Prayer" does not treat forgiveness as an equalizing gesture or quid pro quo. Instead, forgiveness becomes a provocation: the boycott *does not have to be forgiven*.

In the third stanza, "And lead us not into shame, / But deliver us from LOEB," the addressee is COME. The organization, in leading the strike actions and the protests, is placed in the structural position God occupies in the Our Father, but with measurable accountability. COME is not understood as all-powerful, but rather as precarious and dependent on its members and supporters. GerShun Avilez, in his examination of the "disruptive inhabiting" contained within the radical aesthetics of Black nationalist art and poetry, argues that we must attend to "the purposeful adoption of political ideology because of its potential for progressive social analysis," and must also understand that "this adoption is paired with the active attempt to unhinge components of the ideology that threaten to constrain expressions of identity."[33] COME was not aligned directly with Black nationalist politics, but Avilez's important point holds for the poem: a position is adopted and "paired with the active attempt to unhinge" the poem's point of view from absolute identification with any single political position. Indeed, the line "And lead us not into shame" functions less as a request than as a directive—COME is understood as responsible and accountable. This insistence on coalitional accountability as an active effort toward freedom embodies Christina Sharpe's question from *In the Wake*: "How can we think (and rethink and rethink) care laterally, in the register of the intramural, in a different relation than that of the violence of the state?"[34] Turning on Sharpe's question, the declaration that "OURS is justice, jobs and dignity" understands care as an alternative to the violence of the state and its anti-Black civic institutions. The unnamed poet—whose poetry was, is, and shall be collective—understands a different arc of sovereignty, one that cannot ever depend on the state's anti-Black vision of the world.

The poem's final lines remove "the kingdom, the power, and the glory" from the dominion of both Loeb and COME. They declare, "For OURS is justice, jobs and dignity"—these things are no one's to give and no one's to control. In shifting the address away from the "you," the poem turns toward its constitutive communal voice. Indeed, playing on and revising the future-oriented finality of the "Amen" of the Lord's Prayer (which also appears at the end of "The 23rd Slum"), the final line of the "Sanitation Workers' Prayer" shouts "FREEDOM!" Freedom is announced and inhabited in its announcement—it is both a promise and a presence. It is an enunciation of what is, not of what will be—it is, was, and ever shall be. As such, "FREEDOM!" is not a conclusion, but an initiation; not a summing up, but an invocation. This final moment works against a "politics [that] secures its hegemony through time by claiming the future as its unassailable property and excluding (and devaluing) any other conception of time that challenges this temporal ordering."[35] Following Calvin Warren, the conclusion to "Sanitation Workers' Prayer" declares the opening of the future, rather than encapsulating its inevitability.

Unlike the two anonymous sanitation strike poems just discussed, the poems I now turn to have author bylines. The first, by a young student named Joe L. McKinnie, has no title, and was typed up and turned in as part of a larger grouping of poems written by high-school students collected at the University of Memphis's special collections. For that reason, I refer to McKinnie's poem by its first line ("Why should we sit and wait?") or as "McKinnie's untitled poem." The second, by a Memphis State University college student named Morgan McCraw, was featured in the student publication *Black Thesis*, a central voice of the Black Student Association at the university.

McKinnie's and McCraw's poems do not generate meaning through public-facing, biblically anchored critique. Instead, they offer pointed, collectively introspective ruminations on the effects of solidarity and the political consequences of mass determination. Both are poetic declarations of mass protest, thinking with and beside the strike's famous "I AM A MAN" placards. Collectively introspective rumination would initially appear to be a contradiction—but rather than being an irresolvable antinomy, this contradiction contains a constancy and fierceness of resistance that I want to consider, especially given the bad reputation resistance has picked up in literary studies in the wake of twenty-first-century surface reading debates.[36]

Like the previous two poems, neither of these next two poems functions straightforwardly as a lyric, as each situates its poetry as a possible expression of mass collectivity. Like the previous poems, they were produced in the midst of the sanitation strike—right before the assassination of Dr. King and the strike's resolution—and each offers a manifestation of a specific public's poetry, or of a poetry public at a specific time and place in history. Certainly, this is a poetry that *can* be read as emerging from a counterpublic, but that phrase is not discerning or true enough—to do so would require thinking of white readers, academia, or postwar modernism as "the public," and of Black Memphians, protest, and vernacular poetry as "counterpublics." Such a hierarchy of publication and readership would unreasonably and without warrant destabilize the idea of Memphis's centrality to 1968 by relegating its cultural production to marginality and reactivity, rather than acknowledging its transformative and generative potential. This poetry imagines itself as emerging from and engaging with a public—not a counterpublic—and we ought to attune ourselves to this crucial (if subtle) distinction.

There is no biographical or situational information on who Joe McKinnie is, whether he wrote more poetry, or how this poem found its way into the archive at the University of Memphis, other than a reasonable inference that McKinnie was a Memphis high schooler in 1968.[37] His poem is collected with other poems from the strike, specifically those written by high schoolers in response to the strike, and to the fateful events of March 28, 1968, when a police riot violently ended the day's planned march in support of the striking workers. The poem may have been circulated and read, though there's no telling how widely. Because it may well have been written as an assignment, there's a possibility it was read in class, or in a larger institutional setting. There is no definitive context in the archive, however, and the scale and scope of the poem's circulation in Memphis 1968 are impossible to determine. In the face of this uncertainty, however, we find a text whose vision of mass determination is expressed through ruminative yet rousing lyrical expression; this highly rhymed poem sets forth a determined argument with a deliberate pace and sound (figure 4).

The poem's first two lines immediately establish the crux of the problem. One verb—"wait"—signals passivity; the other—"stay"—signals activity. This distinction between passive and active forms of presence generates the poem's critical force. Although it might seem to be splitting hairs, McKinnie claims "stay" as a firmly active, deliberate, and deliberative form of protest that demands recognition. This suggests, as Fleming Jr. does, how "civil rights activists repurposed black patience by transforming the wait into a time and a performance of black political possibility."[38] McKinnie's paradoxical combination of "march and stay" potently indicates motion within a larger sense of resistance, and also contains a prosodic microhistory of the civil rights tac-

```
Why should we sit and wait?
Why shouldn't we march and stay?
For if we stay King Henry will move
All pressure away.

He'll open jobs for you
Jobs that you have not been able to do.
And if we stay
King Henry will move all pressure away.

All these things and others too
Are things that only faith can do.
If you but truly believe
Then Henry can do nothing to deceive.

Let us all take a part,
In the things that are deep in our hearts.
Then let us all together fight,
For the things that we know are right.
                                    By Joe L.
```

Figure 4. "Why should we sit and wait?" Joe L. McKinnie, 1968. The Search for Meaning Archive, Special Collections Department, University Libraries, University of Memphis.

tics that Fleming Jr. describes as a transformative repurposing of "the wait." Harvey Young's *Embodying Black Experience: Stillness, Critical Memory, and the Black Body* offers a similar insight to McKinnie's; specifically, how stillness and silence can function as performances of protest.[39] McKinnie, by linking "stay" to "march," imagines that together these actions can create the condition in which "King Henry will move / All pressure away." By repeating "stay" in the very next line—"do" is crossed out in the typescript and replaced with "stay"—the poem makes emphatic the need to not be moved out of place, and is in this way suggestive of the classic protest song "We Shall Not Be Moved." To refuse is to resist the tyrannical power of mayor Loeb—here nominated "King Henry," an allusion to the famous "Sanitation Workers' Prayer" and its opening apostrophe "Our Henry."

This first stanza does not establish the poem's overall rhyme scheme, which otherwise is a fixed quatrain of rhyming couplets. Why in the first stanza McKinnie uses the scheme *aaba* is unclear; however, the rhyme scheme *does* dramatize the difference between "wait" and "stay," particularly as *one* of these actions will make Loeb "move / All pressure away." By insisting on the primacy of this distinction, McKinnie argues that active resistance and insistence will generate a successful strike. However, the possible overlap between "wait" and "stay" is dangerous, so he uses rhyme to show how only one will lead to victory. Notice how "wait" is an imperfect rhyme with "away," and so wouldn't produce the desired effect or closure—this is what "stay" corrects. "Stay" generates "away," while "wait" does not and cannot. In addition, by noting that to "march and stay" will compel Loeb to "move" political and economic pressure "away," the poem linguistically renders two things out of place: "wait" and "move." Neither of the words has a rhyme throughout the rest of the poem, whereas every other line has an end rhyme. In other words, McKinnie makes his political argument decisively through poetic form.

While it is certainly in vogue to question "resistance" as a paradigm in literature, we can safely say that in this poem's case, resistance is central to its argument. To put a point on it: "stay" is rhymed with the phrase "King Henry will move all pressure away" in two instances (the first and second stanzas), and this repetition emphasizes the poem's argument about cause and effect: victory through resistance. Yet the resistance within the poem is nuanced. Resistance isn't the poem's overwhelming, totalizing meaning: the conjunction "and," used to join the verbs in "march and stay," suggests a complexity of action and intent, a contradictory unity at the heart of the poem. I suggest this nuance in light of Kevin Quashie's *Sovereignty of Quiet*, in which he argues for a mode of attentive reading that does not *reduce* aesthetics to resistance, that understands "a black expressiveness without publicness as its forbearer, a black subject in the undisputed dignity of its humanity."[40] McKinnie's poem offers an intriguing look into expressiveness with publicness as *part* of its project, but not its ultimate goal or its stumbling block: instead—and this becomes clear as the poem continues—public expressions of resistance are coupled with attention to interiority, to an expression of desire that can be fulfilled through protest and resistance, but that does not exist in the first place as a result of protest and resistance. The priority of this desire for dignity—of desire as *dignity itself*, in this case—cannot be reduced or replaced. I am reminded here of how Marlon D. Ross sees Linden Barrett's scholarship as exploring how "even as desire fuels visible . . . subjects conducive to the market's ingenuity . . . it also powers other, less recognizable flows of energy inimical both to monetary exchange and to familiar fixities of sociality."[41] The desire present in McKinnie's poetry, routed through Fleming Jr., Young, Quashie, and Barrett as interpreted by Ross, is atomistic as well as part of a larger molecule: the mass collectivity of the Memphis Sanitation Strike.

In this vein, the second stanza continues from the end of the first: with positive consequences of marching and staying, embodied in staying and fighting Loeb's administration. For McKinnie, a victorious strike means the attainment of its initial objectives: the opening of city government jobs, especially higher-paying jobs. This stanza inaugurates the poem's use of "you," an apostrophic address that reappears a single time in the third stanza. "You," as it appears, refers to the desire that precedes the strike, and this is made clear by the second stanza's turn to the question of jobs, justice, and civil rights. One could argue that this is the poem's neoliberal turn—its acknowledgment of individual, subjective desire. But such a claim would miss the straightforward appeal to dignity that the poem elaborates at both the individual and the collective level. Importantly, the "you" offers an important addition to the "we" and "us" of the poem's initial apostrophic thrust, especially given that it hails *the same collectivity* as the "we" and "us." In this second stanza, "you" is a call to collectivity as well, but with a caveat: "you" can participate in the protest, or "you" can accept isolation by trusting that Loeb will "open jobs for you." The reappearance of "you" in the third stanza clarifies this point, since "If you but truly believe" in the strike's objectives, you cannot be deceived by Loeb.

The poem's distinction between desire and dignity, if it exists, is precisely where and how *speaking with* can enter the poetry. Or, perhaps, this is the place for a favorite term of Muriel Rukeyser's and Robert Hayden's: *the wish*. The wish, with its lovely interiority and its anchoring in human dignity, is what Rukeyser and Hayden use to indicate a longing that is the mark of humanity and that both precedes and cuts through the uneven structure of rights. This is where McKinnie's poem turns in its final stanza. With that stanza's rhyming of "part" and "hearts" in its first two lines, the poem again aligns collective action with individual dignity, not fully *equating* one to the other, instead insisting on fully *relating* one *with* the other. The poem's attachments to "faith" and to acting according to what is within the protesting public's "hearts" indeed convey a shared metaphysical understanding—one that points to a particular conception of a human being's a priori, pre-social dignity. Importantly, doing one's "part" leads to the formation of a collectivity related through every protester's "heart," enabling a fuller human flourishing. As Michael Lackey as shown, debates over metaphysics were particularly resonant in the 1960s: the question of whether there was an essential, metaphysical sense of being Black undergirded African American art practices, as well as the question of whether there should be a narrowed understanding of aesthetics as the result of cultural and social formation at the level of national language.[42] While baldly humanistic terms like "flourishing" and "dignity" may seem overwrought, this is what the poetry of the Memphis Sanitation Strike insists upon. Even more: McKinnie's poem, along with the rest of the sanitation strike poems, suggests the middle ground that Lackey makes the case for, in which genuine conversations about Black power and the Black Arts Movement could rely on, but did not entirely give way to, a set of metaphysical claims about flourishing and dignity according to a new humanistic framework.

Resistance is couched within faith in the third stanza, an important metaphysical turn within what is until this point a solidly materialist poem. The poem seems to suggest that "march and stay"—part of "All these things and others too"—is contained within what "only faith can do," an interesting claim that might initially seem contradictory. As I have argued up to this point, though, in the context of the Memphis Sanitation Strike (and more broadly) metaphysics and materiality cannot be separated. Thus the turn toward metaphysics is not a departure from materialist concerns, but instead an attention to a foundational assumption of belief that the poem makes. McKinnie follows up his claim about faith with a rhyme between "believe" and "deceive," which, when paralleled to "All these things . . . that only faith can do," makes clear the inseparability of spiritual questions from political actions. If you keep the faith, McKinnie suggests, "then Henry can do nothing to deceive." Believing is seeing, in other words. In this way, "march and stay" is extended to become an elaboration of faith and belief, whereas "sit and wait" becomes further mired in negativity: it leads to susceptibility and resignation.

The poem concludes with a reemphasis of its collective vision, by once again apostrophizing to the collective. Thus, having begun with a question addressed to the "we," and then having turned to the shifting "you" of the second and third stanzas (with a brief return to "we" in "And if we stay"), the poem now resolutely commits to the first-person plural in each line of the final stanza. The pronominal sensibility of McKinnie's poem calls to mind, and offers crucial caveats to, Bonnie Costello's rousing conclusion to *The Plural of Us*, in which she insists that "poetry's first-person plural suggests how the genre might propose or project open, reflective, splayed community, create a sense of potential in 'us' that is not predicated on consensus, domination, or the mentality of the crowd."[43] Not all crowd mentality or collectivity is domineering, just as populism is not inherently good (and can certainly be quite malevolent). Yet "Why should we sit and wait?" does "propose" and "project" an "open, reflective, splayed community," one that nonetheless comes "all together" to "fight, / For the things that we know are right." As with Woody Guthrie's emphatic philosophy of union, as pointed out by Stadler, the mass collectivity on offer in McKinnie's poem demands an openness to others while explicitly denouncing forms of harm antithetical to human dignity. This is not a paean about containing multitudes, but instead an invitation to act together against racism and union busting. The assemblage is not ever-shifting, in other words, even as it is not fully enclosed.

This sense of collective sensibility finds another, more significantly Black nationalist perspective in the following poem. Morgan McCraw's "A Black Poem" (see figure 5) comes from the publication *Black Thesis*, a newsletter produced by the Black Student Association at Memphis State University. It appears in the sixth issue of *Black Thesis*, entitled "Who Am I?"—produced in late March 1968, right before MLK Jr.'s assassination on April 4.

McCraw's "black understanding" that "soaks the mind" is loudly (in visual terms) proclaimed through the contradictory image of quiet at the poem's conclusion ("WITHOUT OPENING THE MOUTH"), furnishing a link to McKinnie's "march and stay." The understood sense of collective being and belonging functions through action. Just as McKinnie links "march" and "stay," McCraw understands "Black" as "a thing from within" that performs its actions as a deliberate poetic extension of the example it offers: it "soaks" and "sets," thus putting its metaphysical and material assumptions into poetic motion. "Black," in the poem, "sets every Man / T-O-G-E-T-H-E-R," unifying the final six lines as continuous exemplifications of the first two lines. In

> Definition of the week:
>
> Each week we will present a word that is also used in today's language, but not really understood. The dictionary may give a contrite or out dated meaning to the word. We shall modernize the word to our standards of today's usage and living.
>
> <u>Jim Crow</u>—is like a starfish. You cut one arm off of the starfish, he does not die, but grows another leg. You attempt to kill Jim he grows even larger. Many times he comes in various disguises. JIM is even greater than a starfish. You cut off one leg, two more grow back. How to kill Jim Crow? Today's black generation of youth will take care of that, or die trying. This means <u>you</u>!
>
> <u>A BLACK POEM</u>   Morgan McCraw
>
> Black is not just a color,
> But a thing from within.
> It soaks the mind
> With pride and unity
> And sets every Man
> T-O-G-E-T-H-E-R
> In a black understanding
> WITHOUT OPENING THE MOUTH.

Figure 5. "A Black Poem." Morgan McCraw, 1968. The Search for Meaning Archive, Special Collections Department, University Libraries, University of Memphis.

Being Numerous, Oren Izenberg considers a set of experimental poems that "demand that our concepts of personhood identify something *real*: not political fictions we could come to inhabit together, or pragmatic ways of speaking we might come to share, but a ground on which the idea of a 'we' might stand."[44] For Izenberg, a crucial example can be found in the Language poets, who he argues "are *experimental*" for the reason that "they treat their poems neither as semantic tokens nor as aesthetic objects but as experiments or examples."[45] McCraw's poem is a treatment of this very idea, just slightly prior to Language poetry's emergence—likely due to the Black Arts Movement's indelible influence on midcentury experimental American poetry.

McCraw's poem participates in a larger network of poetic experiment in which the Black Arts Movement plays a central role. But to call the poem experimental is not quite right, either. Shockley's favoring of "innovative" over experimental makes quite a bit of sense in this context: "all avant-garde poetry is innovative (or aspires to be!), but not all innovative work is created within the context of an avant-garde." Shockley notes that her preference for "innovative" over "experimental" is couched in her desire "to respect the fact that poets working within a wide range of aesthetics undertake experimentation in their efforts to achieve their desired effects."[46] McCraw's poem innovatively imagines the social reality it poetically elaborates, and "T-O-G-E-T-H-E-R" examines the Memphian specificity of what Izenberg above calls the "ground on which the idea of a 'we' might stand." As Izenberg asserts, "Language poems are *social* in that what they take poems to be examples of is the unique capacity to produce language altogether, and thus to announce—as nothing else at the present moment seems to be able to do with the same persuasiveness—the existence of something fundamentally human on which the very possibility of social life can be predicated."[47] McCraw's poem, prior to and beside Language poetry, makes specific "the existence of something fundamentally human": it is "Black," the poem's inaugural word, that sets the social ground of the poem into motion. Thus inhabiting the aesthetic and political logic of the Memphis Sanitation Strike's most famous visual icons—"I AM A MAN"— McCraw transforms that declaration of being and belonging by unfurling it into a poetic statement of collective understanding that brings "every Man / T-O-G-E-T-H-E-R." The capitalization of "Man" seems a direct nod to the signs, and it gestures not to gender exclusivity but to the iconicity of the larger Memphian social-political context.

Thus "T-O-G-E-T-H-E-R," eight letters strung together and defamiliarized, expands the field of collective possibility ten years before $L=A=N=G=U=A=G=E$ magazine, with its eight-letter title, put into institutional practice the ethos of the Language poets. Notwithstanding Phillip Brian Harper's caution that "to claim poetry as the prime site for linguistic experimentation is potentially to limit the impact of that experimentation by circumscribing it within a realm where it already appears routine," McCraw's poem works at a distinctively innovative angle toward a Black Arts–informed poetic vision.[48] The four Memphis Sanitation Strike poems discussed here— "The 23rd Slum," "Sanitation Workers' Prayer," McKinnie's untitled poem, and McCraw's "A Black Poem"—are not written "within a realm where [experimentation] already appears routine"; instead, they open up important new spaces where poetry emerges and matters, and where innovation and experiment take place in unexpected (and often quite refreshing) ways.

These four poems of the Memphis Sanitation Strike, while not totalizing of the archive, are quite representative. There are a number of other significant poems collected in the University of Memphis's Search for Meaning Archive. On January 24, 1970, a certain Dorothy J. Royston of Memphis had an elegy to Dr. King published in the *Tri-State Defender* newspaper (part of the larger *Defender* African American media conglomerate), entitled "A Tribute to the Late Great Dr. King." An instructor at Memphis State University, William Page, published "Stretching Us Back into Time" in *Pembroke Magazine*. Seventeen-year-old Barbara Knight wrote a poem on April 11, 1968, still raw from King's assassination a week earlier. Her poem, "There Was a Man," was read and discussed at Hamilton High School, especially after it was published and circulated in a newsletter at the school (figure 6). Her teacher, Freda Marr, wrote notes to herself as reminders to encourage students to engage with the poem widely.

Another poem, anonymously written "by the poetess of Germantown," appeared on August 31, 1968, in a short-lived magazine entitled *The Liberator*:

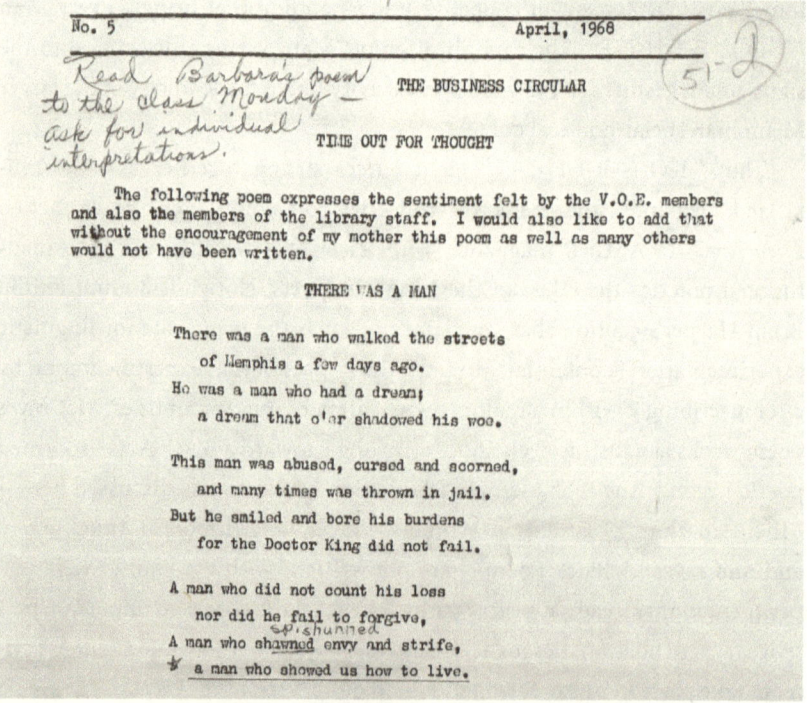

Figure 6. "There Was a Man." Barbara Knight, 1968. The Search for Meaning Archive, Special Collections Department, University Libraries, University of Memphis.

A Voice for <u>Labor</u>, the <u>Negro</u>, and <u>Intelligentsia</u>. The poetess's work is striking for its rigid rhyme scheme, its cynicism, and its humor (often indicated by parenthetical interruptions and asides); the only note we have about the author appears at the end of the poem: "She writes that she is a 'white housewife' and a Charter member of the old-line establishment." All of these additional poems tell a larger story about the Memphis Sanitation Strike and its resonances. A sensitive formalism, based on attending to how *speaking with* occurs in a diverse set of collectively oriented poetry, sees these many poetic responses as part of a coalitional aesthetics organized through the sanitation strike's local specificity as well as its global audience. Indeed, turning to the interactivity of these poems with their known and unknown audiences, with marchers and archival researchers, with academics and people who remember these poems (including teachers who taught the poems and people who recited them), means attending to the decidedly lyrical forms they worked through. For Gillian White, accounting for how the position of the midcentury lyric poem has been understood as overly personal or perhaps shameful means conceptualizing reception as an outcome of the "dynamics in modes of *reading* rather than in individual poems or authors' canons . . . or phases of a genre."[49] Although I do not read the Memphis Sanitation Strike poems as shameful or embarrassing, or as the products of tyro poetics, I do see them as difficult to parse given the elusive and sideways manner in which they enable engagement with broader arguments about poetry. For this reason, the poems offer an opening up: they transform our assumptions about 1968, midcentury poetry, and vernacular instances of lyric forms. They generate a new context for an expanded literary historical account of the influence of the Black Arts Movement. In this very same vein, I turn to the poetry of Gwendolyn Brooks.

Gwendolyn Brooks's Warpland

In June of 1968, Gwendolyn Brooks's collection *In the Mecca* appeared, announcing a decidedly militant poetic wager: a commitment to aesthetic innovation would also mean a commitment to political lyrical expression attuned through Black nationalism. This position does not produce singularity or exclusivity, but is instead a gesture of openness. Contrary to its dominant academic reception, Black nationalism is not inherently exclusive or oppressive. Of course, as GerShun Avilez shows, following Angela Davis and others, Black nationalism's forms of exclusion—while not totalizing—tended to theorize masculinity as central to communal identity. Yet, as Avilez shows, "aesthetic radicalism names a method that acknowledges the value of political frameworks rooted in collectivity (i.e. common racial circumstances) while also recognizing fragmentation within that collective."[50] Locating other genealogies of radical expression within Black nationalism's sphere of influence, Avilez notes the importance—and the openness—of Black nationalism, especially as artists engaged with it in their divergent ways. I acknowledge this may be a willful and recuperative reading of Black nationalism; yet, as Avilez notes, the idiomatic possibilities within Black nationalism allow alternative communal imaginations to index themselves within a larger, quite diverse collective sensibility. In a related interpretive gesture, Diana Fuss demonstrates how Frantz Fanon's complicated decolonial masculinism reveals that "identification is never outside or prior to politics, that identification is always inscribed within a certain history: identification names not only the history of the subject but the subject in history."[51]

Looking to Gwendolyn Brooks's three "Sermon on the Warpland" poems, we can see a poet thinking at a crucial moment in history—1968—and considering the adequacy of poetic forms. In this vein, the Memphis Sanitation Strike poems provide new insight into Brooks's poetry, especially given each Memphis poem's emphatic ongoingness, as well as the melding of religious knowledge with sacred and secular poetics. Turning to Brooks's "Warpland" poems, I build on the foundation established by the Memphis Sanitation Strike poetry to understand transformation and generation as integral versions of *speaking with*. The "Warpland" poems fall at the very beginning of the post–Fisk Conference period of Brooks's biography: after attending the second Black Writers' Conference at Fisk University in 1967 (in Nashville, Tennessee), Brooks began to shift her poetry's ethos and aesthetics toward an explicitly Black nationalist orientation. Yet, as Mary Helen Washington argues, this is "a conversion tale" that is very likely "apocryphal and misleading—and that, most problematically, required the rewriting of her earlier left-wing radicalism."[52] Turning to an interview between Brooks and Claudia Tate, Washington further points out that "Brooks eventually expressed her annoyance with these pronouncements about the 'change' in her work."[53] Much like Washington, I do not see the post-1967 shift as a total break with her previous work;

instead, I see an important transformation of her poetry that maintains elements of her past political experiences, even as she envisions a poetry that can express a shifting aesthetics of collective belonging. This shift maintains a coalitional aesthetics informed by her leftist tendencies even as it rejects the Popular Front's extraordinary political optimism, and what emerges is a collective lyrical language. The contours of this language are difficult to parse, but understanding the poems as offering a collective lyric imaginary—rather than characterizing them straightforwardly as polyvocal or dialogic, even as those descriptions certainly fit—means seeing the poems in an entirely new context.

The "Warpland" poems come from her collection *In the Mecca* and her chapbook *Riot*. Obviously connected by title and theme, these texts form a poetic, political, and theological trio. I call them a trio rather than trilogy, preferring not to think of them directly as a narrative sequence but instead as a set of texts that labor and *speak with* each other. For that reason, I discuss the poems in backward order, beginning with the third and ending with the conclusion of the first. I do not claim for Brooks's poems a conceptual undermining of time or narration, even if they *do* undermine linearity. Instead, I argue that the poems enact a very distinct and directed form of presence, of being together.

As poetic sermons, the poems call forth a number of formal assumptions that shape their collective lyrical imaginary: there is call-and-response, there is a directed theological argument, there is a larger textual embedding for the poems (including scripture and song), and there is a communal space in which the sermons will be sounded and heard. As Lesley Wheeler points out, in this trio of sermon poems, Brooks's "alternate geography also suggests the 'warped land' or even the 'Waste Land' of a racist and riot-torn America; it refers, especially in the first poem, to the 'war planned' by black nationalists against white America, and even a 'warplane,' a carrier for this militant message."[54] The multiplicity of what "warpland" could mean strains interpretive possibilities. As Jenni Rinner suggests, amid the many possibilities, there is a certainty that "Brooks's 'Warpland' names the land around her, which has been 'warped' by the race wars in America. In the 'Warpland' poems, Brooks provides perhaps less 'moral guidance' and more a call to survive together in this new place that is no place."[55] Indeed, Brooks points out to George Stavros in a 1970 interview that her intention for the poems is not to be "apocalyptic or prophetic"; instead, she sees them as "little addresses to black people, that's all."[56]

"The Third Sermon on the Warpland" (henceforth "Third Sermon") begins by defining the word "phoenix." Reminiscent of Rukeyser's relineated letter by Mearl Blankenship, this epigraph fragments the lines from *Webster's Dictionary*. This nod to documentary poetry, couched in an ominous sense of death and rebirth, gives way to an initial observation on the world's beauty: "The earth is a beautiful place. / Watermirrors and things to be reflected. / Goldenrod across the little lagoon."[57] Given that the "Second Sermon" ends with the line "Conduct your blooming in the noise and whip of the whirlwind,"[58] this opening to the "Third Sermon" offers up what will be destroyed in the rising fire of the whirlwind (with its biblical resonances, given the Books of Nahum, Exodus, Job, Habakkuk, and Lamentations, among others[59]), which grows to enormous proportions and becomes the natural expression of the riot Brooks conceptualizes as "A Poem in Three Parts." As the second poem in *Riot*, "Third Sermon" is both the bridge between the first and third poems of that chapbook and a continuation of *In the Mecca*, the longer collection published in 1968 that contains the first two "Warpland" poems.

The second and third stanzas in "Third Sermon" are spoken by "The Black Philosopher," who insists upon separating oneself from the dying spiritual and epistemological world that has produced chattel slavery and continuing oppression. The lines are world historical and domestic at the same time: "Our chains are in the keep of the keeper / in a labeled cabinet / on the second shelf by the cookies, / sonatas, the arabesques . . ."[60] The Black Philosopher's speech ends with a conditional exhortation:

> You do not hear the remarkable music—'A
> Death Song For You Before You Die.'
> If you could hear it
> you would make music too.
> The blackblues.[61]

Like "watermirrors" earlier, "blackblues" condenses words to create a neologism. This tendency, while present in Brooks's earlier work (especially her novel *Maud Martha*), becomes increasingly important to her writing in and after 1968. (The famous elegy "Malcolm X," from *In the Mecca*, begins with: "Original. / Ragged-round. / Rich-robust.")[62] Because this compound-nouning exists prior to 1968, however, it cannot be understood as constitutive of a distinct formal shift; as Washington suggests, the oft-proclaimed shift in Brooks's poetry might be an artifact of Haki Madhubuti's impressive marketing for Third World Books and the move Brooks would make away from Harper & Row after *In the Mecca* and *For Illinois 1968: A Sesquicentennial Poem*, both from 1968. Washington pointedly notes that "in view of the political directness of *The Bean Eaters*, it is stunning that so many of Brooks's critics insisted that she became 'political' only after 1967 and that her poems from the 1940s and 1950s were apolitical and directed at a white audience."[63] Following and extending Washington's point, *Riot* and *In the Mecca* are not radical breaks from an earlier style or marks of political emergence for the poet. The books continue Brooks's "determination to expose the way conventions of respectability, Christian norms, racism, and classism dominate and oppress working-class and racialized subjects."[64] The formation of the "Sermon on the Warpland" poems through the textual implications of the sermon form speak directly to the interests Washington notes; though she is remarking upon *The Bean Eaters* and previous works, her insistence upon understanding the continuities in Brooks's critical and aesthetic commitments offers important context for her sermonically inflected poems.

"Third Sermon" casts its lyrical eye far outside the realm of the sacred, and the spatial implications of the sermon form are made irrelevant. The poem even stretches the idea of call-and-response, substituting a more diffuse and indescribable form of polyvocality, mostly predicated on a roving lyrical eye, incorporated and named voices, and pop culture references. Stanzas 6 and 7, for example, describe a "clean riot" by stating what it is not and couching this within several musical allusions:

> A clean riot is not one in which little rioters
> long-stomped, long-straddled, BEANLESS
> but knowing no Why
> go steal in hell
> a radio, sit to hear James Brown
> and Mingus, Young-Holt, Coleman, John,
>   on V.O.N.
> and sun themselves in Sin.

> However, what
> is going on
> is going on.⁶⁵

"BEANLESS" is certainly a reference to *The Bean Eaters*. After this self-reflexive allusion, which extends the distance between "not one in which little rioters" and "go steal in hell / a radio," the poem imagines *what* the purpose of the radio would be: to "sit to hear" a number of popular artists. The seventh stanza might seem to be a reference to Marvin Gaye; but, importantly, the poem is written three years prior to the recording of "What's Going On?" Perhaps, then, "what / is going on / is going on" is a way to couch the reciprocal Kiswahili greeting "Habari gani?" (literally, "What is the news?") and a broader pan-Africanist ethos within the poem. The repetition of "is going on" also functions as a repudiation of the idea of a "clean riot," especially within the context of *Riot* as a chapbook. Thus, the lines "what / is going on / is going on" serve to emphasize that the "little rioters" *are* sitting down to "hear James Brown / and Mingus, Young-Holt, Coleman, John, on V.O.N." VON, importantly, is a radio station, WVON (now known as "the Voice of the Nation"), founded in 1963 to be "the Voice of the Negro."⁶⁶

In addition to The Black Philosopher, the poem's expansive lyrical attention incorporates the voices of the following: "A White Philosopher"; "Motherwoman"; "Yancey"; the Chicago *Sun-Times*; "Peanut"; "The Disciples," who "confer / with ranging Rangermen"; and, finally, "they / who say also 'It's time. / It's time to help / These People.'" Although discussing Brooks's earlier long poem "The Anniad" in particular, Shockley brings attention to "the strategies which together create polyvocality" in her work, such that Brooks can "manage the delicate balancing act necessary to achieve the legitimacy she wants." To achieve this in "The Anniad," Shockley argues, "Brooks creates a speaker who can be heard as addressing at least three different audiences simultaneously—the effects of which were not entirely predictable or manageable. Polyvocality, then, is a key source of both the work's brilliance and its deeply mixed reception, as well as its long critical history of partial misreadings and grudging admiration."⁶⁷ For Shockley, this polyvocality is part of a long career of innovative formal work, and although it continues in many forms (from "The Anniad" in 1949 to Brooks's longest poem, "In the Mecca," from the collection of the same title), in "Third Sermon" this polyvocality becomes both attenuated and riotous. It has been transformed within the poem, generating a diffused collective and indeed coalitional lyric form that remains ungathered until the first three lines of the final poem in *Riot*, "An Aspect of Love, Alive in the Ice and Fire: LaBohem Brown," which follows "Third Sermon": "It is the morning of our love. // In a package of minutes there is this We. / How beautiful."[68] As the conclusion to *Riot*, "An Aspect of Love, Alive in the Ice and Fire: LaBohem Brown" imagines an emergent collective sensibility that can be expressed, in the Memphian poet Morgan McCraw's words, "WITHOUT OPENING THE MOUTH." Thus, we read:

> There is a moment in Camaraderie
> when interruption is not to be understood.
> I cannot bear an interruption.
> This is the shining joy;
> the time of not-to-end.
>
> On the street we smile.
> We go
> in different directions
> down the imperturbable street.[69]

Against often-apocalyptic notions of revolution and upheaval, Brooks thinks of the end of *Riot* as "the shining joy; / the time of not-to-end." The continuity of the community, of the "we" who "go / in different directions / down the imperturbable street," is a necessary condition for imagining conclusion. There cannot be an end and the street cannot be erased, because this would mean the catastrophic erasure of the community she spent her entire career writing with and *speaking with*. The street must be kept intact and "imperturbable," resonant with possibilities and a space of action, interaction, and continuance.

Split into four numbered sections, "The Second Sermon on the Warpland" (henceforth "Second Sermon") begins and ends with life. The first section—the poem's shortest—begins with a declaration: "This is the urgency: Live! / and have your blooming in the noise of the whirlwind."[70] This poem, which concludes *In the Mecca*, finishes with a return to the opening gesture toward life: "It is lonesome, yes. For we are the last of the loud. / Nevertheless, live. //

Conduct your blooming in the noise and whip of the whirlwind."[71] The imperative "live" appears in each of the poem's four sections, each time an invocation. Thus, in its final appearance, "live" repeats yet transforms the opening "urgency," having undergone progressive shifts across the poem.

The whirlwind, too, transforms: it begins as an intrusion of natural chaos, and, as the poem develops, it becomes defined in slightly more knowable ways. In the second section, "the whirlwind is our commonwealth"; and in the third, the lyric voice tells the audience—of the sermon, presumably—to "Live and go out. / Define and / medicate the whirlwind."[72] The world is not utter chaos, but instead something that one can "medicate." This has additional power when considered in the context of the biblical Book of Job: the whirlwind, in the desert, is where Yahweh resides. When the whirlwind appears in Job, we are told that "the LORD answered Job out of the whirlwind." This whirlwind, in "Second Sermon," is the representation of chaos as well as a sacred space of divine speech. Thus to suggest the whirlwind can be defined and medicated means that the poem understands the transformative possibilities of collective action against injustice. As part of a larger tradition of Black theology, this poetic vision sees action as a form of material resistance, related to what Ashon Crawley calls "enfleshment," which is "distinct from embodiment" and "is the movement to, the vibration of, liberation." For Crawley, this distinction is important, since "embodiment . . . presumes a subject of theology, a subject of philosophy, a subject of history."[73] "Second Sermon" suggests that to be *in* the whirlwind, rather than awaiting an answer from it, means to take up a hitherto banned creative force. To recall the "Third Sermon," to be in the whirlwind is to find the chains "in the keep of the keeper" and to insist on the power to "make music too. / The blackblues."

"The Sermon on the Warpland" (henceforth "First Sermon"), the most formally sermon-like of the trio, begins with a complicated image of coalescence, in which many are condensed into one. After an epigraph by Ron Karenga (the originator of Kwanzaa), the poem starts with a hazy sense of direction before leading to a potent sermon: "And several strengths from the drowsiness campaigned / but spoke in Single Sermon on the warpland. // And went about the warpland saying No."[74] These lines condense the "Single Sermon" into "No," but what follows in the rest of the poem is encapsulated, direct discourse: the sermon, expanded, elaborates on what it means by "saying No." Carl Phillips notes that the first three stanzas of "First Sermon," beginning with "And" and concluding with "the clear obscure!" are governed by "a rhyme scheme . . . , one that unites these fourteen lines into a stylized sonnet."[75] Phillips suggests that "First Sermon" begins with traditional prosodic tendencies while inaugurating Brooks's shift away from the traditional bounds of rhyme and meter within specific poetic forms. He argues that Brooks "won't abandon the traditional English prosody that she so clearly loves. But she seems to have seen its limitations, if not made to adapt to cultural change."[76]

As in the second and third "Warpland" poems, Brooks lovingly turns to the earth's beauty but insists upon rebuilding the human cultural form. The world—culturally and environmentally—is under extraordinary duress, and Brooks argues that to ensure its perpetuation, dramatic moves away from coloniality and its capitalist, anti-Black, and ecocidal tendencies are required. Wheeler argues that the poem contains "a new vision of building," a particularly evocative phrase.[77] To build is to transform—but the coloniality that has determined recent historical shifts must not be allowed to happen again. Thus what must be built must be built with new materials—and, as Wheeler points out, these are philosophical and spiritual yet, importantly, *material* materials. I would not go so far as to say Brooks is imagining a new materiality. However, the philosophical and spiritual are considered inseparable from the material in the three "Warpland" poems.

Brooks's final stanza gives directions for building: invocative, demanding, and wondrous, this stanza imagines the paradoxical and rigorous task ahead. The poem's finale conceptualizes revolutionary desire as a fullness that is not yet sated, a political and theological completeness that is nevertheless interested in continuity and further extension. Accreting descriptions of the love with which these new things must be built, the poem uses "with" to enumerate a list of metaphorical possibilities through which this love can appear:

> Build with lithe love. With love like lion-eyes.
> With love like morningrise.
> With love like black, our black—
> luminously indiscreet;
> complete; continuous.[78]

The cascading metaphors multiply the forms of love: love "like lion-eyes," "like morningrise," "like black, our black." Acute, powerful, dawning, and expansive, love's final form is "like black, our black— / luminously indiscreet;

/ complete; continuous." This final line unifies but does not enclose, offering completion without absoluteness, fullness without boundaries. Ending with a richly contradictory image, Brooks imagines completion against containment—as generative and fruitful, energetic and "luminously indiscreet," and thus always open, always vibrant. Brooks's vision of love's completion as neither satisfaction nor self-justification offers a useful framework for interpreting revolutionary Black poetry as both transformative and generative. Quashie reads "the rapturous conclusion" to "First Sermon" as an example of emphatic aliveness. He notes "the impressive chiasmic repetition in the last two lines as 'luminous*ly*' adheres with 'continu*ous*' and 'indiscr*eet*' with 'comp*lete*.'" This shows "how her mouthy syntax wriggles away from simplistic rendering even as she is very much interested in the simple, how her syntax marries words to densify the expressed thing."[79] In Quashie's sense of densification and fullness, I also see the wonderment of what Gerald Vizenor has called "survivance," an "active sense of presence over absence, deracination, and oblivion"; "survivance is the continuation of stories" through alternative grammars of description and being that exceed conclusive and linear logic.[80] The "complete; continuous" sensibility of Brooks's "First Sermon" reminds me quite strongly of the visions of unclosed conclusion in "The 23rd Slum" and "Sanitation Workers' Prayer." "The 23rd Slum" ends with the so-be-it of "Amen" after its angry, prophetic buildup toward the proclamation that Henry Loeb "shall burn in hell forever." In "Sanitation Workers' Prayer," freedom is announced as both a blessing and as a demand, an origin and a collective declaration. "Forever and ever. / FREEDOM!" shouts out the human spirit from the page, with vindication.

In the long struggle for justice and equality, especially in the striking year of 1968, the Memphis Sanitation Strike has too often been displaced by national narratives of mourning and trauma. To turn to the poetry and aesthetics emerging before, during, and after this catastrophe is, then, to listen closely to people who knew and declared the art of their protest, the truth of their lives, and the necessity of their desires. Freedom is not final or conclusive—it is both a desire and a position, not one or the other. It is not only an end in and of itself, but a means that achieves its ends (but never its end) by continuously transforming and regenerating the world in which it is formed.

4 Coalitional Aesthetics against Allegory
Carlos Bulosan's and Tomás Rivera's Migrant Pizcaresques

IN THIS CHAPTER, I TURN to two highly specific examples of migrant-written texts, spaced roughly three decades apart: Carlos Bulosan's *America Is in the Heart* (1946, republished by the University of Illinois Press in 1973; henceforth *America*) and Tomás Rivera's *. . . y no se lo tragó la tierra* (1971, henceforth *Tierra*). Both are often read allegorically, especially given their relation to the United States as source of economic and literary power and influence. Both *America* and *Tierra* engage with early emergences of the language of multiculturalism, which shapes their coalitional sensibilities through direct and experientially anchored critiques of colonialism, empire, racism, and economic degradation. Bulosan, a Filipino migrant to the US who worked across the West Coast, from Los Angeles to Alaska, is often read as narratively accounting for the psychological and economic effects of coloniality on the Philippines and the Filipino diaspora. Rivera, a Chicano academic whose early years as a migrant farmworker informed his work within the university system (first as a professor and then as an administrator, in a career that culminated in becoming the chancellor of the University of California, Riverside), is often understood as allegorically representing the process of growing into Chicanx political consciousness, particularly in response to forms of racial and economic injustice. Each text, within this general framing, has functioned as an ethno-political bildungsroman, or more specifically, as a *Künstlerroman*—a portrait of the ethnic artist.

Both books operate in the shadow of Spanish and US imperialism, and both think deeply about their emergent literary traditions in relation to received literary histories, particularly Spain's *siglo de oro*—the "golden century" or golden age of literary and cultural production from roughly 1492 into the mid-seventeenth century—and the social history of the US novel along with the rise of realism. Both writers were indeed quite knowledgeable about the history of Spanish prose forms: Bulosan's Catholic education in the Philippines cultivated his literary sensibilities, as did his Los Angeles writing milieu, which included Sanora Babb, John Fante, and others; Tomás Rivera was a professor of Spanish Golden Age literature, so he taught and knew canonical Spanish picaresque novels. This is all to say that Bulosan's and Rivera's texts knowledgeably and deliberately engage with—and, importantly, *refuse*—the totalizing discursive structures of allegory, as well as of the bildungsroman. Bulosan and Rivera undermine the possibility of a totally ethnically representative narrative voice, even as they make use of the possibilities contained within allegory, and even as allegory offers a stable set of interpretive paradigms through which to glean resistant meaning. This remains the case even as the narrative structures of both books can certainly be understood as movements toward ultimately impossible allegories, a contradictory impulse that inhabits and destabilizes the narrative conclusions they reach.

However, allegory has a strong upside in studies of multiethnic literature, especially by offering more or less straightforward symbols of political meaning and providing straightforward interpretive lessons. Especially in the context of US multiethnic literature, allegories are often narratives of learning, growth, and transformation, and are easily homologized with the bildungsroman. *America* and *Tierra* are often understood, in this sense, as allegories that participate in the generic structure of the bildungsroman: novels of growth, of process, of development. Importantly, allegory and the bildungsroman, as presumed genres of ethnic literature, are important lodestars of literary history, and there's a significant reward to be had in offering or proving one's ability to participate in recognizable literary historical narratives.

These distinctions have led me to develop a concept, the *migrant pizcaresque*, to name how the two books together demonstrate a particular aesthetic model for representing the stories of farmworkers. One could attempt to identify significant precursors to what I might provisionally—even autoschediastically—call a tradition, such as Daniel Venegas's *Las aventuras de don Chipote, o, Cuando los pericos mamen* (1928), Jose Antonio Villarreal's

Pocho (1959), or Américo Paredes's *George Washington Gómez* (1990, written in the 1930s), which offer picaresque narratives about Latinx migrants. However, Venegas's uproarious novel is a satirical picaresque about the dangers of migration, and both Paredes's and Villarreal's texts imagine their protagonists within the contours of a *Portrait of the Artist* typology of aspirational young men, and are not as thoroughly ensconced in the agricultural, especially at the semiotic level, as *America* and *Tierra*.

The *migrant pizcaresque* is the genre revolution that happens when the centuries-old literary form of the picaresque is remixed with the stories and situations of workers in the *pizca*—the commonly used Mexican Spanish word for "harvest," which is often descriptive of migrant farm labor. The picaresque, as a long-standing literary form defined by peregrination and experiential seriality that was developed in sixteenth- and seventeenth-century Spain, often hinges on the narrative of a *pícaro*—a rogue, outlaw, or adventurer. Often, the rogue or pícaro has been described as the "mozo de muchos amos"—an archaic way of saying "servant to many masters." By combining *pizca* and *picaresque* into *pizcaresque*, I want to provisionally name an as-yet-unacknowledged genre of multiethnic fiction, one that shares certain qualities with road texts such as John Steinbeck's *The Grapes of Wrath*, but whose ethnic inflection is particularized and therefore avoids the totalizing nature of the Joad family's archetypal status.[1] In this sense, *America* and *Tierra* follow the path of specificity that Sanora Babb prefers in *Whose Names Are Unknown*.

A significant question is raised by the migrant pizcaresque framing, which I deliberately set up and then answer at length: What does it mean that these migrant workers are pícaros, rogues, or outlaws solely by dint of colonialism and the racial economics of their farm labor? Bulosan and Rivera answer this question by arguing that illegality and marginalization are outcomes of colonialism and racism, and each elaborates this problematic condition throughout *America* and *Tierra*. My claims here are also an expansion, through comparative analysis, of Steven Yao's provocative invitation to reread Bulosan's book as an "ethnic picaresque." Yao prompts readers to "continue expanding our thinking beyond the conceptual boundaries of the nation and of nationalism by considering Bulosan's text not simply a negation of the *bildungsroman*, but rather in more positive terms."[2] As Yao points out, the "picaresque" describes an early form of prose narrative that originated in sixteenth-century Spain and which presents an episodic sequence of loosely connected adventures by a protagonist of low social class who lives by his wits on the edge of society. In its traditional historical appearances, the "picaro" is a loose character who never works, nor shows any sort of social advancement. In fact, according to some scholarly views, the figure comes close to being a criminal, a position that stands in necessarily fraught relation to dominant social values. Accordingly, the "picaresque" generally focuses on social critique through comedy and satire rather than on individual character development.[3]

This transvaluation of the picaresque from an outlaw, rogue, or criminal into a migrant worker contains a fundamental acknowledgment that migrants are often criminalized and drafted into racialized and racist discursive patterns. For Bulosan and Rivera, adopting and transvaluating the picaresque tradition's formal parameters shows how migrants participate actively and uniquely in literary history. Particularly because characters do indeed develop in *America* and *Tierra*, and also because the payoff occurs through Popular Front–inflected coalitional aesthetics that seek to *speak with* the migrant communities they depict, the picaresque as such does not *quite* fit as a genre for these texts. For this reason, the *migrant pizcaresque* offers the estranging *z* or "zeta," the letter in the middle of the generic form that multiplies the possibilities of the term itself.

The migrant pizcaresque acknowledges the upsides of allegory: given the anticolonial politics thoroughly expressed in each text, the acceptance of which drives the political awakening of central characters, a sense of ethnicity as a political feeling emerges in *America* and *Tierra*. Yet the downsides of allegory are perhaps even more significant in the migrant pizcaresque, since a character becoming an ethnic representative would suggest the oneness of racial belonging, such that an allegorically determined character would *speak for* their ethnic group. As an emergent form, the migrant pizcaresque is strange enough that it allows Bulosan and Rivera to make *speaking with* a signal part of each book's coalitional aesthetics, especially seeing how *America* and *Tierra* examine failed attempts to fully embody the voices of others. *Speaking for* gives way to *speaking with*, as the many voices in both books evade the capture of any single point of narrative focalization. Both books imagine ethnicity as a relation to others—both in terms of degradation (the Anglo other is a chief antagonist for migrant farmworkers in both books, in particular) and in terms of shared experiences of colonialism and oppression. *America*, for example, features multiracial union organizing and constant encounters across ethnic and national groups, and *Tierra* is shaped indelibly by the Korean War and the labor struggles undertaken by farmworkers.

Throughout this chapter, I explore how *Tierra* and *America* are crafted through a sustained attention to how Mexican American and Filipino farmworkers perform improvisatory interventions on the themes of belonging, thus transforming marginalized spaces into empowering and autonomous speaking positions that nevertheless resist allegorical capture. Margins become centers, and this happens through self-actualizing methods of representation practiced in each text. In the particular modes through which they evince *speaking with*, *Tierra* and *America* generate coalitional voice as an imaginative and justice-oriented aesthetic practice that moves through and beside narration. Importantly, both texts use the very problems of allegory to move beyond realism: these are not native informant texts, even as they are meant to give insight into the experiences of Mexican American and Filipino farmworkers. This adjacency to realism gives each text a difficult balance to strike, and each one responds uniquely to this representational challenge.

This chapter's argumentative focus is at once local and transnational, specific and abstract, Chicanx and Filipino and part of a multiethnic coalitional sensibility that arose within each distinctive literary tradition. I take care to understand, as Ramón Saldívar argues in *Chicano Narrative*, that "it is time to see Chicano narrative as something more than a simple mirror of the life and folklore of a heretofore invisible segment of American society," and the same holds true for Bulosan's novel in relation to both social realism and Filipino literary history.[4] As I argue throughout this book, the study of multiethnic literatures must refuse the impulse to read minoritarian texts anthropologically, as ways to enter into or understand "other" cultures and cultural discourses. Saldívar's admonition in *Chicano Narrative* reminds us that Mexican American cultural production moves with an aesthetic and political urgency that troubles methods and norms of representation, rather than suggesting that the act of representation—making visible minoritarian labor and experience—is in and of itself a panacea. While representation in the sense of inclusion is undeniably important, it is just as important to see this visibility for its formal operations and the specific articulations of its content, not simply for the mere fact of being present. *America* and *Tierra* lean deeply into this political and aesthetic argument, refusing singularity in favor of coalitional orientations. Each text emerges as a multiplicity of voices, *speaking with* historical and contemporary activism as well as literary history.

Tierra and *America* imagine Chicanidad and Filipinoness through discourses of tenuousness, fragmentation, and contradictoriness, arguing that these are necessary and vital aspects through which to find voice and to issue empowering language that reconsiders the shape and flow of ethnic belonging. The idea that fragmentation is a constitutive and powerful aspect of Chicanx identity, in particular, is not new. John C. Akers, in "Fragmentation in the Chicano Novel: Literary Technique and Cultural Identity," and Chela Sandoval, in *Methodology of the Oppressed*, show how fragmentation, while commonly seen only as a symptom of (post)modernity and late capitalism, is a potent and politically charged characteristic of so-called Third World literary and cultural production. Rather than being what authors and cultural producers struggle against in their search for artistic "unity," fragmentation, for Sandoval and Akers—as well as Pat Mora and Gloria Anzaldúa, among others—instead describes the world as it must be understood and negotiated. In other words, the world operates through difference, and this difference must be recognized and accepted, rather than unified. Articulating new modes of representation means directly challenging the foundational logic of political representation and suggesting that something is needed in excess of, or beside, representational democracy to create a truly egalitarian, democratic society. In this, I follow Alicia Schmidt Camacho's *Migrant Imaginaries*, in which she "contends that for much of the twentieth century, Mexican migrants exposed the limits of the nation form—meaning its instruments of governance and its structures of legitimation."[5] Yet I also explore how *America* and *Tierra* do more than expose limits. They craft coalitional aesthetics that elaborate new "structures of legitimation" by moving away from national(ist) recognition of personhood and citizenship.

Importantly, each text generates a transformative relation to overarching aesthetic categories, especially those of allegory, the bildungsroman, and the picaresque. In developing their coalitional aesthetics, *America* and *Tierra* transform the picaresque into a new form of critical commentary on agricultural migrant experiences, generating new generic possibilities through and with the migrant pizcaresque. What emerges in each text, as a result, is a deeply coalitional narrative voice whose undeniable multiplicity offers a different way forward for imagining ethnic belonging.

America Is in the Heart and the Roots of the Migrant Pizcaresque

America has been central to the field of Asian American literary studies, offering a particularly important example of Filipino literary innovation in the history of the novel. It is an English-language text and therefore participates within that language's history of the novel; yet, just as importantly, it participates in the Filipino literary tradition, as well as Spanish narrative forms. Johaina K. Crisostomo, Paul Nadal, E. San Juan Jr., and others have detailed this linguistically and culturally complex literary history extensively, particularly the multiple emergences of novels in each language.[6] For Bulosan, therefore, there is a significant investment in prose narrative forms, from the bildungsroman, and its influence on the coming-of-age story across languages, to the robinsonade (that is, novels influenced by Daniel Defoe's *Robinson Crusoe*), the adventure novel, religious rituals and other Catholic liturgical forms, folk stories and local tales, and, most importantly for this chapter, the picaresque novel.

In terms of how *America* has been described as a text, prevailing literary criticism tends to see it as a mix of biography and fiction. San Juan Jr. has labeled Bulosan's book an "ethnobiography," acknowledging the expansive sense of collective responsibility that drove Bulosan.[7] Oscar V. Campomanes and Todd S. Gernes describe *America* as "blending folk forms (such as the tall tale), biography, and fiction," and also as an "autobiography" and as a "collective biography";[8] Allan Punzalan Isaac argues that Bulosan's text is a "composite autobiography," expands this description to a "composite autobiography as a group event," and also calls *America* a "personal history of a Filipino American composite."[9] These scholars are fairly representative of the most significant line of approach to Bulosan's text, which understands the book as generating an important, generically hybrid form. Many have additionally seen *America* as a bildungsroman that provides an allegory of political coming-of-age; Tim Libretti, following this reasoning, argues that the book's psychological "structure allegorizes the role of collective memory in a Third World resistance culture."[10] Joseph Keith calls the text "Carlos's 'Robinsonade' narrative of self-formation and education," part of his argument that the novel's transnational imaginary flips the idea of mainland and island on its head: the Filipino migrant, rather than arriving at the metropolitan center, encounters the US as a series of island-like communities he undertakes his far-flung travels. To achieve this, the bildungsroman structure gets inverted as well. Keith demonstrates that the book's "narrative of development is based on the move from a personal to an impersonal voice—from an individual to a collective experience."[11] Steven Yao goes even further than Keith in rejecting the idea of the bildungsroman, arguing that "from . . . a transpacific vantage, . . . Bulosan's autobiographical narrative can be better understood not as a failed *bildungsroman* or anti-novel, but rather as an example of the 'ethnic picaresque.'"[12] Chris Vials understands *America* as participating in an emergent, Asian American "transnational political aesthetic . . . that struggled for class-conscious, anti-imperial liberation for [authors'] countries of origin and a viable space for Asians living in the United States."[13] In most of these arguments, expansive thinking prevails: the idea, ultimately, is that *America* converts a series of experiences into the singular figure of the narrator. And for anyone who has read the book, this rings true: it is a truly overwhelming narrative, and much of what the narrator undergoes is appalling. There is significant historical evidence, demonstrated by San Juan Jr. and others, that the narrator's expressive life was constructed by incorporating many specific experiences of Filipino migrant workers Bulosan personally knew, thus creating the composite or collage of which scholars have taken note.

Bulosan begins the novel with a bit of an inside joke, showing that he knows how readers will likely approach his work. The main character's name undergoes several shifts throughout the book, but it begins as Allos—his name, he says, in his native tongue. Of course, Allos can be read as one of the root words of *allegory*: *allos*, meaning "elsewhere" or "other." Yet Bulosan goes to great pains to indicate that Allos is not just a cipher for the novel's possible allegorical impulses; even as it sort of *is* that, it is also, very straightforwardly, a Filipino name. The main character's name, as the novel progresses, becomes Carl and then Carlos while he is in the United States. Literary history has, of course, primed us to think of names at the beginning of plot: Robinson Crusoe gives his name and his familial history; Tristram Shandy spends hundreds of pages explaining just how his parents gave him a name he hates, which he believes has essentially ruined his life; the preface to *Don Quixote* stages an elaborate etymological debate about whether the man from La Mancha's surname—Quixote—is perhaps instead Quijada or Quesada or Quejana. *Lazarillo de Tormes* begins with the announcement that before anything else, even before the initiation of the plot, it's important to know about the protagonist's parentage and geographical placement.

"What's in a name?" is of course a significant question in literary history. As a name, Allos estranges that question. Yet rather than turning directly or solely to allegory, Allos, as an observant narrator, collects experiences and relates them to his readers. This is a book of extraordinary detail, and its three-hundred-plus pages are filled with people's names, place-names, labor experiences, hospital scenes, moments of racial violence and police violence, and more. As Sau-ling Cynthia Wong astutely puts it, if the novel's surface-level desire for a more inclusive and expansive set of democratic ideals "had been realized, the narrative would have shown a meaningful arrangement of place names, a trajectory of struggle and triumph. Yet there is no blazed trail, only chaos, a senseless jumble of brutalities."[14] Nadal, in describing Juan C. Laya's 1941 novel *His Native Soil*, offers a contextual apparatus for beginning to approach the "chaos" of *America*. Nadal argues that *His Native Soil* is driven by a formal construction that "proceeds *as if every subplot contained equal force and weight*, investing in each the same measure of significance, as though each and every one were indispensable to the overall meaning of the work. This way of arranging the action has the effect of producing a monotonic intensity whose momentum from beginning to end would seem to overrun the prose."[15] This is not the payoff for Laya, however, and it is not the point for Bulosan either. As Nadal argues, it is the very breakdown of the bildungsroman as a form, especially when attenuated by transnational desires and emplotment, that transforms "monotonic intensity" into "tonal dissonances" that emerge "from the novel's structural design and the unusual combinations it aims to produce."[16] Bulosan's *America*, as countless scholars have noted, has a similarly remarkable "structural design"; what is even more remarkable, as I have suggested, is how often its outcomes are framed through the bildungsroman form and its allegorical trap. Rather than fusing the harrowing experiences into the migrant worker narrator's single voice, *America* instead shows his body breaking down, fainting, disrupting patterns, and veritably transforming into various personalities with often contradictory desires.

America is indeed a difficult book to read, emotionally, and this difficulty is something Bulosan strives for: it details the degrading experiences of Filipino migrant laborers and suggests that they are constantly treated as outlaws solely because they are colonized subjects from America's Pacific empire. Recall that from 1898 until 1946 the Philippines (which was named Las Filipinas after the Spanish king Philip II and ruled by the Spanish Empire for over three hundred years) was a US territory and commonwealth. As a result of this colonial situation, US racial discourses decisively declared the Philippines backward, primitive, and violent, and its people were declared to be beneficiaries of the US's colonial enterprises. It is in this context that Bulosan raises questions about the position of the Filipino migrant as a pícaro, suggesting that the migrant's outsider status and serving of many masters is the result of colonialism and racism. To put as strong an emphasis as possible on it, the "mozo de muchos amos" or "servant to many masters" genre concept of the picaresque becomes central in the migrant pizcaresque as a formal literary critique: migrant farm laborers are made to serve many masters or bosses simply because they move from farm to farm as colonized, racialized, and often illegalized subjects. This is true in Bulosan's novel, and in Rivera's *Tierra* as well.

America begins in the Philippines, on a farm near Binalonan, in Pangasinan province, which is in the Ilocano region of Luzon, the largest and most populous of the Philippines' more than seven thousand islands. One of the first moments in the text is a scene of farm labor: Allos and his father are working in a field, tending to their carabao—their water buffalo—and crops. One of Allos's brothers returns from fighting in World War I as part of a Philippine colonial regiment of the US army. After the first part of the novel set in the Philippines, first in Binalonan and then Manila, Allos eventually makes his way to the US. Allos's first experience there is immediately demoralizing. Almost as soon as he arrives in Seattle, his money is stolen and he gets contracted to work at a cannery in Anchorage, Alaska. Upon arrival, then, the first thing he must do is leave again. After months of hard labor in Anchorage, he returns to Seattle almost penniless: the bosses in the cannery forced him to repay them for travel, lodging, and food. Months of work, no money. This cycle continues for hundreds of pages: work, or gambling, and the brief acquisition of money, and the violent, catastrophic dissolution of whatever Filipino community he is in. Consider this illustrative example:

> We jumped off in Fresno where Filipinos told us that trouble was brewing. Frank wanted to proceed to Alaska for the fishing season, but I told him that conditions there were intolerable. The east was still an unexplored world, so we agreed to take a freight train to Chicago.
>
> When we arrived in Idaho, I changed my plans. The pea fields decided me. Why go to an unknown city where there was no work? Here in this little town of Moscow were peas waiting and ready to be picked. So Frank and I worked for three weeks picking peas. But his heart was already in Chicago. He could not work any more.
>
> I took him to the bus station and gave him a little of my money. I hate slow partings. I patted him on the back and left. I met some Mexican families on their way to the beet fields in Wyoming. I rode on a truck with them as far as Cheyenne, where they stopped off to work for a month.
>
> I went to town and walked around the premises of the Plains Hotel, hoping to see some workers there who might have come from Binalonan. I tried to locate them by peering through the windows, but gave up when some women looked at me suspiciously. I was too dirty to go inside. And I was afraid. My fear was the product of my early poverty, but it was also the nebulous force that drove me fanatically toward my goal.
>
> I caught a freight train that landed me in Billings, Montana. The beet season was in full swing. Mexicans from Texas and New Mexico were everywhere; their jalopies and makeshift tents dotted the highways. There were also Filipinos from California and Washington. Some of them had just come back from the fish canneries in Alaska.
>
> I went to Helena and found a camp of Filipino migratory workers. I decided to live and work with them, hoping to put my life in order. I had been fleeing from state to state, but now I hoped to gather the threads of my life together. Was there no end to this flight? I sharpened my cutting knife and joined my crew. I did not know that I was becoming a part of another tragedy.[17]

Almost always, Allos and his friends are run out of towns by economic need or threat. From paragraph to paragraph, Allos goes from Fresno toward Chicago, but stops off in Moscow, Idaho; from there, he goes to Cheyenne, Wyoming, and then to Billings, Montana, and finally to Helena, Montana. He nevertheless feels driven "fanatically toward" his unnamed "goal." This goal becomes lost in the movement from place to place, from one scene of the pizca to another. Peas, beets, fish canneries, and other industrialized agricultural settings produce a whirlwind narration. Often, as he notes, Bulosan and his friends are put to flight by vigilante mobs and corrupt police; just as often, he meets up with other Filipinos or Mexican Americans. Through it all, Allos hops freight trains and scrunches down in cars so often that *America* becomes a nightmarish road novel. And in each new setting, Allos learns something new: he meets new friends, learns a new method by which American farmers are hoodwinking farmworkers, sees new illnesses, finds people trapped or killed by vicious processes, and so on.

Early on in the novel, Allos alludes to everything that will come. The flashback narratively occurs in the midst of recounting his Binalonan childhood, thus producing an unsettling temporality: he interrupts the chapter's age-anchored perspective to jump forward in time and reflect, from a later vantage point, on what in his childhood would eventually prompt him to become a writer. In a California hospital being treated for tuberculosis, Allos thinks back to his childhood in the Philippines:

> It was midnight and the hospital was in total darkness. Far away in the city the lights were flickering like a string of pearls strung on the huge neck of a dark woman. And far away also, in the workers' republic of Spain, a civil war was going on that a democracy might live. I remembered all my years in the Philippines, my father fighting for his inherited land, my mother selling *boggoong* to the impoverished peasants. I remembered all my brothers and their bitter fight for a place in the sun, their tragic fear that they might not live long enough to contribute something vital to the world. I remembered my own swift and dangerous life in America. And I cried, recalling all the years that had come and gone, but my remembrance gave me a strange courage and the vision of a better life.
>
> "Yes, I will be a writer and make all of you live again in my words," I sobbed.[18]

Retroactively assigning his emergence as a writer to the vast web of people he has encountered and experiences he has undergone or witnessed, Allos sees the purpose of his writings—indeed, of his travels—as "mak[ing] all of you live again in my words." This realization is a structuring moment for the novel, emphasized by the anaphoric litany of "I remembered" that forms his declarations of artistic desire and the influence of fellow migrants; moments like this punctuate the novel's plot, offering a metafictional emphasis on the narrator's growth as an observer and writer while proleptically giving meaning to the often linguistically orphaned "goal" he refers to in various passages. Yet, at crucial inflection points in the novel, the goal is expressed as Allos's desire to become a writer, specifically as a means of revitalization. Moments like this, in *America*, firmly support Cheryl Higashida's claim that Bulosan, among other midcentury Asian American writers such as Hisaye Yamamoto, must "be studied within the multicultural politics of the Popular Front, especially as it pertains to Asian Americans." In Bulosan's time, "new social movements came into being that drew together anti-imperialist, anti-lynching, pro-union and labor feminist activists, and cultural workers. Popular Front multiculturalism flourished as African and Native Americans, immigrants, and their descendants articulated a new vision of democracy by recovering and re-evaluating their heritage."[19] As Allos is in his hospital bed, suffering from tuberculosis, *America*'s language transforms his "swift and dangerous life in America" into "a strange courage and the vision of a better life." The migrant pizcaresque describes precisely the "recovering and re-evaluating" that *America* produces as a textual participant in "Popular Front multiculturalism," at both the metafictional and the thematic level. In this, Allos the burgeoning writer—Bulosan?—shares the aims Hurston, Rukeyser, Babb, and Rivera elaborate in their own coalitional aesthetics of *speaking with*.

A bit later, while in the US, during one of the many bittersweet, sorrowful partings in the novel, Allos thinks directly of the accumulation of experience. There's a hint here, too, of the "composite" biography that scholars such as San Juan Jr., Isaac, and others have referred to:

> "Good-bye, Julio," I said. "And thanks for everything, Julio. I hope I will meet you again somewhere in America."
>
> Then the train screamed and the thought of Julio hurt me. I stood peering outside and listening to the monotonous chugging of the engine. I knew that I could never be unkind to any Filipino, because Julio had left me a token of

friendship, a seed of trust, that ached to grow to fruition as I rushed toward another city.[20]

The accumulation of experience, for Allos, gets emotionally distended through the paradoxical closeness and distance of the passage: the distance of the departure itself, emphasized by the act of "peering outside" and the "chugging of the engine," combines bittersweetly with the proximity of the "token of friendship" and the "seed of trust." This paradoxical feeling is fully encapsulated by the final phrase of that sentence: that seed of trust "ached to grow to fruition as I rushed toward another city." "Another city" is both the destination and the escape—there is a sense of moving closer to that "fruition," yet there is also the reality of departure and loss. Throughout *America*, ambivalence is the chief tenor of the imagery and plot movement.

This becomes remarkably clear when Allos encounters Julio again, in Seattle this time. Discovering that Julio is now a pickpocket, he argues with Julio about the value and morality of theft. Julio's response, however, is to declare that he is "an artist." Allos decides to observe Julio's process, helps him ward off suspicion, and then argues with Julio about what picking pockets could possibly do for fellow migrants. Julio takes an interesting tack: his "'pickings' are works of art."

> I followed him. How swift and nimble he was! Once, in a department store, he was almost caught. I hurried past him whispering in my dialect that he was being watched. His room was filled with inexpensive trinkets.
>
> "Why don't you sell it and use the money for something good?" I said.
>
> "You are distorting the art of picking pockets again," he said. "My 'pickings' are works of art. I use them for artistic expression only."
>
> His "pickings" were neatly arranged on the table, on the floor; and some of the cheap wrist watches were hanging on the bed post. I thought I had understood Julio when we walked across the Rattlesnake Mountains. But I was wrong. He was again a new personality, shaped by a new environment. I felt that I should leave him. I was angry that the old Julio was lost, for he had given me something, a kind of philosophy, which had sustained me for a long time.[21]

Allos describes Julio as a fellow peripatetic pícaro, observing that he had "again a new personality, shaped by a new environment." Julio's use of "again," which appears before the narrator's frustrated observation, indicates the work

Bulosan is doing within and against the picaresque: this is episodic, a continuation of (clearly frustrating) conversations that readers are not always privy to. Importantly, the "pickings" make Julio a *pizcador*—a picker or harvester—in a new setting and in an entirely new way. "Pickings" is a telling word choice, aligning Julio and Allos even as Allos offers critical words. Indeed, the intentional etymological connection made between picking and harvesting in this passage directly links "artistic expression" and labor. Although Allos rejects Julio, this is certainly a significant debate about art and the transvaluation of labor. Allos cannot accept Julio's viewpoint, perhaps because the objects are "arranged on the table, on the floor." Although it's done "neatly," they are not a composite or unified work of art. Allos sees them as too separate from each other, though, of course, these objects are formed into a descriptive collage, since they are united in Allos's focused narration.

Moments like this, of collection, contain particularly intriguing potential as ciphers for forms of collectivity. For scholars such as Benjamin Balthaser, collection speaks to Bulosan's broader ethos, especially as expressed through a journal he edited, *The New Tide*. Pointing out that in *America*, Allos and his friend and fellow labor organizer José print and distribute copies of *The New Tide* to fellow farmworkers (Bulosan describes how he and José "distributed [copies] to some of the more literate farm workers"[22]), Balthaser makes the following comparison:

> Like the stories and poems [in *The New Tide*] themselves, which cover spaces from New York City coffee-pots to colonial armies to immigrants' quarters to the houses of prostitutes, so too does the journal materially attempt to bridge the divide between urban literary Left and workers in the fields. It's also important to note that the journal was so self-consciously multiethnic and cosmopolitan that Bulosan would attribute a "Filipino social awakening" to its development. This kind of paradox for Bulosan, both racially determined and overdetermined at [the] same time, marks a distinct sensibility one witnesses among many of the writers of color in the Popular Front period.[23]

Although Balthaser is focused here on the importance of *The New Tide* to Bulosan's activism and art, it is notable how important the link is between the Popular Front and Bulosan's aesthetic goals, which were guided by the "multiethnic and cosmopolitan" vision of Bulosan's political and communal sensibilities.

Directly after his reencounter with Julio, as Allos recovers from various ailments, he encounters new friends and old family—two of his brothers in particular, who are also on the West Coast. He begins gambling quite a bit, realizing he's excellent at various card games; this helps him spend less time doing farm labor, though he is ambivalent about his gambling: he generally takes money from people who have been doing manual labor. But this is all part of Allos's slow march toward union organizing and becoming a writer, two things for which Carlos Bulosan himself has become famous. In another moment in the book when Allos is recovering from illness, he discovers that, after his significant and voracious reading, he can write pretty well in English.

> Then it came to me, like a revelation, that I could actually write understandable English. I was seized with happiness. I wrote slowly and boldly, drinking the wine when I stopped, laughing silently and crying. When the long letter was finished, a letter which was actually a story of my life, I jumped to my feet and shouted through my tears:
>
> "They can't silence me any more! I'll tell the world what they have done to me!"[24]

He declares that he has found a medium through which to bear witness, to transform his experiences and the experiences of others into language. While this is a declaration that he will "tell the world what they have done to me," it is also an affirmation of the novel's method of transforming many experiences into a single text: Allos is bearing witness to many, and not just on his own behalf. This becomes clear just a few pages later, when he talks to a friend named Jose. Importantly, Allos has started going by Carl at this point. In other words, right when he begins to learn to write in English, he briefly becomes Carl.

> Jose sat beside me on the green lawn. "I know what is in your mind, Carl," he said. "It's hard for me to explain to you. It is a long story. This is a war between labor and capital. To our people, however, it is something else. It is an assertion of our right to be human beings again, Carl. But in order for you to understand what this struggle means to me, I'll begin from the beginning of my life in the United States . . ."
>
> He began to tell me the story of his life, which was similar to mine.[25]

This straightforward summation—"the story of his life, which was similar to mine"—shows us the narrative logic of the novel and how the transformation of experiences occurs in it. Jose tells Allos/Carl that "in order for you to understand," he must tell the story "from the beginning" of his life. The book combines and compiles experiences, less an exercise in analogy and more a development of narrative through coalitional form: similarity is not analogy, in other words, largely because in itself similarity does not contain the argumentative structure of analogy. Similarity, however, does provide the impulse toward coalition: it is solidarity and coalitional recognition, above all else, that drive this union of stories in *America*.

Indeed, right after Jose unburdens himself to Allos/Carl, Allos's older brother Macario gives a speech. This speech, whose final paragraphs are quoted here, contains the heart of the novel's explicit political sensibilities:

> America is also the nameless foreigner, the homeless refugee, the hungry boy begging for a job and the black body dangling on a tree. America is the illiterate immigrant who is ashamed that the world of books and intellectual opportunities is closed to him. We are all that nameless foreigner, that homeless refugee, that hungry boy, that illiterate immigrant and that lynched black body. All of us, from the first Adams to the last Filipino, native born or alien, educated or illiterate—*We are America!*
>
> The old world is dying, but a new world is being born. It generates inspiration from the chaos that beats upon us all. The false grandeur and security, the unfulfilled promises and illusory power, the number of the dead and those about to die, will charge the forces of our courage and determination. The old world will die so that the new world will be born with less sacrifice and agony on the living . . .[26]

Ellipses end the passage and the chapter, suggesting openness or possibility—or, perhaps, the unspeakable, yet-to-come nature of Macario's desire. The language hinges on an apocalyptic vision of a "new world" that might be "born with less sacrifice and agony on the living." Before the image of the new world being born, though, Macario declares, boldly, "*We are America!*" Macario frames democracy in terms of coalition, togetherness, movement, discovery, and violence. This "we," for Macario, is America—for Allos, this is precisely why, as a writer, America *is in the heart*: the act of writing, of producing this coalitional novel, is an expression of spirit and also an aesthetic enactment of Macario's stated aims.

Notably, this passage is a remembered speech. For Allos the writer, the recollection of his brother's speech becomes part of a coalitional practice that sustains political radicalism. As with the "strange courage and the vision of a better life" described earlier in the book, Macario's speech concludes by turning to "courage and determination" in the service of a "new world . . . born with less sacrifice and agony on the living."

For Allos, who briefly becomes Carl and by the end of the novel has become Carlos, writing is a way to build the composite and transformed pícaro who is the subject of the migrant pizcaresque. As he notes near the novel's end, "The time had come, I felt, for me to utilize my experiences in written form. I had something to live for now, and to fight the world with; and I was no longer afraid of the past. I felt that I would not run away from myself again."[27] This coalitional logic of representation suggests a powerful direction that multiethnic fiction can take. Although Colleen Lye suggests that *America* is *not* an example of "critical realism" and is instead characterized thoroughly by "proletarian realism," I would suggest instead that it does fulfill the remit of a "critical realism in which the criticalness of Asian American identity lies in its representation not as a person or thing but as a social relation between persons."[28] Bulosan's migrant pizcaresque offers accretion and multiplicity, a tendency toward affiliation built through the coalitional aesthetics of *speaking with* as a discovery and privileging of a new "social relation between persons." For Keith, Allos/Carlos's "self-formation is thus defined, in the last instance, less by his ability to reassemble the story of his *personal* development than by his ability, ultimately, to *de*personalize himself and his story. Put differently, *America*'s narrative of development is based on the move from a personal to an impersonal voice—from an individual to a collective experience."[29] This is part of Bulosan's "future work," which according to Nadal is "an abiding compositional principle" that hinges on "the imaginative projection of socialist possibilities into the present."[30]

America's conclusion remains one of the most perplexing and talked-about moments in the text. The uplifting but no longer naïve message is hard-won but still seems out of place in a book as critical as *America*. Reading the ending through the idea of the migrant pizcaresque, however, suggests an approach through ambivalence and coalition that tempers the concluding moments. Although the ending is still an odic quasi-celebration of opportunity in the United States, it employs coalitional, collective language.

> The next morning I put my brother Macario's money in the bank, in his name, and went to the bus station. I wanted to catch the last crew of cannery workers in Portland. I looked out of the bus window. I wanted to shout good-bye to the Filipino pea pickers in the fields who stopped working when the bus came into view. How many times in the past had I done just that? They looked toward the highway and raised their hands. One of them, who looked like my brother Amado, took off his hat. The wind played in his hair. There was a sweet fragrance in the air.
>
> Then I heard bells ringing from the hills—like the bells that had tolled in the church tower when I had left Binalonan. I glanced out of the window again to look at the broad land I had dreamed so much about, only to discover with astonishment that the American earth was like a huge heart unfolding warmly to receive me. I felt it spreading through my being, warming me with its glowing reality. It came to me that no man—no one at all—could destroy my faith in America again. It was something that had grown out of my defeats and successes, something shaped by my struggles for a place in this vast land, digging my hands into the rich soil here and there, catching a freight to the north and to the south, seeking free meals in dingy gambling houses, reading a book that opened up worlds of heroic thoughts. It was something that grew out of the sacrifices and loneliness of my friends, of my brothers in America and my family in the Philippines—something that grew out of our desire to know America, and to become a part of her great tradition, and to contribute something toward her final fulfillment. I knew that no man could destroy my faith in America that had sprung from all our hopes and aspirations, *ever*.[31]

At the end, the "my" becomes transformed into "our." The novel's coalitional aesthetics shift the "me" into the "we" continually, and here in the final sentence the sentiment is, ultimately, communal. Nadal also notes this sensibility, arguing that Bulosan's use of "America," at the conclusion, "proffers an affiliative practice, one that amplifies US Popular Front laborism with the 'hopes and aspirations' of the Filipino peasantry."[32] For Balthaser, this concluding moment shows how "Bulosan's politics of inclusion are radically destabilizing, as the 'Americans' that Bulosan includes are the very colonial subjects" who were subjected to the US's extended rule until the very year that *America* was published.³³ Vials similarly reads the ending through unfixity, arguing that the book's conclusion "does not stake a claim to a fixed location in the US ('America' is to be viewed as a sensibility, after all), nor does it position the narrator as the quintessential American." In further focusing on the passage's language of "earth," "digging," "soil," and "broad," Vials argues that "Bulosan, as a Filipino author, is declaring his right to the authorship of a conventional, naturalized aesthetics of US nationalism," identifying a distance between the implications of "quintessential" and "authorship" that he finds crucial to destabilizing the book's potentially essentialist conclusion.³⁴ Notably, the language Vials picks up on is the grounded language of the pizca.

The sum of Allos/Carlos's experiences—summarized as "defeats and successes, something shaped by my struggles for a place in this vast land, digging my hands into the rich soil here and there, catching a freight to the north and to the south, seeking free meals in dingy gambling houses, reading a book that opened up worlds of heroic thought"—is in this final passage shaped through the language of the pizca. The migrant pizcaresque, then, gives form to Allos/Carlos's realization that the series of encounters in the novel have transformed the narratological possibilities of the "mozo de muchos amos" into the critical, coalitional form that *America* resolutely takes up.

Communal Imagination in . . . *y no se lo tragó la tierra*

The common understanding of Tomás Rivera's *Tierra* as an allegory reduces its hermeneutic and political possibilities and, indeed, undermines its coalitional potential by smoothing out the complexities of *speaking with* in favor of a unified aesthetic and political voice that can speak for Chicanxs.³⁵ The critical history surrounding *Tierra* (with several notable exceptions, particularly José E. Limón, John Alba Cutler, Alicia Schmidt Camacho, and Carlos Gallego) suggests that allegory is the surest way to account for the text's cultural specificity as well as its political message.³⁶ That, in other words, allegorization is how the text best expresses its concrete Chicanismo, while also showing that Chicanx struggles are universal human struggles. This critical tendency is achieved largely through the argument that the text represents a year that is lost and then found, "El año perdido / The Lost Year" (the title of the text's first segment), which Ralph Grajeda, in an early critical approach to the book, emblematically calls the book's "introductory selection."³⁷ *Tierra* contains fourteen named sections and thirteen short *estampas*, or impressions, that separate them. However, in the majority of the critical literature, it is argued that the text contains twelve stories, which correspond to the twelve months in a year, though they are seen as disordered rather than consecutively ordered months. The first and last stories are seen as framing stories, with the twelve stories between these two all taking place in the mind of the text's narrator, the unnamed young Chicano whose perspective introduces and then concludes *Tierra*. This is the way the text has been taught and described, for the most part, since its publication in 1971. Julián Olivares, the editor of Rivera's collected works, assumes the "twelve stories" position, as does Ramón Saldívar, whose excellent *Chicano Narrative* remains one of the classic studies of Chicano aesthetics. Julio Ramos and Gustavo Buenrostro, in their scholarly introduction to the text for a Latin American reading public, assert that the first and last sections

> enmarcan 12 historias correspondientes cada una a un mes del año en la vida del joven protagonista de la novela: "el año perdido." Esta intención estructural ya aparecía en un índice preliminar en que Rivera también había asignado al último texto el título alternativo de "El año encontrado."

> (frame 12 stories, each one corresponding to a month of the year in the life of the novel's young protagonist: "el año perdido / the lost year." This intention behind the book's structure was already apparent in a preliminary table of contents in which Rivera himself had assigned the final text the alternative title "The recovered year.")³⁸

Against the grain of this critical consensus (and even the prepublication archival record to which Ramos and Buenrostro refer), I argue that *Tierra* instead contains a vision of community that reimagines universality as relation rather than as substitutive allegory, a process elaborated through the book's coalitional aesthetics of *speaking with*. Moving away from a highly symbolic reading of *Tierra* does not depoliticize its Chicanidad; neither does it weaken the illustrative and identificatory power contained by the text's powerful representations of migrant and Chicanx life. This broadening provides a greater number of entry points and political possibilities, especially if contrasted to a reading that privileges the centralizing subjectivity of *Tierra*'s unnamed framing narrator.

Attending to *Tierra*'s multivocal, multiply dialogic construction reveals a text full of breaks, improvisations, and intimacies, all of which imagine the self within a framework of communal belonging. In what follows, I reassess the book's formal structure and closely track its capacious yet resolute articulations of communal belonging, especially through the untamable, vivifying multivocality of the *migrant pizcaresque*. We see Rivera constructing Chicano identity through a concrete and relational textuality of places, actions, and ideas. *Tierra* widens access to Chicanidad, making space even for marginal characters, voices, and actions in its coalitional process of *speaking with*, articulated in place of the *speaking for* of an ethnic bildungsroman. Particularly since the idea of universality (especially as it is paradoxically articulated through the idea of "the nation") has underwritten the degradation of migrants as unincorporable aliens, as well as the hierarchal racialization of humans and the exclusion or forcible rehabilitation of nonnormative identities, *Tierra* provides a significant model for *speaking with* a community in its shifting, flowing connection to the world and its contemporary contexts. *Tierra* creates and revels in particularity, in finding the small moments of dignity and humanity that undercut totality, even while affirming communal and political unity. Ultimately, in Rivera's text the performance of recollection and the imagination of a community's experiences become material and present rather than abstracted and mythically oriented.[39] Even further, these materialized memories and experiences form a fundament of praxis for building what is not yet known in conjunction with what is already known—and this praxis is communal and concrete, rather than abstract or individualistic.

Published at the height of Chicano nationalism, and winner of the inaugural Premio Quinto Sol, the first nationwide prize for Chicano writing, *Tierra* is written in the argot of Texan-Mexican Spanish. In a decade of widening academic and nonacademic engagement with Chicano literature, Quinto Sol Press's championing of *Tierra* was part of what Dennis López calls "the fight for self-determination, self-government, equality, justice, and political autonomy . . . [which] had to be waged not solely in the fields, on the streets, and in the barrios, but also in the intellectual and literary circles of the Academy and the publishing industry."[40] John Alba Cutler finds that *Tierra*, within the world of Quinto Sol Press and Chicano activism—a world that he argues is focused "not on the maintenance of a monolithic representational ideal of

Chicano/a culture, but the assertion and institutionalization of Chicanos' capacity to *produce* culture in its various forms"—notably "resists any monological reading" and "represents something other than the narrow nationalism that Bruce-Novoa and López ascribe to Quinto Sol."[41] That *Tierra* speaks to audiences in a timely as well as a transcendent fashion shows its enduring linguistic and imaginative power as a text that both instantiates and elaborates a Chicanx world.[42] *Tierra* is a text that, as Manuel M. Martín-Rodríguez argues convincingly, imagines a Chicanx readership by catalyzing a conversation around the question "of experiencing, of creating a shared [Chicanx] reality by reading."[43] In this sense, the migrant pizcaresque offers a metafictional critical form that hinges upon reading as an interpretive act as well as on the somewhat unstable production of meaning within the text itself.

Saldívar argues that "*Tierra* functions aesthetically and ideologically as a memorial to and partial reconstitution of the forgotten history of a people's oppression and struggles," suggesting that Rivera's intention is to monumentalize and therefore reify a materialist history of struggle.[44] Saldívar's deep, sympathetic reading of *Tierra* contributes crucially to the allegorical tendency in the book's literary criticism and at the same time situates the novel as one of the most subtly difficult and provocative texts in the Chicanx canon. Saldívar puts forth the claim that the text operates through a dialectical structure and philosophy in the way it situates ideologies of personal agency and subjectivity in agonistic relation to political awareness and obligation, ultimately synthesizing the poles into a critical historical consciousness. Says Saldívar, "With . . . the active subject's—the proletariat's—creation of the historical world as part of the dialectic of subject and object, comes the possibility of the articulation of an authentic class consciousness. Rivera does not offer us so much a story of personal redemption as an allegory of historical crisis."[45] With this reading of *Tierra* and its dialectical movement between subject and object in the service of creating (instructive or didactic) political allegory, Saldívar alerts us to Rivera's cultural embedding as a Chicano author writing at the height of Chicano nationalism. To monumentalize struggle in this way— imagining the book, not to mention the young narrator, as a memorial—is to encode and solidify it within a monolithic view of history determined by necessity; indeed, the only way this process can occur is through interpreting the young narrator as an allegorical representation of Chicanidad as a whole.

Although I dispute the consequences of Saldívar's claim, I nevertheless find that his criticism elucidates important elements of how ideological reproduction and resistance take place in the particular context of Chicanx letters.

The symbolic construction of the young narrator as an allegorical monument can lead one to make claims, as Scott A. Beck and Dolores E. Rangel do, that acknowledge but qualify the polyvocality of Rivera's text. Beck and Rangel assert that "Rivera responds to this hopeful context [Chicano activism] by presenting . . . a protagonist whose existential crisis leads to a personal liberating freedom rather than to oppressive resignation or social activism."[46] They go on, arguing that by the end of the book this protagonist's "only action is to climb a tree and wave to an imaginary playmate so as to confirm his own existence. Apparently change will come to this boy if he simply establishes his being and waits for the coming dawn."[47] Even as Beck and Rangel assert the complexity of *Tierra* in their essay, in their argument the young boy becomes the sole locus of identification and political possibility. They seem to take at face value, then, that the young narrator is a representative of nascent Chicano nationalism who activates political desires outside of the text.[48] Yet, as I argue, *Tierra* undoes allegory and situates the narrator less as a symbol of his community than as an interlocutor with it.

The book's fourteen multipage stories are separated by brief, untitled, interstitial paragraphs that appear on separate pages between the stories. In homage to the regional literature from which the text emerges, I call these interstitial paragraphs *estampas*, or impressions; Rivera himself called these sections "dialogue[s] or situation[s] . . . cuadros [portraits] which I placed between the stories to give the total work a cohesiveness that I thought was needed."[49] (To a certain degree, *Tierra* is comparable in form to Jean Toomer's 1923 *Cane* and Ernest Hemingway's 1925 *In Our Time*, especially in terms of interstitial, thematically connective sections between the main stories, whether in the form of poems, prose poems, or reflections.) The text begins and ends with a young boy, whom I will refer to as the text's "framing narrator," a descriptor that notes the young boy's presence as a voice in specific portions of the text. "Framing narrator" names a narrative position distinct from a persistently marked focalizing consciousness that appears in every text, thus offering a descriptive alternative to the text's dominant interpretation, which sees the young boy as the symbolic, unifying whole whose thoughts and words are constitutive of the text. Such an overarching allegorical conclusion must certainly be acknowledged as a possibility, but it must also be taken to its hermeneutically contradictory limits and moved beyond. José E. Limón makes a similar point in *Dancing with the Devil*, when he observes what I consider to be the only logical conclusion of the allegorical argument: that it captures only "the blood of masculinist universal reason which, while permitting him to question idealist religious metaphysics and dominating power, is nonetheless, itself, a complicit exercise of power." Limón goes on, arguing, "But before his growth into these final collective emancipating scenes, we recall his sheer indulgence in his Faustian-Mephistophelian moment when his desire to *know* is all. We need to recall his serenity at *his* own victory—*his* triumph. The moon hovered overhead for *him*, not yet for his people, not yet for a collective utopia, and the price for this is his erasure of another, nonutopian, communal, female-centered way of knowledge and politics."[50] I take Limón's point to be that Rivera's text in fact metafictionally considers the idea of the young boy as an allegorical stand-in for Chicanismo and rejects this reading as "sheer indulgence," as Limón puts it.

Rivera's method as a writer, as noted by many critics, was driven by his powerful sense of memory.[51] Eliud Martínez claims, "Tomás . . . was born to witness, to remember and to tell. An unusual memory is clearly evident in his literary work, which established a model for preserving the oral history of our people, in writing."[52] Álvaro Llosa Sanz argues that *Tierra* bears evidence of Rivera's use of a classical rhetorical strategy, which he calls "arte de la memoria": "Se establece por tanto un discurso retórico de arte de la memoria para fijar un pasado y proponer un futuro a partir de los momentos de cambio que sufre una comunidad." ([Rivera] establishes, therefore, a rhetorical discourse of "theater of the memory" in order to establish a past and propose a future that emerges from moments of change undergone by a community).[53] Far more interesting than whether Rivera's aesthetics are based on an inherent quality (his memory) or his erudition (his engagement with classical rhetoric) is the implication of his shifting, flowing position as a writer: he generates a communal and importantly coalitional dialogue that intriguingly refuses absolute authorial control and, as a consequence, the young narrator's control as well. Thus the densely expansive multivocality of *Tierra* bespeaks a matrix of intersecting movements and narratives, producing a map of many flights and trajectories. To maintain these many possibilities and their as-yet-unknown promise, the allegorical impulse must be refused.

When the voices in *Tierra* work themselves out, they break out of the frames of easy intention, *speaking with* each other in anarchic, self-determined ways that create a community of many voices and desires. In one of the estampas, after "La noche buena" and before "El retrato," we see, "Antes que la gente se fuera para al norte, el cura les bendicía los carros y las trocas a cinco dólares el mueble." (Before people left for up north the priest would bless their cars and trucks at five dollars each).[54] The priest makes enough money from these blessings that he's able to go to Spain, returning with letters and postcards in order to motivate his congregants toward his idealized ends: the construction of a new church, inspired by postcard images of what can safely be assumed to be Gaudí's Sagrada Familia. Yet, "Al poco tiempo empezaron a aparecer palabras en las tarjetas, luego cruces, rayas y con safos así como había pasado con las bancas nuevas. El cura nunca pudo comprender el sacrilegio." (It wasn't long before words began to appear on the cards, then crosses, lines, and con safos symbols, just as had happened to the new church pews. The priest was never able to understand the sacrilege.)[55] As Schmidt Camacho argues, "The 'spiritual strength' that Rivera records in the minute articles affixed to the postcards and church pews are not simply articulations of faith but enunciations of presence against erasure. Their small statements of self-possession, 'con safos,' resist the dehumanizing effects of their labor."[56] Schmidt Camacho here points out the nonreifiable actions of the parishioners: their actions or labor remain human in their resistance to the priest's attempts to "grasp" or "get" what they are doing. The people in the parish literally write themselves into the symbols of authority: they create spaces by marking them discursively, and they physically reshape the symbols and trappings of power by surrounding themselves with a semiotic web of their own making, a network that cannot and will not be understood by the priest. The sphere of signification, in other words, resists comprehension, eluding the grasp of the parish priest.

This is because Rivera's book *flows*—it does not stand still. Much like the migrants it depicts, it cannot be stilled. *Tierra* is a powerful and difficult celebration of Chicanx life in its varieties of experience. Thus, while it is certainly true that the young narrator becomes a chronicler of his community, it seems to me that he adds his experience to the many, thus speaking his story along *with* those of his friends and family and neighbors, rather than *for* them or *at* them—in this way, the labors and loves in the text are preserved in their difference, rather than assimilated by the young narrator. Yet the young boy narrator in *Tierra* seems to be the figure whose voice most often appears; after all, most of the estampas and stories *seem* to focus on a young boy's experiences. Not all do, though, and several are overheard stories, with framing dialogue at their conclusions. This is an issue complicated further by the fact that a very small proportion of the focalizing narrative voices are clearly those of older women, as well as older men, reciting memories to and with each other. Although I agree entirely with Saldívar's point that the narrator is a "witness," I find that constructing a dialectic of witness between "personal redemption" and "an allegory of historical crisis," as Saldívar does, distances *Tierra* from its radical political promise as a text of many voices, largely because it depends on the assumption of a single narrative consciousness. To put a fine point on this distinction: there is no unified or single narrator; rather, there are many narrator*s*.

In a passage from "Debajo de la casa / Under the House," the young narrator thinks to himself, "Y tengo tanto en que pensar y me faltan tantos años. Yo creo que hoy quería recordar este año pasado. Y es nomás uno. Tendré que venir aquí para recordar los demás." (And I have so much to think about and I'm missing so many years. I think today what I wanted to do was recall this past year. And that's just one year. I'll have to come here to recall all of the other years.)[57] This moment marks recollection as a specific, willed gesture that takes place in a specific space—beneath a house. Yet the "text-as-year" reading of the novel glosses over the distinction between, on the one hand, *recollection* or *recording*, and, on the other, *recapture*, or, as Grajeda puts it, the idea that "the twelve stories in a general sense are symbolic representations of the year that the protagonist attempts to recapture."[58] Recapture suggests that the memories are exclusively within the young narrator's experience and person—they are there to be *taken* and brought *back into the fold*. Recollection or recording, on the other hand, suggests a certain distance from memory as an object of narrative and the self. In other words, mediation occurs; there is a necessary difference between the self and the memory. Recording and remembering maintain this difference, whereas recapture is an absorptive interpretive metaphor predisposed toward allegory.

The Spanish, perhaps, makes this distinction clearer: the verb used is "recordar," typically translated as "remember" or perhaps "recollect." The narrator and the other voices in the text are equally authorial, creative, and imperfectly rendered, rather than "recaptured" as though they were all unified wholes to begin with. In essence, this distinction between recollecting/remembering/recording and recapture is precisely what the allegorical reading, as epitomized by the cyclical text-as-year reading, erases—and in order to do so, such a reading requires that the voices operate as native informants, rather than resonating on an autonomous frequency. Indeed, as Rivera himself argued in "Chicano Literature: Fiesta of the Living,"

> one has to go beyond prophecy and ritual and seek the nature of this bond in the act of remembering. Remembering, because the past is what we have and it is all we have. It is from the past that we are able to perceive, create, and give life of our ritual; it is from this that we derive strength, that we can recognize our existence as human beings. I think we also come to the realization that life is perhaps not simply a relationship between the world, ourselves, and others, but, in addition, the discovery and recollection of the relationship and these things.[59]

Here, Rivera not only identifies recollection as the act of memory but also gives it a spatial dimension: his use of "recollection" in the final sentence is both cognitive and physical in its connotation, particularly in its communally oriented usage. For Rivera, the self exists in and through relation, especially in "the discovery and recollection" of one's relationship with "the world, ourselves, and others."

Tierra's first story, "El año perdido / The Lost Year," begins with a young, unnamed boy feeling lost and expressing this internal chaos:

> Aquel año se le perdió. . . . Siempre empezaba todo cuando oía que alguien le llamaba por su nombre, pero cuando volteaba la cabeza a ver quién era el que le llamaba daba una vuelta entera y así quedaba donde mismo. . . . Una vez se detuvo antes de dar la vuelta entera y le entró miedo. Se dio cuenta que él mismo se había llamado. Y así empezó el año perdido.

> (That year was lost to him. . . . It always began when he would hear someone calling him by his name but when he turned his head to see who was calling, he would make a complete turn and there he would end up—in the same

place.... One time he stopped at mid-turn and fear suddenly set in. He realized that he had called himself. And thus the lost year began.)⁶⁰

This passage begins with a declaration of loss and a condensed description of interpellation. Initially, the young boy feels called, though he doesn't know by whom. Then he realizes that not only is he the recipient of this hailing, but he himself is also the symbolic figure doing the calling out. This would seem to support an allegorical reading of the text as a bildungsroman. After all, if the boy is alienated from himself, then the only way out is to transcend his alienation by synthesizing the voices and experiences of the text into himself: self and other are separate no longer, and *Bildung* has taken place. Yet I hesitate at this reading, particularly because, rather than opening out, it turns inward—or, I should say, this reading seeks to internalize everything exterior to the text. Indeed, the role of the creator/narrator/author, from this perspective, is self-justifying. In a text that is as antiauthoritarian, agnostic, and communally driven as *Tierra*, turning inward, rather than sublating the voices into a transcendental figure—itself a discomfiting conclusion—would subsume the voices into a speaking authority, a Leviathan-like sovereign made of the bodies of its subjects, which categorically speaks for them in order to empower them. Contrast this to Bartolo, the poet in the text's final estampa, whose poetry is spoken *to* and *with* the community, given his emphasis on reading poetry communally and aloud:

> Y cuando los leía en voz alta era algo emocionante y serio. Recuerdo que una vez le dijo a la raza que leyeran los poemas en voz alta porque la voz era la semilla del amor en la oscuridad.

> (And when he read them aloud it was something emotional and serious. I recall that one time he told the people to read the poems out loud because the spoken word was the seed of love in the darkness.)⁶¹

Vigil-Piñón's translation renders recollection central within this (re)telling, and what becomes clear is that the poems, when read aloud, become "the seed of love in the darkness" precisely because they are spoken with and among others—from one person with and to others.⁶² Importantly, too, Rivera himself based this fictionalized poet on "Bartolo, our town's itinerant poet."⁶³ The importance of Bartolo in the final estampa, right before the final story, shows the importance of multivocality in shaping a community's art, as contained within the voice of the lyric poet.

Bartolo's poetry stands in for *Tierra* more broadly, especially in how echoes of previous stories are represented as *overheard* rather than necessarily experienced by the narrator. In one of the early stories, "La mano en la bolsa / Hand in His Pocket," which seems to be an older man's recollection of a childhood trauma, the clear temporal separation of the narrative from the young framing narrator's experience establishes it as part of the text's communal dialogue.[64] After don Laíto and doña Bone, the story's antagonists, force the story's narrator—whose identity is unknown—to help them bury a migrant they murder, they present him with a small token of their gratitude, which then becomes a symbol of the terrifying hold they have over him:

> Me traían un presente. Un anillo. Me hicieron que me lo pusiera y recordé que era el que traía aquel día el mojadito. Nomás se fueron y traté de tirarlo pero no sé por qué no pude. Se me hacía que alguien se lo hallaba. Y lo peor fue que por mucho tiempo, nomás veía a algún desconocido, me metía la mano a la bolsa. Esa maña me duró mucho tiempo.
>
> (They had a present for me. A ring. They made me put it on and I remembered that it was the one the wetback had on that day. As soon as they left I tried to throw it away but I don't know why I couldn't. I thought that someone might find it. And the worst was that for a long time, as soon as I would see a stranger, I'd slip my hand into my pocket. That habit stayed with me for a long time.)[65]

It is still uncertain just who this narrator is in relation to the book's framing narrator. The story is presented not simply in the first-person perspective but as a story told to another—to the reader, perhaps, or maybe within the hearing of, or even directly to, the book's framing narrator.

Indeed, the story begins,

> ¿Te acuerdas de don Laíto y de doña Bone? Así les decían pero se llamaban don Hilario y doña Bonifacia. ¿No te acuerdas? Pues, yo tuve que vivir con ellos por tres semanas mientras se acababan las clases y al principio me gustó pero después ya no.
>
> (Remember Don Laíto and Doña Bone? That's what everyone called them but their names were Don Hilario and Doña Bonifacia. Don't you remember?

Well, I had to live with them for three weeks until school ended. At first I liked it but then later on I didn't.)[66]

The story begins with the second person: ¿Te acuerdas? Don't you remember? Establishing "La mano en la bolsa" as a recounted story in this way indicates its communal drive; moreover, we get a sense of the story's oral roots: there is inferred conversation, back and forth. "Remember? . . . Don't you remember? Well . . ." This is the beginning of a story, a prodding, an invitation to hear—or perhaps rehear—and engage with the story in order to create a shared space of communal meaning. The immediacy of the second person shows the importance of this story's "spokenness," as well as the oral culture that Rivera is trying to translate onto the page: "¿Te acuerdas?" Remembering, though, is not the only point: the act of telling the story, sharing it, so that it is overheard, activates the communal imagination.

In particular, the communal imagination activated and engaged by "La mano en la bolsa" responds to the story's central traumas: An older man is remembering himself as a young, scholarly boy. In the story, he gets manipulated, abused, and made an unwilling party to a murder by two people who promised his parents, who are traveling with the harvest, that they would give him food and shelter so that he could finish the school year. It is a story told aloud by the speaker in order to work through his trauma, especially as indicated by its conclusion, when he relates that the "hand in the pocket" habit stayed with him for years—it is something that has been laid aside as a secret, as untellable, but by relating it to others the speaker is able to take his hand out of the pocket and voice what has been silenced by fear and oppression. No longer bound and silenced by the ring and the abuse it represents, he is able to speak for himself, to speak himself. His story, no longer encircled by silence, becomes part of the communal fundament and imagination. Throughout *Tierra*, multivocality is constructed such that stories contain multiple others who are referred to directly rather than inferred. Especially at the rhetorical level, a polymorphous, multiply directed apostrophe shapes the possible routes of the text's reception and interpretation.

Multivocality is also expressed in *Tierra* through four estampas written as interstitial dialogues rather than as flash-fiction-like narratives; each of these is sudden, ephemeral, and laden with rumor, and touches on important migrant concerns. I will focus on the first dialogue, after *Tierra*'s second story, "Un rezo / The Prayer." This estampa's dialogue begins with a question: "Comadre, ¿ustedes piensan ir para Iuta?" (Comadre, do you all plan to go to Utah?)[67] In the Spanish, the name of the state is written "Iuta" (a phonetic rendering of the refamiliarizing "Utah" of the English translation), visually expressing its awkward unfamiliarity to the speakers. The other speaker responds, "Se nos hace que no hay ese estado. A ver, ¿cuándo ha oído decir de ese lugar?" (We don't think there's such a state. You tell me, when've you ever heard of that place?) The other speaker argues that since farm labor contractors are spreading the word, it's clear that Utah is, in fact, a real place. There are shades, in this conversation, of the bills and notices that flit in and out of *The Grapes of Wrath*, rumor and labor contracting being two of the hugest—not to mention most exploitative—drivers of migrant labor. The final touch of rumor in the dialogue closes it out, as the speaker who first raised the question of Utah, after being asked where it is, says, "Pos, nosotros nunca hemos ido pero dicen que queda cerca de Japón" (Well, we've never been there but I hear it's somewhere close to Japan).[68] Interestingly enough, Utah is part of the Mexican land that was ceded as a result of the US invasion of Mexico—not to mention the fact that the state is named after its dominant original inhabitants, the Ute nation. Utah is specifically included in the calls for Aztlán's *reconquista* made by some militant Chicanos at the time of *Tierra*'s publication. Yet rather than showing a divorce between proletarian Mexican American farmworkers and revolutionary Chicano nationalists, this dialogue centers its critique on the material labor practices and neoliberal power relations that not only alienate laborers from the means and modes of production but also remove the land, as both a literal and metaphorical place, from the people that live and labor on it. Furthermore, the "queda cerca de Japón" possibly illuminates Utah's connection to Japanese American removal during World War II: the Topaz Relocation Center, located just west of the center of the state, was where a total of over 11,000 people were incarcerated from the fall of 1942 until the fall of 1945.[69]

At this point, I would like to refocus on the fact that *Tierra* contains fourteen stories. Buenrostro notes that when Rivera first sent the book to the Premio Quinto Sol prize committee for consideration, it contained thirteen main stories, which were then expanded to eighteen, after which a final form of fourteen took shape and was published. In addition, as Ramos and

Buenrostro remind us, Julián Olivares (who edited and compiled the definitive edition of Rivera's collected works) has shown that the story initially in the final position was "Cuando lleguemos / When We Arrive"—what is now the penultimate story in the published version.[70] "Cuando lleguemos" is the most demonstrably multivocal of the text's stories: fourteen separate voices speak in this story, all of them belonging to people stuck in a broken-down truck on a migrant journey. The number of voices offers a suggestive parallel, especially given the fact that it was written after all of the other stories. This would certainly emphasize the book's overall coalitional aesthetics, especially given the narrative structure "Cuando lleguemos" takes. Indeed, it is a distinct possibility that these fourteen voices in the truck are connected to the other stories, whether through participation or conversation. If the book had concluded with "Cuando lleguemos" rather than "Debajo de la casa," this would open up a different potential critical history, one that perceived the many voices—expressed both silently and aloud—as separate yet communal, rather than being focalized through the unifying, meditative consciousness of the young boy beneath his neighbor's house in "Debajo de la casa"; this is perhaps a negligible difference, though, given that "Debajo de la casa" emphasizes the art of dissemination and recollection within *Tierra*'s narrative logic, and both Bartolo and the unnamed young boy work through and contain multiple stories in their respective imaginations. Bartolo, as a hinge between "Cuando lleguemos" and "Debajo de la casa," offers multiple, suggestive routes that *speaking with*, as a coalitional aesthetic, can take as *Tierra* works toward the reconstitution of its community.

Additionally, what intrigues me about the number fourteen is that it suggests a sonnet, with each story analogous to a line. I will not call *Tierra* a sonnet in prose form, especially given the sonnet's status as a monovocal expression of the lyric self. However, I will insist that thinking of the book as more *akin* to a sonnet than a year provides a willful, creative, improvisatory mode of hermeneutic entry that attends to the book's dialogic, flexibly connective structure and moves us away from a strict, teleologically oriented and symbolically enclosed narrative. Comparing *Tierra* to a sonnet—while not insisting that this formal structure directly informs the meaning of the text— gives us an idea of it as a unity outside of the teleological and metaphysical inscriptions required by allegory. That is, the text can operate as a community of stories and voices rather than as a unified field represented by a spokesperson who has been formed through allegory. I would like to go further and suggest that *Tierra*, if it is sonnet-like—but, again, not a sonnet as such—uses something like a turn or volta to query, reconsider, and take off from what precedes it; in this way, it is quite unlike the lyrically unified, monologic sonnet of the literary tradition. This unmooring of *Tierra*'s telos—suggesting that the ending is a "turn" rather than a "recapture" or "recapitulation"—moves the idea of unity away from an allegorically reified young boy and toward a more truly communal ethos and aesthetics.[71]

This especially holds true if we consider that the echoes of previous stories are *overheard* rather than necessarily experienced by the narrator. Nicolás Kanellos, in a reading of *Tierra* through his expertise in theater and drama, argues that the idea of dialogue, especially as overheard, rehearsed, and laid out on the page, is the most important function of the book. Says Kanellos, "Thus, of the different narrative devices utilized in [*Tierra*], the one that most effectively and with the greatest impact communicates the life-style, worldview, and culture of the Chicanos is dialog. That is, the testimony of the people themselves, with their most candid and humble voices, is the factor that makes this novel one of the most powerful pieces of Chicano art."[72] The many voices work to construct a topological text that makes connections and revels in intimacies that are not possible within the allegorical mode. The idea of the text as a manifold finds its most startling and intriguing consequence when we read *Tierra*'s final story. In this final story, all of the previous stories are recollected, but new, previously unheard and unread details and voices—many of them from excised stories that appear in earlier drafts of *Tierra*—emerge as each story reemerges. Thinking of the text's rhymes and resonances might also give an indication as to why two of the three estampas that contain dialogue are written directly after stories in which the Korean War figures prominently. Why is dialogue being used after two texts in which sons are lost to war? Is there a reconstituting or ameliorative purpose to the dialogues? In a text that seems overwhelmingly male and overwhelmingly young, there are related sections that focus on the oppression of women and on the ignored wisdom of a community's elders. There are wonderful, emergent possibilities in the idea that the text may be analogized to a sonnet, but one in which the lyric is constructed as communal rather than singular through the presence of an irrepressible number of voices, relationships, and narratives.

Tierra's final story marks recollection as a willed gesture that occurs in a specific place—beneath a house. In his allegorical reading of the text, Grajeda argues that the cyclical nature of the book operates according to a logic of recapture (a conclusion shared by many critics)—the boy must enfold the rest of the text into himself. Says Grajeda, "The voice we hear is not that of an individual hero intent on discovering and expressing his own subjective reality, but of a Mexican American—a *pocho*—in the significant process of discovering and embracing representatively his community's experience and culture. The end toward which the narrative is directed is a social identity."[73] Llosa Sanz argues:

> Sólo entonces nos damos cuenta realmente de que la función de este personaje, personaje que identificamos ya con el del primer capítulo, es el de reunir en sí todo lo anteriormente disperso, mediante un ejercicio de integración que se realiza en la memoria.
>
> (Only then [at the very end of the novel] do we really note that the function of this character, whom we have identified as the character from the first chapter, is to reunite in himself all that previously was scattered; this occurs through an integrative process realized through his memory.)[74]

For both Grajeda and Llosa Sanz, communalism can take place only through the subsumption of the stories into the young boy's consciousness—he is, essentially, a prophetic figure whose "coming into consciousness" is in actuality the creation of a universal and final signifier through which all meanings and narratives are unified. For Olivares, the idea of unity is central to *Tierra*, and he describes the framing narrator's self as growing from an isolated voice to a union of many stories in one "collective personality." This is resonant with the idea of the narrator as a composite, similar to my assessment of Bulosan's *America*:

> Symbolically, the protagonist's revelation points to that unity that Rivera himself searches for in the creative process. The author creates a character who, in turn, is a creator. On recreating the experiences of his people, the youngster creates himself in his own discovery. He arrives at a communion with the "other" which is the collective humanity of his people. The youngster's *I* grows larger than himself, leaving behind the solitary self and becoming a collective personality.[75]

Although it is counterintuitive, reading *Tierra* against the grain of allegory unfetters the text from expected frames of reception and understanding, confronting us with "the discomforting fact that the natives are no longer staying in their frames."[76] The text, as an anarchic dialogue of many voices speaking their own truths, should not be read to ascertain an authentic or heroic Chicano self; rather, it might be taken as an example of how self-determined spaces of speech and action emerge from a communal articulation of Chicanidad in its multiplicity.

In "Debajo de la casa," voices move in and out of the narrative, italicized and separated by ellipses; they appear as fragments of conversation, spoken either to the framing narrator or within his hearing. This narrator is beneath a house—underground, away from society—where he lets memories flow through him.[77] As mentioned above, in this final story all of *Tierra*'s previous vignettes come together within the narrator's consciousness.

> *Bueno, y ¿qué es el precio del estaño ahora? ¿Por qué no se vienen con nosotros la próxima vez? . . . ya se está viniendo el frío. Te apuesto que mañana va a amanecer todo el suelo parejito de escarcha. Y fíjate como las grúas ya pasan cada rato . . . el domingo va a haber casamiento. De seguro nos van a dar cabrito en mole con arroz y luego luego el baile, y el novio bien desesperado porque se venga la noche . . . fíjese, comadre, que nos asustamos tanto anoche que se apagaron las luces. Estábamos jugando con los niños cuando de repente todo oscuro. Y luego que no teníamos ni una velita.*
>
> *(And tell me, what's the price of tin these days? Why don't you all come with us next time we go? . . . The cold weather is setting in. I'll bet you that tomorrow morning the ground will be all covered with frost. And notice how often the cranes fly by . . . There's going to be a wedding Sunday. For sure they'll serve us cabrito in mole sauce, with rice, and then the dance, and the groom, anxious for night to arrive . . . I tell you, comadre, we got so frightened last night when the lights went out. We were there playing with the children when all of a sudden it was pitch dark. And we didn't even have one candle.)*[78]

All of the words in the passage relate to previous stories, and while some repeat information from previous stories, others add on to what we already know. In every case, the words can be considered overheard speech that the framing narrator then remembers. Entirely in italics, this stream-of-consciousness passage contains the actual voices of the storytellers themselves, not the young narrator's as he hides beneath a house, thinking about all the stories he's been told. He does not speak them aloud—rather, he goes over them, he brings the scenes back to life and repeats them—he re-collects them. The difference between the snippets that are anchored in the published text and those that convey words and information not present in the stories or estampas must be taken seriously; that difference marks these memories as active, as evading narratorial and readerly control.

"Debajo de la casa" continues, the river of memories flooding the narrator's mind. The passage below is taken by most critics to be the ethical and political center of the novel, and it has shaped the claim that the young narrator must be read as a symbol for Chicano political consciousness:

> —Quisiera ver a toda esa gente junta. Y luego si tuviera unos brazos bien grandes los podría abrazar a todos. Quisiera poder platicar con todos otra vez, pero que todos estuvieran juntos. Pero eso apenas en un sueño. Aquí sí que está suave porque puedo pensar en lo que yo quiera. Apenas estando uno solo puede juntar a todos. Yo creo que es lo que necesitaba más que todo. Necesitaba esconderme para poder comprender muchas cosas. De aquí en adelante todo lo que tengo que hacer es venirme aquí, en lo oscuro, y pensar en ellos. Y tengo tanto en que pensar y me faltan tantos años. Yo creo que hoy quería recordar este año pasado. Y es nomás uno. Tendré que venir aquí para recordar los demás.
>
> (I would like to see all of the people together. And then, if I had great big arms, I could embrace them all. I wish I could talk to all of them again, but all of them together. But that, only in a dream. I like it right here because I can think about anything I please. Only by being alone can you bring everybody together. That's what I needed to do, hide, so that I could come to understand a lot of things. From now on, all I have to do is to come here, in the dark, and think about them. And I have so much to think about and I'm missing so many years. I think today what I wanted to do was recall this past year. And that's just one year. I'll have to come here to recall all of the other years.)[79]

For Saldívar, this passage indicates the ultimate political coherence of *Tierra*, especially visible in the "great big arms" that "embrace them all." This reading makes perfect sense. Yet I strongly believe that interpreting the novel's ultimate gesture as one of allegorical unification suggests its own erasure. By this I mean that the different voices, if they are unified within the voice and mind of the narrator in the service of allegory, are necessarily melded and made identical; this is the case even, as Saldívar has convincingly shown, as *Tierra*'s complex political portrait of Chicanx self-understanding searches for and finds an aesthetic form that can appropriately shape the ideological imperatives of emergent Chicanidad. For Stuart Hall, in his critique of Althusser, it is important to recognize how "every social practice is constituted within the interplay of meaning and representation and can itself be represented. In other words, there is no social practice outside of ideology. However, this does not mean that, because all social practices are within the discursive, therefore there is nothing to social practice *but* discourse."[80] Where I part ways with Saldívar, then, is that his reading leads—as do most readings of *Tierra*, to be clear—to a symbolic and discursive unification at the end of the book that displaces its actual concluding paragraphs: the symbol of an imagined embrace, which is in fact neither the conclusion nor the final gesture described in *Tierra*.

Indeed, the embrace and the ability to "talk to all of them again, but all of them together," the narrator notes, can occur "only in a dream," reinforcing the immateriality of allegory. Even more, and this is quite important, to suggest that this embrace is the novel's final gesture denies the novel's *actual* ending gesture:

> Había encontrado. Encontrar y reencontrar y juntar. Relacionar esto con esto, eso con aquello, todo con todo. Eso era. Eso era todo. Y le dio más gusto. Luego cuando llegó a la casa se fue al árbol que estaba en el solar. Se subió. En el horizonte encontró una palma y se imaginó que ahí estaba alguien trepado viéndolo a él. Y hasta levantó el brazo y lo movió para atrás y para adelante para que viera que él sabía que estaba allí.

> (He had made a discovery. To discover and rediscover and piece things together. This to this, that to that, all with all. That was it. That was everything. He was thrilled. When he got home he went straight to the tree that was in the yard. He climbed it. He saw a palm tree on the horizon. He imagined someone perched on top, gazing across at him. He even raised one arm and waved it back and forth so that the other could see that he knew he was there.)[81]

The image of connection sketched out is one that maintains difference, suggesting that the connections between nodes of difference—both subjects and objects—form the material of the world. The final gesture in the book is not an embrace but a wave. This gesture hinges on difference, and it does so in a way that suggests a completely alternative creative agency, especially pertaining to others. Martín-Rodríguez argues with respect to this final wave that "we as readers are the ones who see him 'writing' in the air, moving his arm to signal, to affirm our private, soundless communication."[82] Though Martín-Rodríguez labels the wave a "private" gesture between the writer and the individual reader, to me the wave seems larger in scope: it is an extroverted and public gesture. It is a hailing, a calling into communication and discourse, in addition to a readerly affirmation. This recalls Lye's description of a critical realism devoted to building the "social relation between persons," in which, as I have argued against the grain, *America* is a significant predecessor.[83] In *Tierra*, the young boy is a storyteller and artist, a narrator who, like Rivera, speaks *with*, rather than *for*, his *compañeras* and *compañeros*, enunciating a communal politics that insists on fierce particularity. What I offer here is a critique of the means through which allegory is too often used in an instructional or indicative sense, and a suggestion that the novel does something else entirely in its transformative migrant pizcaresque.

To maintain the particularity and dignity of the individual voices in *Tierra* (even if they are unnamed) is not to capitulate to bankrupt ideologies of dehistoricized or sovereign individuality; neither is my criticism of an allegorical reading meant to disestablish the important political work done on the level of the communal and the historical, especially given the foundational Chicanx studies work that emerged thanks to literary critical engagements with *Tierra*. Instead, I would like to situate myself beside this binary and invoke the radical potential of *Tierra* as a text built through and in the service of *speaking with*. In this reading, the possibility of allegory remains, although it is not the only signifying and symbolically determinative narrative operation.[84] Rivera's *Tierra* generates meanings both about and for Chicanxs, and it does this through its aesthetics of *speaking with*. Paying particular attention to the routes of multiplicity in *Tierra* also makes the text a forum that convenes in multiple forms and venues. As Eliud Martínez says, "Rivera's characters feel deeply. They know love and they dream. . . . Rivera the storyteller conveys their bewilderment, the awe and wonder they experience on migrant journeys to unfamiliar places like Utah and Minnesota."[85]

In *Tierra*, Rivera examines, materializes, and makes a geography of interstitial, minor, intimate, urgent moments in order to instantiate what Homi Bhabha calls "those moments or processes that are produced in the articulation of cultural differences . . . [that] initiate new signs of identity, and innovative sites of collaboration."[86] Especially as a migrant author writing about migrant communities, Rivera is careful to create a text that enables dignity—that speaks *with* a community, rather than *for* or *to* it. *Tierra* is irreducible in its multiplicity, and moving away from a monumentalizing, allegorical reading of *Tierra* allows us to see how the characters flow and move. People and voices cannot be easily tracked down, reduced, or reified, and this differential and autonomous strategy is of paramount importance for a community when it comes to asserting its empowerment, its dignity, and its freedom.

All This and More

What *Tierra* and *America* do above all is function through coalition to bring into being spaces for protest and feeling that might not be legible to or accessible from prevailing national and nationalist discourses. Refusing the allegorical impulse when encountering *Tierra* becomes more than merely a reading position or an interpretive claim; this refusal becomes as much an act of creating autonomous spaces for existence and articulation as one of resisting the impulse toward competing, hegemonic essentialisms. This is the reason the picaresque, in Rivera's and Bulosan's hands, becomes the *migrant pizcaresque*. Indeed, there is so much happening within *Tierra* and *America* that to attempt to reify or pin down these texts within a stable, discursive field removes the imagination, empathy, and creativity of both artists, as well as their audiences and their subjects. Vazquez, describing the enormity of archives and the particular methodological challenges inherent to approaching moving (in every sense of the word) texts, uses the term "all this" to gesture to the often overwhelming complexity of the world we live in, and the equally complicated and daring art that attempts to describe it: "By 'all this,' I mean these indescribable but present symptoms of being messed up, the inherited distortions of past and present. . . . I refuse to transform the difficulty of 'all this' to a smooth political utility, to a singular and pragmatic program to correct a situation that demands flexibility and multiple forms and forums."[87] Acknowledging issues of both critical position(ality) and the status of textuality, Vazquez illuminates the need to bring flexibility to the task of interpretation and engagement.

Ultimately, *Tierra* and *America* show that there are new—or, if not new, then largely unacknowledged—modes of communal politics that are not about elaborating obviously Gramscian counterhegemonies or decisively revolutionary vanguards. Instead, these texts are subtler forms of coalition—each author seeks to address counterpublics in such a way that any sort of politics begins from within, even as it is elaborated through solidarity with other movements. These small yet wondrous coalitions move and evade discursive capture in their search for empowerment. In the case of *Tierra*, this means asserting the fundamental dignity of the people who work in America's homes and fields. For *America*, it means creating a capacious engagement with literary history according to which the author can find a way of *speaking with* fellow migrant laborers; the "mozo de muchos amos" fundament of the picaresque protagonist becomes transformed by *America*'s multivocal, coalitional aesthetics.

5. *This Bridge Called My Back* and the Shape of Dialectics to Come

ALTHOUGH IT HAD ALREADY BEGUN in the 1960s and 1970s, the 1980s saw the more or less inevitable transition of the aesthetic strategies of *speaking with*, from a firm couching in the coalition ethos of the long Popular Front to the multiculturalism of institutions, especially academic and political ones. The emergence and consolidation of multiculturalism, however, still maintained a strongly residual—and perhaps, as I show below, competingly dominant—coalitional ethos, especially as a historical antecedent. *This Bridge Called My Back* (henceforth, *Bridge*) is a central connecting thread between coalitional and multicultural aesthetic modes, offering an important combination of the two as a response to the ethnic and racial nationalisms of the 1960s and 1970s, as well as the emergence of cultural studies in and after 1968.[1] As the editors and contributors to *Bridge* noted, however, the transition to academic spaces was anything but easy: women of color were often treated as dilettantes or as ignorant, and the scholarship they produced was often seen as ancillary or as ethnographic or sociological in both intent and practice. *Bridge* contains the friction within, across, against, and outside academic institutions, generating a decidedly coalitional approach of *speaking with* to engage in multiculturalist debates about the constitution of ethnic studies, lesbian and gay studies, gender studies, literary history, theology, poetry, life writing, philosophy, and political theory.

AnaLouise Keating emphasizes the friction *Bridge* worked through, arguing that while "scholars regularly use this book to *illustrate* the diversity and differences among women, they almost never employ the theories within *Bridge as* theory—as part of their own theorizing process. Nor do they integrate contributors' most radical lessons into their own lives and intellectual traditions."² It is not enough to use *Bridge* as a mere stand-in for diversity, difference, and inclusion: we need to take quite seriously the anthology's incisive and radical contributions to theory. That is, the anthology *is not* a receptacle for the encyclopedic entries of a variegated group of native informants, whose words will grant us access to the diverse interiorities of women of color in general and US Third World feminists in particular. The anthology *is not* a checklist, and it *is not* a roll call. Its theoretical work must not be attributed solely to its expansive representation of voices—though this is undeniably important, especially given the enforced exclusion of women of color in so much of academic discourse. As Teresa de Lauretis has noted, *Bridge*, along with the 1982 anthology *All the Women Are White, All the Blacks Are Men, but Some of Us Are Brave*, is a signal part of "the shift in feminist consciousness" that pinpointed and then offered a corrective to "feminism's complicity with ideology, both ideology in general (including classism or bourgeois liberalism, racism, colonialism, imperialism, and, I would also add, with some qualifications, humanism) and the ideology of gender in particular—that is to say, heterosexism."³ Here, de Lauretis distinguishes complicity from adherence, suggesting that complicity is a result of socially reproduced divisions and contradictions. The contributors to *Bridge* offer a key feminist-of-color critique of mainstream feminism's potential coloniality, while also articulating a cross-class and cross-contextual refusal of heterosexism. Michael Hames-García, however, cautions against seeing texts like *Bridge* as emerging simply from or against white feminist movements. Citing de Lauretis, among others, Hames-García notes that too many scholars of queer theory "erase people of color from the center of debate in order to reintroduce them later at the margins of gay and lesbian theory."⁴ *Bridge* is not a reaction, in other words. Shane Phelan has argued that for many women of color theorizing their positions vis-à-vis ideological discourses of power and belonging, there emerges "a unity precisely in their position as nonwhite in a white supremacist society; theirs is a unity of opposition." While this is certainly true in many instances, it is a statement that assumes critique is nontransformative; Phelan, therefore, elaborates this claim by noting that this is "a move forward, away from the dominance of modeling-type theories to a more concrete, more local, but also more specific and comprehensive way of doing theory."⁵ *Bridge*, while often oppositional, is an anthology dedicated to elaborating a coalitional approach to creative writing, political opposition, and original epistemologies through which to understand the world, generate critique, revitalize archival studies, and more.

My intervention in academic and activist discussions of *Bridge*—which are often characterized by the argument that ethnic representation and diversity are in themselves remedies to an enforced universalism based in whiteness, maleness, and straightness—shows how representation is never enough, and that what Anzaldúa and Moraga's radical anthology offers is multiplicity and multivocality as processes, not as products, of radical politics. *Bridge* is enmeshed in an already emergent critique, in other words, not indebted to or springing from a preexisting feminist or leftist intellectual heritage. Indeed, I see *Bridge* as yet another starting point, even as it signals a waning of the Popular Front. As an anthology and as a cultural object of enormous implications, *Bridge* is deeply coalitional, and it is deeply multicultural; it is invested in internationalist feminist visions of race and class relations even as it is linked indelibly to and in deep conversation with US academic and activist enterprises. In this, I counter what Greil Marcus, in *The Shape of Things to Come*, observes regarding American revolutionary discourse: "Out of a throng of selves, what is one body of prophecy? Before it is anything else it is a single American, claiming his or her birthright, as a single body standing in, if only for a moment, for all other Americans."[6] Marcus's book, which studies the fiery and prophetic literature of American "prophets" (from John Winthrop to Allen Ginsberg) from its post–September 11, 2001 vantage point, focuses on those who stand alone and speak out. *Bridge* refuses this typology of singularity and loneliness, as well as the form of unity contained in Marcus's description of "a single body standing in . . . for all other Americans." *Bridge* opts instead for a necessarily coalitional, multiply voiced critique, refusing the temptation to embody a chosen, voice-from-the-mountaintop strain in American speech and writing. The anthology is not quite a jeremiad, in other words, even as it offers rousing condemnations of racism, capitalism, and colonialism.

Bridge ought to be considered a monumental intervention in literary theory and philosophy.[7] This intervention takes place most visibly, though not solely, on the order of the anthology's important work in making visible the experiences, ideas, poetries, and histories of women of color in the US and the Americas. Though this work in representation and representativeness has challenged scholarly norms (especially in terms of pedagogy and inclusion), it is also necessary to take stock of the monumental rethinking of systems and canons of thought that takes place on the order of the book's shape: its argumentative and narrative arc; its organizational tactics, in the sense of how conversations and dialogues are situated and practiced within and throughout the text; and, finally, its radical and radicalizing arguments against verticalized, teleological theorizations of revolution and progress, and its insistence instead on a reevaluation of transformation as a horizontalized praxis of revolution. In these ways, *Bridge*'s formal and thematic construction establishes a praxis for deliberately shaping a critical space in which transformative thought and action can take place through the deliberative acts of *speaking with* staged throughout—and as—the anthology. Indeed, *speaking with* offers a means of interacting with the theoretical approaches suggested by the anthology's contributors, as well as the broader theoretical importance of the anthology's labor.

Coalitional Aesthetics as Mosaics

I will proceed by taking a step back and situating *Bridge* by way of Estela Portillo's September 1973 edited collection of Chicana writers for Quinto Sol Press's journal *El Grito*. Quinto Sol referred to this collection as "Book 1" of the *El Grito* book series, and it was shorter than and numbered differently from its previous journal issues. Importantly, *El Grito* had been a journal releasing four issues a year for six consecutive years, until Portillo's collection inaugurated a new turn toward the publication of four distinct edited collections or anthologies. Most scholars call this fruit of Portillo's editorial work a "special issue" or, sometimes, an "anthology."[8] Portillo, a strange, innovative, and woefully underdiscussed author from El Paso, Texas, was in the 1970s considered a leading Chicana writer, a status reinforced by her honorary mention for the Premio Quinto Sol, a prize that was won, during its brief existence, by Tomás Rivera, Rudolfo Anaya, and Rolando Hinojosa. Regarding the collection's introduction, Naomi Quiñonez argues that "Portillo's analysis clearly shows that before Chicanas embraced and re-inscribed a feminist analysis, women proved to be susceptible to qualifying themselves in traditional terms, even if they were doing something quite revolutionary."[9] Portillo does indeed claim, in her introduction to the edited collection, that women are linked to the Earth in eternal, cyclical patterns, and that their perspective is more naturalistic, carrying within it a "singular degree of verity." Even so, I hesitate to follow Quiñonez's description of Portillo's work in the edited collection as traditionalist, especially when considering the *enacted process of anthologizing* itself, through which she destabilizes initial claims of essentialism or singularity.

In the introduction (figure 7), Portillo relies on terms and repetitions that emphasize a visually inflected rhetoric of interconnectivity through distinction. "Each and every one of the writers," Portillo writes, "mixes a personal reality with a world of inwardness. The evocations of feeling are the vivid colors in the human experience. Each finite center is a mosaic."[10] Portillo's

> shaping "silent thought." Each and every one of the writers mixes a personal reality with a world of inwardness. The evocations of feeling are the vivid colors in the human experience. Each finite center is a mosaic.
>
> There are many other offerings in this book. There is the marvelous physical energy of Adaljiza Sosa Riddell who draws from that same energy to give us a newness of spirit. Her personal idiom is not of abstractions. Her poetry has a magical obedience to life that spells out the genius of a Chicana "que es muy gringa."
>
> The substance of self-assertion as a woman and as a writer varies in the inlaid patterns of each individual reality. From the barrio experience made organic in hope and faith by Ramona González to the inward struggle of Lorenza Calvillo Schmidt in "Birth." Here, a finite center creates a pain that purifies. Her poem is an intimate, temporal condition of death and birth in simultaneous convergence. The pattern is clear . . . from womb darkness, to womb fever, to womb freedom. As bas-relief for our many colored pattern, are the remembrances, simple and brief, of Isabel Flores, Hortencia Susana Pérez, and María Cristina Sánchez. They successfully present lovely framed images. Another differing element is the torrential tale of Socorro Jáuregui's "El Bastardo." It is a swift wind of ill chance and reconciliation.
>
> A very distinct part of the mosaic are the complex forms of Minerva López Caples whose story, "Donde No Hay Pasado" offers a psychological study of memory and "Now," and the poetic, intellectual solidity of Angélica Inda. Both writers deal expertly with counterpuntal motifs. Minerva López Caples intermingles illusion, memory, and reality with acrobatic skill in a tale where "El fantasma de niñez" looks through a series of mirrors that leaves the reader wondering "What is illusion? What is reality?" Angélica Inda speaks of "punctured glass" in one glimpse of life. Her poetry has a surrealistic taste. She offers distorted, but beautiful relationships. Shapes with a depth that counters. One gets the feeling that her poetry must be read silently, like a puzzle, a game where one depth is a door to another depth. "Lo que llamamos arte es juego," says Octavio Paz. And the game, he believes, is the attempt to erase the barriers between art and life. Angélica Inda plays the game intellectually well.
>
> Included in the patterned pieces, is an excerpt from my three-act musical comedy, *Morality Play*. It too makes a game of Civilization

Figure 7. Partial reproduction of "Introduction" to *Chicanas en la literatura y el arte*, El Grito Book Series No. 1, page 6. Estela Portillo, September 1973. Open Door Archive at Northwestern University, https://opendoor.northwestern.edu/archive/items/show/378.

generalizing statement—"each and every one of the writers"—becomes elaborated and also contradicted through a rhetoric of distinction, in which "each finite center" creates "a mosaic." Portillo continues, suggesting that each piece varies according to "the inlaid patterns of each individual reality," noting how multiple contributions contain "counterpuntal [sic] motifs" and "patterned pieces."[11] This visual language perhaps recalls the collage aesthetics of modernism, which would be in keeping with Portillo's longer aesthetic arc (especially, as I have argued elsewhere, after her turn away from her earlier, aesthetically experimental and politically didactic writing in favor of what she considered a broader humanism).[12]

Bookending the anthology, Portillo concludes with a shape poem entitled "After Hierarchy" (figure 8). Near the end of this concluding poem, as part of a cascade of progressively indented lines, she writes, "The tracing of a dead / *The tracing of a dead* / People speaks / *Art speaks* / Of our Humanity, / *Of our Humanity,* / A gentle soft greenness / *A gentle soft greenness* / That denies tradition, / *That denies tradition.*"[13] The end of the poem, which takes the shape of a crooked tree or a pyramid, offers a new vision emerging from "A COMMON GROUND."

The ideas of "ground" and "nature" are, in Portillo's specific usage across her work, decolonial concepts that push against Chicano nationalism by painfully acknowledging and then rejecting settler desires and impulses held by Chicanxs within the context of the US and its foundations in land theft and dispossession. In this poem, indeed, Portillo makes "common ground" into a figurative and visible commons—the concrete poem, from the top of the image, goes from the title ("After Hierarchy") to the ground, manifesting its argument by "making the common ground" both the fundament and the endpoint of the poem. The poem's lowest visual point, which might be thought of as a seedling or as the beginning of the path, is the poem's end, a constantly regenerating concept. While I work between treating the poem's form as a tree and as a pyramid to suggest the instability of shape poetry, Melina Vizcaíno-Alemán has found extensive archival evidence of Portillo's reliance on pyramids as part of a larger aesthetic project. Vizcaíno-Alemán finds the pyramid image at the center of Portillo's truly idiosyncratic humanistic philosophy, a set of ideas that undergird Portillo's collage-like, coalitional ideas about aesthetics.[14]

AFTER HIERARCHY

Two

Dimensional,

The sacrophagi says,

Of Egypt's art and ant-like

Climbing, up to gods of orchestrated

Terror, strained from flesh and blood on Pharoah's

Tomb, one of seven horrors called the wonders of an ancient

World, where all in a day's work, soldier ants practice power dynamics,

Dully digging catacombs of sterile fear like Aztecs carving reverently the live,

Warm tendon of a heart still spurting blood in last breath, a "tally ho!" to run the one

Chase of Death. . . le malade imaginaire? Civilization? More a plot against all of Mankind. . . . .

Wait!

Have you heard of. . . .

The Etruscans?
Cosmic Unity?
Artists, lovers of earth,
God, Omega Pulse,
In millenia of simplicity
With life-surge pulls
Left lasting Beauty. Primitives
Man's coattails. Evolution
Making love like religion, mixed
Shedding scales like carp, knows
A blood-dye, forbidding human drainage of kin.
Why the Superman casts off Civilization. . . . .Hierarchy.
Their color is sister to hyacinth, Persian melon, persimmon. . . . . .See?
Natural law is brother to trust, balance, unity, forever. . . . .See?
Black bucchero wears
   Utopia lives inside
      The red, undying grain. . . . . .
         The knowing Man.
            Their legacy, a wild
               New promise, wild
                  Leap in Art, is free. . . .
                     Leap in Life is free.
                        No Puritan restraint.
                           No Fear barrier.
                              The tracing of a dead
                                 The tracing of a dead
                                    People speaks
                                       Art speaks
                                          Of our Humanity,
                                             Of our Humanity,
                                                A gentle soft greenness
                                                   A gentle soft greenness
                                                      That denies tradition,
                                                         That denies tradition,
Knowing the Sun Day is the .   . . .   Whole of Man, A Self Real,

LOOKING FOR A COMMON GROUND

Figure 8. Reproduction of "After Hierarchy," in *Chicanas en la literatura y el arte*, El Grito Book Series No. 1, page 84. Estela Portillo, September 1973. Open Door Archive at Northwestern University, https://opendoor.northwestern.edu/archive/items/show/378.

Cordelia Candelaria, John Alba Cutler, and Maythee Rojas have taken up Portillo's work from a theoretical perspective that finds her embedded in a longer feminist conversation (Candelaria and Rojas) and a historicist view of Chicanx literature's status in academia (Cutler). Rojas states, "If woman is nature, argues [Portillo], it is a nature that has been exploited and commodified by men and male culture, and one that ultimately has the power to overwhelm, poison, and subsume its (male) human aggressors and their attempt to impose a false and one-sided sense of order."[15] This nascent ecofeminism, in other words, is more complicated than a straightforward identification with the Earth. In her dialogue with Juan Bruce-Novoa, published in his important 1980 collection of interviews, *Chicano Authors*, Portillo even notes that "people who review *Rain of Scorpions* [her collection of stories] say I am a woman's liberationist, which I didn't see, but when I look through the whole thing, well what do you know, I am."[16] Surprised by herself, Portillo affirms a wonderful sense of self-estrangement, actualizing Maurice Blanchot's speculation that "the writer never reads [their] work. It is, for [them], illegible, a secret. [They] cannot linger in its presence. It is secret because [they are] separated from it. However, [their] inability to read the work is not a purely negative phenomenon. It is, rather, the writer's only real relation to what we call the work."[17] This idea of surprise and the powerful image of a literary text as the interactive, relationally rediscovered thing Blanchot calls "the work" will emerge as some of *Bridge*'s most important philosophical and institutional contributions to the anthology as a form.

Shaping Coalitional Aesthetics

Portillo's *El Grito* special issue, as an artifact of the Chicanx 1970s, prefaces the institutional process of transition represented, rather fittingly, by *Bridge*. Especially because the special issue hinges on a language of communal construction through difference while establishing a pedagogically and institutionally oriented language for describing Chicana literature, it offers a path leading up to *Bridge*. As Cutler has pointed out, "Chicano/a literature as a field emerges via twin commitments to institution building—or literary cultural capital—and the singularity of literary discourse. But while much Chicano/a literary scholarship regards the 1970s as the most important era in the development of Chicana/o literature, it was in the post-Movement 1980s that the field consolidated around these ideas of literariness."[18] *Bridge* fits and doesn't fit within this literary historical arc, though it shows that the contestations Cutler observes are precisely the point, especially because "literariness" as a category is hotly contested by many of the anthology's contributors, especially in relation to publishing, scholastic, and activist institutions. For example, in one of *Bridge*'s poems, Jo Carillo writes,

> And when our white sisters
> radical friends see us
> in the flesh
> not as a picture they own,
> they are not quite as sure
> if
> they like us as much.
> We're not as happy as we look
> on
> their
> wall.[19]

Carillo's examination of pictures, in this poem, speaks to what inclusion means, especially in terms of who or what gets portrayed within extant institutional frames. In addition, the concept of pictures gets picked up later in the anthology, such as in section 3, entitled, like Carillo's poem, "And When You Leave, Take Your Pictures with You: Racism in the Women's Movement," or in one of Anzaldúa's essays, "La Prieta," in which she examines how her non-Chicana friends "have substituted a negative picture the white culture has painted of my race with a highly romanticized, idealized image. . . . Though the power may be real, the mythic qualities attached to it keep others from dealing with me as a person and rob me of my being able to act out my other selves." Anzaldúa continues, bemoaning "the many names of power—pride, arrogance, control. I am not the frozen snow queen but a flesh and blood woman with perhaps too loving a heart, one easily hurt."[20] Carillo and Anzaldúa make critical interventions in being with and *speaking with* each other, especially when one has been reproduced as an "idealized image" unified through a possessive gaze. This shows, Héctor Calderón has noted, how *Bridge* "was a product of grass-roots organizers, conference participants, women who wanted to tell their personal stories and bear witness on behalf of many, as in the Latin American testimonio tradition."[21] Suggestively placing *Bridge* in the testimonio tradition, Calderón makes a fascinating connection that hints at the transnational nature of the coalitional—and thus large-scale—organizing impulses of US Third World feminism. And, indeed, this is one of the signal ways in which *Bridge* shapes literary history: it is a coalitional text that becomes a keystone of multiculturalism, specifically in its direct engagement with the emergent discourse of identity politics. In other words, the text helps us understand the shift from the large-scale, nationally and transnationally couched language of *coalition* to the institutional orientation of *multiculturalism*, especially in its formation as the "liberal multiculturalism" of the 1980s and 1990s.[22]

In the lead-up to its publication in 1981, *Bridge* was constructed through the enormous efforts of Chicana lesbian feminist editors Gloria Anzaldúa and Cherríe Moraga, alongside the contributing authors, all of whom wielded quite a bit of autonomy. Toni Cade Bambara wrote the foreword, Audre Lorde contributed two essays, Chrystos's poetry is included in every section but one, and among the other contributors are Pat Parker, Nellie Wong, the Combahee River Collective, Barbara and Beverly Smith, Norma Alarcón, Rosario Morales, Mitsuye Yamada, and Kate Rushin. The anthology is made up of six parts: "1. Children Passing in the Streets: The Roots of Our Radicalism"; "2. Entering the Lives of Others: Theory in the Flesh"; "3. And When You Leave, Take Your Pictures with You: Racism in the Women's Movement"; "4. Between the Lines: On Culture, Class, and Homophobia"; "5. Speaking in Tongues: The Third World Woman Writer"; and "6. El Mundo Zurdo: The Vision." There seems to be a "narrative structure," since the anthology moves from childhood to womanhood, yet upon further examination this arbitrary structure falls apart: there is no section devoted to adolescence, an odd omission. There are no sections devoted to elderhood; regardless, the anthology's beginning couches the entries firmly—but not *solely*—within knowledge gained through experience. In terms of theory and action, the discrete sections seem to address discrete concerns. However, a few things stand out regarding the section titles: the first four are framed through relational language—that is, they allude to forms of self-other relation—and the last two have to do with theoretical practice and theoretical vision. As a whole, all of the sections are concerned with lived experiences and the radical praxis born out of this knowledge of the world: what emerges is a series of essays and poems that think relationally about difference as a mode of traversing and theorizing the world.

The construction of the anthology follows Anzaldúa's decisively coalitional philosophy. Matthew Beeber's brilliant formulation of coalitional aesthetics in 1930s anthologies, noted earlier, guides my thinking here. Beeber describes coalitional aesthetics as "a set of formal techniques that emphasizes rather than smooths over incongruities between constituent parts, attesting to the disparity of these parts and putting pressure on the unity of the volume as a whole. Distinctly coalitional, these collectivist collections model prospective social formations through their own modes of organization."[23] This description resonates entirely with *Bridge* and its emphasis on thinking with and through difference rather than producing a unified singularity. Even the specificity of the demonstrative adjective "this" and the singular pronoun "my" in *Bridge*'s title gets attenuated and redistributed across the anthology's contributions. Picking up on the literary history of coalitional aesthetics Beeber has identified and contextualized with exceptional clarity, I find that *Bridge* reconsiders the social reproduction of feminist praxis as it stood at the time, intervening in the debate to model its own "prospective social formations" by rethinking the premise of how anthologies could and ought to be organized. In this, *Bridge* becomes, recalling Gwendolyn Brooks, "luminously indiscreet; / complete; continuous"—or, as Sara Marcus suggests, the impulse guiding the anthology is toward a "feminism that attains a condition of perfected incompletion."[24]

Theorizing the Self in Coalition

Most of the poems in *Bridge* offer an attenuated and multidirectional lyric self, often apostrophizing others within an author's own community, other women of color, what Anzaldúa earlier called "my other selves," and, often, white feminist scholars and activists. In each case, the poems turn the lyric into a communal mode that still puts pressure on community as a common-sense concept. As discussed in the introduction to this book, Cherríe Moraga's "The Welder" builds its imagery through an active, constructivist lyric voice. Moraga is "interested in the blend / of common elements to make / a common thing," while nevertheless noting, farther on, that we cannot reduce difference to find commonality. We cannot avoid the "fact that we bend / at different temperatures."[25] Moraga does not reject origins altogether, but she suggests that attention to specificity helps to weld together a community. She emphasizes this critical stance by offering a sonic differentiation between "common" in the first stanza and "come from," which appears in the third stanza (four lines later): "We plead to each other, *we all come from the same rock / we all come from the same rock.*"[26] The polysemy of "common" in the poem suggests both "widespread" and "held by many," and forms an echo to Portillo's "common ground." The poem's use of assonance—"common," "come from"—offers identity *as well as* distinction, formalizing the poem's argument that "a welder" can only produce union through different—but common—things. Keating names this type of coalitional logic in *Bridge* "commonalities," which are "not synonymous with sameness. . . . Commonalities offer pathways into relational investigations of difference—difference defined not as deviation *from* an unmarked norm but as alterations interrelated *with* this norm."[27] Kayann Short has noted that "[the] differential movement between 'naming specific differences' (identity politics) and 'crossing over' (coalition politics) forms the structure of *This Bridge Called My Back*"; this is a process exhibited in Moraga's poem in miniature.[28] The anthology's mode, more broadly, suggests bridging and linking, rather than synthesis, as the means of forming cohesion.

In another of her essays, Gloria Anzaldúa offers a related, but swerved, vision of Moraga's "welding": "The danger in writing is not fusing our personal experience and world view with the social reality we live in, with our inner life, our history, our economics, our vision. What validates us as human beings validates us as writers. What matters to us is the relationships that are important to us whether with our self or others. We must use what is important to us to get to the writing. *No topic is too trivial.* The danger is in being too universal and humanitarian and invoking the eternal to the sacrifice of the particular and the feminine and the specific historical moment."[29] Anzaldúa arrives at her point through nearly overwhelming repetition, transforming repetitive diction so that it shifts from valorizing the concrete to upholding the abstract within nearly the same grammatical and linguistic gesture, thus elaborating a conceptual contradiction that shapes her dialectical vision of writing as a personal, spiritual craft. This puts a fine point on how, for example, Theodor Adorno has critically approached the dialectic, especially when he clarifies that "dialectical thought opposes reification in the further sense that it refuses to affirm individual things in their isolation and separateness: it designates isolation as precisely a product of the universal."[30] Consider, in this light, Andrea Canaan's early theorization of "brownness" in *Bridge*, in which she critiques understandings of the idea of subjective separation. Subject and community must be considered relationally, Canaan argues, and she offers a dialectical distinction between "unit" and "isolate" to make this point: "I must nurture and develop brown self, woman, man, and child. I must address the issues of my own oppression and survival. When I separate them, isolate them, and ignore them, I separate, isolate, and ignore myself. I am a unit. A part of brownness."[31] Theorizing brownness from her position as a Black thinker, Canaan offers a means of theorizing Patricia Hill Collins's call for "intellectual leadership," which "requires collaboration among diverse Black women to think through what would constitute Black women's autonomy." Collins is interested in describing "autonomy" in an abstract sense and turns dialectically toward a definition that requires social and historical grounding: "Autonomy to develop a self-defined, independent analysis means neither that Black feminist thought has relevance only for African-American women nor that we must confine ourselves to analyzing our own experiences."[32] Collins, in elaborating the necessity of coalition building from one's position in deliberate relation with others, speaks to the importance of "Black feminist contextualizations," which undergird the theoretical innovation of describing power through the idea of "intersecting oppressions," from Sojourner Truth and Ida B. Wells to Lorraine Hansberry, Angela Davis, Valerie Smith, and Kimberlé Crenshaw, and into the future.[33]

In dialectical tension with Moraga's demand for concreteness, Anzaldúa and Canaan theorize abstract (but still materially grounded) reasons for coalition building, which align with autonomy as Collins defined it two decades later. Indeed, Anzaldúa warns against too quickly moving away from the abstract and eternal. But note how she gets there: "No topic is too trivial," she says. We must take care to avoid "*not* fusing our personal experience and world view with the social reality we live in," she insists. This is also the urgency of Canaan's "brownness," which by the end of her essay becomes an opposition to patriarchies of every color that crush liberation "in order to decrease their stress and difficulty in visualizing difference and selfhood as revolution and revolution as positive and necessary for cohabitation on this planet."[34] The oppositional, for Canaan, is "positive and necessary," more than simply a negation of negation. The creative force in brownness, then, is not merely descriptive, but a philosophical articulation of a mode of ecocritical coalitional thinking geared toward "cohabitation on this planet."

As these examples from Anzaldúa and Canaan show, *Bridge* provides insight into how midcentury coalitional tendencies still maintained significant descriptive and theoretical force, even as they were gradually being transformed into multiculturalism and, since the heyday of multiculturalism, into the language of intersectionality. Cheryl Higashida calls *Bridge* "one of the first anthologies of multicultural feminism" while also pointing out that the anthology picks up on and elaborates the Combahee River Collective's "A Black Feminist Statement" by asserting "that identity politics is *constitutively* coalitional," a claim that "bears repeating precisely because one of the main reasons for [identity politics'] dismissal by the Right and by the Left has been its supposed and real narrowness, its inability or unwillingness to speak beyond its own concerns or to effect systemic transformation."[35] As Higashida notes, both the Combahee River Collective statement and *Bridge*, which published a copy of that statement, powerfully argue for the "rooting of identity politics in anti-capitalist and anti-imperialist critique, something . . . that gets lost in most subsequent formulations of identity politics."[36] Colleen Lye has noted that this same statement has a "Janus-facing historical quality, as a stepping stone or switch point between the New Communism of the early 1970s and the Critical Race Theory of the late 1980s," and argues that "the reliance on 'intersectionality' as a way to variously describe the meeting of multiple oppressions reflects the fact that their social relationality is hard to think."[37] I fully align with Higashida's and Lye's positions here, and I would add that *Bridge*'s participation in a long tradition of leftist critique—exemplified, partially, by the Combahee River Collective statement's presence in its pages—by necessity aligns it with a robust coalitional aesthetics that thinks firmly against empire. Linda Garber argues that the long-standing ignorance surrounding the way texts like *Bridge* fit within a longer continuum has to do, mostly, with the racist assumptions embedded in literary historical models, such that "commentators rarely extend the litany [of influential leftist political movements] beyond the early 1970s, treating [civil rights, Black power, antiwar, women's liberation, and gay liberation] movements as definitive of an era of direct-action politics." Indeed, notes Garber, most "queer theorists have obscured this genealogy" informing *Bridge*, since the preference too often runs toward critical and literary theory derived from continental philosophy.[38]

In *Bridge*, we see dozens of unique voices come together through the manifold processes of speaking out, in, and through dialogue—a continuous process of *speaking with*, of generating coalition. The dialogue at work in the anthology offers interactive spaces for writerly ruminations and readerly responses—in fact, the work necessitates an engaged and flexible hermeneutic approach. Anzaldúa and Moraga's anthologizing practice thus bespeaks their commitment to dialogism and an antitranscendental dialectic—what, in honor of Anzaldúa's broader philosophy, might be called abiding within contradiction. Garber puts it simply: "Anzaldúa seeks not to transcend differences but to inhabit them in all their messy multiplicity."[39] As a philosophical principle, this antitranscendental dialectic demands that concreteness and abstraction be held together while maintained distinctly, *speaking with* each other in order to elaborate each other. This notion of the antitranscendental dialectic offers a mode of action and language that refuses the discursive progressions that threaten subsumption or teleological completion. While I do not want to discount the idea of the dialectic altogether, it is the transcendence or sublation at the end of dialectical reasoning that *Bridge* prompts us to reconsider. For Anzaldúa, especially six years later in *Borderlands / La Frontera*, abiding within contradiction becomes a distinctively Latinx mode of thought and creativity. This signal contribution of hers—which is based on how she interprets the Aztec deities Coatlicue and Coyolxauhqui as metaphorical images at the heart of attentive, embodied aesthetics—depends on a rootedness that does not want to reject or do away with identity and experience. M. Jacqui Alexander, picking up on this commitment to theorizing the contradiction, suggests that *Bridge* offers "not a transcendent vision, but one . . . rooted in transforming the mundaneness of lived experience, the very ground on which violence finds fodder."[40] This "very ground on which violence finds fodder" must be transformed, argues Alexander, in a powerful echo of the "common ground" that Estela Portillo understood, above, as emerging from "A gentle soft greenness / A gentle soft greenness / That denies tradition, / *That denies tradition*."

Bridge enacts the antitranscendental dialectic of abiding within contradiction as its organizational and philosophical principle, insisting on concreteness of experience and particularity of voice, while emphasizing—and indeed giving form to—the need for an abstracted communal politics to generate transformative theory. Together, this concreteness of voice and abstracted, transformative theory crafts a praxis in the sense Paulo Freire meant in *Pedagogy of the Oppressed*: praxis as "reflection [derived from experience and knowledge] and action upon the world in order to transform it."[41] For de Lauretis, texts such as *Bridge* demonstrate "the possibility, already emergent in feminist writings of the 1980s, to conceive of the social subject and of the relations of subjectivity to sociality in another way: a subject constituted in gender, to be sure, though not by sexual difference alone, but rather across languages and cultural representations: a subject en-gendered in the experiencing of race and class, as well as sexual, relations; a subject, therefore, not unified but rather multiple, and not so much divided as contradicted."[42] This means movement between available spaces of belonging and desired, alternative discourses that can generate different possibilities of social and political being. This movement, paradoxically expressed by abiding within contradiction (an abiding that is quite similar to the idea of staying as distinguished from waiting in Joe McKinnie's Memphis Sanitation Strike poem), shows how *Bridge*, in compiling the voices of US Third World feminists, constructs a marvelous coalition of voices that spreads every which way and suggestively gestures in multiple directions toward multiple nodes of transformation.

As Audre Lorde argues in "The Master's Tools Will Never Dismantle the Master's House," "difference must be not merely tolerated, but seen as a fund of necessary polarities between which our creativity can spark like a dialectic.... Only within that interdependency of different strengths, acknowledged and equal, can the power to seek new ways to actively 'be' in the world generate, as well as the courage and sustenance to act where there are no charters."[43] For Lorde, theorizing and organizing through difference continuously creates power—abiding within the contradiction maintains creative resistance and critique, and generates radical visions of transformative justice. Furthermore, difference, according to Lorde, means that "new ways to actively 'be' in the world generate." In fact, this syntactically interesting clause makes "generate" into an intransitive verb: "generate" signals back to itself in reference only to "new ways to actively 'be' in the world"—not to generating anything else. Lorde's use of "generate" here is about being in and transforming the world, rather than transcending it and its terms. What, indeed, could be more radical than abiding within generation in this sense, within the quest to find new ways to actively be in the world, to generate for the sake of creating a more just world?[44]

Reassessing Coalitional Horizons, Theorizing Surprise

However, such a triumphalist tone is not quite justified, given the historical record since 1981, when the anthology was first published. Some of the terms just used—"coalition" and "contradiction," in particular—seem irrecuperable in nearly every mode of political discourse in the current moment. How can investments in the norms that have produced this world be critiqued? Especially if holding on to these philosophical investments, as Lauren Berlant argues, means death by repetition: "the *affective structure* of an optimistic attachment involves the sustaining inclination to return to the scene of fantasy that enables you to expect that *this* time, nearness to *this* thing will help you or a world to become different in just the right way."[45] The structure of the fantasy is maintained—it *must* be maintained—in order for legible (that is to say, controllable) life to be produced under late capitalism.

In her interview with Frank Wilderson, Saidiya Hartman precisely names what's at stake: "What then does this language—the given language of freedom—enable? And once you realize its limits and begin to see its inexorable investment in certain notions of the subject and subjection, then that language of freedom no longer becomes that which rescues the slave from his or her former condition, but the site of the re-elaboration of that condition, rather than its transformation."[46] In other words, how can any supplications or polemics ever truly liberate us, especially if they are crafted within and addressed to discourses of colonialism, enslavement, and capital? If we address power or utilize its terms, are we not hailing it, calling it into being? The eternal and central problem of recognition within Hegel's "master-slave"/"lord-bondsman" image of the revolutionary dialectic confronts us here—and the problem seems further compounded by the inescapable factor that access to voice always already renders one a subject of discourse.[47] Indeed, when Spivak rigorously critiques the codes and capacities of visibility and comprehensibility contained within ideology in "Can the Subaltern Speak?" she shows that "giving voice" or "speaking for" is never enough. Norma Alarcón argues that, even in *Bridge*, "it must be noted, however, that each woman of color cited here, even in her positing of a 'plurality of self,' is already privileged enough to reach the moment of cognition of a situation for herself. This should suggest that to privilege the subject, even if multiple-voiced, is not enough."[48]

These are all quite serious reservations, and I think that one of the answers *Bridge* offers us, which I will now describe, must be found in the relation between the text and the reader. If, as Audre Lorde famously warned, "the master's tools will never dismantle the master's house . . . [and] will never enable us to bring about genuine change," then can *Bridge* offer a way of understanding justice and power beside, rather than outside, the sovereign frameworks (both theoretical and political) that have perpetuated oppression? This relationship is difficult and active, even as it is based on communication and dialogue: on the transformation of each through the other. Transformation, as a horizontal and differential figuration of change (as opposed to transcendence, a vertical and eruptive figuration), reconfigures the very premises of historical thought, political action, and philosophical inquiry. Transformation shows possibilities against inevitability—it generates the ability to locate other possibilities and alternatives, rather than seeing history as a singular or straightforward progression.[49] Transformation opposes inevitability.

In her description of coalitional work, Bernice Johnson Reagon notes the extreme groundedness that coalition requires. For Reagon,

> Coalition work is not work done in your home. Coalition work has to be done in the streets. And it is some of the most dangerous work you can do. And you shouldn't look for comfort. Some people will come to a coalition and they rate the success of the coalition on whether or not they feel good when they get there. They're not looking for a coalition; they're looking for a home! They're looking for a bottle with some milk in it and a nipple, which does not happen in a coalition. You don't get a lot of food in a coalition. You don't get fed a lot in a coalition. In a coalition you have to give, and it is different from your home. You can't stay there all the time. You go to the coalition for a few hours and then you go back and take your bottle wherever it is, and then you go back and coalesce some more. It is very important not to confuse them—home and coalition. Now when it comes to women—the organized women's movement—this recent thrust—we all have had the opportunity to have some kind of relationship with it.[50]

Reagon's point is that coalition is a process and a form of labor, and not in and of itself a form of being. It is an actively constructed *thing*, something with which one must enter into "relationship." It is discomfiting and "dangerous," especially existentially. It is something made together and thus takes shape according to one's labor, one's orientation to that labor, and one's needs. Ewa Majewska, a feminist Polish activist of the twenty-first century, suggests, following Rosa Luxemburg, that "failure is inevitable, and it should be experienced as a part of the process of building alternatives to capitalism, not as proof of the futility of such efforts. Genuine social change might not happen all at once; it starts with failures, and it will most likely be attacked."[51] Indeed, as Pat Parker notes, "we will disagree; we will get angry; we will fight. This is good and should be welcomed. Here is where we should air our differences but here is also where we should build. In order to survive in this world we must make a commitment to change it; not reform it—revolutionize it."[52] The result, then, is a form of production that cannot be neatly captured by capitalism's imperatives of exchange-value and profit.

We can see this demand for a different accounting of value in Chrystos's *Bridge* poem, "Ceremony for Completing a Poetry Reading," which begins, "This is a give-away poem / You have come gathering / You have made a circle with me."[53] The word "give" appears at least twelve times in the poem, enumerating objects and observations in a ritual of gathering and loving, since the poet has "more to give   this   basket is very large."[54] The giving and gifting continues until, at the poem's end, Chrystos writes that she cannot leave until "everything / and the basket which held" the poem have been taken. "When my hands are empty / I will be full."[55] This surprising contradiction, elaborated as a critique of capitalist values of giving and taking, as well as of voluntarism and obligation, revalues even notions of "empty" and "full," suggesting an ecocritical consciousness whose goal, finally, is pleasure gained through surprise.

These astonishing forms of transvaluation might also be understood through the concept of improvisation, which also turns on notions of surprise. Improvisation, as established in the relationship between the reader and *Bridge*, becomes a *speaking with* that generates surprise and astonishment through an interpretive encounter. Albert Murray—describing the process of jazz improvisation and the attendant philosophical ramifications more than the difficult work of coalition (though improvisation within a small jazz ensemble might fruitfully be theorized through coalition, similarly to how Daniel Fischlin, Ajay Heble, and George Lipsitz understand collaboration and co-creation in *The Fierce Urgency of Now*[56])—provides insight into the work of surprise as an ethical position vis-à-vis others. Surprise "is precisely this disjunction which is the moment of truth. It is on the break that you 'do your thing.' The moment of greatest jeopardy is your moment of greatest opportunity. . . . It is when you establish your identity; it is when you write your signature on the epidermis of actuality. That is how you come to terms with the void."[57] As Keating states, surprise is a heuristic befitting a world in which "life is filled with startling shifts, unexpected changes, unseen energies, and unpredictable complexities."[58] Taking these ideas of "coming to terms with the void" and the "startling shifts, unexpected changes, unseen energies, and unpredictable complexities" of life, we can see how *Bridge*'s theory and philosophy takes a distinctly ethics-oriented approach. Taking Spivak's invitation to give space to other modes of meaning-making without "speaking on their behalf," without "getting it"—and I mean to highlight the possessive physicality of literally "getting it" here, in that the metaphorical way in which we often make sense of "understanding" relies on possessiveness—we can begin to see the outlines of how such a theoretical approach might be established. What is needed is a space in which meaning can be created and distributed differently. As Adrienne Rich has suggested, "Let us insist on kinds of process which allow more women to speak; let us get back to earth—not as paradigm for 'women,' but as place of location."[59] Privileging situatedness rather than embodiment as such, *Bridge* interrogates the very foundations of a discourse that distinguishes the masculine as mind and the feminine as flesh. Rich's emphasis on earth as "place of location" suggests a realm of relation and interaction, of a nearly utopian unboundedness.[60] Rich's insight, if we take it into consideration when regarding *Bridge*'s intervention in the paradigms of theory, gives us a means of understanding the text's approach to experience as a surprising and contingent process of encounter rather than strictly as embodiment. In other words, experience is unbounded and relational, rather than corporeally bounded and untranslatable.

What emerges in *Bridge* is a differential version of totality—an alternative and uncertain one, in that it is not bound to a teleologically predetermined version of unity—in which what matters is the complex journey and the complex relations, rather than a monument of totalization. Édouard Glissant gives us a means of spotting this differential vision of unity: "one who is errant (who is no longer traveler, discoverer, or conqueror) strives to know the totality of the world yet already knows [they] will never accomplish this—and knows that is precisely where the threatened beauty of the world resides. . . . The thinking of errantry conceives of totality but willingly renounces any claims to sum it up or to possess it."[61] *This* is a means of witnessing without grasping, of relating without subsuming or consuming. To take up errantry as an improvisatory and flexible approach to the world grounded in situatedness (especially in the sense in which Glissant means it) is to understand our role as readers in the interpretive encounter with *Bridge*. This suggests a new grounds for mapping out the routes taken by coalitional aesthetics, sharing in Mary Pat Brady's framing of the process of reading as not producing a map of understanding but rather functioning as "an anticartography—one that does not conceive of space as a thing to be possessed or a set of rationalized relations to be mapped."[62] This is a spatial imaginary that must not be shaped by mapping as a means of possessing; it is an unsettling of colonial knowledge and expectations. For Roderick A. Ferguson, this means that in "a period of hegemonic affirmation, the question for us has to be how best to maneuver an especially flexible social artifact [the literary text] to disrupt dominant forms of institutionality."[63] Flexibility, then, can function as a form of errantry that enables an anticartographic critical praxis.

As an anthology built on surprise and the radical juxtaposition of texts, *Bridge* suggests an eternally open circuit—contingency and necessity furnish the nodes of that sparking anti-dialectic, generating new ways of considering the world. Commenting on Rosario Morales's prose poem "We're All in the Same Boat," Keating argues, "As with the unexpected, rule-breaking gaps in her prose, Morales's politics remain open to the possibility of surprise."[64] This means that "resisting the certainty and control (*as well as the limitations!*) a precise definition might supply, our common ground must be created tentatively and (perhaps) temporarily, through our interactions."[65] For Sara Marcus, "common ground can be mapped among diverse experiences of disappointment, despite the admitted risks of doing injustice to the specificities of each."[66] It might surprise us, in other words, how important it is to maintain certain forms of attachment in, through, despite, and *with* disappointments. As Anzaldúa and Moraga note, "We begin by speaking directly to the deaths and disappointments. Here we begin to fill in the spaces of silence between us. For between these seemingly irreconcilable lines—the class lines, the politically correct lines, the daily lines we run down to each other to keep difference and desire at a distance, the truth of our connection lies."[67]

These are journeys that cannot be mapped, because mapping them would reveal them.[68] There's a specific refusal to overcome required by this theoretical paradigm, an antipossessive, nongrasping praxis that moves *beside* the discourses that bind us, because it knows that working *through* them means working *for* them. José Muñoz, describing what he calls "a queer utopian hermeneutic," argues, "This hermeneutic would then be *epistemologically and ontologically humble* in that it would not claim the epistemological certitude of a queerness that we simply 'know' but, instead, strain to activate the no-longer-conscious and to extend a glance toward that which is forward-dawning, anticipatory illuminations of the not-yet-conscious."[69] Although Muñoz describes this hermeneutic in terms of humbleness, I am loath to name the refusal to overcome in *Bridge* as humility—instead, the book seems to be accessing a different mode of knowing, a different circuit of recognition, and a different process of empowerment than one predicated upon overcoming and transcendence. It suggests, simply, that readers *listen* (in detail, qua Vazquez, or in coalition, qua Sara Marcus), rather than grasp and comprehend. For example, *Bridge* does not ignore or refuse white supremacy, and it does not humbly listen to supremacy's elaborations and justifications: instead, *Bridge* envisions a world in which the very terms of white supremacy and patriarchy shall not be sublated in a transcendence of contradictions. White supremacy cannot and must not be reconceptualized or its terms marked as residual—no, it must be destroyed. The sparking of the dialectic provides the fire for white supremacy's destruction, not the possibility for its redescription or reuptake.

As an analytic mode, surprise has a deep history in literary theory, especially as a necessary component of hermeneutics as a process (and not just as a discipline) dedicated to education and discernment. Hans-Georg Gadamer, in *Truth and Method*, argues that the horizon of the hermeneutic circle can only be expanded by incorporating experience as an analytic for knowledge over time.[70] It may be a stretch to suggest that this mode of experience always operates through surprise, or that surprise can in any way operate as a shorthand for Gadamer's important intervention in the field of hermeneutics. However, there is perhaps no better way to describe the process of discovering something intriguing within a text—repetitions that echo throughout it, a metaphor that catches you in its strangeness, a connection that seems impossible except through the unique experience of reading and learning that you're engaged in. *Bridge*, in its insistent juxtapositions, creates situations of tension and surprise. Indeed, the very situation of the anthology as a curated object suggests that surprise is perhaps the most salient experiential category through which to move through the text. The goal is not infinite newness; it is, instead, to generate imaginative connections through as many ontological and epistemic avenues as possible. For Alexander, these sorts of connections undergird the interplay of the past, the present, and the hoped-for future. She asks, and then builds on, a question about one's relationship to collective memory:

> Can we *intentionally* remember, all the time, as a way of never forgetting, all of us, building an archeology of living memory, which has less to do with living in the past, invoking a past, or excising it, and more to do with our relationship to Time and its purpose? There is a difference between remembering *when*—the nostalgic yearning for some return—and a living memory that enables us to remember what was contained in *Bridge* and what could not be contained within it or by it. What did it make possible? What else did we need? All are part of this living memory, of moments, of imaginings, which have never ended. And they will never end so long as we continue to dare yearning for each other.[71]

The effortful, coalitional promise of *Bridge* and the possibilities that emerge from its building of spaces for being and belonging within an often cruel world transform the notions of space that seem to inhibit and entrap us. Remembering this promise, Alexander imagines *Bridge* emerging as a "living memory" that can persist if "yearning" continues. Against the clutches of a discourse that reinscribes dominant ideals of subjectivity and that demands "some return" to a rigidified past, Alexander suggests that *Bridge*, as a literary text and as a "living memory," has the power to persistently surprise its readers. The anthology's invitation to situate each readerly encounter as an act of interactive meaning-making sees power generate in uncapturable, ungraspable, and transformative ways. We are not given a blueprint for proceeding. Instead, we are left with instigations, with insurgent urgency, with imaginative lines of flight that refuse possession, domination, or even comprehension.

This transformation of the past, attuned through and to coalitional aesthetics, means approaching the process of collective intellectual labor with a different goal than absolute knowledge in mind. Turning back to Muñoz, "Astonishment helps one surpass the limitations of an alienating presentness and allows one to see a different time and place."[72] All of this is to say that improvisation, astonishment, and surprise are specifically crafted into the experience of reading *Bridge*, and this is precisely what Anzaldúa and Moraga seem to have had in mind when establishing the order of the texts in the anthology. There are pieces arguing for lesbian separatism and others that vehemently disagree with separatism; some pieces revel in the mystical and others in the hard rationality of dialectical materialism; Barbara and Beverly Smith, twins and co-conspirators and intellectual sparring partners, mix humor and hard-hitting analysis as they record a conversation around a kitchen table, which they then submit, with transgressions and digressions, to Anzaldúa and Moraga. There's something heady and confusing, joyous and liberating, overwhelming and humbling, about reading *Bridge* in its entirety. You do not come away with a specific protocol or a blueprint for revolution—but what you've gotten is a glimpse of a space where justice has taken many forms and suggested many possibilities, and what you must do is witness, listen.

Bridge generates a means of navigating discursive spaces in ways that move beside, or differently than, structures of power that seek to capture and reify, particularly through a transforming and transformational approach to discourse. As part of this process, we are given blueprints for crafting modes of knowledge that do not function through possession and subsumption, that do not depend upon transcendence in order to change the world. Alicia Schmidt Camacho argues, in *Migrant Imaginaries*, that for "migrants, the defense of rights has entailed a renewed search for form—for a politics that might carry forward their desires for justice and preserve the integrity of their communities across the border. The demand for a different framework of governance doubles as a search for political and aesthetic forms that can perform the work of representation in all its senses."[73] What Schmidt Camacho calls the "renewed search for form" is about crafting spaces for justice, rather than trying to find the precisely fitting, already existing political framework; for, to recall Hartman, adhering to the extant protocols of value might mean a "re-elaboration of [one's] condition, rather than its transformation."[74] *Bridge* offers a transformational approach to aesthetic and political revolutionary action that is less about articulating counterhegemony in a Gramscian sense, and more about finding alternative terms of sovereignty that resist reification and reelaboration—alternative sovereignties that do not need to hail power, thus confirming it and reifying oneself within its discursive thrall, in order to resist it. Indeed, as Canaan notes, too often "we think liberation a fixed quantity, that there is only so much to go around. That an individual or community is liberated at the expense of another. *When we view liberation as a scarce resource, something only a precious few of us can have, we stifle our potential, our creativity, our genius for living, learning and growing.*"[75] *Bridge*'s contributors insist that we generate power and reimagine liberation through new visions that arrive in often ungraspable, astonishing, surprising ways.

Coda: Multiculturalism, Advocacy, and Coalitional Forms beyond the Long Popular Front

The shifting ground of coalitional aesthetics, from the large vision of interorganizational and indeed internationalist-inflected sensibilities to the organizationally oriented language of multiculturalism, is not by necessity a story of declension or destruction. It is, above all, a story of shifting tactics, of the movement of a movement from one form of imagining and representing forms of relation to a different one. If this were a longer or different project, there would also be an argument about the transformation of the organizational scope of multiculturalism shifting into the individual orientation of intersectionality: the *experiences* of class, ethnicity, race, sexuality, gender, age, and ability—or, perhaps, put more finely, coalition within the self—become the actionable purview of intersectionality.

Multiculturalism certainly offers a powerful narrative for reconceptualizing belonging away from hegemony. Even with its strengths, however, I find that, especially in comparison to the Popular Front–influenced aesthetics of coalition, multiculturalism cedes important ground to the onward march of capital within the structure of the ossified nation-state. Its powerful vision is (and can perhaps only be) reform-oriented: multiculturalism seeks to re-conceive representation in more equitable, just ways, within the preexisting structure of its organizational parameters. While this impulse is laudable, it has been functionally deployed against critique. Jodi Melamed, for example, argues, "Although liberal multiculturalism appeared antiracist in contrast to Great Books discourse and neoconservatism, it trained Americans to come to terms with racial inequality to flourish based on the increasing prerogative of wealth."[76] The compromise, as Melamed potently sums it up, meant that as "multicultural ideas of integration, representation, and recognition in culture (the last narrowly construed as aesthetics) became the horizon for knowing race and antiracism, they deflected attention from the devastating and accelerating consequences of private capital's economic prerogatives for black and brown lives. It thus became possible for multiculturalism to become a strategy for racial abandonment."[77] Roderick A. Ferguson argues that multiculturalism and postcolonialism, as institutional formations, became "part of the general elements and presuppositions of the US political economy—that is, ones constituted by the intersections of academy, state and capital—and became part of the protocols of an affirmative mode of power. This sort of incorporation would work to narrow multiculturalism and postcoloniality's possibilities."[78] Multiculturalism's very structure accepts the shape of the organization to which it belongs. Couched through a gradually shifting sense of what and how relation could be developed and expressed, multiculturalism went from emergent to dominant in the 1980s and 1990s, especially after the rise of Reaganism. In the 2000s, a muscular nation-state asserted its own version of multiculturalism in order to quash geopolitical enemies. The War on Terror was prosecuted partially in defense of the multicultural state (and the multicultural citizen, in an echo of Roland Barthes's *Mythologies*, has often been represented as a soldier).

In the 1980s, Jesse Jackson's Rainbow Coalition offered a notable, visible progressive alternative to Reaganism. There are two caveats here, though. First, as Jakobi Williams has shown, the "original" Rainbow Coalition emerged directly from the Chicago chapter of the Black Panther Party and was keyed directly to the 1968 revolts against the Democratic National Convention in Chicago. Bridging critiques of the police, of the Vietnam War, and of the big two national political parties through the intersecting language of ideological analysis attentive to race and class, this Rainbow Coalition gathered Black,

Latinx, and white youths under the banners of migration, class, and revolution.[79] This coalition was instrumental in shaping Chicago politics, as "Harold Washington used it as a base for his successful bid for mayor of Chicago in 1983."[80] Importantly, Jesse Jackson worked on Washington's campaign, and in 1984 he would launch his own version of the Rainbow Coalition. Second, Jackson's work on his Rainbow Coalition ought to be understood as different from, rather than as a direct outgrowth of, his 1960s and 1970s politics, especially his presence at the National Black Political Convention in 1972, held in Gary, Indiana, with Amiri Baraka as the organization's secretary-general. As Lee Sustar argued in 1988 about the politicians and philosophers who gathered in Gary that March in 1972, "the Black radicals of that era envisioned a national Black political party independent of both the Republican and Democratic Parties."[81]

Also in 1988, Andrew Kopkind outlined the contradictions of the 1980s Rainbow Coalition quite plainly. In the pages of the *New Left Review*, Kopkind argued:

> The populist part of Jackson's project was that his movement would be built from the bottom up rather than the top down, and the leadership would be made accountable to its base. That, of course, is the problematic part. The Jackson "movement," which is both more and less than the "Rainbow Coalition" which he leads, is much more authentic an expression of popular demands than any other campaign in America since the original Populist efforts at the turn of the century, but it is also a traditional Democratic Party campaign, and it is doubtful that the "bottom" will ever control the "top."[82]

The Rainbow Coalition's move was to effectively rebuild the machinery of the Democratic Party by offering a populism that could compete with the Republican coalition of libertarians and Christian evangelicals. The Rainbow Coalition was rather easily subsumed and shifted into the Democratic Party, which theorized its inclusion of Jackson's populist ethos as an appropriate acceptance of the party's multiculturalism. This perhaps follows inevitably, as Michael Szalay has emphasized, from the Democratic Party's reliance on "the middle."[83] Indeed, as Sustar angrily reported in 1989, this move to the middle admitted nefarious concessions, including backpedaling on the necessity of antiracism in the coalition.[84]

Coalition, in its institutional incorporation, was beginning to look a lot like multiculturalism. Yet, even in the 1980s, residual coalitional elements began asserting themselves in increasingly convincing ways. The AIDS Coalition to Unleash Power (ACT UP), which emerged in 1987 and is still extant, "was a combination of old-time activists with developed analyses and strategic experience, and newly politicized first-time activists with enormous change and openhearted creativity," observes Sarah Schulman; this intragenerational and interracial ethos "was central to its success, even if this dynamic was complex, difficult, and sometimes rancorous."[85] Schulman's list of the organizations, cultural milieux, and influences that contributed to ACT UP activists is truly extraordinary, including groups such as the Congress of Racial Equality (CORE), religious organizations, specific leftist tendencies, student groups, the Gay Liberation Front, Puerto Rican anticolonial groups, nurses, artists, and more.[86] For Bettina Aptheker, a long-standing communist and activist, "one of the most innovative features of ACT UP was its complex committee structure and affinity groups";[87] this complexity of committees and ways of belonging to the organization was driven, as Schulman phrases it, "by a strategy of difference facilitating simultaneity of response."[88] As a purposeful coalition, ACT UP was driven to stave off death, especially as more and more people died of AIDS-related illnesses—including, as many activists pointed out, of willful neglect and homophobia. Yet the limits of ACT UP, as Schulman and others have shown, were largely due to its radical success and visibility, which could bring it into tension with non-LGBT groups who worried about building bridges with a queer organization. As a result, ACT UP had to rely on the politics of visibility and, often, spokesmanship, particularly in Larry Kramer. This was a double-edged sword that focused the message but also, unfortunately, gave the impression that ACT UP was "exclusively, instead of predominantly, white and male." This subtle but crucial distinction "was misrepresented over and over by the national media," which often affiliated whiteness and gayness, as Joseph Beam, Essex Hemphill, and Marlon Riggs, among others, pointed out at the time.[89]

Yet, especially if we turn beyond national parameters, we can see activists in Argentina and Poland elaborating feminist antifascisms, informed powerfully by the Combahee River Collective, *Bridge*, and Black feminist philosophers; their dancing, singing, massed solidarities, and activist strategies conspicuously theorize coalition in important new directions. The Movement for Black Lives, in the US, may not be as visible in 2024 as it was in the preceding ten years, but its urge to think transnationally has led to persistent alliances with Palestinians, rural Mexicans, and others. The immigration activists of Europe and Africa, arrayed against the violence of Fortress Europe, build coalitions not only to catalogue the countless dead, but also to save the living and to desperately care for those who are under threat of death. Indigenous activists in the Americas fold together movements against femicide and ecocide, enacting a place-based politics that demands not only settler acknowledgment but settler complicity in unmaking settlement.

Perhaps the problem has been that the Popular Front, in each national instance, was geared toward and shaped by decidedly narrow conversations, often (but, importantly, not always) in single languages. The transnational point of view has always exceeded the bounds of a Popular Front imaginary, and this is the lesson taught by Hurston's diasporic (and especially Caribbean) influences, Rukeyser's devotion to Spain, Guthrie's grand historical bum, Babb's refusal to narrow the idea of union, Bulosan's transnational socialism, Memphis's decidedly world-historic influence (even if not acknowledged), Brooks's Warpland, Rivera's multinational literary historical influences, and *Bridge*'s Third World US feminism. These are coalitional texts that draw deeply from the well of the Popular Front, yet they take that water toward fields full of a multitude of seeds, sowing and gathering bountiful harvests. Here at the end, even as I acknowledge the Popular Front's shortcomings as a coalitional model, I cannot help but see literary criticism now, and in the future, being shaped by the astonishing, surprising lessons of *speaking with*. The work ahead must be done, as Sara Marcus has so elegantly put it, by "coalitional listening," which "entails generosity, care, distanced intimacy, and attentive presence in the face of difference, even the seeming difference between living and dead; it is a practice capable not just of tuning in to the voices generated within preexisting identities but of building new collectivities as well."[90]

What comes next? I continue to see the legacies of coalitional aesthetics living on, particularly through the idea of *speaking with*, which has become an active, manifold inheritance that continues to inform poetics in particular. In an emergent body of poetry, I have found *speaking with* in the idea of lamentation as an ancient yet ever-renewing mode of collective grief.[91] Lamentation refuses the singularity of elegy by developing innovative techniques of multiplicity, and in the poetry of Aracelis Girmay, John Murillo, Yesenia Montilla, Ada Limón, Roberto Carlos Garcia, and Martín Espada, among others, I have found a rageful solace in their expansions of lyrical voice toward new coalitions. They've emerged after multiculturalism and have been writing poetry in the wake of the confessional lyric, as well as breathing the ancient air of elegy. Yet while they have found respite, repast, and sustenance in those various poetic houses, they have gathered together in an unmapped elsewhere, building a poetry of lamentation that exceeds the singular voice of the elegiac, the persona of confessionalism, and the representational logics of multiculturalism. They have searched out new lyric possibilities sustained by coalition and its multitudes, and in their own pursuit of *speaking with*, they continue to move in uncharted, exciting directions.

Notes

Introduction

1. Martín Espada, *Floaters* (W. W. Norton, 2021), 6.

2. John Murillo, "Some Thoughts after Re-reading Hughes' 'I, Too, Sing America,'" *Q & A: American Poetry*, Poetry Society of America, 2010, accessed January 20, 2020, https://poetrysociety.org/poems-essays/q-a-american-poetry-1/john-murillo.

3. Karma R. Chávez, *Queer Migration Politics: Activist Rhetoric and Coalitional Possibilities* (University of Illinois Press, 2013), 146.

4. Matthew Beeber, "Nancy Cunard and the 1930s Coalitional Anthology," *Comparative Literature* 74, no. 4 (2022): 449.

5. María Eugenia Cotera, *Native Speakers: Ella Deloria, Zora Neale Hurston, Jovita González and the Politics of Culture* (University of Texas Press, 2010), 10–11. Consider also Dean J. Franco, *Ethnic American Literature: Comparing Chicano, Jewish, and African American Writing* (University of Virginia Press, 2006); and Dalia Kandiyoti, *Migrant Sites: America, Place, and Diaspora Literatures* (University Press of New England, 2009).

6. Chávez, *Queer Migration Politics*; Ki Namaste, "The Politics of Inside/Out: Queer Theory, Poststructuralism, and a Sociological Approach to Sexuality," *Sociological Theory* 12, no. 2 (July 1994): 220–31; Erin M. Adam, "Intersectional Coalitions: The Paradoxes of Rights-Based Movement Building in LGBTQ and Immigrant Communities," *Law & Society Review* 51, no. 1 (March 2017): 132–67; Elena Gambino, "'A More Thorough Resistance'? Coalition, Critique, and the Intersectional Promise of Queer Theory," *Political Theory* 48, no. 2 (2020): 218–44. Deborah Gould provides a case study and a critical-theoretical approach to the history of coalitional theory in her article "Becoming Coalitional: The Perverse Encounter of Queer to the Left and the Jesus People USA," *S&F Online* 14, no. 2 (2017): n.p.

7. Gould, "Becoming Coalitional," n.p.

8. Frédéric Neyrat, *Atopias: Manifesto for a Radical Existentialism*, trans. Walt Hunter and Lindsay Turner (Fordham University Press, 2017), 9.

9. Neyrat, 9.

10. Neyrat, 36.

11. Although the literature on the relationship between author, text, and audience is quite lengthy, I find C. Namwali Serpell's meditations on the concept of a "mode" enormously fruitful. Serpell, in her account of the complex structure of relation formed by author, text, and audience, emphasizes the flexibility of "mode" as a critical term. As she points out, "the term *mode* conjoins the critical investments adumbrated above: aesthetics, affect, ethics; the reading experience; a sense of diversity; an emphasis on time; and an argument for resonance." C. Namwali Serpell, *Seven Modes of Uncertainty* (Harvard University Press, 2014), 20. She later gives what she calls a "phenomenological account" of mode, hinging her definition on Empson: "Mode has fixity, as evinced by its relationship to the *model*. But it also has flex, invoking *modulation*—change over time—as well as affective and grammatical *moods*" (24). I do not give mode a phenomenological rendering in this book, although I certainly do not deny the psycho-physical interactions that produce the act of reading as a social interaction.

12. Michael Denning, *The Cultural Front: The Laboring of American Culture in the Twentieth Century* (1986; repr., Verso, 2011); Bill Mullen, *Popular Fronts: Chicago and African-American Cultural Politics, 1935–46* (1999; repr., University of Illinois Press, 2015); Alan Wald, *Exiles from a Future Time: The Forging of a Mid-Twentieth-Century Literary Left* (University of North Carolina Press, 2002); Lawrence P. Jackson, *The Indignant Generation: A Narrative History of African American Writers and Critics, 1934–1960* (Princeton University Press, 2010); Robert F. Reid-Pharr, *Archives of Flesh: African America, Spain, and Post-humanist Critique* (New York University Press, 2016); Erin Royston Battat, *Ain't Got No Home: America's Great Migrations and the Making of an Interracial Left* (University of North Carolina Press, 2014); Kate A. Baldwin, *Beyond the Color Line and the Iron Curtain: Reading Encounters between Black and Red, 1922–1963* (Duke University Press, 2002); Kimberly Springer, *Living for the Revolution: Black Feminist Organizations, 1968–1980* (Duke University Press, 2005); Cheryl Higashida, *Black Internationalist Feminism: Women Writers of the Black Left, 1945–1995* (University of Illinois Press, 2011); and Bettina Aptheker, *Communists in Closets: Queering the History 1930s–1980s* (Routledge, 2023).

13. Mary Helen Washington, *The Other Blacklist: The African American Literary and Cultural Left of the 1950s* (Columbia University Press, 2014); Cristina Pérez Jiménez, "Los Amigos de Wallace: Henry Wallace's 1948 Presidential Campaign and the Bid to Capture the Latino Vote," *Latino Studies* 19, no. 3 (2021): 286–309; Benjamin Balthaser, *Anti-imperialist Modernism: Race and Transnational Radical Culture from the Great Depression to the Cold War* (University of Michigan Press, 2016); Margo Natalie Crawford, *Black Post-Blackness: The Black Arts Movement and Twenty-First-Century Black Aesthetics* (University of Illinois Press, 2017); James Smethurst, *The Black Arts Movement: Literary Nationalism in the 1960s and 1970s* (University of North Carolina Press, 2005); and, especially, James Smethurst, *Behold the Land: The Black Arts Movement in the South* (University of North Carolina Press, 2021).

14. Michael Kazin, *What It Took to Win: A History of the Democratic Party* (Farrar, Straus and Giroux, 2022), 185.

15. Michael Szalay, *Hip Figures: A Literary History of the Democratic Party* (Stanford University Press, 2012).

16. Szalay, 14.

17. Andy Hines, *Outside Literary Studies: Black Criticism and the University* (University of Chicago Press, 2022), 43.

18. Denning, *Cultural Front*, 26–27.

19. Denning, 27.

20. Muriel Rukeyser, "Absalom," in *The Collected Poems of Muriel Rukeyser*, ed. Janet E. Kaufman and Anne F. Herzog (University of Pittsburgh Press, 2005), 84.

21. Cherríe L. Moraga, "The Welder," in *This Bridge Called My Back*, ed. Cherríe L. Moraga and Gloria E. Anzaldúa (1981; repr., Third Woman Press, 2002), 245.

22. Shu-mei Shih, "World Studies and Relational Comparison," *PMLA* 130, no. 2 (2015): 434.

23. Balthaser, *Anti-imperialist Modernism*, 7.

24. Crawford, *Black Post-Blackness*; Robin D. G. Kelley, *Hammer and Hoe: Alabama Communists during the Great Depression* (University of North Carolina Press, 1990).

25. Alan Wald, "The 1930s Left in U.S. Literature Reconsidered," in *Writing from the Left: New Essays on Radical Culture and Politics* (Verso, 1994), 110.

26. Smethurst, *Behold the Land*, 36.

27. Rachel Ida Buff, *Against the Deportation Terror: Organizing for Immigrant Rights in the Twentieth Century* (Temple University Press, 2017), 1.

28. Buff, 19.

29. See Hungerford's lecture on *The Woman Warrior* from her course "The American Novel since 1945," in the Yale Open Courses archive, https://oyc.yale.edu/english/engl-291/lecture-14 (accessed May 1, 2016).

30. Édouard Glissant, *Poetics of Relation*, trans. Betsy Wing (University of Michigan Press, 1997), 172.

31. For more on "the fractal" as an aesthetic and philosophical category, see Mayra Santos-Febres, *Sobre piel y papel* (Ediciones Callejón, 2005). Convincing arguments have been made regarding the necessity of geographically contextualizing the work of Glissant and other Caribbean philosophers and authors, such as Sylvia Wynter, M. Jacqui Alexander, and Mayra Santos-Febres. Furthermore, the relations and acts of generation I analyze produce connections that remake geographical possibilities and continuities—new unities and disunities constantly emerge.

32. Glissant, *Poetics of Relation*, 139.

33. "Undercommons" refers here to Stefano Harney and Fred Moten's *The Undercommons: Fugitive Planning and Black Study* (Minor Compositions, 2013). I am suggesting that my interpretations of work by Guthrie are conversant with, but not entirely beholden to, the protocols of literary studies and musicology. In this, I align

myself with Gustavus Stadler's reassessment of Guthrie in *Woody Guthrie: An Intimate Life* (Beacon Press, 2020).

34. Monika Gehlawat, *In Defense of Dialogue: Reading Habermas and Postwar American Literature* (Routledge, 2020), 37.

35. Joshua L. Miller, *Accented America: The Cultural Politics of Multilingual Modernism* (Oxford University Press, 2011), 20.

36. Sara Marcus, *Political Disappointment: A Cultural History from Reconstruction to the AIDS Crisis* (The Belknap Press of Harvard University Press, 2023), 23.

37. Jessica Berman, *Modernist Commitments: Ethics, Politics, and Transnational Modernism* (Columbia University Press, 2012), 238–39.

38. Alexandra T. Vazquez, *Listening in Detail: Performances of Cuban Music* (Duke University Press, 2013), 7.

39. See Hortense Spillers, "Black, White, and In Color, or Learning How to Paint: Toward an Intramural Protocol of Reading," in *Black, White, and In Color: Essays on American Literature and Culture* (University of Chicago Press, 2003).

40. James Baldwin, "Everybody's Protest Novel," in *Notes of a Native Son* (1955; repr., Beacon Press, 2012), 15.

41. Gayatri Spivak, "Can the Subaltern Speak?," in *Marxism and the Interpretation of Culture*, ed. Cary Nelson and Lawrence Grossberg (Macmillan, 1988), 274.

42. For a convergent criticism applied to literature as such, one might turn to Wayne Booth, *The Rhetoric of Fiction (University of Chicago Press, 1961)*, or to William Stott, *Documentary Expression and Thirties America (Oxford University Press, 1973)*. Booth's trenchant critique of early and mid-twentieth-century literary criticism, levied in particular against purely New Critical textual approaches as well as purely biographical approaches, focuses on the inherent "rhetoric" of all writing: every piece of fiction reveals the positionality of the author and their attempt to communicate this knowledge of the world.

43. Rey Chow, *Writing Diaspora* (Indiana University Press, 1993), 29.

44. Simone Weil, "The *Iliad* or the Poem of Force," trans. Mary McCarthy, in *Simone Weil: An Anthology*, ed. Siân Miles (Grove Press, 2000), 192.

45. Paula M. L. Moya, *The Social Imperative: Race, Close Reading, and Contemporary Literary Criticism* (Stanford University Press, 2016), 40.

46. Sanora Babb, *Whose Names Are Unknown* (University of Oklahoma Press, 2002), 222.

47. Harney and Moten, *Undercommons*, 19.

Chapter 1

1. *The Book of the Dead* is the first of three sections in Rukeyser's *U.S. 1*, and it contains twenty poems. Throughout this chapter, I refer to *The Book of the Dead* as a suite of poems, and I italicize its title in order to distinguish the whole from the individual, titled poems within it. In this, I follow Tim Dayton's convention in *Muriel Rukeyser's "The Book of the Dead"* (University of Missouri Press, 2003).

2. Rowena Kennedy-Epstein, *Unfinished Spirit: Muriel Rukeyser's Twentieth Century* (Cornell University Press, 2022), 137. Kennedy-Epstein's excellent work on Rukeyser's unfinished and unpublished Boas biography can be found in chapter 6 of *Unfinished Spirit*, "Pillars of Process: Franz Boas, Birth, and Indigenous Thought." Unfortunately, Kennedy-Epstein does not cite major accounts of Hurston's influence on her mentor, Boas, including María Eugenia Cotera's *Native Speakers: Ella Deloria, Zora Neale Hurston, Jovita González, and the Poetics of Culture* (University of Texas Press, 2010) and Sonnet Retman's *Real Folks: Race and Genre in the Great Depression* (Duke University Press, 2011), or prior work exploring Hurston's influence on non-Harlem modernists, such as Erin Royston Battat's *Ain't Got No Home: America's Great Migrations and the Making of an Interracial Left* (University of North Carolina Press, 2014); all of these texts influenced my argument connecting Rukeyser and Hurston in my 2016 PhD thesis, "Migrant Modalities: Radical Democracy and Intersectional Praxis in American Literatures, 1923–1976." Still, Kennedy-Epstein's focus on Boas and Rukeyser sheds important light on important possible paths for the continued study of Rukeyser's work.

3. Mary Helen Washington, *The Other Blacklist: The African American Literary and Cultural Left of the 1950s* (Columbia University Press, 2015), 6.

4. James Smethurst, *Behold the Land: The Black Arts Movement in the South* (University of North Carolina Press, 2021), 36.

5. Jonathan Freedman, *Klezmer America: Jewishness, Ethnicity, Modernity* (Columbia University Press, 2008), 6.

6. Alan Wald, *The New York Intellectuals: The Rise and Decline of the Anti-Stalinist Left from the 1930s to the 1980s* (University of North Carolina Press, 1987), 29.

7. Michael Denning, *The Cultural Front: The Laboring of American Culture in the Twentieth Century* (Verso, 1997), 9.

8. Alain Locke, *The New Negro: Voices of the Harlem Renaissance* (1925; repr., Touchstone Press, 1999), 6–7.

9. The Harlem Renaissance has long been an imperfect moniker for this movement made through many coteries in various regional iterations. See Davarian Baldwin and Minkah Makalani, eds., *Escape from New York: The New Negro Renaissance beyond Harlem* (University of Minnesota Press, 2013). Davarian Baldwin, in his introduction to the volume, makes especially clear that the New Negro Renaissance was an internationally inflected movement with a strong sense of both historical obligation and future orientation.

10. Steven S. Lee, *The Ethnic Avant-Garde: Minority Cultures and World Revolution* (Columbia University Press, 2015), 4.

11. Monika Gehlawat, *In Defense of Dialogue: Reading Habermas and Postwar American Literature* (Routledge, 2020), 27.

12. The documentary tendency is certainly present in most of Hurston's work, even if that might not be how Hurston herself would describe her ethnographic method. Indeed, it is a bit inaccurate to call Hurston's work documentary per se, especially

because doing so might legitimize an unfortunate tendency to read Hurston through a reductive mimesis, most often captured in the term "authenticity."

13. Cotera shows how Hurston's work was innovative and provocative in its time, turning to Boas's private correspondence with Hurston. Boas did not have a great amount of faith in Hurston's scholarly techniques and expressed strong discomfort with her approach to fieldwork, especially since he felt it did not adhere to the objective anthropology he was trying to establish. See Cotera, *Native Speakers*, 71–82.

14. Rosemary V. Hathaway, "The Unbearable Weight of Authenticity: Zora Neale Hurston's *Their Eyes Were Watching God* and a Theory of 'Touristic Reading,'" *Journal of American Folklore* 117 (2004): 175.

15. Gehlawat, *In Defense of Dialogue*, 41.

16. Zora Neale Hurston, *Mules and Men* (1935; repr., Harper Perennial Modern Classics, 2008), 64–65.

17. Daphne A. Brooks, "'Sister Can You Line It Out?': Zora Neale Hurston and the Sound of Angular Black. Womanhood," *Amerikastudien / American Studies* 55, no. 4 (2010): 622.

18. Hurston, *Mules and Men*, 65.

19. Retman, *Real Folks*, 175. See also Retman, 172–75, in which she describes Hurston's experience at a "toe party," perhaps the most famous scene from *Mules and Men*. Hurston builds suspense through her telling, describing her own feelings and experiences, thus involving the reader in a very deliberate way. Hurston's own footnotes throughout the text, which often give the reader a rundown of terms with which they may not be familiar, also contribute to this participatory ethic.

20. James Ford III, *Thinking through Crisis: Depression-Era Black Literature, Theory, and Politics* (Fordham University Press, 2019), 208.

21. Hurston, *Mules and Men*, 94–95.

22. Hurston, 95.

23. Hurston, 95.

24. David Todd Lawrence, "Folkloric Representation and Extended Context in the Experimental Ethnography of Zora Neale Hurston," *Southern Folklore* 57, no. 2 (2000): 122.

25. Lawrence, 127.

26. See Michelle Wallace, *Invisibility Blues: From Pop to Theory* (1990; repr., Verso Press, 2008), especially pages 172–86.

27. Retman, *Real Folks*, 24.

28. Retman, 3.

29. Franz Boas, "Introduction," in Hurston, *Mules and Men*, xiii; emphasis added.

30. John Laudun, "Reading Hurston Writing," *African American Review* 38, no. 1 (2004): 49.

31. Autumn Womack, "'The Brown Bag of Miscellany': Zora Neale Hurston and the Practice of Overexposure," *Black Camera* 7, no. 1 (Fall 2015): 117.

32. Womack, 119.

33. Hurston, *Mules and Men*, 17, 37, 57, 142, 179.

34. Hurston, 246.

35. Retman, *Real Folks*, 136.

36. Tim Dayton, "Lyric and Document in Muriel Rukeyser's *The Book of the Dead*," *Journal of Modern. Literature* 21, no. 2 (Winter 1997-98): 224.

37. For a thorough account of the media, legal, and public-health responses to the Hawks Nest disaster, see William "Rick" Crandall and Richard E. Crandall, "Revisiting the Hawks Nest Tunnel Incident: Lessons Learned from an American Tragedy," *Journal of Appalachian Studies* 8, no. 2 (Fall 2002): 261-83.

38. Although the town is spelled both "Hawk's Nest" and "Hawks Nest" in various sources, and both are used seemingly interchangeably, I use "Hawks Nest" in accordance with the State of West Virginia's usage.

39. Cherniak's *The Hawk's Nest Incident* (Yale University Press, 1989) approaches the industrial disaster from a public health perspective. As an interdisciplinary work written by a trained doctor, the text works as a political analysis, a medical analysis oriented through a public health approach, a sociological survey, and a historiography of what remains the deadliest industrial disaster in American history. Dayton, in *Muriel Rukeyser's "The Book of the Dead"*, contextualizes Rukeyser's role in relation to the larger story of Gauley Bridge and the tunnel. Dayton concisely provides an overview of the classist, racist nature of the disaster, recognizing the environmental racism at play in every single aspect of what happened to the workers, from labor recruitment to death.

40. Dayton, *Muriel Rukeyser's "The Book of the Dead"*, 19.

41. Sara Judy, "Singing in the Late Season: Prophetic American Poetry in the Postwar Period" (PhD diss., University of Notre Dame, 2022), 93.

42. Matthew Baigell, *Social Concern and Left Politics in Jewish American Art: 1880-1940* (Syracuse University Press, 2015), 6.

43. This same antifascist presentism motivated her coverage of the Scottsboro trial, prompting an unpublished piece entitled "Women and Scottsboro," found in the Library of Congress, in which she sees the people involved in and touched by the Scottsboro nightmare as motivated, emotional individuals whose consciousness was drawn toward more expansive notions of class and race—thus representing a clear desire for democracy—rather than as a new source of proletarian anger to be swayed and captured. For more on this, see Alan Wald, *Exiles from a Future Time: The Forging of the Mid-Twentieth-Century Literary Left* (University of North Carolina Press, 2001), especially 299-306; and Anne F. Herzog and Janet E. Kaufman, eds., *How Shall We Tell Each Other of the Poet?* (Palgrave Macmillan, 1999). The latter is a beautifully wrought and carefully compiled collection dedicated to exploring and sharing Rukeyser's life and artistic output, and includes submissions from Adrienne Rich, Richard Howard, Denise Levertov, Gerald Stern, and Rukeyser's son William, among many others.

44. John Wheelwright, "U.S. 1," *Partisan Review* 4, no. 4 (March 1938): 54.

45. Alan Wald, *Constituting Americans: Cultural Anxiety and Narrative Form* (Duke University Press, 1995), 302.

46. Julius Lobo, "From 'The Book of the Dead' to 'Gauley Bridge': Muriel Rukeyser's Documentary Film at the Crossroads of the Popular Front," *Journal of Modern Literature* 35, no. 3 (Spring 2012): 80.

47. Baigell, *Social Concern and Left Politics*, 147.

48. Wheelwright, "U.S. 1," 55.

49. Wheelwright, 56.

50. Walter Kalaidjian, "Muriel Rukeyser and the Poetics of Specific Critique," *Cultural Critique* 20 (Winter 1991–92): 70.

51. Kalaidjian, 70.

52. Lisa Siraganian, *Modernism and the Meaning of Corporate Persons* (Oxford University Press, 2020), 10; emphasis original.

53. Muriel Rukeyser, "West Virginia," in *The Collected Poems of Muriel Rukeyser*, ed. Janet E. Kaufman and Anne F. Herzog (University of Pittsburgh Press, 2006), 74.

54. Denning, *Cultural Front*, 131.

55. Rukeyser, "West Virginia," 74–75.

56. Muriel Rukeyser, "Story Outline for *Gauley Bridge*," circa 1939–40. Located in the Muriel Rukeyser Papers housed in the Library of Congress, part 1, box 42, folder 7. All subsequent references to this collection will be listed as *LC* part:box:folder.

57. Letter from Eve Ettinger of the Columbia Pictures Corporation, *LC* 1:42:7.

58. Lobo, "Muriel Rukeyser's Documentary Film," 96.

59. Raphael C. Allison, "Muriel Rukeyser Goes to War: Pragmatism, Pluralism, and the Politics of Ekphrasis," *College Literature* 33, no. 2 (Spring 2006): 5.

60. Christa Buschendorf, "Poet and Reader in the Witness Box: Society on Trial in Muriel Rukeyser's Early Poetry," *Amerikastudien / American Studies* 62, no. 2 (2017): 216.

61. Allison, "Muriel Rukeyser Goes to War," 8–9.

62. The letter upon which "Mearl Blankenship" is based is now located in Rukeyser's papers at the Library of Congress, and was sent on March 13, 1926, to an unspecified denizen of "Room 10005–245 Seventh Ave, New York, NY." *LC* 1:42:7.

63. Catherine Venable Moore, "The Book of the Dead," *Oxford American*, no. 94 (Fall 2016), accessed April 23, 2024, https://oxfordamerican.org/magazine/issue-94-fall-2016/the-book-of-the-dead.

64. Muriel Rukeyser, "Mearl Blankenship," in *Collected Poems*, 82–83.

65. Dayton, *Muriel Rukeyser's "Book of the Dead,"* 42.

66. Lobo discusses how "Story Outline for *Gauley Bridge*" makes further changes for the visual medium: "Instead of extending the document and placing the letter within the larger fabric of juxtaposed materials . . . she presents the Blankenship letter . . . as part of the scene unfolding between husband and wife. The letter sits amidst the remains of a partially eaten dinner, presented by Rukeyser as an addendum to their conversation and an outgrowth of their lives after the silicosis disaster." Lobo, "Muriel Rukeyser's Documentary Film," 88.

67. Michael Thurston, "Documentary Modernism as Popular Front Poetics: Muriel

Rukeyser's 'Book of the Dead,'" *Modern Language Quarterly* 60, no. 1 (March 1999): 69.

68. William Stott, *Documentary Expression and Thirties America* (University of Chicago Press, 1973), 57.

69. Stott, 62.

70. Rukeyser, "Mearl Blankenship," 83.

71. Muriel Rukeyser, "George Robinson: Blues," in *Collected Poems*, 88.

72. Muriel Rukeyser, "Alloy," in *Collected Poems*, 95.

73. Dayton, *Muriel Rukeyser's "Book of the Dead"*, 71-77.

74. Muriel Rukeyser, "Praise of the Committee," in *Collected Poems*, 79-80.

75. Rukeyser, "Praise of the Committee," 80.

76. Rukeyser, 80.

77. Rukeyser, 81.

78. Rukeyser, 81.

79. Siraganian, *Modernism and the Meaning*, 3.

80. Muriel Rukeyser, "Absalom," in *Collected Poems*, 84-85.

81. Rukeyser, "Praise of the Committee," 81-82.

82. Thurston, "Documentary Modernism," 195.

83. Stephanie Hartman, "All Systems Go: Muriel Rukeyser's *The Book of the Dead* and the Reinvention of Modernist Poetics," in Herzog and Kaufman, *How Shall We Tell Each Other*, 211.

84. Rukeyser, "Praise of the Committee," 82.

85. Muriel Rukeyser, "The Bill," in *Collected Poems*, 106.

86. For a history of the song "John Brown's Body," consult Roger L. Hall's "The Story of the John Brown Song," American Music Preservation, 2012, updated 2022, accessed July 31, 2024, https://www.americanmusicpreservation.com/JohnBrownSong.htm.

87. Muriel Rukeyser, "The Soul and Body of John Brown," in *Collected Poems*, 247.

88. Muriel Rukeyser, "The Book of the Dead," in *Collected Poems*, 107.

89. Thurston, "Documentary Modernism," 199.

90. Rukeyser wrote an article for *New Masses* about her trip to the "People's Olympics" in Barcelona, which abruptly ended before they started at the outbreak of the Spanish Civil War. She also wrote several poems about the Spanish Civil War, including "Mediterranean," originally published as a pamphlet and then chapbook to raise money for the Spanish Republic's war effort. See Rowena Kennedy-Epstein's introduction to Rukeyser's novel *Savage Coast*, published by the Feminist Press in 2013 after its careful recovery by Kennedy-Epstein, as well as Kennedy-Epstein's article "'Her symbol was civil war': Recovering Muriel Rukeyser's Lost Spanish Civil War Novel" in *MFS: Modern Fiction Studies* 59, no. 2 (Summer 2013): 416-39. Kennedy-Epstein also recovered and introduced Rukeyser's poem "Barcelona, 1936."

91. Rukeyser, "Book of the Dead," 110-11.

92. Sarah Ehlers, *Left of Poetry: Depression America and the Formation of Modern Poetics* (University of North Carolina Press, 2019), 90.

93. Hartman, "All Systems Go," 215.

94. Ehlers, *Left of Poetry*, 68.

95. Ehlers, 72.

96. Buschendorf, "Poet and Reader in the Witness Box," 215.

97. Ehlers, *Left of Poetry*, 74.

98. Gwendolyn Brooks, "The Sermon on the Warpland," in *Blacks* (Third World Press, 1987), 452.

99. Audre Lorde, "The Master's Tools Will Never Dismantle the Master's House," in *This Bridge Called My Back*, ed. Gloria Anzaldúa and Cherría Moraga (1981; repr., State University of New York Press, 2015), 95.

100. Édouard Glissant, *Poetics of Relation*, trans. Betsy Wing (University of Michigan Press, 1997), 20. See Yomaira C. Figueroa-Vásquez, *Decolonizing Diasporas: Radical Mappings of Afro-Atlantic Literature* (Northwestern University Press, 2020); and John E. Drabinski, *Glissant and the Middle Passage: Philosophy, Beginning, Abyss* (University of Minnesota Press, 2019).

101. Kandice Chuh et al., "Being with José: An Introduction," *Social Text* 32, no. 4 (2014): 1–7.

102. Figueroa-Vásquez, *Decolonizing Diasporas*, 3.

103. Glissant, *Poetics of Relation*, 139.

104. Caroline Levine, *Forms: Whole, Rhythm, Hierarchy, Network* (Princeton University Press, 2017), 6. For Levine's more thoroughgoing definitional work, see pp. 2–11, 16–24, and 49–53.

105. Chela Sandoval, *Methodology of the Oppressed* (University of Minnesota Press, 2000), 140.

106. Lauren Berlant, *Cruel Optimism* (Duke University Press, 2011), 2.

Chapter 2

1. Henry Hill Collins Jr., *America's Own Refugees: Our 4,000,000 Homeless Migrants* (Princeton University Press, 1941), 4–5.

2. Henry Nash Smith, *Virgin Land: The American West as Symbol and Myth* (1950; repr., Harvard University Press, 1978), 123.

3. Abigail G. H. Manzella, *Migrating Fictions: Gender, Race, and Citizenship in U.S. Internal Displacements* (Ohio State University Press, 2018), 69–70.

4. Sarah D. Wald, *The Nature of California; Race, Citizenship, and Farming since the Dust Bowl* (University of California Press, 2016), 67.

5. S. Wald, 52.

6. Manzella, *Migrating Fictions*, 21.

7. S. Wald, *Nature of California*, 53.

8. S. Wald, 53.

9. Gustavus Stadler, *Woody Guthrie: An Intimate Life* (Beacon Press, 2020), 67.

10. Robbie Lieberman, *"My Song Is My Weapon": People's Songs, American Communism, and the Politics of Culture, 1930–1950* (University of Illinois Press, 1989), 5.

11. Michael Denning, *The Cultural Front: The Laboring of American Culture in the Twentieth Century* (1986; repr., Verso, 2011), 37.

12. Denning, 38.

13. Michael Kazin's 2011 contribution to the history of the Popular Front is tightly packed and informative; in particular, Kazin explains how the "white-led radical movement" took charge in the interwar civil rights movement but also made civil rights subservient to the Communist International. This accords with Ellison's critique of the Communist Party in *Invisible Man*. See Michael Kazin, "This Land Is Our Land," *Humanities* 32, no. 3 (May/June 2011), accessed April 23, 2024, http://www.neh.gov/humanities/2011/mayjune/feature/land-our-land; and Michael Kazin, *American Dreamers: How the Left Changed a Nation* (Vintage Books, 2011).

14. Kazin, *American Dreamers*, 170.

15. Lieberman, *My Song*, 38.

16. The Coen brothers' 1991 film *Barton Fink* (starring John Turturro and John Goodman) satirizes the "proletcult" style to great effect. Turturro's character, Barton Fink, an extreme version of playwright Clifford Odets (*Waiting For Lefty*, 1935), sets up shop in Los Angeles and tries to write a script "about the common man" even while ignoring the stories of a common man, John Goodman's traveling insurance salesman.

17. Lieberman, *My Song*, 41.

18. While I engaged with Sonnet Retman's work on Hurston in particular, *Real Folks* also delves into the politics of representing and maintaining folk culture more broadly. WPA pamphlets and propaganda, as well as Alan Lomax and his associates' collection of folk music across the United States, were very invested in setting apart certain parts of the country—putatively unalloyed regions that were meant to remain untouched and unspoiled. Rural electrification, for example, did much to homogenize popular culture and aesthetics, and this incredible material benefit to rural people and peoples was often seen as destructive of folk purity. Sonnet Retman, *Real Folks: Race and Genre in the Great Depression* (Duke University Press, 2011).

19. Sanora Babb, *Whose Names Are Unknown* (University of Oklahoma Press, 2002), 146.

20. Babb, 147.

21. About Redding, Guthrie writes, "In a bend of the Sacramento [River] is the town of Redding, California. The word had scattered out that twenty-five hundred workers was needed to build the Kenneth Dam, and already eight thousand work hands had come to do the job. Redding was like a wild ant den. A mile to the north in a railroad bend had sprung up another camp, a thriving nest of two thousand people, which we just called by the name of the 'jungle.' In that summer of 1938, I learned a few little things about the folks in Redding, but a whole lot more, some way, down there by that big jungle where the people lived as close to nature, and as far from everything natural, as human beings can." Woody Guthrie, *Bound for Glory* (E. P. Dutton, 1943), 45.

22. Guthrie, 252.

23. Guthrie, 252–53.

24. Guthrie, 253.

25. Guthrie, 254.

26. Of immediate import to the slogan on Guthrie's wartime guitar: Jimmy Longhi, who along with Cisco Houston and Guthrie briefly joined sailors on a US Navy ship in order to provide entertainment, has written a long anecdote relating to Guthrie's insistent, defiant demand that the ship's Black sailors be allowed to join the white sailors on deck to enjoy the entertainment. Longhi describes a scene in which the Black commanding officer, Daniel Rutledge, was given Guthrie's guitar: "When Woody offered to let Rutledge play his guitar, the black officer noticed Woody's slogan—this machine kills fascists—and improvised a sermon on the connection between the war against Hitler and the struggle against American racism. . . . When the men responded 'Change! Change!' Rutledge held Woody's guitar 'above his head like a weapon' and hammered home the main point of the movement that returning black veterans would help define and carry through: 'An' the walls will come tumblin' down!'" See Craig Werner, "Democratic Visions, Democratic Voices: Woody as Writer," in *Hard Travelin'*, ed. Robert Santelli and Emily Davidson (Wesleyan University Press; University of New England Press, 1999), 75; Longhi's longer anecdote is related on 75–76. See also Jim Longhi, *Woody, Cisco, and Me: Seamen Three in the Merchant Marine* (University of Illinois Press, 1997). The phrase "the walls will come tumblin' down," referencing the battle of Jericho, becomes a powerful symbol in Odetta's "Joshua Fit the Battle of Jericho." Another connection Guthrie made between antifascism and antiracism is noted in Dave Marsh and Harold Leventhal's edited collection of Guthrie archival materials, *Pastures of Plenty: A Self-Portrait* (Harper Perennial, 1992). On a calendar page from Monday, August 31, 1942, underneath enormous block letters proclaiming, "Beat Fascism!" we find a drawing of a tombstone upon which is written, "Here lies Jim Crow."

27. Bryan Garman, "The Ghost of History: Bruce Springsteen, Woody Guthrie, and the Hurt Song," *Popular Music and Society* 20, no. 2 (1996): 70–71.

28. Garman, 69–70.

29. Mark Allan Jackson argues that when listening to Guthrie's songs, it is important to note that, "rather than stand as pure history, these songs and their subject matter provide access to the past for a purpose. Guthrie wanted those who encountered his songs to take in the tale and then recognize the example of resistance inherent in each." Mark Allan Jackson, *Prophet Singer: The Voice and Vision of Woody Guthrie* (University of Mississippi Press, 2007), 14.

30. Richard Reuss, "Woody Guthrie and His Folk Tradition," *Journal of American Folklore* 83, no. 329 (July–September 1970): 275.

31. For a brief history of his time at KFVD, see https://woodyguthrie.org/biography.htm (accessed August 7, 2024). Guthrie was an extremely popular radio personality until his employment was cut short in 1940 due the fact that his unapologetic on-air support for Joseph Stalin became too aggravating for the station owner to bear. See Will Kaufman, *Woody Guthrie, American Radical* (University of Illinois Press, 2011);

and Ronald Briley, "'Woody Sez': Woody Guthrie, the 'People's Daily World,' and Indigenous Radicalism," *California History* 84, no. 1 (Fall 2006): 30–46.

32. Edwin Cohen, "Neither Hero nor Myth: Woody Guthrie's Contribution to Folk Art," *Folklore* 91, no. 1 (1980): 13.

33. Serge Denisoff, *Great Day Coming: Folk Music and the American Left* (University of Illinois Press, 1971), 25.

34. Denisoff, 136.

35. Gene Bluestein, *Poplore: Folk and Pop in American Culture* (University of Massachusetts Press, 1994), 88–89.

36. "So even to this day, major artists of the past (as well as such contemporaries as Woody Guthrie and Pete Seeger) are either excluded from evaluation or selectively examined in such a way as to avoid evidence of such issues as the influence of non-folk sources on their work and the powerful individualism of their expression. Folklore, in my view, needs to be understood in a new way. Here I use the term *poplore* as a positive rather than pejorative expression. Folklorists generally consider poplore an invasion of folk tradition by insidious popular and commercial materials." Bluestein, *Poplore*, 6.

37. Bluestein, 89.

38. Will Kaufman gives a brief account of the Guthrie and Lead Belly collaborations in *Woody Guthrie, American Radical*, noting Guthrie's discussion with Henrietta Yurchenco: "[Guthrie] convinced Henrietta Yurchenco [sic], host of the WNYC program *Adventures in Music*, to give Lead Belly a chance on the air. Learning from Lead Belly, Guthrie told her, was 'one of New Yorks [sic] greatest pleasures'—particularly for his reinforcement of plain speaking and singing in what Guthrie perceived as an overwhelmingly timid and politically evasive broadcasting culture. . . . In Lead Belly's music, Guthrie saw an entire people and an entire political revolution stirring. . . . Thus to leave Lead Belly out of the broadcasting mix, Guthrie told Yurchenco, was 'like leaving the alcohol out of the wine or leaving the spring out of the clock'" (51).

39. Bluestein, *Poplore*, 90.

40. Raymond Williams, *Keywords: A Vocabulary of Culture and Society* (1976; repr., Oxford University Press, 1983), 180. The entire quote, from which I've taken a snippet, is: "Popular [in the early twentieth century] was being seen from the point of view of the people rather than from those seeking favour or power from them. Yet the earlier sense has not died. Popular culture was not identified by *the people* but by others, and it still carries two older senses: inferior kinds of work (cf. popular literature, popular press as distinguished from *quality press*); and work deliberately setting out to win favor (popular journalism as distinguished from *democratic journalism*, or popular entertainment); as well as the more modern sense of well-liked by many people, with which of course, in many cases, the earlier senses overlap. The sense of popular culture as the culture actually made by people for themselves is different from all these" (180).

41. Joe Klein, *Woody Guthrie: A Life* (Delta Trade Paperbacks, 1980), 208.

42. Werner, "Democratic Visions," 74.

43. Here is an instructive passage, in which Denisoff works hard to distinguish John L. Handcox and Jim Garland through the measure of purity versus contamination: "Both Handcox and Harlan refugee Jim Garland provided artifacts of proletarian culture, not contaminated by commercialism, which fitted into the folk consciousness of the late 1930s. The musical forms or vehicles both employed were from their natural genre. It was only when both perceived themselves as *conscious* spokesmen of the 'folk' that their traditional role was transformed into that of a folk entrepreneur (one who exploits a market outside the original folk group). This is an essential point. When Handcox sang his songs in the ranks of the STFU, he was not using folk song to be a proletarian. Rather, the Negro preacher was singing the tunes he and his listeners were born and raised with. Handcox was expressing his social indignation in a genre endemic and natural to his community. This is a far cry from his role in the North; there he became, in the eyes of Marxists, a spokesman for proletarian culture." Denisoff, *Great Day Coming*, 36. While historically notable, the interpretation is frustrating. The fault he finds seems to not lie with Handcox, Garland, or anyone else in their position; rather, it seems to come about through their idealization by others. Taking advantage of this situation does not seem, to me, quite as bad as Denisoff makes it out to be. Though Denisoff ultimately seems to place blame with the Marxists in the North, he still seems to place the significant heft of blame on Handcox and Garland, since both "perceived themselves as *conscious* spokesmen."

44. Denisoff, *Great Day Coming*, 68.

45. Denisoff, 6.

46. Interested persons would write to Guthrie's Brooklyn address, and he would send a copy of his *Ten Songs* to the indicated return address. Often he would include doodles, small sayings, aphorisms, personal notes, and other marginalia.

47. Reuss, "Woody Guthrie and His Folk Tradition," 288.

48. Woody Guthrie, "Why, Oh Why," on *This Land Is Your Land: The Asch Recordings, Vol. 1*, Smithsonian Folkways, 1997; available at https://www.youtube.com/watch?v=fOAz3uCsS-E (accessed July 31, 2024).

49. Josh Kun, *Audiotopia: Music, Race, and America* (University of California Press, 2005), 17.

50. Cornel West, *Race Matters* (Beacon Press, 1993); and Cornel West, *Democracy Matters: Winning the Fight Against Imperialism* (Penguin Books, 2004).

51. Greil Marcus, *The Shape of Things to Come* (Farrar, Straus and Giroux, 2006), 15.

52. Woody Guthrie, "Farmer-Labor Train," on *Hard Travelin': The Asch Recordings, Vol. 3*, Smithsonian Folkways, 1998. The song is also released on *Long Ways to Travel: The Unreleased Folkways Masters, 1944–1949* (Smithsonian Folkways, 1994). There is no date for the recording, though given where it appears in *The Asch Recordings*, one could infer it was recorded in 1944 or 1945. Lyrics taken from http://www.woodyguthrie.org/Lyrics/Farmer-Labor_Train.htm (accessed July 31, 2024). The Woodyguthrie.org website maintains Guthrie's original spellings, line breaks, and grammar.

53. Woody Guthrie, "1913 Massacre," on *Hard Travelin': The Asch Recordings, Vol. 3*, Smithsonian Folkways, 1998. Lyrics from https://www.woodyguthrie.org/Lyrics/Nineteen_Thirteen_Massacre.htm. All subsequent quotes and descriptions of "1913 Massacre" follow the performance and lyrics cited in this note. Guthrie's lyrics vary in several of the performances (particularly his verb tenses), as does his vocal performance. In *The Live Wire: Woody Guthrie in Performance 1949* (Woody Guthrie Archives, 2007), Guthrie plays the song in a far more lilting fashion, with chords played as blocks, rather than arpeggiated, as they are in *Hard Travelin': The Asch Recordings, Vol. 3*.

54. Jonathan Freedman draws out Guthrie's connection to Judaism by noting how The Klezmatics, a group "that conspicuously combines radical musical innovation with radical cultural and social politics," has issued "albums of songs written by Woody Guthrie on Jewish themes, inspired by the mother of Guthrie's second wife." Jonathan Freedman, *Klezmer America: Jewishness, Ethnicity, Modernity* (Columbia University Press, 2008), 19.

55. Given the available information, it appears that Guthrie plays the guitar on this track.

56. The scandal of the Italian Hall massacre reverberated throughout the United States. After the incident, the leader of the striking workers, Charles Moyer, was shot and "deported" from the state of Michigan under mysterious circumstances. See, from the *Chicago Daily Tribune* archives, "Moyer, Wounded, Sticks to Battle [. . .]," *Chicago Daily Tribune*, December 28, 1913, accessed July 31, 2024, www.proquest.com/historical-newspapers/moyer-wounded-sticks-battle/docview/173733371/se-2; and "Moyer Tells of His Deportation [. . .]," *Chicago Daily Tribune*, March 11, 1914, accessed July 31, 2024, www.proquest.com/historical-newspapers/moyer-tells-his-deportation/docview/173789767/se-2.

57. Klein, *Woody Guthrie*, 10. Kaufman points out, "It is impossible to tell whether one of the grinning white faces in the photographed mob is that of Charley Guthrie, Woody's father; Ed Cray's biography makes no mention of Guthrie's presence, although he refers to the lynching by way of a footnote. Joe Klein's biography is categorical: Charley Guthrie, proud member of the Ku Klux Klan, was part of the lynch mob. (There is in face no documentary evidence to establish conclusively Charley Guthrie's Klan membership.)" Kaufman, *American Radical*, 145. Although Kaufman is right to note the lack of absolute archival evidence, Klein's claim is built on a careful examination of Charley Guthrie's infamous politics and his desire to lead crowds into fervent action through oratory and writing, a quality that the Oklahoma Democratic Party used to its great benefit in propounding a nativist, anti-Black, anti-Indigenous populism. For his fuller argument, see Klein, *Woody Guthrie*, 7–18.

58. Harvey Young, "The Black Body as Souvenir in American Lynching," *Theatre Journal* 57, no. 4 (2005): 642.

59. Stadler, *Intimate Life*, 164–86; see also the book's final chapter.

60. Werner, "Democratic Visions," 70.

61. Robert Cantwell, *Ethnomimesis: Folklife and the Representation of Culture* (University of North Carolina Press, 1993), 135.

62. Much work on Babb comes from news media and books. See, for example, Kenneth Burns's *The Dust Bowl* PBS documentary (2012); the Harry Ransom Center's website dedicated to Babb, http://www.hrc.utexas.edu/exhibitions/web/babb/intro (the Ransom Center also houses most of Babb's papers, along with her sister Dorothy's photographs of migrant workers in California; accessed July 31, 2024); a website dedicated to Babb, http://www.sanorababb.com/, run by Joanne Dearcopp, Babb's literary executor (still updated as of 2024; accessed July 31, 2024); and Ed Vulliamy, "The Vindication of Sanora Babb," *New York Review of Books*, August 19, 2021, accessed August 7, 2024, https://www.nybooks.com/articles/2021/08/19/vindication-of-sanora-babb/. An overview of Babb's work can be found in Douglas Wixson, "Radical by Nature: Sanora Babb and Ecological Disaster on the High Plains, 1900–1940," in *Regionalists on the Left*, ed. Michael C. Steiner (Oklahoma University Press, 2013), 110–33.

63. Babb's personal history is quite extraordinary. She was born in Oklahoma and moved to southeastern Colorado as a youth. She worked for the FSA as a social worker. With her sister, she documented the migrant workers in California, especially in camps. In the 1930s, she was romantically involved with William Saroyan and Ralph Ellison. She was the bride in one of the first official interracial marriages in California history when she married James Wong Howe in 1937. She was blacklisted for her political beliefs in the 1940s and moved to Mexico City. This is not even half of her story, though. Babb's memoir, *An Owl on Every Post* (1970), and her largely autobiographical novel *The Lost Traveler* (1958) detail more of her vast and interesting life.

64. As Paula M. L. Moya points out, a key feature of Mikhail Bakhtin's idea of heteroglossia emerges from "a multivoicedness that is accomplished artistically in any given novel through the characters' dialogue, the authorial voice(s), and the incorporation of other genres such as letters, news articles, poems, and so forth, all of which bring with them their own schemas." Paula M. L. Moya, *The Social Imperative: Race, Close Reading, and Contemporary Literary Criticism* (Stanford University Press, 2016), 55.

65. Babb, *Whose Names*, 128.

66. Watching *The Dust Bowl* convinced me that Babb's writing should be engaged with more widely. While the Steinbeck-Guthrie connection is quite evident (Guthrie's *Dust Bowl Ballads* have songs named after the Joads, for example), the connection between Babb's style and Guthrie's is just as worthy of examination.

67. In her 2004 review of the novel, Pamela J. Annas notes, "In one of those shifts of fate familiar to writers, especially new writers—and this was Babb's first novel—when she turned her manuscript in to Bennett Cerf [co-founder of Random House and the leading figure in the landmark court case *United States v. One Book Called Ulysses*, 1933] in 1939, Steinbeck's *The Grapes of Wrath* had already hit the bookstore shelves and become a bestseller. Cerf, and subsequently editors at Scribner, Colliers, and Viking, turned down *Whose Names Are Unknown*, saying another novel on the same subject wouldn't sell." Pamela J. Annas, "Unknown No More," *The Women's Review of Books* 21, no. 10/11 (July 2004): 10.

68. In addition to Wixson's work, cited throughout this chapter, see Abigail G. H. Manzella's dissertation, *Permanent Transients: The Temporary Spaces of Internal Migration in Four 20th-Century Novels by U.S. Women Writers* (PhD diss., University of Tulsa, 2010), which Manzella has turned into a book, *Migrating Fictions*, that I cite throughout the chapter; and Jennifer Marie Harrison's dissertation, *Oppositional Narratives: Embedded Tales, Social Justice, and the Reader* (PhD diss., University of Maryland Baltimore County, 2013).

69. "Deeply socialized by the same postfrontier conditions that historically had fostered individualism and conservative politics, Babb reconnected with her childhood and youth in the tent camps and along the dirt roads in California where new arrivals squatted in their cars until they found work. Initiating cooperative arrangements for their children's education and health, organizing labor demonstrations for better conditions, and recording the refugees' stories, she was able to enter the intimacy of the dispossessed farmers' lives and share their experiences." Douglas Wixson, "Introduction: The Babb Sisters," in *On the Dirty Plate Trail: Remembering the Dust Bowl Refugee Camps*, by Sanora Babb, photographs by Dorothy Babb, ed. Douglas Wixson (University of Texas Press, 2007), 6.

70. Babb, *Dirty Plate Trail*, 92.

71. Wixson, "Radical by Nature," 125.

72. Babb, *Whose Names*, 200.

73. Paul Virilio, *Speed and Politics*, trans. Mark Polizzotti (Semiotext(e), 2006), 34.

74. See especially James N. Gregory's history of migration from the Dust Bowl, *American Exodus: The Dust Bowl Migration and Okie Culture in California* (Oxford University Press, 1989). Gregory's work undoes the myth of absolute poverty among migrants from the Dust Bowl, while still maintaining the discursive importance of environmental and agricultural devastation. Even while Gregory critiques the idea that *all* Dust Bowl migrants were impoverished yeoman farmers, he nonetheless proves that a still astonishing number of the migrants *were*, in fact, small landowners and farmers. Gregory's work is especially important in revealing the class distinctions that enabled certain migrants to access economic privilege (for particulars, refer to pp. 6–35). Woody Guthrie's important and popular song "Do Re Mi," in fact, was a pointed criticism of the fact that the LAPD at one point took it upon themselves to act as state border patrol agents, demanding that migrants have a specific amount of funds ($500) in order to enter the state of California and seek work.

75. Babb, *Whose Names*, 174–75.

76. Wixson, "Radical by Nature," 126.

77. Wixson, 127.

78. Denisoff, *Great Day Coming*, 14.

79. Babb, *Whose Names*, 220. I argue for this tendency most strenuously in chapter 4 of this book, especially in my section on Tomás Rivera's *. . . y no se lo tragó la tierra* (1971).

80. An unfortunately persistent issue, the erasure of Filipino labor organizers in the literature and filmic representations of California and migrant labor has been

a truly disappointing aspect of progressive art, from Steinbeck to the recent Cesar Chavez biopic.

81. S. Wald, *Nature of California*, 53.

82. Babb, *Whose Names*, 160.

83. See, in particular, E. San Juan Jr., "Excavating the Bulosan Ruins: What Is at Stake in Re-discovering the Anti-imperialist Writer in the Age of US Global Terrorism?," *Kritika Kultura* 23 (2014): 154–67.

84. In the vein of Guthrie's song "Vigilante Man," named after the vigilante men in *The Grapes of Wrath*, I refer to these strikebreakers as vigilante men. Listen to Guthrie's version, recorded and released on his 1940 album *Dust Bowl Ballads* (Smithsonian Folkways, 1964): https://www.youtube.com/watch?v=S-tXikT2DZA (accessed July 31, 2024); listen also to Ry Cooder's slide guitar performance of the song in London on the program "The Old Grey Whistle Test," recorded in the BBC Television Theatre (March 20, 1973): https://www.youtube.com/watch?v=MhPw6cHzyWU (accessed July 31, 2024).

85. Babb, *Whose Names*, 154.

86. Babb, 154.

87. Babb, 184–85.

88. Babb, 185.

89. Jane Adams and D. Gorton, "This Land Ain't My Land: The Eviction of Sharecroppers by the Farm Security Administration," *Agricultural History* 83, no. 3 (Summer 2009): 323–51. Adams and Gorton point out that the FSA, in its efforts to "modernize" rural America, often resorted to displacement and resettlement tactics to make space for new model communities. Although they focus on Mississippi and Louisiana, their article provides considerable insight into how legal and de facto segregation informed FSA policy: "When the FSA developed the nine-thousand-plus-acre Transylvania Plantation [in East Carroll Parish, Louisiana] as an all-white project, displacing the plantation's long-established African-American settlement, the African-American sharecroppers' protest would reverberate throughout the black press, which was taken seriously by the New Deal" (324). Though Adams and Gorton point out that not all projects involved resettlement, in every case the land utilized, if not inhabited, was either previously worked over or agriculturally developed. In addition, the Library of Congress points out that FSA camps were often segregated by race. With regard to Mexican and Mexican American agricultural workers, these camps were set apart specifically to prevent racial violence against the workers: https://www.loc.gov/teachers/classroommaterials/presentationsandactivities/presentations/immigration/mexican6.html (accessed April 23, 2024).

90. Julia Dunne's father, known as "Konkie," is often depicted as communicating through a "sideways nod," one of the novel's repeated gestures conveying empathy toward others.

91. Babb, *Whose Names*, 187.

92. Babb, 194.

93. Maund's Scottsboro- and *Canterbury Tales*–influenced novel was reissued by the University of Illinois Press in 1999.

94. This overall observation is perhaps due to my training as a literary scholar. I believe it is definitely not a specious point, even as I argue that it does not entirely obviate what Babb is trying to do. The framework of Hegelian recognition and subject formation that Babb provides, for example, is quite radical when compared to her fellow white writers of the time. Considering how widespread the dialectal rendering of white migrant speech was, especially in the 1930s and 1940s, it seems clear that the failure is Babb's and not Milt Dunne's, and thus cannot be attributed to or explained away by the simple claim that a character is flawed.

95. Babb, *Whose Names*, 54–56.

96. In Julia Dunne's diary, April 14 is not the worst day of the dust storm, which is why I hesitate to positively identify the date as 1935.

97. Lawrence Svobida, *Farming the Dust Bowl: A First-Hand Account from Kansas* (1940; repr., University of Kansas Press, 1986), 147.

98. Babb, *Whose Names*, 90.

99. Babb, 213.

100. Babb, 220.

101. Babb, 220.

102. Manzella, *Migrating Fictions*, 107.

103. S. Wald, *Nature of California*, 66.

104. Erin Royston Battat, *Ain't Got No Home: America's Great Migrations and the Making of an Interracial Left* (University of North Carolina Press, 2014), 63.

105. Babb, *Whose Names*, 203.

106. Babb, 221.

107. S. Wald, *Nature of California*, 73.

108. May Joseph, *Nomadic Identities: The Performance of Citizenship* (University of Minnesota Press, 1999), 17.

109. Woody Guthrie, *Pastures of Plenty: A Self Portrait*, ed. Dave Marsh and Harold Leventhal (Harper Perennial, 1992), 248.

Chapter 3

1. Margo Natalie Crawford, *Black Post-Blackness: The Black Arts Movement and Twenty-First-Century Black Aesthetics* (University of Illinois Press, 2017); Robin D. G. Kelley, *Hammer and Hoe: Alabama Communists during the Great Depression* (1990; repr., University of North Carolina Press, 2015).

2. James Smethurst, *Behold the Land: The Black Arts Movement in the South* (University of North Carolina Press, 2021), 8–9, 36.

3. Andy Hines, *Outside Literary Studies: Black Criticism and the University* (University of Chicago Press, 2022).

4. Julius B. Fleming Jr., *Black Patience: Performance, Civil Rights, and the Unfinished Project of Emancipation* (New York University Press, 2022), 25.

5. Robert Rodgers Korstad, *Civil Rights Unionism: Tobacco Workers and the Struggle for Democracy in the Mid-Twentieth-Century South* (University of North Carolina Press, 2003), 11.

6. Michael K. Honey, *Southern Labor and Black Civil Rights: Organizing Memphis Workers* (University of Illinois Press, 1993), 291.

7. See especially Honey, *Southern Labor*, 13–43.

8. Michael Szalay, *Hip Figures: A Literary History of the Democratic Party* (Stanford University Press, 2012), 39. In making this observation, Szalay situates Robert Penn Warren's work in relation to Huey Long, the enormously popular and eventually assassinated Louisiana governor who inspired (and troubled) Warren to write *All the King's Men*. Szalay notes that Long bucked the trend of white racist political organization (up to a point) and that, as a result, "Warren's novel attributes responsibility for this assassination and analyzes its larger significance, especially in light of Long's interracial coalition" (40).

9. Ashon Crawley, *Blackpentecostal Breath: The Aesthetics of Possibility* (Fordham University Press, 2016), 4.

10. Smethurst, *Behold the Land*, 8.

11. Smethurst, 8–9.

12. Benjamin Balthaser, "Exceptional Whites, Bad Jews: Racial Subjectivity, Anti-Zionism, and the Jewish New Left," *Shofar: An Interdisciplinary Journal of Jewish Studies* 41, no. 2 (2023): 43.

13. See Laurie B. Green, "Race, Gender, and Labor in 1960s Memphis: 'I AM A MAN' and the Meaning of Freedom," *Journal of Urban History* 30, no. 3 (March 2004): 465–89. See also Green's book *Battling the Plantation Mentality: Memphis and the Black Freedom Struggle* (University of North Carolina Press, 2007); Steve Estes, *I Am a Man! Race, Manhood and the Struggle for Civil Rights* (University of North Carolina Press, 2005); and Joseph B. Atkins, *Covering for the Bosses: Labor and the Southern Press* (University Press of Mississippi, 2008).

14. Green, "Race, Gender, and Labor," 467.

15. Lynn Festa, *Sentimental Figures of Empire in Eighteenth-Century Britain and France* (Johns Hopkins University Press, 2006), 4.

16. Alexandra Vazquez, *Listening in Detail: Performances of Cuban Music* (Duke University Press, 2013), 7.

17. Vazquez, 95.

18. Theodor Adorno, "On Lyric Poetry and Society," in *The Lyric Theory Reader: A Critical Anthology*, ed. Virginia Jackson and Yopie Prins (Johns Hopkins University Press, 2014), 350.

19. Typescript of poem "The 23rd Slum," 1968, container 5, folder 15, Memphis Search for Meaning Committee Records, University of Memphis Special Collections, Memphis, TN.

20. This is the famous psalm that begins with "The Lord is my Shepherd; I shall not want" and contains the lines "Yea, though I walk through the valley of the shadow of death, / I will fear no evil."

21. Mike Chasar, *Everyday Reading: Poetry and Popular Culture in Modern America* (Columbia University Press, 2012), 8.

22. Chasar, 18.

23. Evie Shockley, *Renegade Poetics: Black Aesthetics and Formal Innovation in African American Poetry* (University of Iowa Press, 2011), 9–11. Shockley prefers "innovation" over either "avant-garde" or "experimental" because of the racist, misogynist, and capitalist exclusions the latter terms have been used to perpetuate in the academy.

24. Anthony Reed, *Freedom Time: The Poetics and Politics of Black Experimental Writing* (Johns Hopkins University Press, 2016), 6.

25. Fred Moten, *Black and Blur* (Duke University Press, 2017), 10.

26. Fred Moten, *Stolen Life* (Duke University Press, 2018), 243.

27. Sonya Posmentier's concept of "lyric ecology" offers a clarifying framework for beginning to understand how Memphis becomes a site of catastrophe and trauma, and how Memphis as a space affects representational practices. Sonya Posmentier, *Cultivation and Catastrophe: The Lyric Ecology of Modern Black Literature* (Johns Hopkins University Press, 2017). Memphis, in 1968, could certainly be understood as an instance of what Posmentier calls "spaces of bounded aesthetic innovation" which, importantly, generate "lyric modes of representation [that] allow us to comprehend the spatiotemporal displacements that have originated and perpetuated this time and place of modernity" (3, 17).

28. While the Lord's Prayer also appears in Luke, the version in Matthew is used far more broadly.

29. Typescript of "Sanitation Workers' Prayer" by Anonymous, 1968, container 5, folder 15, Memphis Search for Meaning Committee Records, University of Memphis Special Collections, Memphis, TN. Multiple editions exist, and I have selected these two for their exemplarity. As can be seen from the two images included here, orthographic and typographic differences are quite evident. Because I focus on the version entitled "Sanitation Workers' Prayer" (on the bottom, with the apostrophe), I will adhere to its material specifics, other than the ink stains.

30. The Committee On the Move for Equality functioned as one of the primary organizers of strike support during the Memphis Sanitation Strike. Made up of clergymen and labor leaders, COME played a central role in strike and protest activities throughout the duration of the strike. The committee invited Martin Luther King to Memphis and organized the march on March 28, the subsequent strike actions to protest police brutality, and the march to commemorate King's life. As noted by Michael K. Honey in his in-depth history of the Memphis Sanitation Strike, COME was formed on February 24 at the Mason Temple. Michael K. Honey, *Going Down Jericho Road: The Memphis Strike, Martin Luther King's Last Campaign* (W. W. Norton, 2008). Thirty-nine days later, on the day before he was assassinated, King gave his final speech, "I've Been to the Mountaintop," at the Mason Temple.

31. Thank you to Donal Harris for noting this subtle distinction in the line.

32. Crawley, *Blackpentecostal Breath*, 77.

33. GerShun Avilez, *Radical Aesthetics and Modern Black Nationalism* (University of Illinois Press, 2016), 12.

34. Christina Sharpe, *In the Wake: On Blackness and Being* (Duke University Press, 2016), 20.

35. Calvin Warren, "Black Nihilism and the Politics of Hope," *CR: The New Centennial Review* 15, no. 1 (2015): 223.

36. See especially Rita Felski's *The Limits of Critique* (University of Chicago Press, 2015); as well as Stephen Best and Sharon Marcus's "Surface Reading: An Introduction," *Representations* 108, no. 1 (2019): 1–21.

37. Several efforts, beginning in 2019, to locate Joe L. McKinnie were unsuccessful.

38. Fleming Jr., *Black Patience*, 13.

39. Harvey Young, *Embodying Black Experience: Stillness, Critical Memory, and the Black Body* (University of Michigan Press, 2010).

40. Kevin Quashie, *The Sovereignty of Quiet: Beyond Resistance in Black Culture* (Rutgers University Press, 2012), 26.

41. Marlon D. Ross, "Imagining Collectively: Identity, Individuality, and Other Social Phantasms; Introduction," in *Conditions of the Present: Selected Essays*, by Lindon Barrett, ed. Janet Neary (Duke University Press, 2018), 167.

42. Michael Lackey, "A Brief History of the Haverford Group," in *The Haverford Discussions: A Black Integrationist Manifesto for Racial Justice*, ed. Michael Lackey (University of Virginia Press, 2013), xi–xlvi.

43. Bonnie Costello, *The Plural of Us: Poetry and Community in Auden and Others* (Princeton University Press, 2017), 225.

44. Oren Izenberg, *Being Numerous: Poetry and the Ground of Social Life* (Princeton University Press, 2011), 4.

45. Izenberg, 142.

46. Shockley, *Renegade Poetics*, 11.

47. Izenberg, *Being Numerous*, 142.

48. Phillip Brian Harper, *Abstractionist Aesthetics: Artistic Form and Social Critique in African American Culture* (New York University Press, 2015), 15.

49. Gillian White, *Lyric Shame: The "Lyric" Subject of Contemporary American Poetry* (Harvard University Press, 2014), 5.

50. Avilez, *Radical Aesthetics*, 12.

51. Diana Fuss, *Identification Papers: Readings on Psychoanalysis, Sexuality, and Culture* (Routledge, 1995), 39.

52. Mary Helen Washington, *The Other Blacklist: The African American Literary and Cultural Left of the 1950s* (Columbia University Press, 2014), 174–75.

53. Washington, 176.

54. Lesley Wheeler, "Heralding the Clear Obscure: Gwendolyn Brooks and Apostrophe," *Callaloo* 24, no. 1 (2001): 231.

55. Jenni Rinner, "From Bronzeville to the Mecca and After: Gwendolyn Brooks and the Location of Black Identity," *MELUS* 40, no. 4 (Winter 2015): 168.

56. Gwendolyn Brooks and George Stavros, "An Interview with Gwendolyn Brooks," *Contemporary Literature* 11, no. 1 (1970): 5–6.

57. Gwendolyn Brooks, "The Third Sermon on the Warpland," in *Blacks* (Third World Press, 1987), 472.

58. Gwendolyn Brooks, "The Second Sermon on the Warpland," in *Blacks*, 470.

59. Thank you to Sara Judy for pointing this out at the Post45 workshop in 2019.

60. Brooks, "Third Sermon," 472.

61. Brooks, 472.

62. Gwendolyn Brooks, "Malcolm X," in *Blacks*, 441.

63. Washington, *Other Blacklist*, 192.

64. Washington, 192.

65. Brooks, "Third Sermon," 474.

66. From the station's own web page: "For over six decades, WVON has been the voice of the city and urban community. The station has performed as a platform of Real influence, including the political campaign sector in President Barack Obama's election. The Original owners of Chess Records, Leonard and Phil Chess, first carved out the canvas of WVON in 1963, a station designed to be 'The Voice of the Negro.' Later they assembled the dynamic group of Radio personalities, The Good Guys. This group had the title of the *Top 3 Radio Stations in Chicago*. Political activism and cultural awareness became the nationwide recognition attached to WVON. To magnify the station's capabilities, in 1977, WVON was bought by Midway Broadcasting owners Wesley South and Pervis Spann. Today the station is continuing to flourish with Melody Spann-Cooper's radio expertise in Chicago." See more at https://www.wvon.com/about-wvon/ (accessed April 25, 2024).

67. Shockley, *Renegade Poetics*, 28–29.

68. Gwendolyn Brooks, "An Aspect of Love, Alive in the Ice and Fire," in *Blacks*, 480.

69. Brooks, "Aspect of Love," 480.

70. Brooks, "Second Sermon," 453.

71. Brooks, 456.

72. Brooks, 454, 455.

73. Crawley, *Blackpentecostal Breath*, 6.

74. Gwendolyn Brooks, "The Sermon on the Warpland," in *Blacks*, 451.

75. Carl Phillips, "Brooks's Prosody: Three Sermons on the Warpland," *Poetry* 210, no. 3 (June 2017): 247.

76. Phillips, 252.

77. Wheeler, "Heralding the Clear Obscure," 167.

78. Brooks, "Sermon," 452.

79. Kevin Quashie, *Black Aliveness, or a Poetics of Being* (Duke University Press, 2021), 152. Emphasis original.

80. Gerald Vizenor, "Aesthetics of Survivance: Literary Theory and Practice," in *Survivance*, ed. Gerald Vizenor (University of Nebraska Press, 2008), 1.

Chapter 4

1. Chris Vials, in *Realism for the Masses: Aesthetics, Popular Front Pluralism, and U.S. Culture, 1935–1947* (University Press of Mississippi, 2009), indeed reads *America* and *The Grapes of Wrath* as each offering distinct views of the "people" as a structuring category of analysis, and therefore "forming two streams within the Popular Front, each with its popular and official adherents" (xxiv).

2. Steven Yao, "The Motions of the Oceans: Circulation, Displacement, Expansion, and Carlos Bulosan's *America Is in the Heart*," *Atlantic Studies* 15, no. 2 (2018): 193.

3. Yao, 193.

4. Ramón Saldívar, *Chicano Narrative: Dialectics of Difference* (University of Wisconsin Press, 1990), 6.

5. Alicia Schmidt Camacho, *Migrant Imaginaries: Latino Cultural Politics in the US-Mexico Borderlands* (New York University Press, 2008), 10.

6. Johaina K. Crisostomo, "'Self-Reliance, Self-Sacrifice': Translating Ethics across Empires in Maximo M. Kalaw's *The Filipino Rebel* (1930)," *American Quarterly* 73, no. 3 (2021): 535–56; Paul Nadal, "A Literary Remittance: Juan C. Laya's *His Native Soil* and the Rise of Realism in the Filipino Novel in English," *American Literature* 89, no. 3 (September 2017): 591–626; E. San Juan Jr., *The Philippine Temptation: Dialectics of Philippines-U.S. Literary Relations* (Temple University Press, 1996).

7. San Juan Jr., *Philippine Temptation*, 137.

8. Oscar V. Campomanes and Todd S. Gernes, "Two Letters from America: Carlos Bulosan and the Act of Writing," *MELUS* 15, no. 3 (Autumn 1988): 17, 23, 23.

9. Allan Punzalan Isaac, "Displacing Filipinos, Dislocating America: Carlos Bulosan's *America Is in the Heart*," in *Racially Writing the Republic: Racists, Race Rebels, and Transformations of American Identity*, ed. Bruce Braum and Duchess Harris (Duke University Press, 2009), 234, 242, 234.

10. Tim Libretti, "First and Third Worlds in U.S. Literature: Rethinking Carlos Bulosan," *MELUS* 23, no. 4 (Winter 1998): 141.

11. Joseph Keith, "Invisible Islands: Remapping the Transpacific Archipelago of US Empire in Carlos Bulosan's *America Is in the Heart*," in *Archipelagic American Studies*, ed. Brian Russell Roberts and Michelle Ann Stephens (Duke University Press, 2017), 184.

12. Yao, "Motions of the Oceans," 186–87.

13. Vials, *Realism for the Masses*, 111.

14. Sau-ling Cynthia Wong, *Reading Asian American Literature: From Necessity to Extravagance* (Princeton University Press, 1993), 134.

15. Nadal, "Literary Remittance," 604; emphasis original.

16. Nadal, 612.

17. Carlos Bulosan, *America Is in the Heart* (University of Washington Press, 1973), 148–49.

18. Bulosan, 56–57.

19. Cheryl Higashida, "Re-signed Subjects: Women, Work, and World in the Fic-

tion of Carlos Bulosan and Hisaye Yamamoto," *Studies in the Literary Imagination* 37, no. 1 (Spring 2004): 36.

20. Bulosan, *America*, 112.
21. Bulosan, 175–76.
22. Bulosan, 193.
23. Benjamin Balthaser, *Anti-imperialist Modernism: Race and Transnational Political Culture from the Great Depression to the Cold War* (University of Michigan Press, 2016), 189.
24. Bulosan, *America*, 180.
25. Bulosan, 186; ellipses original.
26. Bulosan, 189; ellipses original.
27. Bulosan, 305–6.
28. Colleen Lye, "Asian American Cultural Critique at the End of US Empire," *American Literary History* 34, no. 1 (2022): 246.
29. Keith, "Invisible Islands," 184.
30. Paul Nadal, "Carlos Bulosan, Socialist?," *Verge: Studies in Global Asia* 9, no. 1 (2023): 65.
31. Bulosan, *America*, 326–27.
32. Nadal, "Carlos Bulosan, Socialist?," 66.
33. Balthaser, *Anti-imperialist Modernism*, 191.
34. Vials, *Realism for the Masses*, 144.
35. I use both "Chicano" and "Chicanx," although not interchangeably. I mean for "Chicano" to signal a specific intersection of masculinity, politics, and philosophy, as well as Rivera's own historical usages and sensibilities. In using "Chicanx," I signal a linguistically inclusive Chicanidad that contains within it *Chicano, Chicana, Chicane, Chicanø,* and *Chican@,* seeking to avoid the grammatical genders of -*a/o*. Although new terms will certainly arise, this note stands in for my thinking at the time of publication.
36. Bill Gleason, professor of English at Princeton University, recalls quite clearly that at UCLA in the late 1980s, *Tierra* was taught as a paradigmatic example of political allegory. This recollection took place during a conversation in 2016.
37. Ralph F. Grajeda, "Tomás Rivera's . . . *y no se lo tragó la tierra*: Discovery and Appropriation of the Chicano Past," *Hispania* 62, no. 1 (1979): 71. This suggestion has taken the shape of an assumption in the critical literature. In addition to Grajeda, consult: Erlina González-Berry and Tey Diana Rebolledo, "Growing Up Chicano: Tomás Rivera and Sandra Cisneros," *International Studies in Honor of Tomás Rivera* (*Revista Chicano-Riqueña*) 13, no. 3–4 (Fall–Winter 1985): 109–19; Teresa B. Rodríguez, "Nociones sobre el arte narrativo en . . . *y no se lo tragó la tierra* de Tomás Rivera," *Bilingual Review / La Revista Bilingüe* 13, no. 1/2 (January–August 1986): 130–35; Julián Olivares, "The Search for Being, Identity and Form in the Work of Tomás Rivera," *International Studies in Honor of Tomás Rivera* (*Revista Chicano-Riqueña*) 13, no. 3–4 (Fall–Winter 1985): 66–80; Julián Olivares, "Introduction," in *Tomás Rivera: The*

Complete Works (Arte Público Press, 1992); Saldívar, *Chicano Narrative*; Álvaro Llosa Sanz, "Artes de la memoria y universo chicano: La memoria como técnica estructural en . . . *y no se lo tragó la tierra*," *Romance Quarterly* 54, no. 4 (2007): 280–89; Scott A. Beck and Dolores E. Rangel, "Representations of Mexican American Migrant Childhood in Rivera's . . . *y no se lo tragó la tierra* and Viramontes's *Under the Feet of Jesus*," *Bilingual Review / La Revista Bilingüe* 29, no. 1 (January–April 2008-9): 14–24; and Julio Ramos and Gustavo Buenrostro, "Prólogo a la edición argentina," in . . . *y no se lo tragó la tierra*, by Tomás Rivera, ed. Julio Ramos and Gustavo Buenrostro (Corregidor Press, 2012). Kimberly Socha, while largely adhering to the single-narrator argument, notes that *Tierra* "is at once one story and multiple stories. It is intensely personal to the unnamed narrator while also presenting communal experiences. In other words, it is paradoxical via its ability to represent the particular and the general." Kimberly Socha, "'To Discover and Rediscover': The Textualization of Individual and Communal Memory in Tomás Rivera's . . . *y no se lo tragó la tierra* / . . . *And the Earth Did Not Devour Him*," *Hipertexto* 9 (2009): 71.

38. Ramos and Buenrostro, "Prólogo a la edición argentina," 186. Other than Evangelina Vigil-Piñón's 1995 translation of *Tierra*, all translations from Spanish in this chapter are my own.

39. In other words, *Tierra* undoes the idea that racial or ethnic memory is a process of nostalgic mythmaking that finds its analogue in self-creation through memory's recapture; instead, it is a text that offers a vision of community built through differential experiences. Mexican American ethnic memory, then, is not reducible to the desire for the long-lost, idealized, and perhaps unknown homeland Aztlán, the mythic origin of the Aztecs (even as this is an important political claim). This memory is, rather, about the irreducible contours of concrete experience and life in the geographical space of Aztlán.

40. Dennis López, "Good-Bye Revolution—Hello Cultural Mystique: Quinto Sol Publications and Chicano Literary Nationalism," *MELUS* 35, no. 3 (2010): 184.

41. John Alba Cutler, "Quinto Sol, Chicano/a Literature, and the Long March through Institutions," *American Literary History* 26, no. 2 (2014): 264, 274.

42. Though he focuses on one particular passage of (mis)translation in the earliest edition of the book, John Alba Cutler's description of *Tierra* captures the overall spirit of the book. He argues that in asides, conversations, and moments of vernacular philosophy, we find "not merely an ethnographic transcription of local idioms. [This particular example] calls the speakers into existence within the fictional world, and its appearance as a fragment within a larger narrative lends it an aphoristic force, so that what reads initially as a joke (what do we have to lose?) continues to resonate as an existential meditation on the despair of poverty." Cutler, "Quinto Sol," 274.

43. Manuel M. Martín-Rodríguez, *Life in Search of Readers: Reading (in) Chicano/a Literature* (University of New Mexico Press, 2003), 26.

44. Saldívar, *Chicano Narrative*, 77.

45. Saldívar, 84.

46. Beck and Rangel, "Representations," 17.

47. Beck and Rangel, 18.

48. For Kimberly Socha, *Tierra*'s reconstruction of memory is a way to cope with trauma. Although she notes at multiple points in her essay that many of the sections "are fleeting stories that the child has heard but that do not necessarily affect him personally," she also argues that "the lessons learned, however, do relate to him and to all Chicanos." Socha, "To Discover and Rediscover," 68.

49. Ramos and Buenrostro, "Prólogo a la edición argentina," 249.

50. José E. Limón, *Dancing with the Devil: Society and Cultural Poetics in Mexican-American South Texas* (University of Wisconsin Press, 1994), 204.

51. James H. Abbot, ". . . *Y no se lo tragó la tierra*: With Tomás Rivera in Spain and Personal Memories," *International Studies in Honor of Tomás Rivera* (*Revista Chicano-Riqueña*) 13, no. 3–4 (Fall–Winter 1985): 26–29; Nicolás Kanellos, "Language and Dialog in . . . *y no se lo tragó la tierra*," *International Studies in Honor of Tomás Rivera* (*Revista Chicano-Riqueña*) 13, no. 3–4 (Fall–Winter 1985): 53–65; Luis Leal, "Tomás Rivera: The Ritual of Remembering," *International Studies in Honor of Tomás Rivera* (*Revista Chicano-Riqueña*) 13, no. 3–4 (Fall–Winter 1985): 30–38; Brooke Fredericksen, "Cuando Lleguemos / When We Arrive: The Paradox of Migration in Tomás Rivera's '. . . *y no se lo tragó la tierra*,'" *Bilingual Review / La Revista Bilingüe* 19, no. 2 (1994): 142–50; Mary A. Seliger, "Colonialism, Contract and Community in Américo Paredes's *George Washington Gómez* and . . . *And the Earth Did Not Devour Him* by Tomás Rivera," *Latino Studies* 7, no. 4 (Winter 2009): 435–56; Llosa Sanz, "Artes de la memoria"; and Socha, "To Discover and Rediscover."

Rivera's writing method is reminiscent of Zora Neale Hurston's, whose ethnographic methods enabled her to recount words and actions with powerful accuracy (although not without a little bit of creativity, which is another important point of similarity between the two). *Mules and Men* (1935) and *Tierra* are texts often, to their great detriment, excavated or taught for their ethnographic information. Both texts reveal the stakes of the literary, especially as an art with the discursive flexibility to illuminate imaginative, creative models of encountering and theorizing ethnic belonging, particularly in spaces that deny the dignity of migrants.

52. Eliud Martínez, "Tomás Rivera: Witness and Storyteller," *International Studies in Honor of Tomás Rivera* (*Revista Chicano-Riqueña*) 13, no. 3–4 (Fall–Winter 1985): 42.

53. Llosa Sanz, "Artes de la memoria," 288. "Theater of memory" is Llosa Sanz's own translation of "arte de la memoria," as he describes it in the abstract to his article. In this article, Llosa Sanz goes on to argue that each of the twelve stories functions as an "imagen o cuadro" (image or painting), in the style of Roman Catholic religious images (285). Vexingly, Llosa Sanz sticks to the "twelve stories" structure, even though arguing that there are fourteen stories would allow him to compare *Tierra* to the Stations of the Cross (in the Catholic tradition, there are fourteen Stations of the Cross), which would in turn strengthen the connections he wants to draw between *Tierra* and Catholic religious art.

54. Tomás Rivera, . . . *y no se lo tragó la tierra* / *And the Earth Did Not Devour Him* (1971; 3rd ed., Arte Público Press, 1995), 59, 135. The currently canonical translation, published in a bilingual edition by Arte Público Press, is by Evangelina Vigil-Piñón. I use this edition exclusively. While I prefer the third edition, published in 1995, the most commonly taught *Tierra* is the fourth edition, published in 2015; the pagination differs between the editions.

55. Rivera, *Tierra*, 59, 135.

56. Schmidt Camacho, *Migrant Imaginaries*, 8.

57. Rivera, *Tierra*, 74, 151.

58. Grajeda, "Discovery and Appropriation," 72.

59. Tomás Rivera, "Chicano Literature: Fiesta of the Living," *Books Abroad* 49, no. 3 (1975): 440.

60. Rivera, *Tierra*, 7, 89.

61. Rivera, 71, 147.

62. It is with regard to this emphasis on identity that I differ strongly with Carlos Gallego's reading of the text. See Carlos Gallego, "Topographies of Resistance: Cognitive Mapping in Chicano/a Literature," *Arizona Quarterly* 70, no. 2 (Summer 2014): 21–53. Gallego argues that *Tierra* contains an "emphasis on cognitive mapping as a type of epistemological praxis that precedes political action. It is precisely the desire for totality underlying cognitive mapping that I find privileges an economic or geopolitical reading over a cultural or identity-based analysis" (29). Gallego turns away from "identity-based analysis," which he later calls one of the "tired themes of Chicana/o community consciousness and identity formation" (33). That said, Gallego's argument that *Tierra* represents a nonallegorical political principle of totality, which in its particularity is geared "toward an alternative interpretive model capable of sustaining a critique of capitalism's totalizing effects," is quite convincing.

63. Rivera, "Fiesta of the Living," 440.

64. The late Rolando Hinojosa-Smith, in fact, claimed that this horrifying incident happened to Rivera himself. That said, I do not believe that Rivera means for *Tierra* to be explicitly or exclusively autobiographical; regardless, all of Rivera's own indications place the book within fiction as a genre, rather than nonfiction. Rolando Hinojosa-Smith, "Tomás Rivera: Rememberances [*sic*] of an Educator and a Poet," *Confluencia* 1, no. 1 (Fall 1985): 92.

65. Rivera, *Tierra*, 25, 101.

66. Rivera, 22, 98.

67. Rivera, 15, 91. The other passages quoted in this paragraph are on the same pages.

68. Rivera, 15, 91.

69. Daniel Valella has read *Tierra* within a larger sphere of what he terms "Japanese/American" and "Mexican/American" solidarities and influences. This argument focuses in particular on shared languages of incarceration and "conditions of forced relocation." See Daniel Valella, "Crystal City's 'Alien' Farmworkers: Tomás Rivera's . . .

y no se lo tragó la tierra and the Shared Histories of Chicanx and Japanese American Detention," *MELUS* 48, no. 1 (Spring 2023): 115–41 (quote at 134).

70. Gustavo Buenrostro, "Introducción a los anexos," in . . . *y no se lo tragó la tierra*, ed. Julio Ramos and Gustavo Buenrostro (Corregidor, 2012), 185.

71. When I have taught this text in the past, I often place it on a syllabus that includes Claude McKay's *Harlem Shadows* (1922) and Gwendolyn Brooks's *Annie Allen* (1949), both of which utilize the sonnet to great effect, especially in order to illuminate African American life in and against the frames of classical literature. As in McKay's and Brooks's poems, there is a cracking open of the formal frames of historical literary forms. There is another interesting connection—and I am eager to further research this—between *Tierra* and books of a similar construction, such as Jean Toomer's *Cane* and Ernest Hemingway's *In Our Time*. *Cane* contains fourteen stories and interstitial poems; *In Our Time* switches between "impressions" and short stories. *My Name Is Aram* (1940), William Saroyan's quintessential Armenian American short story collection, also contains fourteen stories.

72. Kanellos, "Language and Dialog," 54.

73. Grajeda, "Discovery and Appropriation," 72.

74. Llosa Sanz, "Artes de la memoria," 282.

75. Olivares, "Search for Being," 70.

76. Rey Chow, *Writing Diaspora: Tactics of Intervention in Contemporary Cultural Studies* (Indiana University Press, 2003), 28.

77. This aspect of the text is strikingly reminiscent of Ralph Ellison's *Invisible Man* (1952) (including the anonymity of the narrator), except that in Ellison's text the narrator has surrounded himself with bright, perpetual lights as he goes about recollecting the narrative that becomes the novel—a narrative that, like *Tierra*, resists, or in fact refuses, allegory. There is also a connection to Juan Rulfo's *Pedro Páramo* (1955), a connection well-noted by Saldívar in particular, as well as by Rivera himself in discussions of his influences and his striking literary style. The Ellison connection is unnoted, however, and perhaps evocative given the anonymity of that novel's protagonist and the anonymity of the young boy at the end of *Tierra*. Teresa B. Rodríguez, in addition to pointing out the connection to Rulfo's *El llano en llamas* (1953), also suggests we consider *Tierra* alongside Miguel Ángel Asturias, Alejo Carpentier, Carlos Fuentes, Gabriel García Márquez, and Ernesto Sábato. See T. Rodríguez, "Nociones," 130–35.

78. Rivera, *Tierra*, 74, 150; ellipses original.

79. Rivera, 74, 151.

80. Stuart Hall, "Ideology and Ideological Struggle," in *Cultural Studies 1983: A History*, ed. Jennifer Daryl Slack and Lawrence Grossberg (Duke University Press, 2016), 136.

81. Rivera, *Tierra*, 75, 152.

82. Martín-Rodríguez, *Life in Search of Readers*, 26.

83. Lye, "Asian American Cultural Critique," 246.

84. The allegorical reading, regardless of my critique, still provides a powerful interpretation of the book, especially since it is perhaps the most straightforward, or readily available, explanation for the narrator's memorialization and literal incorporation of his community's stories.

85. Martínez, "Witness and Storyteller," 49.

86. Homi K. Bhabha, *The Location of Culture* (Routledge, 1994), 2.

87. Alexandra T. Vazquez, *Listening in Detail: Performances of Cuban Music* (Duke University Press, 2013), 208.

Chapter 5

1. My first and favored copy of *Bridge* is the 2002 version published by Third Woman Press, which has an Ana Mendieta cover and full-color reproductions of images. For ease of access, in this chapter I refer to and cite the widely available 2015 edition published by the State University of New York Press.

2. AnaLouise Keating, *Transformation Now! Toward a Post-oppositional Politics of Change* (University of Illinois Press, 2013), 20.

3. Teresa de Lauretis, *Technologies of Gender: Essays on Theory, Film, and Fiction* (Indiana University Press, 1987), 10–11.

4. Michael Hames-García, "Queer Theory Revisited," in *Gay Latino Studies: A Critical Reader*, ed. Michael Hames-García and Ernesto Javier Martínez (Duke University Press, 2011), 25.

5. Shane Phelan, *Getting Specific: Postmodern Lesbian Politics* (University of Minnesota Press, 1994), 29.

6. Greil Marcus, *The Shape of Things to Come* (Farrar, Straus and Giroux, 2006), 14–15.

7. Not to mention historiography and anthropology, though I will avoid a granular discussion of either field in this chapter.

8. The digital archive of *El Grito* is housed at Northwestern University's website: opendoor.northwestern.edu (accessed January 8, 2023).

9. Naomi H. Quiñonez, "Re(Riting) the Chicana Postcolonial: From Traitor to 21st Century Interpreter," in *Living Chicana Theory*, ed. Carla Trujillo (Third Woman Press, 1997), 137.

10. Estela Portillo, "Introduction," in *Chicanas en la literatura y el arte*, ed. Estela Portillo, El Grito Book Series No. 1 (Quinto Sol, 1973), 6.

11. Portillo, 6.

12. Francisco E. Robles, "Unsettling Monuments of Chicanx Masculinity in Estela Portillo Trambley's 'Rain of Scorpions,'" in *Decolonizing Latinx Masculinities*, ed. Frederick Luis Aldama and Arturo Aldama (University of Arizona Press, 2020), 228–47.

13. Estela Portillo, "After Hierarchy," in Portillo, *Chicanas en la literatura y el arte*, 84.

14. Melina Vizcaíno-Alemán, "Chicana Letters: Writing Back, con Safos," *Pasados: Recovering Histories, Imagining Latinidad* 1, no. 1 (Spring 2024): 29–49.

15. Maythee Rojas, "Violent Acts of a Feminist Nature: Estela Portillo Trambley's Striking Short Fiction," *MELUS* 33, no. 3 (Fall 2008): 72.

16. Juan Bruce-Novoa, *Chicano Authors: Inquiry by Interview* (University of Texas Press, 1980), 167.

17. Maurice Blanchot, *The Space of Literature*, trans. Ann Smock (University of Nebraska Press, 1986), 23.

18. John Alba Cutler, *The Ends of Assimilation: The Formation of Chicano Literature* (Oxford University Press, 2015), 118.

19. Jo Carillo, "And When You Leave, Take Your Pictures with You," in *This Bridge Called My Back*, ed. Gloria E. Anzaldúa and Cherríe Moraga (1981; repr., State University of New York Press, 2015), 60–61.

20. Gloria Anzaldúa, "La Prieta," in Anzaldúa and Moraga, *Bridge*, 204.

21. Héctor Calderón, "'A New Connection, a New Set of Recognitions': From *This Bridge Called My Back* to *this bridge we call home*," *Discourse* 25, no. 1 (2003): 300.

22. Jodi Melamed, *Represent and Destroy: Rationalizing Violence in the New Racial Capitalism* (University of Minnesota Press, 2011), 1.

23. Matthew Beeber, "Nancy Cunard and the 1930s Coalitional Anthology," *Comparative Literature* 74, no. 4 (2022): 449.

24. Sara Marcus, *Political Disappointment: A Cultural History from Reconstruction to the AIDS Crisis* (The Belknap Press of Harvard University Press, 2023), 130.

25. Cherríe Moraga, "The Welder," in Anzaldúa and Moraga, *Bridge*, 219.

26. Moraga, 219.

27. Keating, *Transformation Now!*, 19.

28. Kayann Short, "Coming to the Table: The Differential Politics of *This Bridge Called My Back*," *Genders* 19 (1994): 30.

29. Gloria E. Anzaldúa, "Speaking in Tongues: A Letter to Third World Women Writers," in Anzaldúa and Moraga, *Bridge*, 168.

30. Theodor Adorno, *Minima Moralia: Reflections from Damaged Life*, trans. E. F. N. Jephcott (1974; repr., Verso, 2005), 71.

31. Andrea Canaan, "Brownness," in Anzaldúa and Moraga, *Bridge*, 234.

32. Patricia Hill Collins, *Black Feminist Thought* (2000; repr., Routledge Classics, 2009), 41.

33. P. H. Collins, 138.

34. Canaan, "Brownness," 236.

35. Cheryl Higashida, "Not Just a 'Special Issue': Gender, Sexuality, and Post-1965 Afro Asian Coalition Building in the *Yardbird Reader* and *This Bridge Called My Back*," in *Afro Asia: Revolutionary Political and Cultural Connections between African Americans and Asian Americans*, ed. Fred Ho and Bill V. Mullen (Duke University Press, 2008), 224, 227.

36. Higashida, 227.

37. Colleen Lye, "Criticism/Self-Criticism and Identity Politics," *South Atlantic Quarterly* 119, no. 4 (October 2020): 711, 705.

38. Linda Garber, *Identity Poetics: Race, Class, and the Lesbian-Feminist Roots of Queer Theory* (Columbia University Press, 2001), 176.

39. Garber, 148.

40. M. Jacqui Alexander, *Pedagogies of Crossing: Meditations on Feminism, Sexual Politics, Memory, and the Sacred* (Duke University Press, 2006), 279.

41. Paulo Freire, *Pedagogy of the Oppressed*, trans. Myra Bergman Ramos (Continuum, 2010), 51.

42. De Lauretis, *Technologies of Gender*, 2.

43. Audre Lorde, "The Master's Tools Will Never Dismantle the Master's House," in Anzaldúa and Moraga, *Bridge*, 95.

44. Deleuze and Guattari describe something similar: "*Between* things does not designate a localizable relation going from one thing to the other and back again, but a perpendicular direction, a transversal movement that sweeps one *and* the other away, a stream without beginning or end that undermines its banks and picks up speed in the middle." Gilles Deleuze and Félix Guattari, *A Thousand Plateaus*, trans. Brian Massumi (University of Minnesota Press, 1987), 25.

45. Lauren Berlant, *Cruel Optimism* (Duke University Press, 2011), 2.

46. Saidiya V. Hartman and Frank B. Wilderson, "The Position of the Unthought," *Qui Parle* 13, no. 2 (2003): 185.

47. For a provocative history of the dialectic, including a remapping of the famous "master-slave" opposition into the feudal "lord-bondsman" relation, see Andrew Cole, *The Birth of Theory* (University of Chicago Press, 2014).

48. Norma Alarcón, "The Theoretical Subject(s) of *This Bridge Called My Back* and Anglo-American Feminism," in *The Postmodern Turn: New Perspectives on Social Theory*, ed. Steven Seidman (Cambridge University Press, 1994), 152.

49. This is certainly related to how José Muñoz uses the work of Ernst Bloch, in particular the idea of "potentiality" in *The Principle of Hope*, which Muñoz activates. Deborah Gould describes potentiality, as Muñoz uses it vis-à-vis Bloch, beautifully: "The not-yet exists in the present as potentiality, meaning that rather than seeking transcendence, we can look to the world *as it is* for sources of change. The unrealized potentialities of the past—what we might call the not-yet of politics—provide a storehouse of live possibilities for the now." Deborah Gould, "Becoming Coalitional: The Perverse Encounter of Queer to the Left and the Jesus People USA," *S&F Online* 14, no. 2 (2017): n.p.

50. Bernice Johnson Reagon, "Coalition Politics: Turning the Century," *Feministische Studien* 33, no. 1 (2015): 117. Originally published in *Home Girls: A Black Feminist Anthology*, ed. Barbara Johnson (Kitchen Table Press, 1983).

51. Ewa Majewska, *Feminist Antifascism: Counterpublics of the Common* (Verso, 2021), 19.

52. Pat Parker, "Revolution: It's Not Neat or Pretty or Quick," in Anzaldúa and Moraga, *Bridge*, 242.

53. Chrystos, "Ceremony for Completing a Poetry Reading," in Anzaldúa and Moraga, *Bridge*, 190.

54. Chrystos, 190.
55. Chrystos, 191.
56. Daniel Fischlin, Ajay Heble, and George Lipsitz, *The Fierce Urgency of Now: Improvisation, Rights, and the Politics of Cocreation* (Duke University Press, 2013).
57. Albert Murray, "Improvisation and the Creative Process," in *The Jazz Cadence of American Culture*, ed. Robert O'Meally (Columbia University Press, 1998), 112.
58. Keating, *Transformation Now!*, 55.
59. Adrienne Rich, "Notes toward a Politics of Location," in *Feminist Postcolonial Theory: A Reader*, ed. Reina Lewis and Sara Mills (Routledge, 2003), 32.
60. I am also inspired, in pursuing the question of location, by Christina A. León's examination of position and positionality in her discussion of *Bridge*, especially Moraga's essay "La Güera." To listen to León's lecture: https://youtu.be/YeqrIzMx7RU?si=aRX86ZgQ0cYACHYX&t=1936 (accessed April 21, 2024).
61. Édouard Glissant, *Poetics of Relation*, trans. Betsy Wing (University of Michigan Press, 1997), 20, 21.
62. Mary Pat Brady, *Extinct Lands, Temporal Geographies: Chicana Literature and the Urgency of Space* (Duke University Press, 2002), 139.
63. Roderick A. Ferguson, *The Reorder of Things: The University and Its Pedagogies of Minority Difference* (University of Minnesota Press, 2012), 230.
64. Keating, *Transformation Now!*, 41.
65. Keating, 54.
66. S. Marcus, *Political Disappointment*, 12.
67. Gloria Anzaldúa and Cherríe Moraga, "Between Lines: On Culture, Class, and Homophobia," in Anzaldúa and Moraga, *Bridge*, 102–3.
68. Here, I am echoing quite deliberately the passage from James Baldwin's essay "Notes of a Native Son": "But that battered word, truth, having made its appearance here, confronts one immediately with a series of riddles and has, moreover, since so many gospels are preached, the unfortunate tendency to make one belligerent. Let us say, then, that truth, as used here, is meant to imply a devotion to the human being, his freedom and fulfillment; freedom which cannot be legislated, *fulfillment which cannot be charted*." James Baldwin, "Notes of a Native Son," in *Notes of a Native Son* (1955; repr., Beacon Press, 2012), 12; emphasis mine.
69. José Esteban Muñoz, *Cruising Utopia: The Then and There of Queer Futurity* (New York University Press, 2009), 28.
70. Hans-Georg Gadamer's insights into hermeneutics as a method of encounter suggest that interpretation and understanding move bidirectionally yet in concert, persistently (re)producing the process of meaning: "A person trying to understand something will not resign himself from the start to relying on his own accidental foremeanings, ignoring as consistently and stubbornly as possible the actual meaning of the text until the latter becomes so persistently audible that it breaks through what the interpreter imagines it to be. Rather, a person trying to understand a text is prepared for it to tell him something. That is why a hermeneutically trained consciousness must

be, from the start, sensitive to the text's alterity." Hans-Georg Gadamer, *Truth and Method*, trans. Joel Wensheimer and Donald G. Marshall (Bloomsbury Academic, 2004), 269. The hinge of Gadamer's observation, importantly, is that the text *speaks*. If it is ignored, he argues, "the actual meaning of the text" will stop functioning as a process, and as a result "becomes so persistently audible that it breaks through what the interpreter imagines it to be"; indeed, he says, we must be "prepared" for the text "to tell" us its meaning—this is a subtle but quite radical displacement of textuality as a processual operation rather than as a stable enterprise.

71. Alexander, *Pedagogies of Crossing*, 278.

72. Muñoz, *Cruising Utopia*, 5.

73. Alicia Schmidt Camacho, *Migrant Imaginaries: Latino Cultural Politics in the U.S.–Mexico Borderlands* (New York University Press, 2008), 12.

74. Hartman and Wilderson, "Position of the Unthought," 185.

75. Canaan, "Brownness," 235.

76. Melamed, *Represent and Destroy*, 116.

77. Melamed, 97.

78. Ferguson, *Reorder of Things*, 174.

79. Jakobi Williams, *From the Bullet to the Ballot: The Illinois Chapter of the Black Panther Party and Racial Coalition Politics in Chicago* (University of North Carolina Press, 2013), 127–59.

80. J. Williams, 126.

81. Lee Sustar, "The National Black Political Convention," *Socialist Worker*, April 1988, accessed April 22, 2024, https://socialistworker.org/2013/03/22/the-national-black-political-convention.

82. Andrew Kopkind, "The Jackson Moment," *New Left Review*, no. 172 (November/December 1988): 87–88.

83. Michael Szalay, *Hip Figures: A Literary History of the Democratic Party* (Stanford University Press, 2012).

84. As a result of these concessions, Sustar pointed out, "Jackson's selection of Ron Brown as his chief negotiator at the 1988 Democratic National Convention showed where Jackson had taken the Rainbow. Brown was a California Democrat with no history at all in grassroots struggles, but a long record of working inside the party machine. He had once made his living as a lobbyist for Jean 'Baby Doc' Duvalier during Duvalier's murderous dictatorship in Haiti." Lee Sustar, "Jesse Jackson and the Rainbow Coalition," *Socialist Worker*, February–March 1989, accessed April 22, 2024, https://socialistworker.org/2013/04/12/jesse-jackson-and-the-rainbow.

85. Sarah Schulman, *Let the Record Show: A Political History of ACT UP New York, 1987-1993* (Farrar, Straus and Giroux, 2021), xviii.

86. Schulman, 14–15.

87. Bettina Aptheker, *Communists in Closets: Queering the History 1930s–1980s* (Routledge, 2023), 224.

88. Schulman, *Let the Record Show*, xxvi.

89. Schulman, 16.

90. S. Marcus, *Political Disappointment*, 23.

91. This work has been published in *Post45: Contemporaries*, *Killing the Buddha*, *Chiricú*, and the *Routledge Handbook of Latinx Life Writing* (ed. Christine Fernández and Maria Villaseñor).

Index

"23rd Slum, The," 129, 132–37, 140, 149, 160; Biblical language in, 132–37; rage in, 136–37

activism, 14, 18–19, 24, 30, 120, 130, 166, 173, 184, 229, 255n66; and Bulosan, Carlos, 175; Chicano, 183–84; civil rights, 121–22, 124, 142; feminist, 212, 229; housing, 5; immigration, 230; Indigenous, 230; internationalism of, 14, 32, 119. *See also* AIDS Coalition to Unleash Power (ACT UP); Memphis Sanitation Strike

AIDS Coalition to Unleash Power (ACT UP), 30, 229

Adam, Erin M., 5

Adams, Jane, 250n89

Adorno, Theodor: on the dialectic, 214; on lyric poetry, 131

aesthetics: of affect, 116; Black, 32; coalitional, 3–4, 6, 9–10, 12–14, 16, 18, 21, 23–24, 26–27, 29–30, 32, 33, 35, 71–72, 82, 114, 119, 122–23, 130, 151, 153, 164, 166, 173, 178–79, 181, 193, 201, 212, 215, 222, 225, 226, 230; embodied, 216; and inheritance, 230; and politics, 16, 22, 36; and the Popular Front, 175

affect, 85, 116, 234n11

agriculture, 78–80, 99, 106, 111, 163, 167, 170, 172; farm labor, 163, 170, 176, 190; land use, 250n89

Akers, John C., 166

Alarcón, Norma, 211

Alexander, M. Jacqui, 216, 235n31

allegory, 17, 162, 166–69; in *America Is in the Heart* (Bulosan), 17, 161–65; limits of, 20, 24, 199; in *. . . y no se lo tragó la tierra* (Rivera), 24, 161–65, 180–81, 183–84, 187, 193–94, 196, 198, 257n36, 261n77

Allison, Raphael C., 59

America Is in the Heart (Bulosan), 19–21, 24, 28, 161–80; as *migrant pizcaresque*, 162–64, 167, 170, 173, 178, 180; coalitional logic of, 177–79; and Popular Front aesthetics, 175

American Federation of Labor (AFL), 34

analogy, 4, 52, 177; limits of, 4, 9

Anderson, Sherwood: *Winesburg, Ohio*, 24

Annas, Pamela J., 248n67

anti-Blackness, 126–27, 137

anticommunism, 7, 14, 119–20

antifascism, 34, 55, 80, 119, 230, 239n43, 244n26

269

Anzaldúa, Gloria, 6, 166, 204, 210–216, 223, 225; *Borderlands/La Frontera*, 216; *This Bridge Called My Back*, 3, 5, 6, 10, 11, 17, 20, 26, 29, 202–205, 209–17, 219–26, 229, 230; "La Prieta," 210
Aptheker, Bettina, 7, 229
Asian American studies, 167
Atkins, Joseph B., 123
authority: collectivized, 21, 23, 56, 66, 189; dispersed, 37, 50, 63, 72, 74; and ethnography, 40; rethinking of, 32
Avilez, GerShun, 125, 140, 151–52

Babb, Sanora: *Whose Names Are Unknown*, 3, 8, 9, 17, 25, 27, 45, 79–82, 98–117, 162, 163, 173, 249n69, 251n94
Baigell, Matthew, 55
Bakhtin, Mikhail, 248n64
Baldwin, Davarian, 237n9
Baldwin, James: "Everybody's Protest Novel" 21–22; "Notes of a Native Son," 265n68
Baldwin, Kate A., 7
Balthaser, Benjamin, 8, 13, 126, 175, 179
Bambara, Toni Cade, 32, 211
Barrett, Linden, 145
Barton Fink (Coen), 243n16
Barthes, Roland, 109, 116; on myth, 43, 227
Battat, Erin Royston: *Ain't Got No Home*, 7, 34, 100, 103, 113–14, 237n2
Beam, Joseph, 229
Beck, Scott A., 184
Beeber, Matthew: on "coalitional aesthetics," 4, 212
Benjamin, Walter, 131
Berlant, Lauren: on "cruel optimism," 76, 218
Berman, Jessica, 21
Bhabha, Homi, 200
bildungsroman, 17, 28, 161–63, 166–69, 182, 189; ethnic, 182

Blanchot, Maurice, 209
Black Arts Movement, 14, 119, 125–26, 130, 146, 148, 151
Black nationalism, 120, 121, 122, 125, 151–52
Black Panther Party, 126, 227,
"Black Poem, A" (McCraw), 147–49
Bloch, Ernst: *The Principle of Hope*, 264n49
Bluestein, Gene: on folk authenticity, 89, 245n36
Boas, Franz, 37, 43, 48, 49, 237n2
Book of the Dead, The (Rukeyser): 10, 20, 24, 26, 31, 35–36, 53–76, 118, 239n39; "Absalom," 10–12; "Alloy," 63; criticism of, 55–56; "George Robinson: Blues," 63, 67; "Mearl Blankenship," 59–64; polyvocality in, 59–61; as poetry of witness, 54, 59, 67–69, 71, 72; as "proletcult" verse, 62; "Praise of the Committee," 63–68; "The Soul and Body of John Brown," 57, 68; and *speaking with*, 59–61
Booth, Wayne: The Rhetoric of Fiction, 236n43
Brady, Mary Pat, 222
Bridge Called My Back, This (Moraga and Anzaldúa), 3, 5, 6, 10, 11, 17, 20, 26, 29, 202–205, 209–17, 219–26, 229, 230; argumentative and narrative arc of, 29, 205; coalition in, 29, 204, 212; multivocality as process in, 20, 204; and white supremacy, 223
Brooks, Daphne, 41
Brooks, Gwendolyn, 2, 3, 9, 73, 151–60, 212; "An Aspect of Love Alive in the Ice and Fire: LaBohem Brown," 157; *Annie Allen*, 261n71; *The Bean Eaters*, 155–56; "In the Mecca," 156; *In the Mecca*, 28, 122, 151, 153, 154, 155; *Maud Martha*, 154; *Riot*, 28, 122, 153–57; "The Second Sermon

on the Warpland," 154, 157–58; "The Sermon on the Warpland," 158–60; "The Third Sermon on the Warpland," 154–55, 157, 158
Brown, John, 57, 68
Bruce-Novoa, Juan, 183, 209
Buenrostro, Gustavo,181, 192–93
Buff, Rachel Ida, 14–15
Bulosan, Carlos, 3, 8, 9, 24, 28–29, 45, 103, 106, 161–80; *America is In the Heart*, 19–21, 24, 28, 161–80
Burns, Ken: *The Dust Bowl*, 99–100, 102
Buschendorf, Christa, 59, 72

Cahan, Abraham: *Forverts*, 19
Calderón, Héctor, 210–11
Campomanes, Oscar V.,167
Canaan, Andrea, 214–15, 226
Candelaria, Cordelia, 209
Cantwell, Robert, 97
Carillo, Jo: "And When You Leave, Take Your Pictures with You: Racism in the Women's Movement," 210
Catlett, Elizabeth, 119
Cervantes, Miguel de: *Don Quixote*, 169
Chasar, Mike, 132
Chávez, Karma R., 3, 5
Cherniak, Martin, 53, 239n39
Chicano nationalism, 182–84, 192, 207
Chow, Rey, 23
Chrystos: "Ceremony for Completing a Poetry Reading," 211, 220
Chuh, Kandice: on "being with," 73
Civil Rights Movement, 9, 15, 120, 122, 125, 127, 243n13
coalition, 3–6; and contemporary politics, 218; and the Democratic Party, 8–9, 17; groundedness required of, 219–22; and multiculturalism, 30, 202, 211; and the Popular Front, 30, 80, 202, 222; Rainbow Coalition, 227–28
Cohen, Edwin, 88

collectivity: and Black nationalism, 152; in *The Book of the Dead* (Rukeyser), 70; in Memphis Sanitation Strike poetry, 141, 145–47
Collins, Patricia Hill, 214
Collins, Tom, 27, 99, 101
Collins Jr., Henry Hill, 77
Combahee River Collective, 211, 215, 229; "A Black Feminist Statement," 215
Committee On the Move for Equality (COME), 137, 253n30
Congress of Industrial Organizations (CIO), 8, 10, 34
Congress of Racial Equality (CORE), 229
Corwin, Norman, 81
Costello, Bonnie: *The Plural of Us*, 147
Cotera, María Eugenia, 4, 37, 238n13
Crawford, Margo Natalie: *Black Post-Blackness*, 8, 14, 119, 125
Crawley, Ashon: *Blackpentecostal Breath*, 125, 139, 158
Crenshaw, Cornelia, 129
Crenshaw, Kimberlé, 214
Crisostomo, Johaina K.,167

Dayton, Tim, 53–54, 61, 64, 70, 239n39
Defoe, Daniel: *Robinson Crusoe*, 167
de Lauretis, Teresa, 203, 217
Deleuze, Gilles, 22, 116, 264n44
democracy, 24, 81, 90, 94, 102, 113, 172, 173, 177, 239n43; direct, 102; and music, 94, 97; radical, 115–17; representational, 166; and whiteness, 82
Denisoff, Serge, 88–92, 104, 246n43
Denning, Michael, 7, 8, 10, 12, 33, 34, 57
direct action, 27. *See also* activism; Memphis Sanitation Strike
documentary poetics, 32, 54, 116
Dos Passos, John, 24
Drabinski, John E., 73
Dunbar, Paul Laurence, 32

Ehlers, Sarah, 71–72
elegy, 1, 150, 155, 231; refusal of, 1
Eliot, George: *Adam Bede*, 105
Ellison, Ralph, 243n13, 248n63, 261n77
Espada, Martín, 1–3, 231; "Floaters," 1–3
Estes, Steve, 123
ethnicity, 5, 9, 28, 164, 226
ethnic literature, 15–16, 74, 162; reception of, 16
ethnic studies, 16, 120, 202
ethnography, 24, 36–39, 41,44, 48–49, 50; participatory, 39–40, 44, 47

failure, 20, 25, 35, 80, 109, 220
Fante, John, 9, 103, 162
farm labor, 78–79, 94, 108, 163, 170, 175–76, 192, 170, 176, 192
Farm Security Administration (FSA), 98
Faulkner, William: *The Sound and the Fury*, 25
feminism, 203, 212, 217; Black, 214–15, 229; of color, 203; internationalist, 204; labor, 173; multicultural, 215; US Third World, 211, 230; white, 203, 212
Ferguson, Roderick A., 222, 227
Festa, Lynn,127, 128
Figlerowicz, Marta: *Flat Protagonists*, 39
Figueroa-Vásquez, Yomaira C., 73–74
Fischlin, Daniel, 221
Fleming Jr., Julius B., 121, 142–43, 145
folklore, 48, 52, 165, 245n36. *See also* poplore
folk music, 42, 80, 81, 87–92, 243n18, 246n43
Ford III, James E., 45
Foucault, Michel, 22, 56
Freedman, Jonathan, 33, 247n54
Friere, Paulo: *Pedagogy of the Oppressed*, 217
Fuss, Diana, 152

Gadamer, Hans-Georg: *Truth and Method*, 223, 265n70
Gallego, Carlos, 180, 260n62
Gambino, Elena, 5
Garber, Linda, 215–16
Garcia, Roberto Carlos, 231
Garman, Bryan: on the "hurt song," 87
Gay Liberation Front, 229
Gehlawat, Monica, 19, 35–36, 40
gender, 2, 5, 9, 12, 15, 29, 149, 203, 217, 226
gender studies, 202
Gernes, Todd S., 167
Ginsberg, Allen, 93, 204
Girmay, Aracelis, 2, 231
Glissant, Édouard: geographical contextualization of, 235n31; on relation, 17–18, 73–74; on totality, 222
Gorton, D., 250n89
Gould, Deborah, 5, 6, 233n6, 264n49
Grajeda, Ralph, 180, 187, 195, 257n37
Great Depression, 78, 82
Green, Laurie B., 123, 127, 128
Gregory, James N., 249n74
Guattari, Felix, 264n44
Guthrie, Woody, 3, 9, 17, 19, 21, 27, 79–98, 116–18, 235n33, 243n21, 244n26, 244n29, 245n36, 245n38; "1913 Massacre," 91, 95, 247n53; *Bound for Glory*, 84–87; diary entries of, 117–18; *Dust Bowl Ballads*, 91, 103, 248n66; "Farmer-Labor Train," 94–95; and folk authenticity, 89; performance ethos of, 89, 92–93; and thick description, 85–86; utopianism of, 93–94

Habermas, Jürgen, 35
Hall, Stuart: on ideology, 198
Hames-García, Michael, 203
Harlem Renaissance, 26, 32, 33–34, 237n9

Harney, Stefano, 25, 235n33
Hartman, Saidiya, 218, 226
Hartman, Stephanie, 66, 71
Hathaway, Rosemary V.: on "touristic reading," 38–39
Hayden, Robert, 145
Heble, Ajay, 221
Hegel, G.W.F.: on the "master-slave" dialectic, 107, 116, 218
Hemingway, Ernest: *In Our Time*, 184, 261n71
Hemphill, Essex, 229
Herzog, Anne F., 58, 70
Higashida, Cheryl, 7, 173, 215
Hines, Andy, 9, 120
Hinojosa-Smith, Rolando, 205, 260n64
Holmes, Odetta ("Odetta"), 8, 244n26
Honey, Michael K., 2, 122–24, 253n30
hope, 4, 20, 25–26, 58, 75, 82, 87, 113
Houston, Cisco, 90, 244n26
Hughes, Langston, 32
Hungerford, Amy: on "the identity plot," 16
Hurston, Zora Neale, 3, 9, 17–20, 26–27, 31–53, 55, 59, 71, 74–76, 82, 98, 104, 109, 173, 237n12, 238n13, 238n19, 243n18; *Mules and Men*, 6, 20, 21, 24, 26, 31, 35, 36–53, 72–74, 76, 88, 238n18, 259n51; authenticity in, 42, 49–50, 238n12; *Tell My Horse: Voodoo and Life in Haiti and Jamaica*, 41

imperialism, 161, 203
intersectionality, 13–14, 215, 226
Isaac, Allan Punzalan, 167, 173
Izenberg, Oren: *On Being Numerous*, 148–49

Jackson, Jesse, 228
Jackson, Lawrence P., 34
Jackson, Mark Allan, 244n29
Johnson, James Weldon, 32

Jones, Gayl, 2, 32
Joseph, May: on "nomadism," 116
Judy, Sara, 54

Kalaidjian, Walter, 56, 59, 62
Kanellos, Nicolás, 194
Kaufman, Janet E., 58
Kaufman, Will, 245n38, 247n57
Kazin, Michael, 8, 80, 243n13
Keating, AnaLouise, 202, 213, 221, 222
Keith, Joseph, 168, 178
Kelley, Robin D. G.: *Hammer and Hoe*, 14, 119
Kennedy-Epstein, Rowena, 32, 237n2
King Jr., Martin Luther, 120–21, 124, 127, 136, 141, 150, 253n30
Klein, Joe, 90–91, 96–97
Kopkind, Andrew, 228
Korstad, Robert Rodgers, 121
Kun, Josh, 93
labor, 9, 12, 15, 16, 29, 46, 52, 53, 70, 81, 82, 98, 104–109, 113, 115, 120–27, 129, 132, 153, 165, 169, 173, 175–76, 186, 192; anti-, 91, 96; of coalition, 4, 220; demonstrations, 249n69; dignity of, 74, 124; farm, 78–79, 94, 108, 163, 170, 175–76, 192, 170, 176, 192; exploitation, 45; intellectual, 18, 225; migrant, 192, 250n80; poetic, 11; politics, 3, 5, 34, 80, 121; power, 24; strikes, 27, 253n30; textual, 205; and voice, 36. *See also* Memphis Sanitation Strike; Popular Front
Lackey, Michael, 146
lamentation, 230–31
Lange, Dorothea, 101
Latinx studies, 8, 216
Laudun, John, 50
Lawrence, David Todd, 47–48
Laya, Juan C.: *His Native Soil*, 169
Libretti, Tim, 168
Lee, Steven S., 34

Leventhal, Harold: *Pastures of Plenty*, 117
Levine, Caroline, 75
Lieberman, Robbie, 81–82
Limón, Ada, 231
Limón, José E.: *Dancing with the Devil*, 180, 185
Lipsitz, George, 221
listening, 21, 71, 84–88, 93, 131, 173, 230
literary form, 2, 4, 12, 15, 23, 56, 64, 75, 144, 163–64, 207; and deformation, 24, 36; and sermon form, 122. *See also* bildungsroman; lyric; picaresque; migrant pizcaresque; *. . . y no se lo tragó la tierra* (Rivera): *estampas*
Llosa Sanz, Álvaro, 185, 195, 259n53
Lobo, Julius, 55, 58, 240n66
Locke, Alain: on the Harlem Renaissance, 32–34
Long, Huey, 252n8
Longhi, Jimmy, 244n26
López, Dennis, 182–83
Lorde, Audre, 2, 211, 217, 219; "The Master's Tools Will Never Dismantle the Master's House," 217, 219
Lorentz, Pare, 81
Los Lobos, 8
Luxemburg, Rosa, 220
Lye, Colleen, 178, 199, 215
lyric, 10–11, 28, 35–36, 54, 60–61, 63, 66, 71–72, 90, 122–23, 130–31, 135, 139, 141, 151, 153, 157–58, 190, 193–94, 212, 231, 253n27; collectivity, 11, 130, 153

Majewska, Ewa, 220
Make Way for Tomorrow (McCarey), 81
Maltz, Albert: "Man on the Road," 53
Manzella, Abigail G.H.: *Migrating Fictions*, 78, 79, 103, 113
Marcus, Greil: *The Shape of Things to Come*, 93, 204

Marcus, Sara: on disappointment, 20, 212, 222, 223, 230
Marsh, Dave: *Pastures of Plenty*, 117, 244n26
Martínez, Eliud, 185, 199
Martínez, Valerie, 2
Martín-Rodríguez, Manuel M., 183, 199
Masters, Edgar Lee; *Spoon River Anthology*, 24, 54
Maund, Alfred: *The Big Boxcar*, 109
Maxwell, Bill, 34
McCraw, Morgan, 129, 141, 147–49, 157; "A Black Poem," 147–49
McKay, Claude: *Harlem Shadows*, 261n71
McKinnie, Joe L., 129, 141–47: "Why should we sit and wait?," 130, 141–47
Melamed, Jodi, 227
memory: in *America is In the Heart* (Bulosan), 107, 112, 168; in *The Book of the Dead* (Rukeyser), 11, 69; in *This Bridge Called My Back* (Anzaldúa and Moraga), 224; collective, 168, 224; ethnic, 258n39; in *Mules and Men* (Hurston), 43, 45; in *. . . y no se lo tragó la tierra* (Rivera), 28, 185–88, 195; and Woody Guthrie, 86–87, 93
Memphis Sanitation Strike (1968), 3, 18, 21, 24, 27–28, 121–23, 127, 129–52, 160, 253n30; and Black nationalism, 120, 121, 122, 125, 151–52; history of, 123–29; and Memphis churches, 124–25; poems of, 9, 17, 21, 24, 28, 122–23, 129–52, 217
migration, 5, 9, 12, 16, 24, 27, 31, 34, 58, 75, 77–78, 105, 122–23, 228; Black, 31, 52, 73, 98, 123; dangers of, 163; Dust Bowl, 77–78, 105; legacies of, 126; to Memphis, 122–23
migrant literature, 28
migrant pizcaresque, 28, 162–64, 167, 170, 173, 178, 180, 182–83, 199–200

Miller, Joshua L., 19
modernism, 10, 13, 142, 207; Fordist, 80; multilingual, 8, 19; Yiddish, 19
Montilla, Yesenia, 231
Moore, Catherine Venable, 60
Mora, Pat, 166
Moraga, Cherríe, 6, 9, 11–12, 211–13, 223, 225; "The Welder," 11–12. See also *Bridge Called My Back, This* (Anzaldúa and Moraga)
Morales, Rosario, 211, 222; "We're All in the Same Boat," 222
Moten, Fred, 25, 125, 136–37, 235n33
movement: politics of, 97
Movement for Black Lives, 230
Moya, Paula M. L., 24, 248n64
Mules and Men (Hurston), 6, 20, 21, 24, 26, 31, 35, 36–53, 72–74, 76, 88, 238n18, 259n51; authenticity in, 42, 49–50, 238n12; authority in, 40; 37–51; endings in, 38, 51–52; as experimental ethnography, 37–40; lies in, 42–49, 52; and problematization of folk, 39; truth in, 39, 42, 44, 49–50
Mullen, Bill, 7, 14, 34, 119
multiculturalism, 3, 7, 12–13, 15, 29–30, 161, 173, 202, 211, 215, 226–31; coalitional ethos of, 15, 29, 202, 211; critique of, 3, 30; representational logic of, 74, 166, 178, 231
Muñoz, José E., 73, 223, 225, 264n49
Murillo, John: "the tradition of the witness," 2
Murray, Albert, 220

Nadal, Paul, 167, 169, 178, 179
Namaste, Ki, 5
nationalism: Black, 120–22, 125–26, 151–52, 163; Chicano, 183–84, 207; US, 180
New Deal, 8, 77, 81, 122, 250n89

Neyrat, Frédéric: on atopianism, 5–6
nomadism, 116

Olivares, Julián, 181, 193, 195

Paley, Grace, 40
Parker, Pat, 211, 220
Pérez Jiménez, Cristina, 8
Phelan, Shane, 203
Phillips, Carl, 158–59
picaresque, 28, 162–64, 167–68, 170, 175, 200, 201. See also *migrant pizcaresque*
poetry. See documentary poetics; lyric; Memphis Sanitation Strike: poetry of,
poplore, 89, 245n36
Popular Front, 3–4, 7–10, 13–15, 29–30, 32–34, 55, 57, 80–82, 98, 100, 107, 113, 119–20, 122–23, 126, 164, 173, 175, 179, 202, 203, 226, 230; cultural resonances of, 7–10, 30; racial politics of, 80; and transnationalism, 230
Portillo, Estela, 9, 205–209, 216; "After Hierarchy," 207–208; "Introduction" to *El Grito* Book Series No. 1, 205–206, 209
Posmentier, Sonya: "lyric ecology," 253n27

Quashie, Kevin: *Black Aliveness*, 160; *Sovereignty of Quiet*, 144–45, 160
queerness, 5, 223, 229
queer theory, 73, 203, 216
Quiñonez, Naomi, 205–206

race, 4–5, 9, 12, 15, 125, 204, 226, 227; in "The 23rd Slum," 132; in *This Bridge Called My Back* (Anzaldúa and Moraga), 204, 210, 217; and the Popular Front, 80–82, 121–22; –welding, 33–34; in *Whose Names are Unknown* (Babb) 105–10. See also whiteness

Rainbow Coalition, 227–28
Ramos, Julio, 181, 192
Rangel, Dolores E., 184
Reagon, Bernice Johnson: on coalition work, 219
Reed, Anthony, 136
Reid-Pharr, Robert, 7, 34
religion, 55, 121–25, 132, African Methodist Episcopal (AME) Church, 124; Pentecostalism, 124, 139
Retman, Sonnet, 41, 44, 48–49, 52, 62
Reuss, Richard, 88, 92
Reznikoff, Charles: *Testimony*, 54
Rich, Adrienne, 221
Riggs, Marlon, 229
Rinner, Jenni, 153
Rivera, Tomás, 3, 9, 19–21, 24, 28–29, 45, 161–66, 170, 173, 180–201, 205, 258n39, 258n42, 259n51, 259n53, 260n62, 260n64, 261n71, 261n77; "Chicago Literature: Fiesta of the Living," 188; "La mano en la bolsa," 190–91; *. . . y no se lo tragó la tierra*, 19–21, 24, 28, 161–66, 170, 180–201, 258n39, 258n42, 259n51, 259n53, 260n62, 260n64, 261n71, 261n77
Rodríguez, Teresa B., 261n77
Rojas, Maythee, 209
Roosevelt, Franklin Delano, 8, 9, 77
Ross, Marlon D., 144–45
Rothstein, Arthur, 101
Rukeyser, Muriel, 3, 8, 9, 10–11, 17–20, 26–27, 31–37, 45, 53–76, 82, 98, 104, 145, 173, 237n2, 241n90; "Absalom," 10–12, 64, 66, 69; "Alloy," 63; *The Book of the Dead*, 10, 20, 24, 26, 31, 35–36, 53–76, 118, 239n39; "George Robinson: Blues," 63, 67; "Mearl Blankenship," 59–64; "Praise for the Committee," 63–68; "The Soul and Body of John Brown," 57, 68; *U.S. 1*, 31, 53, 55, 236n1; "Story Outline for *Gauley Bridge*," 57–58; "West Virginia," 56–57
Rulfo, Juan: *El llano en llamas*, 261n77; *Pedro Páramo*, 261n77
Rushin, Kate, 211

Saldívar, Ramón: *Chicano Narrative*, 165, 181, 183–84, 187, 198
Salt of the Earth (Biberman), 58, 81, 119
Sandburg, Carl: *Chicago Poems*, 24, 54
Sandoval, Chela: *Methodology of the Oppressed*, 75, 166
"Sanitation Workers' Prayer," 129, 137–41, 143, 149, 160; Biblical language in, 137–41; collectivity in, 139
San Juan Jr, E., 167–68, 173
Santos-Febres, Mayra, 235n31
Saroyan, William: *My Name is Aram*, 248n63, 261n71
Schmidt Camacho, Alicia: *Migrant Imaginaries*, 166, 180, 186, 225
Schulman, Sarah, 229
Sedgwick, Eve: *Touching Feeling*, 73
Serpell, C. Namwali, 234n11
Shahn, Ben, 9, 55
Sharpe, Christina: *In the Wake*, 140
Shih, Shu-mei, 13
Shockley, Evie, 125, 136, 148–49, 156
Short, Kayann, 213
Singer, Isaac Bashevis, 19
Singer, Israel Joshua, 19
Siraganian, Lisa: on Muriel Rukeyser's literary form, 56, 65
Smethurst, James, 8, 14, 32–33, 119, 123, 125–26
Smith, Barbara, 211, 225
Smith, Beverly, 211, 225
Smith, Henry Nash: *Virgin Land*, 77–78
Socha, Kimberly, 258n37, 259n48
social realism, 123, 165
solidarity, 13, 107, 109, 113, 114, 177, 201; in *America Is in the Heart* (Bulosan),

177, 201; effects of, 141; and Guthrie, Woody, 90, 93; interracial, 114; and the Popular Front, 13; racial 109; and vernacular poetry, 62; in *Whose Names Are Unknown* (Babb), 109; . . . *y no se lo tragó la tierra* (Rivera), 201
sovereignty, 15, 19, 116, 140, 226
Spillers, Hortense, 21
Spivak, Gayatri Chakravorty: "Can the Subaltern Speak?," 218; on representation and re-presentation, 22–23
Springer, Kimberly, 7
Stadler, Gustavus, 80, 96–97, 147
Steinbeck, John: *The Grapes of Wrath*, 91, 99, 103, 104, 105, 115, 163, 192, 248n67
Sterne, Lawrence: *Tristram Shandy*, 169
Stott, William, 62
Sullivan's Travels (Sturges), 81
surprise, 209, 220–25
Sustar, Lee, 228, 266n84
Svobida, Lawrence: *Farming the Dust Bowl*, 110
Szalay, Michael: *Hip Figures*, 8–9, 124, 228, 252n8

"There Was a Man" (Knight), 150–51
Thurston, Michael, 62, 66, 69
Toomer, Jean: *Cane*, 184, 261n71

Valella, Daniel, 260n69
Vazquez, Alexandra: "listening in detail," 21, 131
Venegas, Daniel: *Las aventuras de don Chipote, o, Cuando los pericos mamen*, 162–63
Vials, Chris, 168, 180
Villareal, Jose Antonio: *Pocho*, 163
violence: in *America Is in the Heart* (Bulosan), 177; anti-Black, 96–97, 135, 139–40; in *This Bridge Called My Back* (Anzaldúa and Moraga), 216; in *Mules and Men* (Hurston), 49; police, 169; racial, 12, 169, 230, 250n89; in "The Soul and Body of John Brown" (Rukeyser), 68
Virilio, Paul: on migrant "enclosure," 102
Vizcaíno-Alemán, Melina, 207
Vizenor, Gerald: on "survivance," 160

Wald, Alan, 7, 33, 55
Wald, Sarah D.: *The Nature of California*, 78–79, 100, 103, 105–106, 113–15
Walker, Margaret, 32
Wallace, Henry, 94, 119
Wallace, Michele, 48
Warren, Calvin, 141
Warren, Robert Penn, 252n8
Washington, Mary Helen, 7, 8, 14, 32, 34, 119, 152, 155
Wedgwood, Josiah, 127–28
Weil, Simone: on aesthetic "force," 23–24
Werner, Craig, 91, 97
West, Cornel, 93
Wheeler, Lesley, 153, 159
Wheelwright, John, 55–56
White, Gillian, 151
whiteness: and ACT UP, 229; and Dust Bowl migration, 77–79; and lynching, 97; of Popular Front political imagery, 81, 98; as problem, 82; as enforced universalism, 204; in *Whose Names Are Unknown* (Babb), 105, 106, 107, 113, 114
Whitman, Walt: *Leaves of Grass*, 19, 24–25, 54
Whose Names Are Unknown (Babb), 20, 21, 24–25, 25, 80, 82–, 98–116; dialect in, 109; hope in, 25; intimacy in, 110–11; music in, 83–84; racial solidarity in, 105–109; representation of people in, 98, 100, 104

"Why should we sit and wait?" (McKinnie), 141–47; collectivity in, 141–42, 145–47; passivity in, 142–43; rhyme in, 143–46
Williams, Jakobi, 227
Williams, Raymond, 245n40
Wixson, Douglas, 100–104
Woloch, Alex: *The One vs. the Many*, 39
Wong, Nellie, 211
Wong, Sau-ling Cynthia, 169
Worsham, Robert, 129
Wright, Richard, 38

Yamada, Mitsuye, 211
Yamamoto, Hisaye, 8, 173
Yamashita, Karen Tei, 2
Yao, Steven, 163–64, 168
... *y no se lo tragó la tierra* (Rivera), 19, 20, 21, 24, 28, 161–66, 170, 180–201, 258n39, 258n42, 259n51, 259n53, 260n62, 260n64, 261n71, 261n77; beyond allegory, 180–84, 186, 196, 198; "Debajo de la casa," 196–97; diasporic consciousness in, 195–96; *estampas* in, 184–85; form in, 192–94; memory in, 185–88, 196; multivocality in, 186–87, 191–92, 195, 198
Young, Harvey: Embodying Black Experience, 97, 113

Myka Tucker-Abramson, *Cartographies of Empire: The Road Novel and American Hegemony*

Michael Shane Boyle, *The Arts of Logistics: Artistic Production in Supply Chain Capitalism*

Adam Kelly, *New Sincerity: American Fiction in the Neoliberal Age*

Adrienne Brown, *The Residential Is Racial: A Perceptual History of Mass Homeownership*

Patrick Whitmarsh, *Writing Our Extinction: Anthropocene Fiction and Vertical Science*

Rebecca B. Clark, *American Graphic: Disgust and Data in Contemporary Literature*

Palmer Rampell, *Genres of Privacy in Postwar America*

Joseph Darda, *The Strange Career of Racial Liberalism*

Jordan S. Carroll, *Reading the Obscene: Transgressive Editors and the Class Politics of US Literature*

Michael Dango, *Crisis Style: The Aesthetics of Repair*

Mary Esteve, *Incremental Realism: Postwar American Fiction, Happiness, and Welfare-State Liberalism*

Dorothy J. Hale, *The Novel and the New Ethics*

Christine Hong, *A Violent Peace: Race, U.S. Militarism, and Cultures of Democratization in Cold War Asia and the Pacific*

Sarah Brouillette, *UNESCO and the Fate of the Literary*

Sophie Seita, *Provisional Avant-Gardes: Little Magazine Communities from Dada to Digital*

Guy Davidson, *Categorically Famous: Literary Celebrity and Sexual Liberation in 1960s America*

Joseph Jonghyun Jeon, *Vicious Circuits: Korea's IMF Cinema and the End of the American Century*

Lytle Shaw, *Narrowcast: Poetry and Audio Research*

Stephen Schryer, *Maximum Feasible Participation: American Literature and the War on Poverty*

Margaret Ronda, *Remainders: American Poetry at Nature's End*

Jasper Bernes, *The Work of Art in the Age of Deindustrialization*

Annie McClanahan, *Dead Pledges: Debt, Crisis, and Twenty-First-Century Culture*

Amy Hungerford, *Making Literature Now*

J. D. Connor, *The Studios After the Studios: Neoclassical Hollywood (1970–2010)*

Michael Trask, *Camp Sites: Sex, Politics, and Academic Style in Postwar America*

Loren Glass, *Counterculture Colophon: Grove Press, the* Evergreen Review, *and the Incorporation of the Avant-Garde*

Michael Szalay, *Hip Figures: A Literary History of the Democratic Party*

Jared Gardner, *Projections: Comics and the History of Twenty-First-Century Storytelling*

Jerome Christensen, *America's Corporate Art: The Studio Authorship of Hollywood Motion Pictures*

For a complete listing of titles in this series, visit the Stanford University Press website, www.sup.org.

The authorized representative in the EU for product safety and compliance is:
Mare Nostrum Group B.V.
Mauritskade 21D
1091 GC Amsterdam
The Netherlands
Email address: gpsr@mare-nostrum.co.uk

KVK chamber of commerce number: 96249943

The authorized representative in the EU for product safety and compliance is:
Mare Nostrum Group
B.V Doelen 72
4831 GR Breda
The Netherlands

www.ingramcontent.com/pod-product-compliance
Lightning Source LLC
Chambersburg PA
CBHW030610230426
43661CB00053B/1919